Fifth Edition

Community-Based Strategic
POLICING IN CANADA

Brian Whitelaw
City of Calgary, Calgary Transit, Public Safety

Rick Parent
Simon Fraser University, School of Criminology

NELSON

NELSON

Community-Based Strategic Policing in Canada, Fifth Edition

by Brian Whitelaw and Richard B. Parent

VP, Product Solutions, K–20:
Claudine O'Donnell

Publisher, Digital and Print Content:
Leanna MacLean

Marketing Manager:
Claire Varley

Content Manager:
Gail Brown

Photo and Permissions Researcher:
Natalie Barrington

Production Project Manager:
Jaime Smith

Production Service:
SPi Global

Copy Editor:
Matthew Kudelka

Proofreader:
SPi Global

Indexer:
SPi Global

Design Director:
Ken Phipps

Higher Education Design PM:
Pamela Johnston

Interior Design:
deboraH brock

Cover Design:
Jen Spinner

Cover Image:
Dan Janisse/Windsor Star

Compositor:
SPi Global

**Library and Archives Canada
Cataloguing in Publication**

Whitelaw, Brian, author Community-
based strategic policing in Canada/
Brian Whitelaw and Rick Parent. --
Fifth edition.

Includes index. First published under
title: Community policing in Canada/
Curt Taylor Griffiths, Richard B. Parent,
Brian Whitelaw. Issued in print and
electronic formats. ISBN 978-0-17-
670002-7 (softcover).—ISBN 978-0-
17-685382-2 (PDF)

1. Community policing—Canada—
Textbooks. 2. Textbooks.I. Parent,
Richard B., 1958-, author II. Griffiths,
Curt T. (Curt Taylor), 1948- . Community
policing in Canada III. Title.

HV7936.C83G74 2018
363.2'30971
C2017-905700-6
C2017-905701-4

ISBN-13: 978-0-17-670002-7
ISBN-10: 0-17-670002-1

To Lida, Sebastian, Koen and Austin—my community
—Brian Whitelaw

To my wonderful wife Cathy and my incredible daughters Jennifer and Janeen
—Rick Parent

Brief Contents

Contents

UNIT 2:   UNDERSTANDING COMMUNITY POLICING 51
CHAPTER 3: WHAT IS COMMUNITY POLICING? 53

UNIT 3: CRIME PREVENTION AND CRIME RESPONSE WITHIN A COMMUNITY POLICING FRAMEWORK 85

CHAPTER 4: RESPONDING TO AND PREVENTING CRIME WITHIN A COMMUNITY POLICING FRAMEWORK 87

CHAPTER 5: PROBLEM-ORIENTED POLICING 127

UNIT 4:   THE KEY PLAYERS IN COMMUNITY POLICING 177
CHAPTER 6: THE COMMUNITY POLICING POLICE SERVICE 179

CHAPTER 7: IMPLEMENTING COMMUNITY POLICING 211

CHAPTER 8: THE COMMUNITY POLICE OFFICER 251

CHAPTER 9: RESTORATIVE JUSTICE WITHIN A COMMUNITY POLICING FRAMEWORK 287

CHAPTER 10: THE COMMUNITY AND COMMUNITY POLICING 313

Preface

INTRODUCTION

In *Community-Based Strategic Policing in Canada,* we describe a model of community policing in Canada that is evolving. Changes in Canadian society, particularly in terms of immigration and population demographics, the nature of crime in society, and the proliferation of new technologies are transforming the relationship the police have with multiple and diverse communities.

Since the release of the fourth edition, there have been a number of important developments both nationally and internationally that have altered the basic blueprint of community policing described simplistically in Sir Robert Peel's principle, "The police are the public and the public are the police." Incidents in the United States such as the fatal shooting of African Americans leading to the establishment of Black Lives Matter, along with countless lethal force incidents occurring across North America, have raised some fundamental questions about the relationship between police and the community. In Toronto, for example, while the fatal shooting of Sammy Yatim by a Toronto police officer has raised many important questions about police training, there is a larger issue related to the attitudes police have about policing communities. Are the efforts of policing as an institution at the frontlines truly integrative, or is policing something that is done *to* a community as opposed to *with* the community? This is in keeping with growing concerns over the militarization of policing and the many images and videos depicting police in full combat gear ready to quell disorder. This state of affairs calls for a new model of engagement with the community.

The Community Mobilization and Engagement Model developed in Ontario and now being applied all across Canada in various forms offers a promising future in the development of the next phase of community policing. Through the use of "situational tables" or "Hubs" in provinces including British Columbia and Saskatchewan, the basic problem-solving model is becoming more strategic, leveraging the support of multidisciplinary partners to address high-risk community safety and well-being issues. As this model of cooperation continues to evolve, it has the potential to reduce crime and disorder in our communities by focusing on "root causes" that are crime generators.

In the last ten years, a question has surfaced as to whether community policing has been replaced by a new model of policing. Some of the features of this "new" model include "intelligence-led policing," where quantitative measures determine policing priorities and expenditures, and strategies are tailored to this analysis. Technology is performing a key role in identifying and responding to problems, and police work has become "smarter." In our view, this new model is nothing other than a more advanced, strategic form of community policing. This revision of community policing will continue to require police services to examine how service is delivered and by whom. Under the umbrella of public safety, there is a strong leadership role for Canadian police services to coordinate the resources necessary to address community problems effectively without having to be solely responsible for solving them.

Ethical and professional conduct, based on organizational core values, must be standard practice within every police service. While selection, training, and effective leadership are fundamental to professionalism, community-based policing provides the necessary framework to further this process. Public involvement in police service delivery is a key component of community safety, and in securing public confidence and support.

We hope you find this textbook a great learning experience, and that it provides a solid foundation of the approaches and research in the practice and study of community policing in Canada.

WHAT'S NEW IN THE FIFTH EDITION

The following is an overview of the key revisions and updates throughout *Community-Based Strategic Policing in Canada*. As well, feature boxes have been relabelled to better identify their purpose and relevance.

Chapter 1

- Introduction of new concepts—*policing by consent* and the *legitimacy of the police* in Canada
- Expanded discussion on the evolution of the role of police, with an emphasis on the historic differences between Canadian policing and policing in the United States
- Expanded discussion on the emergence of women in policing in Canada New feature on the Toronto Police Service—the largest municipal police service in Canada

Chapter 2

- Updated statistics on the social and demographic attributes of communities
- Updated data and statistics on policing in Canada (Table 2.1)
- Updated statistics on Indigenous policing in Canada

Chapter 3

- Emphasis on the issue of intelligence-led policing being a collaborative enterprise based on improved intelligence operations and community-oriented policing and problem solving, which includes engaging the public with an exchange of information using the Internet and social media

Chapter 4

- New section on cybercrime and community policing
- New feature on citizen volunteer bicycle patrol programs
- Updated discussion on technology in crime prevention
- New discussion on the Northern and Aboriginal Crime Prevention Fund (NACPF), which serves to facilitate culturally sensitive initiatives that foster the development and implementation of crime prevention approaches in Indigenous communities, both on- and off-reserve
- A new end-of-chapter case study on how social media assisted police in rescuing an abducted newborn

Chapter 5

- Revised and updated information on CAPRA, the problem-solving model used by the RCMP
- New feature on problem-oriented policing in New Brunswick
- New feature illustrating problem-solving and intervention in the case of pharmacy robberies

Chapter 6

- New features on police leadership
- New feature on police services vision and values
- New discussion on the delivery of police services through integrated units
- Updated material on the RCMP's strategies and priorities
- Expanded discussion on community policing service delivery deployment
- New discussion on community policing and the HUB model

Chapter 7

- Updated material on Surrey Mobilization and Resiliency Table (SMART) model
- Updated information on Edmonton Police Service and Service de police de la Ville de Montréal
- Updated material on the Surrey RCMP Service Delivery Model
- Updated data for municipal policing resource indicators (Table 7.3)

Chapter 8

- Expanded discussion of the emerging issues related to the recruitment of individuals into policing, including preferred qualifications
- Updated discussion on the evolving issues of diversity and today's police recruit
- New feature boxes on becoming a Toronto police officer, training with the Ontario Provincial Police, and the Ontario Police Fitness Award Program
- Updated material on the RCMP's Aboriginal Pre-Cadet Training Program (APTP)
- New material on trending training courses for Canadian police service personnel, including crisis intervention training and implicit bias awareness training

Chapter 9

- Updated data on Indigenous incarceration rates in Canada
- Revised and updated material on the Indigenous Justice Program (IJP)— formerly the Aboriginal Justice Strategy (AJS)—including the Community-Based Justice Fund and the Capacity Building Fund

Chapter 10

- New feature boxes on Vancouver Community Policing Centres and on the RCMP serving Canada's Indigenous peoples
- New discussion surrounding the Black Lives Matter movement in the United States, which has established chapters in Canada, as well as the controversial practice of "carding" and police involvement in the deaths of civilians Andrew Loku and Sammy Yatim
- New discussion on the levels of public satisfaction with police, as well as police services' new "customer service" approach
- Expanded discussion on the Ontario Provincial Police model of community policing

KEY FEATURES

A Closer Look provides a more detailed look into different aspects of community policing.

A CLOSER LOOK 9.1

THE INDIGENOUS JUSTICE PROGRAM

The Indigenous Justice Program (IJP) supports Indigenous community-based justice programs that offer alternatives to mainstream justice processes in appropriate circumstances. The objectives of the Indigenous Justice Program are:

- to assist Indigenous people in assuming greater responsibility for the administration of justice in their communities;

- to reflect and include Indigenous values within the justice system; and

- to contribute to a decrease in the rate of victimization, crime, and incarceration among Indigenous people in communities with community-based justice programs funded by the IJP.

The Indigenous Justice Program consists of two funding components: the Community-Based Justice Fund and the Capacity-Building Fund.

Community-Based Justice Fund

The Community-Based Justice Fund supports community-based justice programs in partnership with Indigenous communities. Programs are cost-shared with provincial and territorial governments and designed to reflect the culture and values of the communities in which they are situated. The IJP currently funds 197 community-based programs that serve over 750 communities. The objectives of the Community-Based Justice Fund component are:

- to allow Indigenous people the opportunity to assume greater responsibility for the administration of justice in their communities;
- to help reduce the rates of crime and incarceration among Indigenous people in communities with cost-shared programs; and,
- to foster improved responsiveness, fairness, inclusiveness, and effectiveness of the justice system with respect to justice and its administration so as to meet the needs and aspirations of Indigenous people in the areas of appropriate models for:

  - diversion;
  - development of pre-sentencing options;
  - sentencing alternatives (circles);
  - use of Justices of the Peace;
  - family and civil mediation; and
  - additional community justice services such as victim support and offender reintegration services that support the overall goals of the IJP or, where affiliated with a successful program under any of the above.

Capacity Building Fund

The Capacity-Building Fund is designed to support capacity-building efforts in Indigenous communities. With a focus on building increased knowledge and skills for the establishment and management of community-based justice programs, the objectives of the Capacity-Building Fund are:

- to support the training and/or developmental needs of Indigenous communities that currently do not have community-based justice programs;
- to supplement the ongoing training needs of current community-based justice programs where the cost-shared budget does not adequately meet these needs, including supporting evaluation activities, data collection, and sharing of best practices and useful models;
- to support activities targeted at improved community reporting in IJP communities and the development of data management systems;
- to support the development of new justice programs, paying particular attention to:

  - the current geographic/regional imbalance in programming;
  - the commitment to develop new programs in the underrepresented program models, such as dispute resolution for civil and family/child welfare; and

- to support one-time or annual events and initiatives (as opposed to ongoing projects and programs) that build bridges, trust and partnerships between the mainstream justice system and Indigenous communities.

Sources: Department of Justice, Indigenous Justice Program, http://www.justice.gc.ca/eng/fund-fina/acf-fca/ajs-sja/index.html. Department of Justice Canada, 2017. Reproduced with the permission of the Department of Justice Canada, 2017.

Critical Perspectives provide a critical analysis of theories and practices in community policing.

CRITICAL PERSPECTIVES 4.5

TECHNOLOGY VERSUS PRIVACY RIGHTS: WALKING A SLIPPERY SLOPE

Proponents of CCTV argue that law-abiding citizens have nothing to fear from being monitored by CCTV cameras. Opponents fear that the technological monitoring of public spaces represents an unjustified intrusion on a citizen's right to privacy. What do you think? If technology could prevent all crime or identify all offenders, would it be worth the investment? Now think about other forms of current technology that can track our every movement—from biometric scanning devices such as facial recognition software in Heathrow Airport to gunshot detection systems in Chicago, from so-called black boxes in motor vehicles to global positioning systems (GPSs). Another technological system is a photo-radar grid system that calculates the speed and distance travelled by a motor vehicle between several points. If the motor vehicle passes another camera located in the grid earlier than predicted, then a speeding ticket is issued. All of these examples of technology are in use around the world. In Canada, provincial and federal privacy bodies (i.e., Ontario Office of the Information and the Privacy Commissioner) recommend that all public bodies, including the police, prepare Privacy Impact Assessments in order to achieve a balance between intrusive technology and privacy rights.

In Your Community highlights specific examples of community policing.

IN YOUR COMMUNITY 10.2

POLICE–COMMUNITY PARTNERSHIPS

Vancouver's ten community policing centres hold a unique position among crime prevention initiatives in North America, because of their strong partnership with the community. Unlike their counterparts in other cities, these centres are not satellite police stations—they are actually operated, staffed, and governed by members of the community.

Source: *Courtesy of the Vancouver Police Department*

Vancouver Aboriginal Community Policing Centre Society

The Vancouver Aboriginal Community Policing Centre Society (VACPCS) was incorporated in 2006 as a non-for-profit society by the Vancouver Indigenous community. It was created to address social justice issues, improve safety for Indigenous people, and build the relationship between the Vancouver Police Department (VPD) and the Indigenous community through education, awareness, and open dialogue.

The positive link between the Vancouver Indigenous community and the VPD provides an avenue to engage and support Indigenous people so that they better understand and utilize the services of the VPD. This link is supported by the presence of an assigned member of the VPD, a Neighbourhood Police Officer at VACPC who participates in activities and is available to support the specific needs of the Indigenous community in Vancouver.

VACPCS is governed by a board of directors elected by and from members of the Vancouver Indigenous community. Working in partnership with Indigenous community members, Indigenous and non-Indigenous organizations, and all levels of government, VACPC seeks to provide resources, services, and programs that support the safety and security of Vancouver's Indigenous community.

Source: *Courtesy of Vancouver Aboriginal Community Policing Centre Society*

Situations and Strategies highlight real-world case studies at the end of each chapter to illustrate community policing in practice.

Case Study 7. Abducted Baby Now with Family after Facebook Spurs Search

Day-old Victoria is back with her family this morning, thanks to four friends who went hunting for the baby after they saw a Facebook alert about her abduction last night from a hospital in Trois-Rivières, Que.

In a Facebook post also thanking the three women and one man for their help, Victoria's mother, Mélissa McMahon, on Tuesday expressed the family's horror of having the newborn taken from the maternity ward at the Sainte-Marie pavillion of the Centre hospitalier régional de Trois-Rivières (CHRTR) the night before.

"Yesterday we experienced the worst time of our lives. It was a feeling that nobody should have to live through. The helplessness in this situation was difficult to accept," wrote McMahon.

Quebec provincial police said that just before 7 p.m. ET Monday, a woman dressed as a nurse showed up at the hospital and entered the maternity ward.

Police said the woman took the baby from the mother, and left the room with the newborn wrapped in a blue blanket.

"She walked calmly down the hall, wearing a nurse's uniform. No one asked any questions about who she was," a hospital employee told Radio-Canada.

Amber Alert

Police issued an Amber Alert around 7 p.m., looking for a red Toyota Yaris hatchback with a "Bébé à bord" ("Baby on Board") sticker.

Sgt. Martine Asselin with provincial police says many people were contacting police with tips after the Amber Alert went out.

"The media really helped us put out the picture and the description fast. We could see on the TV, on the media, on Facebook, everything we needed and very fast ... the public was able to call us and give us information," said Asselin.

The baby was found three hours later after the four young adults learned of the abduction through Facebook. Police had shared a photo on social networks of the woman police were seeking.

The four say they went looking for the vehicle of the woman at the centre of the hunt, and found one that fit the description—then called police.

"We saw [the alert] on Facebook, and decided to go looking for red cars, and we saw the woman. We recognized her," said 20-year-old Mélizanne Bergeron.

21-Year-Old Suspect Arrested

Police say they arrested a 21-year-old woman at her home. They found baby Victoria, and returned her to hospital. On Tuesday, Victoria was taken home to her family. McMahon said in her Facebook post that it was social media that helped save the baby:

"Thousands of people shared the photo of the woman on social networks," McMahon wrote. "Know that this is what has saved our little Victoria. Each click, each share made the difference. Four wonderful people, who we had the chance to meet, identified the woman through Facebook."

The 21-year-old woman picked up by police is in hospital for a psychiatric evaluation, they say. She may appear in court later Tuesday.

INSTRUCTOR RESOURCES

The **Nelson Education Teaching Advantage (NETA)** program delivers research-based instructor resources that promote student engagement and higher-order thinking to enable the success of Canadian students and educators. Visit Nelson Education's **Inspired Instruction** website at www.nelson.com/inspired/ to find out more about NETA.

The following instructor resources have been created for *Community-Based Strategic Policing in Canada*, Fifth Edition. Access these ultimate tools for customizing lectures and presentations at www.nelson.com/instructor.

NETA Test Bank

This resource was written by the textbook's authors, Brian Whitelaw and Rick Parent. It includes over 130 multiple-choice questions written according to NETA guidelines for effective construction and development of higher-order thinking. Also included are approximately 50 true/false, 100 short-answer, and 30 essay-type questions. Test Bank files are provided in Word format for easy editing and in PDF.

NETA Answer Key

Answers to the end-of-chapter Questions and Key Ideas (multiple-choice questions) are provided for each chapter in *Community-Based Strategic Policing in Canada*. For the Questions, the page number where the material appears in the textbook is also included. The Answer Key also provides suggested responses for the Exercises: Knowledge into Practice section.

NETA Instructor's Manual

The Instructor's Manual to accompany *Community-Based Strategic Policing in Canada* has been prepared by the textbook's authors Brian Whitelaw and Rick Parent. This manual contains learning objectives, a list of key terms with page references, and extensive discussion points for engaging students in the classroom.

NETA PowerPoint

Microsoft® PowerPoint ® lecture slides have been created for every chapter. There is an average of 35 slides per chapter, many featuring key figures and tables from *Community-Based Strategic Policing in Canada*. NETA principles of clear design and engaging content have been incorporated throughout, making it simple for instructors to customize the deck for their courses.

ACKNOWLEDGMENTS

In preparing this edition, we have been very fortunate to have had the exceptional support of a very talented and motivating editorial team at Nelson, comprised of Gail Brown, Content Manager; Leanna MacLean, Publisher; Claire Varley, Marketing Manager; Daniela Glass, Project Manager, Rights Acquisition & Policy; Jaime Smith, Production Project Manager; and Natalie Barrington, Copyright Licensing and Photo Researcher. We can't thank these individuals enough for their encouragement and assistance in taking our ideas and presenting them in a very engaging and learner-focused textbook.

We would also like to thank our long-time colleague Dr. Curt Griffiths at Simon Fraser University, who gave us our start in sharing our insights with the Canadian police academic community. Curt has been an important contributor to the study and practice of policing and his keen insights have helped us develop the evolving model of community-based policing in Canada.

We would also like to thank Sandra Kurdziel, Hamilton Police Service, who shared with us information about Hamilton's award-winning Social Navigator Program; Tammi Simcoe of the Ontario Provincial Police, who shared with us how the model of Community Mobilization and Engagement is implemented in the Ontario Provincial Police; and Chief Robert A. Keetch of the Sault Ste. Marie Police Service, who has demonstrated strong leadership commitment to the advancement of the Ontario Model of Community Mobilization and Engagement. It is always a pleasure working with progressive, strategic thinkers committed to the evolving model of community policing in Canada. Our thanks also go out to the police services in Canada that supported this edition by granting permission to use their material in this textbook. It is the collective efforts of various sources that allows Canadians to benefit from some of the finest policing in the world.

Finally, a special thanks to the faculty and students at universities and colleges, as well as the serving police officers across Canada, who continue to utilize this textbook. We appreciate your continuous support and the valuable feedback that you provide as we attempt to continually enhance the concepts and practice associated with community-based strategic policing in Canada.

Brian Whitelaw, Calgary Police Service, retired
Rick Parent, School of Criminology, Simon Fraser University

About the Authors

Brian Whitelaw

Brian Whitelaw is currently Superintendent in charge of Calgary Transit Community Peace Officers. Brian retired from the Calgary Police Service as Inspector in 2011. In 2012, he won the Province of Alberta Solicitor General Crime Prevention Award. Brian has a Master's degree in Public Policy, Law and Administration and is the author of a number of national policing courses and peer-reviewed journal articles. His primary research interest is organizational effectiveness in public safety organizations.

Rick Parent

Rick Parent is an Associate Professor at the School of Criminology at Simon Fraser University. Rick is a former police officer, having completed 30 years of service with the Delta Police Force (BC), and a former police recruit instructor at the Justice Institute of British Columbia–Police Academy. He has a Ph.D. in criminology, and his research interests include international policing, police ethics and accountability, police use of deadly force, and the phenomenon of "suicide by cop." Rick is frequently utilized in court proceedings as an expert witness in regards to police shootings, in Canada and the United States.

UNIT 1

S. Forster/Alamy Stock Photo

Policing in Canada

Evolution of Canadian Policing

Sir Robert Peel was the father of contemporary policing, who envisioned policing as it is today.

Source: Pictorial Press Ltd/Alamy Stock Photo

Learning Objectives

After completing this chapter, you should be able to:

- Identify the key historical developments in policing,
- Discuss the emergence of police services,
- Discuss how Sir Robert Peel has influenced modern policing,
- Describe how the role of police in France differed from that in England, and
- Discuss the emergence of women in policing.

INTRODUCTION

In this chapter, we provide a brief overview of the evolution of policing. The materials in this chapter are designed to provide you with a backdrop against which to study the emergence and practice of community policing and will be useful in understanding both the possibilities and the obstacles confronting the delivery of policing services within a community policing model. A historical overview provides us with valuable insights into the values, beliefs, and traditions of a community. Furthermore, history plays an important role in how communities define their own identities and how they interact with their local police. In this way, important implications for how policing is delivered in communities can be more fully understood.

THE ORIGINS AND EVOLUTION OF POLICING

The development of full-time, state-sanctioned police forces enforcing sets of codified laws is a relatively recent phenomenon. Prior to the emergence of the state and governmental arrangements with centralized authority, order among groups was maintained through a system of self-policing. Those whose behaviour contravened established folkways and customs faced personal, group, and tribal retaliation. In these rural, agrarian societies, which were concerned primarily with day-to-day subsistence and survival, there were no individuals or organizations charged with the task of law enforcement.

As societies increased in complexity, however, the effectiveness of these self-policing arrangements diminished. Systems of codified laws were enacted, such as the Hammurabi Code in 1200 BC and similar codes of law in the Shang (1500 BC) and Chou (1000 BC) dynasties. These codes of law, enforced by military authority, outlined prescribed rules of conduct and penalties for noncompliance. The enactment of these codes of law signalled a shift in the enforcement of conduct away from the individual and group level towards the level of centralized authority.

Several centuries later, in the Greek city-states and in the Roman Empire, similar developments occurred. In Greece, a system of self-policing called *kin-police* was implemented. In Imperial Rome, the law was codified in the Law of the Twelve Tablets (450 BC), and officials were assigned the task of law enforcement. At the height of the Roman Empire, there were distinct police forces. In both Greece and the Roman Empire, the military was charged with policing. The Romans were the first to use nonmilitary units, the *vigiles*, to assist in maintaining order and to fight fires. The *vigiles* in the Roman Empire and the kin-police in the Greek city-states are early examples of policing; however, it was in England that the institution of policing was to develop, and this would have a profound effect upon Canadian policing.

The Development of Policing in England

Prior to the Industrial Revolution and the development of capitalism, England was a feudal society made up of villages. Policing was a *community responsibility* (hold this thought until we return to a discussion of community policing in Chapter 2). Order was maintained under the principle of "hue and cry," which invested in every able-bodied man the responsibility to assist in the pursuit and apprehension of law violators. Failure to respond to the **hue and cry** could result in punishment of the derelict citizen, often a punishment equal to that imposed on the law-breaker.

Under the reign of Alfred the Great (871–901), the responsibilities of local communities for peacekeeping and order maintenance were strengthened. Lacking a standing army to maintain order and not having the financial resources to create a force specifically for peacekeeping, Alfred instituted the **frankpledge system** (see Figure 1.1). This system was based on the principle of the mutual responsibility of each man to his neighbours. Under

Figure 1.1 Frankpledge System in Feudal England

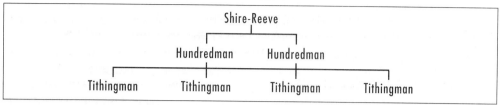

Source: Critchley (1978).

the frankpledge system, all free men between the ages of 15 and 60 were required to enrol in groupings of 10 families, called *tithings*. In each tithing, a tithingman was responsible for keeping order, and citizens were required to report crimes to him and to respond to his hue and cry (commonly heard as "Halt! Who goes there?").

Stenning (1981, 17) notes that the tithingman was "an elected community spokesman, responsible for all aspects of local government within his community, and … entirely responsible to the community that elected him as its representative." The tithingman also had the authority to collect fines from those charged with breaching the peace, and to demand surety or bail. Each adult male in the community was required to accept a turn in the position of tithingman.

As the size and population of villages grew, tithings were formed into *hundreds* (groups of 10 tithings), each headed by a hundredman. *Constables*, generally considered to be the first real police officers, were appointed by local noblemen and placed in charge of the equipment and weapons of the hundred. Hundreds were combined to form *shires* (parishes or counties), which were administered by officials known as *shire-reeves* (sheriffs). Shire-reeves were appointed by the king to represent his interests and to uphold the authority of the Crown. The shire-reeve was invested with considerable military, civil, and judicial powers and made periodic visits to each hundred to ensure that the system of local policing was operating properly.

This locally based system of crime control evolved from the concept of mutual responsibility by individual residents. Although it invested the tithingmen and hundredmen with a certain amount of authority for maintaining order in communities, an important attribute of the frankpledge system was that it was organized from the ground up. The tithingmen and hundredmen were chosen from within the community, were responsible to that community, and could be removed for dereliction of duty. This system of peacekeeping was in sharp contrast to the policing arrangements that existed at the time in Continental Europe, where the police were directly attached to centralized, autocratic rule.

After the Norman Invasion of England in 1066, William the Conqueror continued the frankpledge system, despite a movement away from community responsibility for maintaining peace (as established by the tithing system) towards a concept of state responsibility. To assist in the implementation of Norman policing, the shire-reeves were invested with considerable powers, which were often used to collect unjust and oppressive fines and taxes from the community. Military officers were assigned the responsibility for maintaining order in specified areas.

By 1252, under the reign of Henry III, the position of constable had come to be applied to the local law enforcement officers—previously known as tithingmen—and a "watch and ward" system had been introduced in communities to maintain order. Critchley (1978, 6) notes that the watch and ward system provided for two watchmen to supplement the duties of the constable: "A watch of up to sixteen men … was to be stationed at every gate of a walled town between sunset and sunrise, and the watchmen were given the power to arrest strangers during the hours of darkness." All able-bodied men in the town were required to serve a term on watch, reinforcing the responsibility of individual citizens to participate in policing.

Between the 13th century and the passage of the Police Act in 1829, two important statutes were enacted that structured both the nature of policing and the role of constables in England. The **Statute of Winchester**, passed in 1285, "sought to rationalize and redefine the police system that had been gradually developed over preceding centuries" (Stenning 1981, 23). The statute assigned to each hundred responsibility for all offences committed within it, revived the hue and cry, and reinforced the watch and ward system. In 1361, the **Justice of the Peace Act** centralized peacekeeping duties under justices of the peace, who were appointed directly by the king and who were superior in power and authority to the constables. The justice of the peace replaced the shire-reeve as peace officer while also acting in a judicial capacity. This development marked the first instance in which the police had been subordinated to the judiciary—an arrangement that resulted in considerable injustice and corruption.

By the 1500s, the system of community-based policing had begun to deteriorate, due in large measure to the growth of cities such as London, the increased mobility of the population, and the beginnings of the shift from a primary agricultural economy to one based on industry. As communities were transformed by these events, individuals avoided serving as constables, paying others to assume their duties. This practice had disastrous consequences; often only the unemployed and uneducated were willing to take on the constable's duties. The long-standing system of community-based policing was thereby undermined.

As a consequence of the vast changes occurring in English society, the increasing corruption of justices of the peace, and the reluctance of citizens to serve as constables, many towns and cities, including London, were unpoliced by the 1800s. Merchants and industrialists grew more and more fearful of the "dangerous classes" and the threat they posed to law and order. Businesses began to employ private police to protect their establishments and to assist in maintaining order. Against this backdrop—the deterioration of community-based policing and the increasing class distinctions between the propertied business people and industrialists on the one hand and the propertyless peasants on the other—modern policing as we know it developed.

Policing Developments in France

The evolution of policing followed a different path in France, and cast the police in a different light among its citizens. During the 17th century, King Louis XIV maintained a small, central police organization consisting of some 40 inspectors who, with the help of numerous paid informants, supplied the government with details about the conduct of private individuals. The king could then administer a kind of summary justice as he saw fit. This system continued during the reigns of Louis XV and Louis XVI. After the French Revolution (1789–1799), two separate police bodies were set up, one to handle ordinary duties and the other to deal with political crimes. The French Revolution brought about significant reform to French governmental structures but left lingering fears among the citizenry that the police represented an arm of the absolute monarchy whose primary role was essentially to "spy" on citizens and report back to the king. Based on the French experience with police, Londoners understandably were fearful and suspicious about the role and intentions of a full-time police force in England.

As the French settled in New France, now Quebec, they brought with them systems of security and policing modelled after those in France. One custom in particular that they continued was the practice of granting wealthy persons large tracts of land. Around 1633, this practice resulted in a wave of immigrants coming to New France as settlers who hoped to obtain land of their own.

The history of early policing in Quebec provides a valuable lesson for contemporary policing in Canada, particularly since 11 September 2001, when the role of the police grew to include what Murphy (2005) calls "security policing." We will examine this in greater detail in the next chapter.

THE DEVELOPMENT OF MODERN POLICING

Modern policing is based on principles first set out in England in the early 1800s. One of the first organized attempts to address the increasing problem of disorder was made in London in 1748 by the magistrate (and novelist) Henry Fielding. To enforce the decisions of his court, Fielding created the Bow Street Runners, named after the street on which his court was located. The Bow Street Runners were the first organized body of police. However, although Fielding had recruited men of high calibre and paid them well, the efforts of the force were not sufficient to stem the rising tide of social disorder and chaos produced by the emerging Industrial Revolution.

During the late 1700s and early 1800s, London was beset by a series of riots, many of which were caused by workers protesting rising prices and by the displacement of workers as a result of increased mechanization. Despite these developments, there continued to be strong resistance to the formation of an organized, 24-hour police force. In 1822, however, Britain's new Home Secretary, **Sir Robert Peel**, set out to establish a full-time police force. Unsurprisingly, his initial efforts met with considerable opposition.

Between 1822 and 1828, no fewer than 17 parliamentary subcommittees studied the need for reform of the system of law enforcement. There was concern about the concentration of power that would accrue to such a police force. Despite the widespread opposition to the formation of a police force, by the late 1820s the fear of crime and disorder had overshadowed the potential threats to liberty inherent in an organized police unit, at least among the propertied classes. In 1829, the **Metropolitan Police Act** was enacted and a full-time, unarmed police force of 1,000 men was established in London. Peel's new officers were known popularly as "bobbies" or "peelers," characterizations that were intended as derisive by a largely skeptical public.

Peel sought to legitimize the new police force by arguing that the police would serve the interests of *all* citizens, would include the prevention of crime as part of their mandate, and would recruit officers from the working class. In a determined effort to create a professional police force and to reduce public suspicion and distrust of the police, Peel instituted high standards of recruitment and training and selected constables from the community. He also introduced the concept of police stations spread throughout the community.

Peel formulated several principles for law enforcement that have remained the basis for professional police work (see A Closer Look 1.1). Although these principles were set out early in the 19th century, they are still very much alive and well today and are reflected in the philosophy and practice of community policing. Although Peel's principles were first set down nearly 200 years ago, they provide the foundation for community policing as it is implemented today. This is fascinating, given the immense changes that have occurred in society since the early 1800s.

With this brief historical introduction completed, we can now turn our attention to the development of policing in Canada, a process that was very much influenced by events in England.

A BRIEF HISTORY OF CANADIAN POLICING

Early police work in Canada was characterized by a considerable degree of diversity. Prior to Confederation in 1867, each region of the country had its own policing arrangements, which depended on the size of the settlements, the characteristics of the population, and the specific needs of communities. In areas settled by the French, for example, major town centres were policed under the traditional French system of captains of militias. In Upper Canada, by contrast, the influence of the English was evident, with the policing system based on the common law and carried out by sheriffs, high constables, constables, and

A CLOSER LOOK 1.1

THE PRINCIPLES OF SIR ROBERT PEEL

1. The basic mission of the police is to prevent crime and disorder.

2. The ability of the police to perform their duties depends upon public approval of their actions.

3. Police must secure the co-operation of the public in voluntary observance of the law in order to secure and maintain the respect of the public.

4. The degree of public co-operation with police diminishes proportionately to the necessity of the use of physical force.

5. Police maintain public favour by constantly demonstrating absolutely impartial service, not by catering to public opinion.

6. Police should use physical force only to the extent necessary to ensure compliance with the law or to restore order only after persuasion, advice, and warnings are insufficient.

7. Police should maintain a relationship with the public that is based on the fact that the police are the public and the public are the police.

8. Police should direct their actions toward their functions and not appear to usurp the powers of the judiciary.

9. The test of police efficiency is the absence of crime and disorder, not the visible evidence of the police dealing with them.

Source: Charles Reith, *The Principles of Sir Robert Peel Oliver and Boyd, A new study of police history* (1956).

---

justices of the peace. Historians have made the important observation that communities and settlements created formal police forces only when there was a "felt need" to do so.

Early attempts to establish a formal system of justice, including police, met with failure in Upper Canada and Quebec precisely for this reason (Talbot, Jayewardene, and Juliani 1983, 84). This highlights one of the key issues in the emergence of formal policing in Canada: Much like their British counterparts, early Canadians were hesitant to create police forces that had authority and power over the population.

In alignment with Peel's Principles, Canadian policing evolved with the approval, respect, and cooperation of the public. Often referred to as **policing by consent**, police powers have the common consent of the Canadian public instead of being imposed by the state. This has led to the **legitimacy of the police** in Canada—the general belief that police should be permitted to exercise their authority to manage conflicts, maintain social order, and solve problems in the community.

Other developments beginning in the late 20th century and continuing into the early 21st century include a concerted effort to reinvolve community residents in preventing and responding to crime and social disorder. The view that professional police forces can, on their own and without the assistance of community residents, prevent and solve problems of crime and disorder is fading rapidly. How to re-engage the community in identifying and responding to crime and social disorder is the subject of our discussion in Chapter 10.

Municipal Policing

Prior to the development of organized police forces, community residents performed a sort of informal law enforcement. In Halifax, for example, tavern owners were charged with maintaining order. These arrangements, however, were ultimately insufficient to meet the problems of an increasingly urbanized and industrialized society. It was in the eastern regions of the country that the first appointed police constables appeared, their role most likely being restricted to night watch duties. Eastern port cities such as Halifax and St. John's relied on militias and the navy, while other, less populated regions of the country remained largely unpoliced. As more settlers moved west, however, the need to control disorder—usually related to drinking, prostitution, and gambling—increased.

The historical record indicates that the first police constables were appointed in Quebec City in the mid-1600s and in Upper Canada (now the Province of Ontario) in the early 1800s. In 1835, the City of Toronto replaced its night watch system with six full-time police constables; in 1858, legislation was enacted in Upper Canada that authorized towns and cities to create boards or commissions to oversee the activities of police forces. Given the vast distances and sparse populations, municipal police forces developed much later in the western regions of the country.

In 1845, a bylaw in the newly created town of St. Catharines provided for "pound-keepers and constables," citizen volunteers who provided assistance when it was required and were paid according to a fee schedule. The activities of this "police force" were supervised by a police board, which also served as the town council. The volunteers were paid according to a fee schedule that included a payment of five shillings each for issuing a summons, making an arrest under a warrant, and assisting in an arrest; escorting a prisoner to jail earned 15 shillings. The town hired its first full-time police officers in 1856 (Niagara Regional Police Service 2000).

Police constables were generally assigned other duties as well. In Sudbury, Ontario, for example, the first constable was the jailer, tax collector, sanitary inspector, truant officer, firefighter, bailiff, chimney inspector, and animal pound caretaker (Juliani, Talbot, and Jayewardene 1984, 326). In 1826, Kingston appointed its first paid constable, Henry Wilkinson, who also held the position of street surveyor.

The mandate of early municipal police forces covered three primary tasks: (1) policing conflicts that developed between labourers and business owners; (2) attempting to maintain moral standards by enforcing laws against drunkenness, prostitution, and gambling; and (3) apprehending criminals (Juliani, Talbot, and Jayewardene 1984). The historical record indicates that the five-man Kingston police force created in 1841 spent most of its time dealing with drunk and disorderly persons (McCullough 1997).

Provincial Police

All the regions that ultimately became part of Confederation had police forces. These forces were most often created in response to disorder emerging from the opportunities and challenges of exploration and settlement—for example, the disorder that emerged with the discovery of gold in British Columbia and Ontario. The earliest provincial force was established in Quebec in 1870, three years after it entered Confederation. In BC, police forces formed in the colonies of Vancouver Island and British Columbia as early as 1858. A large number of these early police officers were Black immigrants from California. In 1866, the two police forces united; in 1871, they became the BC Provincial Police when that province entered Confederation.

Provincial police forces created in Alberta, Saskatchewan, and Manitoba encountered a number of difficulties, including poor leadership and a lack of qualified officers; by the late 1920s these provincial forces had been replaced by the Royal Canadian Mounted Police (RCMP, the Mounties). Provincial policing in Ontario followed a different course. On 13 October 1909, an order-in-council authorized the immediate formation of the Ontario Provincial Police Force. By 1950, the RCMP had assumed provincial policing responsibilities in all provinces except Quebec and Ontario; those two provinces continued to operate independent provincial police forces.

A CLOSER LOOK 1.2

TORONTO POLICE SERVICE IN THE MAKING

Well over 150 years have passed since the muddy town of "York" was renamed "Toronto" in 1834. In that year Mayor William Lyon Mackenzie headed the city, which had a population of just 9,000. That same year, the Toronto Police Force had its humble beginnings when the first full-time High Constable was appointed to lead a handful of volunteers. There were no permanent officers, Constables were simply hired as needed. It wasn't until a year later that five paid constables were hired.

1834—First full-time High Constable.

1859—First Board of Commissioners of Police, which assumed control of the city from Municipal council. The Board included the Mayor, the Recorder or County Judge, and the Police Magistrate. New discipline and standards came to the service.

1837—First uniforms, which are forest-green.

1874—First use of communications technology, the telegraph, which links four stations.

1876—First all-night patrols, extending police coverage around the clock.

1880—First police benefit fund. The first beneficiary, who resigned from the service due to ill health, received $29.64 a month for the rest of his life.

1884—First electric streetlights, welcomed by police walking the night beat—and cursed by would-be wrongdoers.

1886—First mounted unit, which patrols outlying areas and controls speeding horses.

1887—First call box.

1894—Bicycles provided for patrols, a first for any police service in North America.

1895—First police boat, to suppress illegal fishing, shooting, and bathing.

1906—First use of fingerprinting.

1907—First parking ticket issued (there were only 1,500 cars in all of Ontario!).

Source: Toronto Police Services. Found at http://www.torontopolice.on.ca/publications/files/misc/history/1t.html

Federal Police

It is worth noting the contribution of the Dominion Police to the evolution of Canadian policing. The Dominion Police were created by an act of Parliament in 1868, although there were only two officers at that time. By 1869, their authority and numbers had grown, although mainly in Ontario and Quebec. Over time their duties evolved to include protecting parliamentary buildings, guarding navy yards, and enforcing laws involving the national interest, such as those against counterfeiting and white slavery. They also established a national fingerprint bureau and a branch that maintained the records of paroled and reporting prisoners. The Dominion Police existed until 1920, when the RCMP assumed a national presence and absorbed its 150 members.

The Mounties

The RCMP, originally known as the North-West Mounted Police (NWMP), was created in 1873 mainly to ensure the orderly settlement of Canada's sparsely settled northwestern territories. Sir John A. Macdonald, the prime minister of the day, wanted Canada to avoid what had happened in the American West, where settlers and miners clashed violently with Indigenous peoples. The model for the proposed force was the Royal Irish Constabulary, which had provided the pattern for many police forces throughout the British Empire. The NWMP were never intended to become a national police force. It was anticipated that once its original objectives had been met in terms of securing peaceful settlement, the responsibility for policing would shift to local communities as areas became more urbanized. However, this did not generally occur.

In 1916, the Royal North-West Mounted Police (RNWMP) announced that contracts with the prairie provinces would be cancelled by the end of that year. Those provinces established their own police forces the following year. For example, the Alberta Provincial Police formed in 1917, following the withdrawal of the RNWMP, and remained the province's police force until 1932. In 1932, the Alberta government reluctantly dissolved the Alberta Provincial Police, mainly due to the economics of the Great Depression, and by the end of that year the now national RCMP had resumed policing in the prairie provinces and the Maritimes. It continues in that role to this day. The 2000 *Report on Policing in the Province of Alberta* examined the role of the RCMP in Alberta and took a serious look at the idea of establishing a provincial police service by 2012 (Government of Alberta 2000).

While the evolution of policing in western Canada favoured provincial police over the RCMP, attempts to phase out the force in the 1920s encountered resistance in many regions. In fact, the later emergence of the RCMP as a national police force involved in policing provinces and municipalities was more the result of historical accident than any

The RCMP were originally known as the North-West Mounted Police. They were created in 1873 to maintain law and order and to ensure orderly settlement of the unpoliced and sparsely settled Canadian Northwest.

Source: Library and Archives Canada/C-042755

master plan'. And as we will see, this has resulted in the Mounties facing unique challenges in developing and implementing community policing.

The duties and activities of the first police constables were highly localized. Officers patrolled on foot, and their primary roles were preventive as well as reactive. As night watchmen, the officers were very familiar with the areas to which they were assigned.

Evolution of the Police Role

From the early 1900s through to roughly 1970, reform efforts in Canadian policing focused on ensuring that police forces functioned free from political influence, operated with strong centralized control, maintained strong discipline, and used both personnel and technology efficiently. Canadian police services remained focused on the Peelian principle that effective policing required community approval and support. Strong leadership ensured that police services functioned with restraint and in accordance with Canadian political traditions. England's Metropolitan Police Act served as the model for policing developments that were to occur in Canada in the 20th century.

In the United States, by contrast, police officers derived their authority from local political power but their ability to obtain citizen cooperation often depended on the policing style of individual officers. Unlike in the British model of policing that Peel had established, American officers were provided with greater individual discretion and were influenced by local politics. This sometimes resulted in policing that was inefficient, corrupt, discriminatory, and subject to political interference. These factors eventually forced federal and state governments in the United States to create their own police organizations.

It is in this context that during this era, described as the **professional era of policing**, efforts were made to increase the control and efficiency of the police in North America (Fleissner and Heinzelmann 1996, 2; Goldstein 1990). During this time frame, three technological innovations radically altered the delivery of policing services, often in response to the growth of urban centres and communities: (1) the expansion of telephone systems into households, (2) the emergence of police patrol cars, and (3) the introduction of the two-way radio. All three innovations precipitated a fundamental change in how police services were delivered. Police officers became reactive, relying on complaints telephoned in by community residents. Officers were dispatched to the scene of a crime by two-way radio in patrol cars. Motorized patrol began to emerge as the primary method of police patrol.

Since officers were now more mobile, they could cover a larger area than foot patrol officers. However, this also meant that officers became more isolated from the communities they policed. The patrol car, rather than the neighbourhood beat, became the "office" of the police officer. This led to the centralization of police command and control. The introduction of additional technologies, including computer terminals in patrol cars and centralized dispatch systems that prioritize calls for assistance, has further distanced officers from the community. The computer screen, rather than the community's residents, has become the primary source of information for officers. This makes it much more difficult for community residents to interact with and communicate their concerns to local police constables. Calls are made to centralized telephone numbers. Dispatchers who are far removed from the neighbourhood and unfamiliar with residents and their concerns prioritize calls for assistance (Reiss 1992).

Gender and Policing

Women played a supporting role in Canadian policing for well over a hundred years; recently, they have become active participants in front-line policing. Since 1974, they have been involved in regular police duties, serving in a variety of roles and ranks, including as senior administrators and police chiefs. In the past decade, gay and lesbian officers have been acknowledged and welcomed within police services, further enhancing the diversity of Canadian police and expanding the community representation of police officers.

A CLOSER LOOK 1.3

THE HISTORY OF 9-1-1 EMERGENCY REPORTING IN CANADA

Canada adopted 9-1-1 in 1972. The first city to implement the system was London, Ontario, in 1974. In Quebec, it was Laval that first put 9-1-1 at the disposal of its residents, in 1977.

University of Manitoba Archives & Special Collections, Winnipeg Tribune fonds PC 18—"999 switchboard at Police Station" dated September 04, 1968

On 24 April 1981, the Communauté urbaine de Montréal public security commission formed a task force with the mandate to coordinate efforts to create an emergency communications centre (9-1-1). The centre began operations on 1 December 1985. It received all emergency calls from the CUM territory and directed them to the appropriate emergency services. It also offered telephone information to the public on services offered by the CUM and the transit corporation.

Source: Service de police de la Ville de Montréal, 911 Emergency Centre-History from https://www.spvm.qc.ca/en/Pages/Discover-SPVM/Who-does-what/911-Emergency-Centre-/History

A CLOSER LOOK 1.4

THE HISTORY OF WOMEN POLICING IN TORONTO

Use of the Toronto Police Services Images. Courtesy of the Toronto Police Services Board

JayLazarin/iStock photo

Courtesy of Toronto Police Museum

1974—Policewomen are placed on regular patrol duties with men and are expected to do the same work. Thirteen policewomen are transferred to the downtown core, where it will be decided whether women can perform the same duties as men. These women are armed with .38 calibre revolvers.

(continues)

1975—The title "Policewoman" is changed to Police Constable (Female).

2011—Of the 5,776 police officers in Toronto, 1,063 are female (Statistics Canada 2011).

Source: Toronto Police Service, Herstory: Milestones in the History of the Toronto Police Service Women, found at http://www.torontopolice.on.ca/museum/herstory-milestones_in_the_history_of_tps_women.pdf

She had to be 25 to 30 years of age and well educated. She had to live near No. 1 Station, to respond promptly to calls. She searched women who had been arrested and attended to them while they awaited court appearances. She was the Police Matron, and the first was a Mrs. Whiddon in 1887. That began a rich history of women in the police service, though it was not until 1913 that Mary Minty and Maria Levitt became Toronto's first policewomen. Besides dealing with female prisoners, they supervised dance halls ("where their visitations have a good moral effect") and handled the regulation of fortune tellers. Still, this was progress. After the original policewomen retired in 1919, three more were hired. In 1921, another two were appointed. They were gradually assigned more and more responsibilities. By 1933, policewomen were an integral part of the Morality Bureau, participating in undercover investigations.

When the Women's Bureau and the Youth Bureau were established in 1958, they were staffed almost entirely by female officers. These two bureaux allowed women to gain experience and demonstrate their competence. Equality in the service has come slowly but steadily. In 1945, the pay scale finally became the same for women as for men. That same year, women adopted the proper blue uniforms and their duties became more wide-ranging.

Women didn't ride in scout cars until 1959. In 1960, policewomen changed their hats to the derby style, after being mistaken for stewardesses or transit guides. Until 1972, a policewoman who had a baby had to resign. It was only in 1974 that policewomen were armed for the first time, carrying their revolvers in specially designed handbags. Today, women serve in every facet of policing and in the most senior positions. From the days when a handful of officers made up the female contingent, there are now more than 600 female officers, over 12 percent of the total. Women also comprise more than half of civilian staff. It has been a long, interesting, and rewarding ride since the days of Mrs. Whiddon.

Source: http://www.torontopolice.on.ca/publications/files/misc/history/4t.html

CHAPTER SUMMARY

As we end this chapter, there are some very important observations to consider when thinking about community policing. Historically, Canadian police have assisted with the formation of new communities, and their primary role has been to guide the peaceful settlement of new areas, particularly in northern and western Canada. In contrast to the United States, where the police were often brought into communities to re-establish order, Canadian policing evolved in a much more peaceful and orderly fashion. As a result, the local police have, to various degrees, shaped the development of many Canadian communities. Understandably, local residents, who had grown accustomed to their own methods of policing, often resisted the changes introduced by more formalized local policing. A major point that emerges from our brief historical review is that there was considerable public opposition—both in Europe during the early 1800s and in early Canada—to the creation of formal police services. Their necessity was questioned, and their role, based on unfavourable experiences in France, was regarded with suspicion. The historical relationship between police and the community is an important factor in contemporary levels of support, cooperation, and citizen involvement. The blueprint for Canadian policing has been shaped to a large extent by the emergence of the modern police service in London, England. However, the model of Canadian policing has also been influenced by policing practices in the United States, France, and Ireland. These influences have combined to give Canadian policing its distinctive character and positive international reputation.

CHAPTER REVIEW

Key Terms

- frankpledge system, p. 04
- hue and cry, p. 04
- Justice of the Peace Act (1361), p. 06
- legitimacy of the police, p. 08
- Metropolitan Police Act (1829), p. 07
- policing by consent, p. 08
- professional era of policing, p. 12
- Sir Robert Peel, p. 07
- Statute of Winchester (1285), p. 06

Key Points

- Prior to the creation of formal police services, communities policed themselves.
- There was opposition to the creation of formal police services.
- The development of full-time police forces, operating under the authority of the state and enforcing sets of codified laws, is a relatively recent phenomenon.
- The foundations of modern policing are the principles set forth by Sir Robert Peel in England in the early 1800s.
- The role of the police in Canadian history differs from that of the United States, where police were often brought in to re-establish order.
- Before Confederation in 1867, each region of the country had its own policing arrangements, depending on the size of the settlements, the characteristics of the population, and the specific needs of communities.
- The mandate of early municipal police forces covered three main tasks: (1) policing conflicts between labourers and business owners; (2) maintaining moral standards by enforcing laws against drunkenness, prostitution, and gambling, and (3) apprehending criminals.
- The provincial police forces created in Alberta, Saskatchewan, and Manitoba experienced a number of difficulties. By the late 1920s these provincial forces had been replaced by the RCMP. In BC, the provincial police were replaced by the RCMP in 1950.
- The RCMP, originally known as the North-West Mounted Police, was created in 1873 primarily to maintain law and order and ensure the orderly settlement of the previously unpoliced and sparsely settled northwest territory.
- The early 1900s to 1970 was the "professional era of policing," during which efforts were made to increase the control and efficiency of the police.
- Women have always been involved in policing, but it was not until 1974 that they began serving as front-line operational officers in Canada.
- History plays a role in how communities see themselves and how they interact with the police.

Self-Evaluation

QUESTIONS

1. Why is **Sir Robert Peel** an important person in our study of community policing?
2. In what way does the **hue and cry** illustrate the involvement of the community in maintaining order?
3. In what way could the **frankpledge system** be called the first type of community policing?
4. What was the significance of the **Statute of Winchester**, enacted in 1285?
5. Why is the **Justice of the Peace Act** (1321) important in our study of the history of policing?
6. The **mandate of early municipal police forces** covered three main tasks. Has this changed over the years?

7. What was the significance of the **Metropolitan Police Act** (1829)?
8. Define and discuss **policing by consent** and the **legitimacy of the police in Canada**.
9. What were the initial objectives of the **NWMP** when it was formed?
10. List some of the characteristics of the **professional era of policing**.
11. Discuss the **three technological innovations** that have radically altered the delivery of policing services in recent times.
12. State some of the **historic moments of women in policing** that have occurred in Toronto since 1959.

KEY IDEAS

1. Who was Sir Robert Peel?
   a. The first Commissioner of the North-West Mounted Police.
   b. The Chief Constable of the first municipal police force established in Canada.
   c. The chief of the first organized police force in London, England.
   d. The first provincial police commissioner in Canada.

2. According to the historical record, where and when were the first police constables in Canada appointed?
   a. Quebec City in the early 1600s.
   b. Halifax in the early 1700s.
   c. Upper Canada in the early 1700s.
   d. The current province of British Columbia in the 1800s.

3. Early Canadians were hesitant to create police forces that had authority and power over the population. What was the result?
   a. Police services were developed in a uniform manner with minimal duties.
   b. Strong support existed for the development of localized municipal police forces.
   c. Law enforcement functions were performed informally by community residents.
   d. The NWMP was created as a national police force to facilitate peaceful settlement.

4. In 1829 a full-time, unarmed police force of 1000 men was established in London. What were these new officers popularly known as?
   a. Cops or coppers.
   b. Officers or NCOs.
   c. Bobbies or peelers.
   d. Detectives or investigators.

5. In the history of policing in France, how were the police considered in general?
   a. As supportive and respectful of human rights.
   b. As spies for the king.
   c. As focused on citizen safety.
   d. As politically neutral.

6. Which police force was the model for the RCMP (originally known as the North-West Mounted Police)?
   a. Victoria Police Department
   b. Royal Irish Constabulary
   c. London Metropolitan Police
   d. New York City Police Department

7. Why did the Alberta government dissolve the Alberta Provincial Police?
   a. A lack of suitable applicants in the province.
   b. Corruption and scandals within the police department.
   c. The economics of the Depression.
   d. A political desire for a national police force.

8. Which term describes the period from the early 1900s through to roughly 1970?
    a. The professional era of policing.
    b. The modern era of policing.
    c. The era of reform and restoration.
    d. The era of technological change.

9. Historically, the neighbourhood beat acted as the "office" of the police officer. Which of the following is considered the police officer's office today?
    a. The community police station.
    b. Departmental headquarters.
    c. Local coffee shops and youth centres.
    d. The patrol car.

10. Which group made up the earliest police force in British Columbia, created in 1858?
    a. Individuals from the logging community.
    b. French Canadians from Quebec.
    c. Black immigrants from California.
    d. Former police personnel from Ontario.

11. Unlike the British model of policing that Peel had established, American officers were:
    a. provided with firearms, a badge, and accommodation.
    b. provided with greater individual discretion and influenced by politics.
    c. provided with stricter guidelines regarding community engagement.
    d. provided with greater freedom to engage in outside employment.

12. The term "policing by consent" refers to the concept that:
    a. individuals have a level of control when responding to a police request.
    b. police powers have the common consent of the elected government, rather than the imposed powers of the monarchy.
    c. police powers have the common consent of the public, rather than the imposed powers of the state.
    d. individuals and the Charter of Rights serve to direct and influence the powers of the police.

Canadian Policing: Situations and Strategies

Case Studies

Case Study 1. The Near-Demise of the RCMP

The RCMP is a unique police force. Its officers are involved in federal, provincial, and municipal policing across the country, and the force itself is one of the most widely recognized symbols of Canada. What is not as well-known is that during the 1920s, when the RCMP was a small police force involved only in federal policing, there was considerable opposition to its expansion into the various regions of the country, and the force was nearly phased out due to political pressure. The emergence of the RCMP as the national police force was more the result of historical accident than the product of a master plan. It certainly went against trends in Britain and the United States, where police services were decentralized. In fact, there were attempts to abolish the RCMP in 1922 and 1923. The decision by the federal government to create the RCMP in 1920 by merging the North-West Mounted Police and the Dominion Police (Canada's first federal police force) was met with considerable opposition, particularly among members of Parliament from the Atlantic region. This is reflected in the arguments made by Robert H. Butts, representing Cape Breton South: "I have been a magistrate, sometimes I have been called a judge, of a town of between 9,000 and 10,000 people. We never had need of Mounted Police down there and we have no need of them now… Do not send hayseed from away across the plains to Nova Scotia… I say that it is dangerous to send them there. I speak for 73,000 people in Cape Breton, and I can say that they will not appreciate any such intrusion." Another MP from Nova Scotia, J.H. Sinclair, echoed these views: "The Federal Government are assuming a duty that they do not require to assume; that the provinces are not asking them to assume, and that the provinces themselves are well able to take care of" (both cited in Macleod 1994, 45–46). Concern on the part of the federal government with increasing labour unrest and "subversives," combined with the ineptitude of provincial police forces, however, provided the Mounties with an opportunity to significantly expand and, ultimately, to become extensively involved in provincial and municipal policing.

Interestingly, much of the opposition to the RCMP arose from concerns that the force was not a local police service, but rather a federal police force that also provided provincial and municipal police services under contract. These issues of local control and accountability continue to be raised today and are particularly relevant in the context of community policing.

REFERENCES

Critchley, T.A. 1978. A History of the Police in England and Wales. London: Constable.

Fleissner, D., and F. Heinzelmann. 1996 (August). "Crime Prevention through Environmental Design and Community Policing." Research in Action. National Institute of Justice. Washington, DC: US Department of Justice.

Goldstein, H. 1990. Problem-Oriented Policing. New York: McGraw-Hill.

Government of Alberta. 2000. "Policing Alberta: A Discussion Paper". Edmonton: Alberta Justice.

Juliani, T.J., C.K. Talbot, and C.H.S. Jayewardene. 1984. "Municipal Policing in Canada: A Developmental Perspective." Canadian Police College Journal 8(3): 315–85.

Macleod, R.C. 1994. "The RCMP and the Evolution of Provincial Policing." In Police Powers in Canada: The Evolution and Practice of Authority, ed. R.C. Macleod and D. Schneiderman. Toronto: University of Toronto Press.

McCullough, E.C. 1997. "150 Years of Service: The Kingston Police Force, 1841-1991." http://www.police.kingston.on.ca.

Murphy, C. 2005. "Securitizing Community Policing: Towards a Canadian Public Policing Model." Canadian Review of Policing Research 1.http://crpr.icaap.org/index.php/crpr/article/view/41/37

Niagara Regional Police Service. 2000. "A Brief History of the Niagara Regional Police Service." http://www.nrps.com.

Reiss, A.J. 1992. "Police Organization in the Twentieth Century." In Modern Policing: Crime and Justice, vol. 15, ed. M. Tonry and N. Morris. 51–95. Chicago: University of Chicago Press.

Statistics Canada. 2011. Police Resources in Canada. Cat. no. 85-225-X. Ottawa.

Stenning, P.C. 1981. Legal Status of the Police. Ottawa: Law Reform Commission of Canada.

Talbot, C.K., C.H.S. Jayewardene, and T.J. Juliani. 1983. The Thin Blue Line: A Historical Perspective of Policing in Canada. Ottawa: Crimcare.

Overview of Canadian Policing

Policing is the largest component of the Canadian criminal justice system. Traditionally, the police mandate has been categorized as follows: crime control (catching criminals), order maintenance (keeping the peace), and service (assisting the public). Increasingly today, a large portion of police work involves gathering and processing information ("knowledge workers") as well as restoring order in conflict situations.

Source: The Canadian Press/Peter McCabe

Learning Objectives

After completing this chapter, you should be able to:

- Discuss the structure of policing in Canada,
- Describe the contemporary roles of the police,
- Identify and discuss the contexts of police work, and
- Describe trends in police work.

INTRODUCTION

In this chapter, we examine the current structure of policing across Canada, including the current arrangements for delivering policing services across the country and the contemporary roles of the police. We consider the various contexts in which police work is carried out in Canada and identify a number of key trends and challenges that are having a significant impact on policing. A clear understanding of the limitations facing contemporary police work makes the case for community-based policing much more compelling. It is these challenges and possibilities that require police agencies to be more strategic in their delivery and that we believe represent an evolving model of policing, which we call "community-based strategic policing."

THE STRUCTURE OF CONTEMPORARY CANADIAN POLICING

Policing is the largest component of the Canadian criminal justice system and, accordingly, receives the biggest slice of funding, at $14.2 billion annually in 2015–16 (Statistics Canada 2017, 11). This works out to $313 per Canadian to cover the costs of policing. In 2015 there were 176 stand-alone municipal police in Canada serving 64 per-cent of the Canadian population (Statistics Canada 2016a), and of those, 117 services have fewer than 25 staff. Five Canadian police services—the RCMP, the Toronto Police Service, the Ontario Provincial Police (OPP), the Sûreté du Québec (SQ), and the City of Montreal Police Service (Service de police de la Ville de Montréal, or SPVM)—account for just over 60 percent of all police officers in Canada (see A Closer Look 2.1). Municipalities across the country, with the exception of those in Yukon, the Northwest Territories, and Nunavut, have a choice as to whether to create and operate their own independent police service or to contract out to a provincial police service.

A CLOSER LOOK 2.1

QUICK FACTS ABOUT POLICING IN CANADA (2016*)

1. Total number of police officers: 68,773

2. Total number of civilian employees: 28,422

3. Total number of private security personnel: 10,200 private investigators and 91,325 security guards (2006)

4. Police strength: 190 officers per 100,000 population (lower than United States [211 in 2012] and England/Wales [252])

5. Police officers per 100,000 population: Yukon (368), Nunavut (353), Manitoba (194), Quebec (191), Ontario (187), Newfoundland (172), Saskatchewan (200), British Columbia (184)

6. Women as a percentage of police officer positions: 21 percent, or slightly more than one in five police officers

7. Visible minorities as a percentage of police officer positions: 9 percent (2012 data)

8. Indigenous persons as a percentage of police officer positions: 5 percent (self-reported) (2012 data)

*Reported on 15 May 2016

Sources: Statistics Canada, Canadian Centre for Justice Statistics, 2017, 2012

Under the ***Police Services Act*** in Ontario, for example, municipalities have a number of options in terms of the provision of policing services. They may:

- have their own independent municipal police force,
- amalgamate their police service with one or more other services,
- share police services with one or more other municipalities, or
- contract with the OPP to provide police services.

Policing in Canada is carried out at four levels: municipal, provincial, federal, and First Nations. See Table 2.1 for additional information on policing in Canada.

In Quebec, communities with fewer than 5,000 residents may sign service agreements with the provincial Ministère de la Sécurité publique for the SQ to provide police services. Municipalities with more than 5,000 residents may enter into similar arrangements with the authorization of the minister.

In Ontario, the Ministry of Community Safety and Correctional Services is responsible for ensuring that adequate and effective policing services are provided to municipalities. The responsibilities of the Minister of Community Safety and Correctional Services (formerly the Solicitor General), as set out in Section 3(2) of the Police Services Act, include developing programs to enhance professional police practices, standards, and training; developing and promoting community policing; and maintaining records and conducting research on police-related issues.

Considerable variation exists among Canadian police services in terms of their size and responsibilities. Most, however, have similar divisions or sections, including:

- *Operational patrol:* patrol division, canine unit, identification squad, traffic, reserve or auxiliary;
- *Investigative:* general investigation (detectives), major crimes, vice offences;
- *Support services:* information technology, communications centre, victim services, community services, and crime prevention;
- *Administrative:* finance and payroll, property office;
- *Human resources:* staff development, recruiting, training; and Office of the chief.

Canadian police services, like their counterparts worldwide, have a rank structure that reflects their paramilitary organization. Most police services have a chief constable, a deputy chief constable, superintendents, and inspectors (often referred to as "commissioned officers," although they are not actually commissioned), and noncommissioned officers, including staff sergeants, sergeants, corporals, detectives, and constables. In recent years, the move towards community policing has resulted in major changes in the organization and rank structure of many police services. We will consider these changes in greater detail in Chapter 7.

Table 2.1 Quick Facts about Policing in Canada (2016)

	BC	Ontario	Yukon	Quebec	Canada
Total number of police officers	8,761	26,168	138	15,869	68,773
Females as a percentage of total officers	21.9	19.1	15.6	24.7	21.1
Number of police officers per 100,000 population	184	187	368	191	190
Total expenditure on policing ($000)	1,562,521	5,308,226	36,145	2,698,722	14,192,608

Source: Police Resources in Canada, 2016. ©2017

Independent Municipal Police Services

Municipal police forces assume responsibility for enforcing the Criminal Code, provincial statutes, and municipal bylaws within the city limits. Across Canada, municipal police services range in size from three members to more than 5,000 officers (the Toronto Police Service has 5,366 plus an additional 2,818 civilian personnel, and the Montreal Police Service has 4,583 and an additional 1,364 civilian personnel), and have jurisdiction within a city's boundaries. Newfoundland and Labrador, Yukon, the Northwest Territories, and Nunavut are the only areas in Canada without municipal police services. In addition to enforcing the Criminal Code, provincial statutes, municipal bylaws, certain federal statutes such as the Controlled Drugs and Substances Act have also come under the jurisdiction of municipal forces. Most police "work" is performed by services operating at this level. In recent years, municipal police services have been critical about the lack of resources the Royal Canadian Mounted Police are able to provide to joint-force operations.

Municipalities can select one of the three options in providing police services: they can create their own independent police service; they can join with an existing municipal police service, which often means becoming involved with a regional police service; or they can contract with the provincial police service (in Ontario and Quebec) or with the RCMP (in the rest of Canada) to provide police services.

Provincial Police Services

The provincial and territorial governments are responsible for the administration of justice and, to this end, oversee police services, prosecute offences, staff courthouses with judges, operate programs for adult and young offenders, and operate correctional facilities for offenders who receive sentences totalling less than two years. Police services generally fall under the purview of provincial ministries of justice or attorneys general.

Provincial police forces are charged with enforcing the Criminal Code and provincial statutes in areas not covered by municipal police services. These areas generally comprise rural areas and small towns. There are three independent provincial police forces in Canada: the Ontario Provincial Police (OPP), the Sûreté du Québec (SQ), and the Royal Newfoundland Constabulary (RNC). The RNC polices only the communities of Corner Brook, Churchill Falls, Labrador City, and St. John's. The RCMP, under contract, polices the remainder of the province.

In Ontario, the OPP is responsible for policing rural areas and the areas outside municipalities, and enforcing provincial laws as well as the Criminal Code. It provides general policing services to more than 2.4 million people (3.7 million during the summer months) throughout Ontario. The OPP deploys 1,845 police officers under contract to 325 Ontario municipalities, constituting 70 percent of all Ontario municipalities (Ontario Provincial Police 2015). The OPP's area of responsibility takes in 993,000 square kilometres of land and 174,000 kilometres of waterways. This wide range of settings presents special challenges, which we will address throughout this text.

A unique component of the OPP is the Aboriginal Policing Bureau, which oversees the delivery of policing services to First Nations communities and provides assistance and training for the transition to self-policing. Pursuant to the Ontario First Nations Policing agreement, the OPP administers policing for 20 First Nations. Indigenous and non-Indigenous constables who are posted to First Nations communities are required to complete specialized training to sensitize them to Native culture and communities.

Royal Canadian Mounted Police

The RCMP is a component (along with the Correctional Service of Canada and the National Parole Board) of the Ministry of Public Safety Canada and is divided into 15 divisions, in addition to its National Headquarters in Ottawa and Training Depot

Figure 2.1 Organization of the RCMP

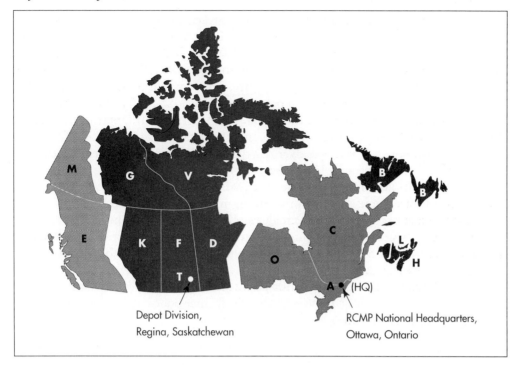

Depot Division,
Regina, Saskatchewan

RCMP National Headquarters,
Ottawa, Ontario

Pacific Region: E Division, Vancouver, British Columbia; M Division, Whitehorse, Yukon

Northwest Region: D Division, Winnipeg, Manitoba; T Depot and F Divisions, Regina, Saskatchewan; G Division, Yellowknife, Northwest Territories; V Division, Iqaluit, Nunavut Territory; K Division, Edmonton, Alberta

Central Region: O Division, London, Ontario; C Division, Montreal, Quebec; HQ and A Divisions, Ottawa, Ontario

Atlantic Region: B Division, St. John's, Newfoundland; H Division, Halifax, Nova Scotia; J Division, Fredericton, New Brunswick; L Division, Charlottetown, Prince Edward Island

Source: Reproduced with the permission of the RCMP.

in Regina (see Figure 2.1). The headquarters of these divisions are generally located in the provincial and territorial capitals and are under the supervision of a Commanding Officer. These divisions are organized into four regions, each under the direction a deputy commissioner (see Figure 2.1).

There is also a deputy commissioner at the national headquarters in charge of the various directorates located there.

The Royal Canadian Mounted Police Act provides the legislative basis for the operations and activities of the RCMP. The RCMP operates as a federal police force in all provinces and territories, enforcing or administering more than 250 federal statutes and agreements including the Controlled Drugs and Substances Act, as well as lesser-known statutes such as the Canada Shipping Act and the Canada Student Loans Act.

Nationwide, approximately 60 percent of RCMP personnel are involved in contract policing. That is, they serve as provincial and municipal police officers under agreements signed between the RCMP and the provinces/territories. However, there is no RCMP contract policing in Ontario or Quebec.

Regional Police Services

A regional police service generally involves the amalgamation of several independent police departments into one large organization. Regional police services have been a feature of policing for many years, and today there are a number of regional police services, including the Peel Regional Police, the York Regional Police, Niagara Regional Police Service, and the Halifax Regional Police. The regional police services of Peel, York, and Niagara serve more than 50 percent of Ontario's population. From 1962 to 2002, the number of independent municipal police services in Ontario has steadily declined from nearly 300 to fewer than 100. In 2010, the Ontario Provincial Police provided frontline policing services to over 322 municipalities, 148 of which had entered into formal policing contracts. In Quebec, the Montreal Police Service (formerly the Montreal Urban Community Police Service [MUCPS]) provides policing services to the City of Montreal and several surrounding municipalities. The Montreal Police Service was created as a result of the amalgamation of the urban communities around Montreal in 1971. An important point to keep in mind is the impact on a community when its local police service is amalgamated into a larger regional organization. We will address this issue later.

The Peel Regional Police was established on 1 January 1974, upon the creation of the Regional Municipality of Peel. It incorporated the former police services of Mississauga, Port Credit, Streetsville, Brampton, and Chinguacousy.

Indigenous Policing

A unique feature of the policing landscape in Canada is "autonomous" Indigenous police forces, which have developed across the country over the past three decades. This is occurring in the context of a broader movement leading towards Indigenous self-government. Under the First Nations Policing Policy (FNPP), Indigenous policing is implemented across Canada through tripartite agreements negotiated among the federal government, provincial or territorial governments, and First Nations. The agreements are cost-shared 52 percent by the Government of Canada and 48 percent by the province involved. Depending on the resources available, the First Nation may develop and administer its own police service, as is the case in most of Quebec and Ontario, or it may enter into a Community Tripartite Agreement (CTA) negotiated between the federal government, the province or territory in which the First Nation is located, and the governing body of the First Nation. Under such agreements, the First Nation has its own dedicated contingent of officers from an existing police service (usually the RCMP). Every effort is made by these police services to have the department staffed by members of the First Nations community (Statistics Canada 2011d). In Ontario, the Aboriginal Policing Bureau manages First Nations policing in the province.

In 2015, there were 186 First Nations policing program agreements in place in Canada, providing policing services to roughly 65 percent of First Nation and Inuit communities nationwide. A total of 1,299 police officer positions receive funding under the FNPP, serving a population of approximately 422,000 in 453 communities. There are single-community services, such as at Six Nations, where there is a population of 10,000. There are also multi-community agreements, such as Nishnawbe-Aski, which serves 35 communities.

Officers in Indigenous police forces generally have full powers to enforce the *Criminal Code* and federal and provincial statutes, as well as band bylaws on reserve lands. The activities of Indigenous police forces are overseen by reserve-based police commissions or by the local band council. There are also band constables who are appointed under provisions of the Indian Act and who are responsible for enforcing band bylaws. Band constables are not fully sworn police officers, and their powers are limited.

Railway and Transit Police

Both the Canadian Pacific Railway and Canadian National Railways maintain their own police services, which have authority to enforce the federal Railway Safety Act. Police in both organizations have the same powers of arrest as police across Canada, although their role is generally restricted to the protection of their property and the safety of people on it. Policing arrangements can be very complex, as both railways run through several US states. This requires a number of legal agreements, called Memoranda of Understanding (MOUs), with police in US states.

Across Canada, a variety of transit policing arrangements are in place, ranging from the local police agency assuming primary policing responsibility in Montreal and Toronto to dedicated police and security services. Translink BC, responsible for the management of the transit system in BC Lower Mainland, employs the South Coast British Columbia Transportation Authority Police Service, which works closely with 21 police jurisdictions that the transit system passes through.

Integrated Policing

Special Constables

Many Canadian provinces employ law enforcement personnel (special constables, sheriffs, peace officers) whose powers are limited. They provide safety and security services at a lower cost than police officers with full authority. Special constables may be found enforcing municipal bylaws and specific provincial or federal statutes. For example, some provide hospital security, or enforce provincial liquor laws. Generally, special constables' authority derives from the province. Public bodies and employers turn to them for dedicated "policing" services that jurisdictional police may not be able to provide. Both Alberta and Manitoba, for example, have hired peace officers, sheriffs, and special constables to perform a variety of functions including surveillance, fugitive apprehension, and traffic enforcement on rural highways. These special constables are not counted as part of the overall police resource estimates by Statistics Canada; however, they play an important role in enhancing public safety. Their overall effectiveness in supplementing the work of the police in Canadian society is thought to be high, although this is an area for further study.

POLICE ACCOUNTABILITY

In jurisdictions across Canada, police activities are overseen both externally and internally. Police commissions, boards, and agencies established under the provisions of the various police acts—or, for RCMP officers, the RCMP Act—exist as a measure of external oversight of policing. Boards and commissions ensure accountability at the municipal and provincial levels. For example, the Edmonton Police Commission oversees the Edmonton Police Service, and the Law Enforcement Review Board in Alberta hears appeals from citizens and police officers related to the disposition of complaints. In Ontario, the Ontario Civilian Committee on Police Services performs this function. In addition, the Office of the Independent Police Review Director (OIPRD), staffed entirely by civilians, plays an additional independent police oversight role. Similarly, civilian oversight of the RCMP is conducted through the Civilian Review and Complaints Commission for the RCMP and through the RCMP External Review Committee, which oversees labour and disciplinary issues. Table 2.2 describes models of police oversight in Canada.

Within police services, there are units often titled "*Professional Standards*" or "Internal Affairs" that investigate allegations of professional misconduct on the part of officers as well as, in rare instances, corruption. Police officers may be held liable for

Table 2.2 Models of Canadian Police Oversight

1. Dependent Model		2. Interdependent Model		3. Independent Model
1.1 Police Investigating Police	1.2 Police Investigating Another Police Force	2.1 Civilian Observation	2.2 Hybrid Investigation	3. Independent Investigation
Represents police investigating police criminal investigations	Represents police investigating another police force	Introduces civilian observation to investigation	Oversight body may choose from various options, which include: may supervise/manage parts of police criminal investigation (beyond monitor/oversee) conducted by police may assume control over police investigation may undertake independent criminal investigation	Oversight body undertakes independent criminal investigation for cases within its mandate
Police fully responsible for the investigation and administration of public complaints	Involves formal arrangements (memoranda of agreement) in place with another police force to handle investigation of police officers in cases of death or serious bodily harm	Civilian observer responsible to monitor criminal investigation (not direct or oversee investigation)		Police are excluded or removed from process of investigating public complaints
No civilian involvement in a criminal investigation	Unlegislated process	Regular reporting on status of investigation required	Oversight body can refer investigation to police force	Hallmark of this system is that civilian personnel are fully responsible for investigation
Oversight body recognizes complaints regarding service, internal discipline or public trust	In place only in select provinces in Canada	Police responsible for investigation, adjudication, and administration of public complaints	Police can be involved in some form of collaboration, cooperation, or coordination of the actual investigation of public complaints with oversight body	Nil ability to refer investigation to police
Oversight body may be an appellate authority				

Source: Civilian Review and Complaints Commission for the RCMP, *Police Investigating Police: Final Public Report* (August 11, 2009). https://www.crcc-ccetp.gc.ca/pdf/pip-finR-eng.pdf

violating the policies and procedures of the police service in which they work. They can also be held liable—administratively, civilly, and criminally—for their conduct. Police officers can be held accountable for their conduct both on and off duty. Over the past 10 years, police officers and police departments have been found civilly liable for negligently supervising employees, conducting deficient investigations, and failing to warn the community about dangerous persons.

Police Boards and Police Commissions

In many jurisdictions, police boards and police commissions play a prominent role in overseeing the activities of police services. This ***governance*** function is intended to provide strategic oversight; by contrast, day-to-day operational decision-making falls under the jurisdiction of the chief of police. Where they exist, provincial and municipal police commissions are involved in developing policing standards, promoting research into police, providing training programs for provincial and municipal officers, and assisting in the preparation of the annual police budget. In the *Alberta Police Act*, for example, the duties of a commission include:

- allocating the funds established by council (the police budget),
- establishing policies providing for efficient and effective policing,
- issuing instructions to the chief in relation to the policies established above, and
- ensuring sufficient persons are employed for the police service for the purposes of carrying out the functions of the police service.

As well, the commission may play a role in police disciplinary matters. In Alberta, for example, the Edmonton Police Commission has appointed a Public Complaints Director, who reviews all public complaints and can make recommendations. The Calgary Police Commission has done the same.

There are also municipal police services boards, composed of community members, that oversee the activities of municipal police services. These boards do not operate in all provinces (they have never existed in Quebec or Newfoundland) or in all municipalities (in Manitoba, only Brandon and Winnipeg have such a board). The activities of municipal police services boards may include hiring the chief constable, preparing and overseeing the police budget, and authorizing increases in police personnel.

In Ontario, the police services boards function as the civilian authority over police services. Every Ontario municipality that has a police force is required to have a police services board responsible for providing adequate and effective services. Section 31(1) of the Police Services Act identifies the duties of these boards, which include appointing the members of the municipal police force, establishing the priorities and objectives of the police services in consultation with the chief of police, recruiting and hiring the chief of police, and allocating and administering police services budgets.

The size of the board varies: three members for communities with fewer than 25,000 people; five for those with greater than 25,000; and seven for communities with populations greater than 300,000. Each municipality appoints the majority of members, including one community representative who is not an elected official or employee of the municipality; the province retains a minority number of appointments. Under the provisions of the Police Services Act, municipalities may also create a joint police services board with one or more other municipalities. Municipalities policed under contract by the OPP may establish a community policing advisory committee to work with the local OPP commander and provide information on community objectives and concerns relating to the delivery of police services.

If this discussion of police boards and commissions seems a little confusing, it is. There is an inconsistency in the work of police boards and commissions across Canada—in some jurisdictions the activities of a commission are similar to those of a board in another locale. The Canadian Association of Police Boards (CAPB), which oversees approximately 75 police boards and commissions across Canada, who themselves oversee some 33,000 municipal police officers, has as its mission to work collaboratively and proactively to improve police governance in Canada and to bring about change that will enhance public safety for all Canadians. It is the only national organization whose mandate is to improve police governance in Canada.

Police Conduct Review Agencies and Adjudicative Bodies

Every Canadian province (except Prince Edward Island) has an office whose task is to receive and review complaints against police officers (excluding RCMP officers policing under contract). These include the Alberta Law Enforcement Review Board, Manitoba's Law Enforcement Review Agency, the Nova Scotia Police Review Board, and the

Office of the Police Complaint Commissioner in British Columbia. Oversight of the RCMP is conducted through the Civilian Review and Complaints Commission for the RCMP and the External Review Committee (ERC) on labour-related matter. In Ontario, the Special Investigations Unit (SIU) and the Ontario Civilian Commission on Police Services (OCCPS) and the Office of the Independent Police Review Director perform these tasks. The role of each oversight body varies, ranging from reviewing complaint investigations and making recommendations to conducting the investigation itself.

The SIU is perhaps the best example of external civilian review of police activities. Established under the provisions of the Police Services Act, it investigates cases involving serious injury, sexual assault, or death that may have been the result of criminal offences committed by police officers. The SIU, which is independent of any police service and operates directly under the provincial attorney general, has the authority to investigate municipal, regional, and provincial police officers. It tries to complete its case investigations within 30 days, although in more complex cases this is not often possible. The director of the SIU has the authority to decide whether charges are warranted in a case, and he or she reports this decision directly to the attorney general. This model of external civilian review has also been established in Alberta through the creation of the Alberta Serious Incident Response Team (ASIRT). ASIRT has a broader mandate than the SIU in that it also investigates sensitive matters. In 2011, the Province of British Columbia created the Independent Investigations Office (IIO), which is similar to the SIU in its role and function.

The primary mandate of the OCCPS is to conduct investigations into the conduct of police officers and police services. More specifically, the OCCPS:

- conducts investigations into police services not in compliance with the standards of service prescribed in the Police Services Act, including the requirements of community policing, on behalf of the Solicitor General;
- receives appeals from municipalities involving the misconduct of police officers;
- reviews public complaints against police officers that have not been resolved to the satisfaction of the complainant at the local level; and
- conducts inquiries on its own relating to complaints and the disposition of complaints.

Professional Standards Units

All police services have internal policies with which police officers must comply, internal units to investigate alleged misconduct on the part of officers, and a disciplinary process that includes a variety of sanctions that can be imposed on officers found guilty of misconduct. Police officers who work in internal investigation units have a difficult and challenging mandate. They must investigate fellow police officers as objectively and neutrally as possible. Critics of this system argue that it is virtually impossible for the police to objectively investigate their own personnel, while those who favour this approach argue that investigations are conducted thoroughly by insiders who know policing.

In certain situations, police services will request that officers from another police service conduct the investigation. It is common practice, for example, for the Montreal Police Service to call upon the Quebec provincial police to conduct investigations, particularly in more serious cases. Police legislation in each province governs how police officers from other departments can be requested.

While misconduct in policing has generally been considered an individual officer phenomenon, the investigation of serious misconduct and criminal acts by police officers acting in concert has required police departments to reorganize their resources to better respond to these emerging problems. The RCMP, for example, has recently established

In Ontario, the Special Investigations Unit conducts investigations where serious injury or death has occurred as a result of an interaction between the police and a member of the public.

Source: Andrew Lahodynskyj/Toronto Star via Getty Images

anti-corruption units in major urban centres. In addition, the Toronto Police Service enhanced its internal investigative capacity after a serious investigation into the misappropriation of money and property in their Drug Unit. To maintain public confidence in policing, investigations must be transparent and open to the public.

THE CONTEMPORARY ROLES OF THE POLICE

Traditionally, the mandate of the police was categorized as crime control (catching criminals), order maintenance (keeping the peace), and service (providing assistance). These distinctions, however, fail to capture the diversity and complexity of the police role in a highly technological, global society. Increasingly, police officers are being viewed as "knowledge workers" who spend a considerable amount of time gathering and processing information. Police work also extends far beyond the street level and cuts across jurisdictional and international boundaries.

Section 4.2 of Ontario's Police Services Act, for example, states that all police services in Ontario must provide adequate and effective police services, including the following:

• crime prevention,
• law enforcement,
• assistance to victims of crime,
• public order maintenance, and
• emergency response.

Note that crime prevention is listed first and that attention to the needs of crime victims is also a stated priority. The act further states that the OPP will be used in those instances when a municipality fails to provide these core policing services.

The next step in considering the role of the police is to ask a very simple yet very important question: "What do you want your police to do?" This question requires us to consider the expectations that community residents have of the police—after all, the police are a public (and often political) agency and are hired to serve the community.

The community policing model is often described as a "full service" model in that it attempts to provide a broad range of comprehensive services to the community. Since the terrorist attacks of 11 September 2001, the role and mandate of the police has broadened to include a significant commitment to controlling terrorism and local extremism, both at home and abroad. The quick passage of public safety legislation, including the Proceeds of Crime (Money Laundering) and Terrorist Financing Act, the Anti-Terrorism Act, and the Immigration and Refugee Protection Act, has placed even greater demands on Canadian police to provide national security. Therefore, the mandate of the police has grown to include "security policing," and with this has come a corresponding need to respond to elevated levels of fear and the management of disorder, which lowers citizens' perceptions of safety.

Public Perceptions and Expectations of the Police

Citizens often have unrealistic and conflicting expectations of the police. Police officers catch crooks and make communities safe from crime. Community residents often assign equal importance to crime prevention, crime control, order maintenance, and service functions, and rarely provide any input into how police resources are to be allocated.

Someone who calls the police wants an immediate patrol car response, regardless of the relative seriousness of the situation. The situation could involve dealing with street prostitution, searching for lost children, apprehending criminals, or working with community residents to solve local problems. To put it bluntly, citizens often want the police to be all things to all people, which is an impossible and unachievable goal.

Compounding these expectations is the fact that in many communities there are differences of opinion among community residents regarding what the priorities of the police should be. This diversity of opinion may be even more pronounced in urban centres with diverse cultural and ethnic populations. The framework of community policing provides the best opportunity for police services to respond to the needs and concerns of individual communities.

THE CONTEXTS OF POLICE WORK

Police work is complex, and one factor that contributes to this complexity is that police officers carry out their tasks in a number of different contexts. Broadly speaking, these contexts include the frameworks created by:

- the types and levels of criminal activity that confront the police;
- legislation;
- the criminal justice system;
- the police service; and
- the demographics of the community.

Each of these contexts, and their implications for policing, are considered briefly below.

The Crime Context

Examining crime patterns provides insights into the demands that are placed on police services and into the policing policies and practices required to address these demands. Traditionally, police services have been organized to combat "traditional" types of crime, such as robberies, assaults, and various types of property crime. Often, police services have attempted to increase their budgets and personnel by arguing that crime rates are increasing. However, not only are the overall rates of crime declining, but police services are also being confronted by new types of criminal activity, such as cybercrime, corporate crime, and organized crime, that may require a rethinking of how police carry out their work. Another factor creating demands on police services is the aging of the population, which is likely to be accompanied by an increasing fear of crime, which police services will need to respond to.

As we will see, community policing is an appropriate model of service delivery for many, though not all, of the challenges confronting police services. Some highlights of Canadian crime are presented in A Closer Look 2.2.

A CLOSER LOOK 2.2

HIGHLIGHTS OF CANADIAN CRIME

1. Police-reported crime, including violent crime, property crime, and sexual assault, has generally been declining over the past three decades, reaching its lowest point in 2011, down approximately 30 percent since it peaked in 1991. In 2015 and 2016, police-reported crime increased slightly but remains 29 percent lower than 2006.

2. In 2016, both the rate of police reported violent crime and severity of violent crime were basically unchanged since 2015 and overall 25 percent lower than 2006. Some crime categories, including sexual violations against children and new violations related to the commodification of sexual activity, increased by 30 percent and 11 percent respectively.

3. Motor vehicle thefts have steadily been decreasing and since 2006 have decreased by 55 percent. In 2016, impaired driving offences decreased for the fifth year in a row.

4. Cannabis- and cocaine-related drug offences have been declining since 2011. However, crimes related to drugs other than cannabis and cocaine (e.g., heroin, methamphetamines, and opioids such fentanyl) have been increasing since the early 1990s.

5. Youth crime continues to decline. In 2016, police reported youth crime had decreased for the seventh year in a row.

6. Since the introduction of the Youth Criminal Justice Act (YCJA) in 2003, more youth have come into contact with the police; however, the proportion of those formally charged declined from 56 percent (pre-YCJA) in 2002 to 45 percent in 2016.

7. Shifts in the age composition of the population are linked to lowered reported crime, as well as changing societal attitudes and police enforcement practices.

8. Large cities generally have lower rates of crime than smaller cities and rural areas, particularly for sexual assault offences, common assault, and weapons offences.

9. Large cities generally have higher crime rates for robbery, break and enter, motor vehicle theft, and prostitution.

10. Violent crime rates in the western provinces and the territories tend to be higher than in other parts of the country. Violent crime rates in the three territories were double the highest provincial rate in 2016, consistent with previous years.

11. Consistent with the drop in the overall crime rate, the rate of crime incidents per officer has generally been decreasing since 1991. In 2010, there were 30.5 incidents per officer, the lowest in over 35 years. While incidents per officer may be decreasing, the time spent investigating incidents is believed to have increased significantly.

12. The General Social Survey (GSS) on Victimization is conducted every five years. The most recent GSS, from 2014, measured both reported and unreported crime and found that only 31 percent of crimes were reported to police. This reporting trend reflects that of all Western countries.

13. While reported crime is declining, the length of time it takes to thoroughly investigate crimes is increasing.

Sources: Statistics Canada, Canadian Centre for Justice Statistics, Police–reported crime statistics in Canada (2010); Statistics Canada, Canadian Centre for Justice Statistics, Exploring Crime Patterns in Canada, (2005); Statistics Canada, Homicide in Canada (2010).

The patterns of crime in a neighbourhood, community, or city have significant implications for how community policing strategies are implemented. Every "task environment" within which the police officer works presents unique challenges. These are even greater in remote and northern areas, where cultural barriers between the officers and the community, coupled with geographic isolation and the relatively short period of time that officers are posted to these communities, undermine the best intentions of police officers.

The Legislative Context

Police officers carry out their tasks within several legislative frameworks that define their roles, powers, and responsibilities. When new legislation is enacted, it may result in increased demands on the police. The more significant pieces of legislation are the following:

- The *Canadian Charter of Rights and Freedoms* is part of the **Constitution Act, 1982**. Canada's constitution is the supreme law of the land and guarantees basic rights and freedoms for citizens. The Charter contains specific sections on fundamental freedoms, legal rights, equality rights, and enforcement. Courts may use the Constitution to strike down legislation and criminal laws as unconstitutional. In 2017, the Charter turned 35; it has had a significant impact on the powers and activities of the police.
- The *Constitution Act, 1982*, sets out the responsibilities of the federal and provincial governments in the area of criminal justice. The federal government has the sole authority to enact criminal laws and to establish the procedures to be followed in criminal cases (Section 91[14]); the provinces are assigned the responsibility for the administration of justice (Section 92[14]).
- The Criminal Code sets out the criminal laws and the procedures for the administration of justice.
- Other federal statutes include the Controlled Drugs and Substances Act, relating to different types of illegal drugs; the Youth Criminal Justice Act, relating to the administration of youth justice; the Canada Evidence Act, pertaining to evidentiary matters in the courts; and the Corrections and Conditional Release Act, which sets out the framework for federal corrections. Recent amendments to the Criminal Code establishing criminal liability for organizations that commit criminal offences also have had a significant impact on police resources. Provincial and municipal acts provide the structure for delivering police services. They set out the process for filing complaints against police officers, establish the procedures for disciplining police officers, and fix the activities of police commissions and municipal police boards.
- The Royal Canadian Mounted Police Act provides the legislative framework for the operations of the RCMP. It contains provisions for the operation of the External Review Committee and the Public Complaints Commission, and for handling officer grievances, discipline, discharge, and demotion.

The Legislative and Regulatory Framework for Policing in Ontario

There are two key pieces of legislation that provide the framework for police services in the province of Ontario. These are the *Police Services Act* and the *Adequacy and Effectiveness of Police Services Regulation*, an amendment to the Police Services Act introduced in 1999. Similar legislative enactments are under way in other provinces as well, including Alberta, where provincial policing standards have been incorporated into the Police Act.

The Police Services Act is divided into several parts that set out the responsibility for police services; the role and activities of the Ontario Civilian Commission on Police Services and the municipal police services boards; the mandate and duties of police officers

A CLOSER LOOK 2.3

PRINCIPLES OF POLICING IN ONTARIO

(1) Police services shall be provided throughout Ontario in accordance with the following principles:

1. The need to ensure the safety and security of all persons and property in Ontario.

2. The importance of safeguarding the fundamental rights guaranteed by the *Canadian Charter of Rights and Freedoms* and the *Human Rights Code*.

3. The need for co-operation between the providers of police services and the communities they serve.

4. The importance of respect for victims of crime and understanding of their needs.

5. The need for sensitivity to the pluralistic, multiracial, and multicultural character of Ontario society.

6. The need to ensure that police forces are representative of the communities they serve.

Police Services Act, Revised Statutes of Ontario, 1990. Copyright © Queen's Printer for Ontario. This is an unofficial version of Government of Ontario legal materials.

and other police staff; the procedure and process for filing, hearing, and resolving complaints against the police; and the provisions for special investigations into policing. A Closer Look 2.3 sets out the principles of policing in Ontario as defined by the *Police Services Act*.

We will engage in a more in-depth discussion of the Police Services Act in Chapter 3. The Adequacy and Effectiveness of Police Services Regulation (Ontario Regulation 3/99, also known as the Adequacy Standards) was designed to establish uniform service standards for police services across the province. The regulation sets out standards for police services in seven areas: crime prevention, law enforcement, victim assistance, public order maintenance, emergency response services, administration, and infrastructure. We will also examine the Adequacy Standards in more detail in Chapter 3.

The Criminal Justice System

Police officers operate at the front end of the criminal justice system. Although the general public may be involved in calling the police and participating in various crime prevention and crime response initiatives, the activities and decision-making of police officers are what determine which individuals and cases become involved further in the justice system. Officers are vested with considerable discretion in responding to incidents and, in that sense, they perform a major screening function.

Even though the police are a cornerstone of the criminal justice system, historically there has been little contact or cooperation between the police and criminal justice and social service agencies. Agencies have tended to work in isolation from each other. This is partly because criminal justice agencies typically maintain separate computer databases. The federal, provincial, and territorial governments realized that information-sharing practices within Canada's criminal justice information system needed to be improved in order to address the long-standing problem of poor communication and failure to share useful information among justice agencies (*including individual police services*). To this end they are collaborating on an Integrated Justice Information Initiative, the goal of which is to integrate the information systems of all partners in Canada's criminal justice system. In the main, this will involve building the Canada

Public Safety Information Network (CPSIN) to serve as the foundation on which a modern, national network of information-sharing will be built. It will be a network of networks and not a mega-database. Another information-sharing initiative is the Police Information Portal (PIP), which allows for the sharing of information among police, public safety, and federal agencies across Canada. PIP is a searchable index of all police agency record management systems across the country and is an important means of gathering information during serial predator investigations, organized crime investigations, and investigations where the subject may move from one jurisdiction to another.

Several provinces have embarked on additional projects to foster closer cooperation and information-sharing among the different components of the justice system. BC's Justice Information System (JUSTIN) and Ontario's Integrated Justice Project are two examples of the pursuit of integrated justice initiatives at the provincial level. Both provinces are working hard to design cost-effective, efficient, and streamlined systems that will allow police to spend more time policing and less time on paperwork. The courts and corrections staff will have the information required to process cases more quickly and effectively.

Ontario's **Integrated Justice System Initiative** is designed to facilitate a seamless flow of information among justice agencies and throughout the justice system, from policing to the courts to corrections. In addition, with today's emphasis on community policing, police officers now often work closely with their professional counterparts in other disciplines to address problems of crime and disorder in communities. Similar initiatives involving information-sharing between police agencies include the Alberta Provincial Information Integration Initiative (API3) and the RCMP Police Records Information Management Environment (PRIME-BC). Throughout this book, we will highlight examples of cooperation and problem-solving.

The Police Service

Police officers work in departments and detachments that are diverse in terms of their structure and activities. This has had a significant impact on how individual police organizations and their officers implement community policing. For example, although an OPP or an RCMP officer may be posted to a small detachment in a remote area, the officer is still accountable to an organizational hierarchy that stretches many kilometres from the detachment to the subdivision to the division headquarters to headquarters. Policies and procedures for the RCMP are formulated in Ottawa and then transmitted on a regular basis to the detachments through the divisional headquarters. The extent of this organizational "reach" is in sharp contrast to the situation faced by a police officer working in a small Indigenous police service with responsibility for a single First Nation.

Although the provincial police acts and the RCMP Act provide a general framework within which police services establish policies and procedures, set goals and objectives, and assess the performance of officers, each police service has its own unique organizational "climate" and its own ways of fulfilling its mandate. There are also differences among police services with regard to the demands and expectations of the communities, the numbers of officers in the department, and the perspectives on police work held by senior police management.

The Social and Demographic Attributes of Communities

Canada has a number of social and demographic attributes that affect the demands that are placed on police officers. Some of these are discussed below.

- *Demographics.* Most Canadians reside in urban centres close to the American border. However, police services must also be provided to smaller regional cities, as well as to rural and remote communities that are often inhabited by First Nations and Inuit peoples. Projections based on census data indicate that Canada's population growth is slowing and that future growth will primarily be due to immigration. In addition, the Canadian population is aging; the first of the baby boomers reached the age of 65 in 2010. These factors will result in a multiracial society that is on average older and longer-living.

• *Cultural diversity.* A defining attribute of Canada as a country is multicultural diversity. The primary source of this diversity is immigration. The census conducted by Statistics Canada in 2011 points to interesting attributes of immigration as follows:

– In 2011, there were 6,775,800 foreign-born citizens in Canada, representing one-fifth (20.6 percent) of the total population. This represents the highest proportion among the G8 countries (Statistics Canada 2013b).

– Two-thirds of Canada's population growth was attributable to net international migration; by contrast, growth of the US population resulted mostly from natural increase, as fertility was higher in the United States than in Canada.

– In 2011, nearly 25 million people, or more than four-fifths of Canadians, were living in urban areas.

– In 2011, nearly 6,264,800 people identified themselves as a member of a visible minority group. They represented 19.1 percent of the total Canadian population.

– Between 2006 and 2011, 1,162,900 people immigrated to Canada. These newcomers made up 17.2 percent of the foreign-born population and 3.5 percent of Canada's 32.9 million total population.

– Recent immigrants (2006 to 2011) born in Asia (including the Middle East) made up the largest proportion of newcomers to Canada in 2011 (56.9 percent).

– Immigrants tend to settle in urban areas. Toronto, Montreal, and Vancouver were home to 62.5 percent of recent immigrants in 2011. By contrast, slightly over one-third (35.2 percent) of Canada's total population lived in these three Census Metropolitan Areas.

– The 2011 Census enumerated 2,537,400 foreign-born people living in Toronto, 913,3000 in Vancouver, and 846,600 in Montreal. These individuals represented 46 percent of Toronto's population, 40 percent of Vancouver's, and 20.6 percent of Montreal's. The proportion of foreign-born people in Toronto surpasses that of cities known for their cultural diversity, including New York, Los Angeles, and Sydney, Australia. It is estimated that by 2031, visible minorities in Toronto will represent 63 percent of the population.

– In 2011, 58.6 percent of immigrants who came to Canada in the last five years were in the prime working age group: 25 to 54. In contrast, 56 percent of the Canadian-born population was in this age group.

– A majority (72.8 percent) of the foreign-born population in 2011 reported a mother tongue other than English or French. Among these individuals, the largest proportion, one in seven (13 percent), reported Chinese languages, followed by Tagalog (Filipino), Spanish, and Punjabi.

– Just over 22.1 million people, two-thirds of Canada's population, reported they were affiliated with a Christian religion; of these, 12.7 million reported Roman Catholic. Slightly more than 1 million individuals identified themselves as Muslim, representing 3.2 percent of the nation's total population.

– Many immigrants come from countries where conflict is present and where the police treatment of its citizens is very poor. Consequently, the police may be feared and avoided. This attitude places unique challenges on a police service attempting to implement the principles of community policing (Metropolitan Toronto Police 1996, 9; Mitchell 1997, A1; Toronto Police Service 2011).

The cultural diversity of Canada and its communities presents major challenges to police services. For example, how can they increase the number of police recruits from cultural and ethnic minorities? How can they ensure that officers receive training that makes them culturally sensitive and aware? And how can they implement strategies that facilitate the development of police–community partnerships? The philosophy of community policing provides a broad framework within which police services can develop strategic partnerships with communities.

- *Indigenous peoples.* Indigenous people comprise 4.3 percent of the Canadian population. This includes Status and non-Status First Nations peoples, Métis, and Inuit. Indigenous people, however, are unevenly distributed across the country; the highest numbers are in Ontario and the western provinces. Most First Nations people reside in rural and remote areas of the country; but there are also significant numbers in the "southern" urban areas of the country, including Toronto, Winnipeg, and Vancouver. In 2011, 1,400,685 people identified themselves as Indigenous; that is, North American Indian (First Nations people), Métis, and/or Inuit. The Indigenous population is younger than the non-Indigenous population: almost half (46 percent) of Canada's Indigenous people are 24 and under, compared to 31 percent of the non-Indigenous population. This makes the Indigenous population an excellent target group for future recruitment to police services (Statistics Canada 2013c).

The Community Context

The community context plays a significant role in determining the demands that are placed on police officers, the role the police assume in the community, and the specific patterns of relationships that exist between the community and the police (which, in turn, will determine the potential for police–community partnerships in preventing and responding to crime).

Communities vary on a number of critical dimensions, including their size; their socioeconomic, ethnic, cultural, and spiritual makeup; the types and levels of crime and disorder; their attitudes towards the police; their expectations of the police; and the levels of citizen interest in becoming involved in police–community partnerships. In Ontario, for example, there are a multitude of policing environments, ranging from the inner-city neighbourhoods of Toronto, to suburban communities, to small towns and remote communities.

A key requirement for effective community policing is that police officers have a thorough understanding of the community they are policing. Officers must be able to identify key resource persons in the community who will facilitate the development of police–community partnerships; they must also be sensitive to potential sources of resistance in the community that may undermine community policing initiatives.

TRENDS IN POLICING

Until the mid-1990s, the police and other public sector institutions enjoyed continual expansion and a seemingly endless resource base. From the mid-1990s through to 2001, however, federal, provincial, and municipal governments underwent a period of fiscal restraint with a clear focus on deficit reduction and reduced spending. In recent years, the federal government has reduced transfer payments to the provinces, and provincial governments—including Ontario—have downloaded fiscal responsibilities onto the municipalities. At the same time, policing costs are steadily increasing. This has resulted in significant changes to the organization and delivery of police services; it has also contributed to many of the trends in policing that we see today. In addition, since the terrorist attacks of 9/11, police have had to place a greater emphasis on community safety. This has caused all levels of government to carefully review the budget requests of police services. While there continue to be fiscal constraints that keep policing costs in check, there is also the fundamental realization that the demands placed on police services have increased. This realization has significantly shaped police services, and will do much to define the future role of the police.

Trend 1: As Crime Goes Down, Costs of Policing Go Up

Earlier in this chapter, we observed that crime rates are falling and that, notwithstanding a temporary spike in crime in 1991, the crime rate has been steadily declining since 1973. In 2010, homicides in Canada were at their lowest in 44 years. This has been accompanied by a decline in the severity of crime. Consequently, the number of criminal investigations per police officer has also been declining. While rates of reported crime are down, policing costs have been increasing steadily over the past 14 years. Police services across Canada point out that the increasing costs are due to police salaries and benefits and the costs associated with policing large events such as the 2010 G8 and G20 summits in Toronto, the 2010 Stanley Cup playoffs, and the Olympic and Paralympic Games. While reported crime is declining, police services are not necessarily any less busy. Responding to calls for service; investigating organized crime; managing the complexities of the legal process, which lengthens time spent on investigations; addressing complex social issues; and responding to the challenges of increased ethnic diversity all place growing demands on policing. According to the study *A 30-Year Analysis of Police Service Delivery and Costing* (2005), the time necessary to handle a case from initial call to acceptance by Crown counsel increased 58 percent for break-and-enter cases between 1983 and 2003; a driving-under-the-influence case required 250 percent more time; and a domestic assault case required 964 percent more time (Centre for Criminal Justice Research 2005). Recognizing this trend, several police services now base their departmental budgets on how many staff it takes to manage predicted workload (i.e., on "staffing to workload" estimates). Halton, Edmonton, Calgary, and Vancouver are all taking steps to justify increases in personnel based on workload activities. Efforts to reduce costs will require that police services and their boards and commissions conduct in-depth analyses of their current model of police service delivery, including an assessment of what constitutes core and non-core service.

Trend 2: Adoption of the Philosophy and Practice of Community Policing

Community policing has been practised in Canada for four decades, yet there remains uncertainty in terms of the role of the police and that of the community and how the two relate. For police services seeking to enhance community safety there is a fundamental recognition that community involvement is necessary; however, that involvement have not moved much past a passive role for the community acting as the "eyes and ears" of the police. At the same time, the police maintain their expert role with regard to *how* police service is delivered to the community. Despite this confusion, the philosophy of community policing is having a significant impact on the structure and delivery of policing services. The increasing emphasis on community policing is reflected in numerous federal government documents and in provincial police acts and legislation.

As we will see in Chapter 3, community policing has firm roots in the principles set down by Sir Robert Peel in 1829. Today, it represents the continuing evolution of police work and has resulted in an increased emphasis on many of the core principles and activities of early policing: a close relationship between the police and the community, geographic assignment of officers to communities, community involvement in addressing problems of crime and social disorder, and providing officers with the authority to address a wide range of problems at the street level.

Community policing is often described as "full service" policing. As a result, the demands for service placed on contemporary police organizations exact a significant toll on individual police officers. Burnout, frustration, and other stress-related issues require police organizations to develop improved strategies for police service delivery. Today's Canadian police organizations find themselves trying to incorporate effective practices with tactics and strategies for increasing community participation and involvement in problem-solving. If anything, greater sophistication has emerged in terms of how police–community relationships are structured. For example, while the police used to be able to attend small Neighbourhood Watch meetings, it is now recognized that the police must prioritize and leverage their resources in more effective ways. The best way of doing this is to provide the knowledge, resources, and leadership to groups and agencies that are capable of fostering crime prevention and community safety initiatives. While this represents a return to the ideals of self-policing, it is easier said than done, as we will see in Chapter 8.

Trend 3: A Growing Crisis in Human Resources

The police sector is facing significant human resource challenges arising from an aging workforce, a smaller youth population with declining interest in policing as a career, and the need to recruit police officers who will reflect Canada's increasingly diverse population.

All police services in Canada are struggling to recruit enough police officers to keep pace with the growing number of retiring baby boomer police officers. In 2015, over 11 percent of police officers across Canada were eligible to retire, and this will only compound a growing experience gap. The most pressing challenge over the next decade will be to hire enough police officers, but simply keeping pace with retirements will not allow police services to increase their capacity to respond to expanding community demands. Surprisingly, police services have done little to develop a nationally coordinated strategy for recruiting and retaining senior personnel. This has led to a dire situation: police services not only compete with one another for new recruits but also actively recruit experienced officers from one another.

The 2007 study "A National Diagnostic on Human Resources in Policing" is very critical of efforts to adequately staff police organizations. The study's authors fear that policing may collapse unless police services begin to act more like one single sector and less like individual competitive entities. Police strength increased between 1999 and 2010; since then, it has declined by 5 percent. Clearly, if community policing is to succeed there must be enough police officers to manage the complex demands placed on it and to strategically work with communities to foster safe environments. To address these concerns, the Police Sector Council (PSC) was founded in 2004 to identify common human resource challenges among police services and to find innovative solutions to urgent human resource issues in the policing community.

Police services need to become more efficient, and this requirement has generated new approaches, such as best practices and the development of community partnerships. The current human resource issues affecting police organizations can be summarized as follows:

1. recruitment of personnel;
2. retention of personnel;
3. retirement of senior personnel; and
4. reinvention of personnel.

These topics will be discussed later in the text.

Trend 4: Technology Creates a Borderless World

Globalization and advances in technology have made policing more complex, increased investigative costs, and increased the time needed to conduct investigations. In addition, the expansion of technology has generated both new venues for committing crime and new sources of evidence for police investigations. For example, the 2011 Vancouver Stanley Cup riots were captured on thousands of smartphone cameras, enabling police to identify hundreds of criminal suspects responsible for damaging and looting downtown Vancouver. Many criminal incidents are uploaded to YouTube. The upside is improved catch rates; the downside is the investigative time and costs associated with evidence retrieval and with the disclosure of this evidence when charges are laid. In fact, criminal cases are likely to be withdrawn if police are aware of the existence of video evidence and fail to seize it. In addition to this, technology enables criminals to live in one country and commit their crimes in another, such as mass marketing fraud and child exploitation. This can present significant jurisdictional challenges for police, who find themselves having to conduct criminal investigations in which the victims and offenders live in different countries. The mobility of criminals requires that Canada have treaties in place with other countries to facilitate investigations throughout the world.

Technology helps police solve crimes by providing stronger analytical tools and generating new strategies; but those tools and strategies run the risk of eroding the fundamental rights and freedoms of Canadians, including privacy rights. This has placed pressure on police to balance their investigative approaches with the constitutional rights and freedoms of all Canadians.

Trend 5: An Increase in the Numbers of Volunteers Involved in Policing

Citizen volunteers play an important role in policing today. Police departments rely on them to staff community police offices and to assist in crime prevention efforts. Volunteers also play an integral role in victim services and mediation programs, and as police reservists and auxiliaries. Police reserves and auxiliaries also help manage the workload of police services. With the aging of the Canadian population, it is anticipated that retiring baby boomers will seek meaningful volunteer opportunities in greater numbers; this offers the opportunity for further reductions in crime and disorder at very low cost. This trend will require police services and police officers to develop skills in recruiting, screening, training, deploying, supervising, and retaining volunteers. It will also require police services to establish parameters regarding what type of work volunteers can do and what information they can access; also, they will have to ensure that controls are in place to maintain the privacy of community residents, the confidentiality of files and records, and the security of sensitive information and firearms. We will address this important component of community policing in Chapter 10.

Trend 6: Increasing Collaboration between Police Services and Other Agencies and Community Organizations

The reduction in fiscal resources available to police services, combined with the emphasis on establishing police–community partnerships within the framework of community policing, has resulted in increased collaboration with social agencies, private sector companies, and community organizations in a variety of police activities. In communities across the country, businesses and service clubs are sponsoring a wide variety of crime prevention programs. To establish effective partnerships with the community, police services and their officers must acquire the skills to work closely with the community, identify areas for collaboration and cooperation, and define the parameters of community involvement.

This collaboration has increased the complexity of delivering police service to the community, for organizations such as health organizations may face restrictions with regard to how much information-sharing can occur between them and the police. Similarly, police must be diligent about protecting confidential police information. This raises questions about the limits of police–community partnerships, an issue we will examine further in Chapter 10.

In an attempt to maximize resources, many police services have entered into collaborative arrangements with government ministries and agencies. This includes the use of integrated service teams in which police officers work with their counterparts in other social service and health areas to address problems. For example, a number of municipalities have paired police officers with social workers to respond to children at risk. *Integrated service delivery* is part of the evolving model we describe as *community-based strategic policing*. These arrangements can be found in every jurisdiction across Canada. In Alberta, for example, a number of integrated police teams are funded under the umbrella of the Alberta Law Enforcement Response Team (ALERT). Nationally integrated proceeds of crime units (IPOCs) targeting money-laundering and criminal organizations, integrated market enforcement units (IMETs) serving to maintain the integrity of Canadian capital markets, and integrated border enforcement units (IBETs) protecting the Canada–US border are all illustrations of integrated policing strategies.

Trend 7: Community Policing 2.0—The Virtual Community

Social media technologies have created new opportunities for both the police and the community and may be transforming the ways the community reports crime and the ways police services respond to it. For police services, the strategic advantages of social media have to do with community notification, crime detection, and crime solving. Almost all police services today make use of social media, whether through Facebook, blogs, Twitter, YouTube, or Instagram. In addition, police services are increasingly using social media to identify criminals and solve crimes. Social networks can help strengthen police–community relations, particularly through police service–endorsed blogs, wikis, and tweets. However, social media can also be used to frustrate law enforcement efforts by identifying the locations of speed traps and Check Stops. While the use of social media by police services has a number of advantages, there are risks as well. Police services must ensure that communication with communities does not violate professional codes of police conduct, and they must be careful that crime reporting through social media does not become a substitute for 9-1-1 emergency calls. Finally, it is important to evaluate the impact of social media in relation to citizen perceptions of crime and personal safety. For example, a tweet reporting an aggressive panhandler can reach thousands of people, which could cause some people to become fearful of their environment. While we identified the need for police to be mindful of Canadians' right to privacy, the same considerations do not apply to private citizens who record the activities of others and themselves and then upload them to social media. It appears that millions of Canadians regularly relinquish concerns they may have about privacy in favour of social networking. The use of social media may very well be a game changer as it relates to community policing, which is why we call it "community policing 2.0."

Trend 8: Emerging Crime and a Broadened Police Mandate

Since 9/11, Canadian police have been under pressure to add more security functions to their traditional crime control/enforcement mandate. This has contributed to shifts in the mandate, structure, and operations of police organizations. The growing security mandate has subtly changed how police services are delivered while also affirming a stronger surveillance role for the community, whose members are now tasked with performing a surveillance role over suspect communities (Murphy 2005). All of this has contributed to elevated levels of fear, which is precisely what the traditional model of community policing was intended to reduce.

The reverberations from 9/11 have broadened the mandate of policing to include a stronger focus on security, a development Murphy (2005) describes as the "securitization of policing." Besides this, immigration is heightening the social isolation of some new Canadians, particularly refugees. When resources and supports are lacking, some individuals may be at increased risk for committing crime. Whether someone is new Canadian or not, social distancing plays a role in radicalization, where individuals plan acts of terrorism domestically. The police have an important role to play in monitoring the activities of these types of individuals.

Emerging forms of crime include mass marketing fraud and a variety of cyber-crimes, including child exploitation, cyberstalking, and identity theft. One need only look at the names and titles of new legislation to grasp the emerging crime environment and the Canadian response to it. For example, the Parliament of Canada website (www.parl.gc.ca) lists the following new legislative acts: Bill C-2, An Act to Amend the Criminal Code (mega-trials); Bill C-49, Preventing Human Smugglers from Abusing Canada's Immigration System Act; and Bill C-10, Safe Streets and Communities Act. While there are many more, these new legislative acts highlight Canadian efforts to criminalize new types of crime.

Trend 9: Adoption of Business-Like Corporate Models and Best Practices by Police Services

The requirement that police services do more work more efficiently with fewer resources has provided the catalyst for a transformation in the organizational structure and operations of many police services. For example, police services are adopting private sector principles and establishing administrative and operational structures within a corporate framework. Among the key components of the corporate model of police organization are the creation of mission and vision statements, the identification of organizational values and objectives, and the development of a capacity for short- and long-term strategic planning and evaluation frameworks to assess the effectiveness and efficiency of service delivery. Much of this development is due to technology, which has greatly enhanced police services' business intelligence. Terms such as *efficiency, effectiveness, client service, total quality management (TQM), Six Sigma, balanced scorecard,* and *risk management* are frequently used by police services and reflect the use of a corporate model. We will examine how these approaches have been implemented in police services that have adopted a community policing framework in Chapters 7 and 8.

Trend 10: The Changing Face of Policing

One of Peel's principles was that the public are the police and the police are the public. This includes the requirement that police services reflect the diversity of the communities they police. You will recall that one of the principles of policing in Ontario, as set out by the Police Services Act, is that police forces must be representative of the communities they serve. Today's police recruit is older (the average age of recruits in the Ontario Police College is 28); more likely to be a woman or a member of a cultural or ethnic minority, or both; and more likely to speak a language other than English (or French); and has a college or university degree. These changes in the composition of police services blend well with a key principle of community policing: police services should reflect the diversity of the communities they serve. The relative merits of this approach will be examined in Chapter 8 in our discussion of the community police officer.

Trend 11: The Rise of Private Security and Collaborative Policing

Private security officers in Canada outnumber public police officers by a ratio of at least 3 to 2 (Statistics Canada 2008b). This pattern has been unchanged for the last decade: according to the 2006 Canadian Census survey there were 101,525 private security personnel compared to 68,000 police officers. While public police services are facing cutbacks because of the government's attempts to reduce costs, the private security industry is growing rapidly. Between 2001 and 2006, private security grew by 15 percent compared to an overall growth of 3 percent in police officers. The increase in the number of private security officers—sometimes called "rent-a-cops" or "robo-cops"—has been precipitated by a number of factors, including the downsizing of police services, the increase in privately owned public spaces such as shopping malls, and the perception by business and property owners that the public police do not have the resources to serve them effectively. In addition, approximately 30 percent of private investigators and 25 percent of private security guards work for municipal, provincial, and federal governments (Centre of Criminology 1996, 12–13).

In some venues, such as sporting events and concerts, private security officers and police officers may work together in a collaborative arrangement. Any community policing strategies developed by a police department must include plans for cooperating with private security firms and must address the suspicion with which private security firms are often viewed by police services.

Police unions across the country have expressed concerns about the entry of private security firms into areas that were traditionally the responsibility of the police. Police unions largely view private security as an unregulated, unaccountable industry guided by the private interests of corporate clients. Some provinces, such as Ontario, Alberta, and British Columbia, have addressed these concerns by developing a legislated regulatory framework for private security. For example, security personnel in Ontario must be licensed under the Private Security & Investigative Services Act (2005).

Despite these concerns, private security is quickly establishing itself as a legitimate low-cost alternative to police services. There is a growing recognition among police agencies and governments that private security is an integral component of public safety. Private security is now often referred to as "private policing." One of the emerging issues is to sort out how a model of community-based strategic policing can incorporate both public and private policing into an effective service delivery model. We will address this point in greater detail later.

Trend 12: Increasing Accountability of the Police

One of the most important dimensions of community-based policing is the accountability of the police service to the community. The police are responsible for the services they provide to the community as well as for their conduct within the community. The days when police officers were viewed as being beyond reproach, and when community residents were reluctant to complain about actions of the police that they perceived as unfair, inappropriate, or unlawful, are over. There are both legislative and administrative frameworks for holding Canadian police officers accountable for their actions. The Canadian Charter of Rights and Freedoms has had a significant impact on police work; since its enactment, a number of major decisions by the Supreme Court of Canada (so-called Charter cases) have further defined the role and powers of the police.

Police officers can be held accountable under the Criminal Code as well as under civil and administrative law for their actions. For example, the police have been held civilly liable for negligent investigations and both negligent supervision and negligent retention of employees. In addition, the various provincial police acts set out mechanisms and procedures for overseeing and reviewing the actions and decisions of police officers. One of the most significant recent developments is the Supreme Court of Canada's decision in *R. v. McNeil* (2009), as a result of which police services must now release a police officer's disciplinary records to defence counsel prior to a criminal prosecution.

Police services and their employees are also held accountable by coroner's inquests or fatality inquiries and by human rights boards and commissions. In addition, freedom of information legislation has established a heightened level of accountability in relation to police records and their management.

Trend 13: A Focus on Leadership and Professionalism

Historically, police services have given little attention to issues of leadership and professionalism. Promotion and security were a function of longevity rather than of education level attained and specific qualifications and achievements. Today, the rigours of policing require police leaders who possess skills in management, administration, and public relations, as well as a global perspective. As a result, there has been an increased emphasis on the need to train police leaders of all ranks, and this has increased the mobility of police professionals. Police agencies are committed to lifelong continuous learning, and educational requirements are being established for senior officers in several Canadian police agencies. The Canadian Association of Chiefs of Police, for example, plays a major role in strengthening the professionalism and leadership skills of senior police personnel by providing research and policy direction on major policing issues as well a commitment to ongoing continuous learning through conferences, information-sharing, and advocacy for legislative reforms.

A number of programs, seminars, and courses are designed to strengthen the leadership skills of police officers. Many of these programs focus on executive development of police leaders and include seminars through the Canadian Police College and the Rotman Police Leadership Program. Outside of Canada, police executives receive leadership training through the FBI National Executive Institute, the Senior Management Institute for Policing sponsored by the Police Executive Research Forum (PERF) in Washington, DC, and the National Policing Improvement Agency in Great Britain.

In addition, as part of the move towards increasing professionalism, there has been an increased emphasis on accreditation by the US Commission on Accreditation for Law Enforcement Agencies (CALEA). This process involves evaluating a police service on a number of standardized criteria related to the management, administration, and delivery of services. Among the police services that have been accredited are the Peel Regional Police and the Winnipeg and Edmonton Police Services.

Trend 14: The Changing Structure of Police Organizations

Community policing is perhaps the most significant development in Canadian policing in the past half-century and has resulted in profound changes in how police services are organized. The traditional police organization was premised on a hierarchical, paramilitary model with very distinct lines of command and control. With the advent of community policing, there has been a "flattening" of police organizations, caused in part by the decentralization of power and the increasing authority and autonomy being given to line officers. We will examine the organizational changes that have occurred (and are occurring) in police services in Chapters 7 and 8.

CHAPTER SUMMARY

This chapter should get you thinking about Canadian policing, the various contexts in which police officers carry out their duties, and some of the more important trends arising in policing today. All of these items have significant implications for the development and implementation of community policing strategies and programs. The currently evolving model of policing is more accurately described as community-based strategic policing because the demands on policing require police work to be delivered in strategic ways. Now, two centuries later, things have come full circle: police services are actively soliciting the involvement of communities in preventing and responding to crime and social disorder, and communities are taking steps to ensure that police officers are held accountable for their actions.

CHAPTER REVIEW

Key Terms

- Adequacy and Effectiveness of Police Services Regulation, p. 32
- Canadian Charter of Rights and Freedoms, p. 32
- community-based strategic policing, p. 40
- Constitution Act, 1982, p. 32
- governance, p. 26
- Integrated Justice System Initiative, p. 34
- integrated service delivery, p. 40
- Police Services Act (Ontario), p. 32
- Professional Standards, p. 25

Key Points

- There are four levels of policing: federal, provincial and territorial, municipal, and First Nations.
- The various contexts in which police officers carry out their tasks provide both opportunities and challenges for community policing.
- Community-based policing has become the primary framework for the delivery of police services, and considerable pressures require police service to be delivered more strategically.
- Trends in police work, including the need to do more with less, the increasing diversity of police services, and the changes that are occurring in police organizations, are related to and affect community policing.
- The police are responsible for the services they provide to the community as well as for their conduct within the community. Accountability of the police service to the community is one of the most important dimensions of community-based policing.

Self-Evaluation

QUESTIONS

1. Why has the **Canadian Charter of Rights and Freedoms** had a profound impact on Canadian police work?
2. What is the **Constitution Act, 1982**, and why is it important in our study of policing?
3. What are the key sections of Ontario's **Police Services Act**?
4. Discuss the mechanisms that exist in Canada to ensure **police accountability**.
5. What is Canada's **Integrated Justice Information Initiative** and what are its objectives?
6. State the two key pieces of **legislation** that provide the framework for police services in the province of Ontario. Explain the purpose of these pieces of legislation.
7. Explain why is it necessary to continually examine the **contemporary roles of the police**.
8. What is **community-based strategic policing**, and how is it different from earlier community-based policing?
9. Explain how recent changes in the **crime context** have resulted in a change in policing.
10. Reflect on the **trends in policing**. What developments are occurring in Canadian society that will likely result in new trends in policing?

KEY IDEAS

1. At which level of policing do most Canadian police officers work?
   a. municipal police services
   b. provincial police services
   c. federal police services
   d. police support services, such as information systems

2. Which statement describes Aboriginal police services and their officers?
   a. They operate exclusively under the supervision of the RCMP.
   b. They do not have the same authority and power as municipal police, provincial police, and RCMP.
   c. They are autonomous and have full power and authority to enforce all laws, including the Criminal Code, on reserve lands.
   d. They are responsible and accountable to the National Aboriginal Police Commission.

3. What is set out in the Canadian Charter of Rights and Freedoms?
   a. The responsibilities of the federal and provincial governments in the area of criminal justice.
   b. The criminal laws and procedures for the administration of justice.
   c. The jurisdiction of the *Criminal Code* and the *Bill of Rights.*
   d. Basic rights and freedoms for citizens.

4. Which trend is indicated by statistics on Canadian crime?
   a. There is an upward trend in reported crime.
   b. There has been a decline in reported crime.
   c. The rates of violent crime have shown an upward trend.
   d. Property crimes have increased.

5. Why did the government create the *Constitution Act, 1982*?
   a. To establish the responsibilities of the federal and provincial governments in the area of criminal justice.
   b. To establish the civil laws of Canada.
   c. To establish the criminal laws of Canada.
   d. To establish legislation that applies only to the RCMP and other federal agencies.

6. What do statistics on visible minorities indicate?
   a. Most new arrivals in Canada settle in rural rather than in urban areas.
   b. Visible minorities, as a percentage of the population, have been declining.
   c. Immigrants to Canada tend to settle in urban areas.
   d. Most visible minorities live in the province of Quebec.

7. Which statement is characteristic of private security officers in Canada?
   a. They outnumber public police officers.
   b. They are permitted to wear side arms.
   c. They have no powers of arrest or detention.
   d. They operate under the supervision of public police services.

8. Which of the following describes community-based strategic policing?
   a. An evolving model of policing in Canada.
   b. The community's response to taking over its own policing needs.
   c. A new policing initiative run by the federal government.
   d. The current model of policing.

9. In Ontario, what was the Integrated Justice System Initiative designed to do?
   a. Prosecute individuals who have committed crimes throughout the province.
   b. Coordinate drug trafficking offences and other serious crimes.
   c. Facilitate a seamless flow of information among justice agencies.
   d. Provide direction to police services in the area of charge approval.

10. Which statement best defines the "growing crisis in human resources"?
    a. The inability of police to attract women and visible minorities to policing.
    b. The requirement for police agencies to establish summer police camps and cadet programs.
    c. The trend for new police officers to select specialty sections over general duty patrol.
    d. The need for recruitment and retention of police officers.

11. The SIU in Ontario is perhaps the best example in Canada of which of the following concepts?
    a. How policing has changed since 11 September 2001.
    b. External civilian review of police activities.
    c. A specialized policing unit.
    d. The contemporary role of policing.

12. What is a defining characteristic of professional standards units within police agencies?
    a. They ensure adequate dress and deportment levels.
    b. They provide direction to the community on levels of police response.
    c. They investigate alleged misconduct on the part of officers.
    d. They ensure that police applicants can meet recruit entry expectations.

EXERCISES: KNOWLEDGE INTO PRACTICE

Exercise 1. The Images of Policing

Consider the images of the police presented on television shows and in the movies. Make a list using the table below to compare these images with the contemporary roles of the police and with the types of activities in which the police in your home community were/are involved. Why is there a discrepancy between what the police actually do and the image that is presented of them?

Image of Police in Media	Actual Police Activity
1. _____	_____
2. _____	_____
3. _____	_____
4. _____	_____
5. _____	_____

Why the discrepancy? _____

_____

_____

_____

_____

_____

Do you think the image of policing on TV could have implications for police officers themselves in terms of how they define themselves and their role?

_____

_____

_____

_____

_____

Exercise 2. Regional Police Services

A predominant feature of policing in eastern Canada is the existence of regional police services. Research suggests that regional police forces are efficient in a number of ways, including reduced per capita policing costs, increased police coverage, higher clearance rates, and increased flexibility in deploying officers. Critics counter that there are often organizational and operational difficulties associated with amalgamating police services and that the size of regional forces makes community policing difficult. What is your view?

_____

_____

_____

_____

_____

Exercise 3: The Relationship between Community Policing and Internal Affairs Investigations

What do you think is the relationship between community policing and the public's trust in the police to investigate complaints against themselves? In parts of Canada where the relationship between police and visible minorities is strained, how essential is it to try to improve this relationship? What can the police and the community both gain by positive and collaborative relationships? Structure your answer using the key terms of _accountability_ and _legitimacy_. If you live in a community where the police have resorted to the use of deadly force against a visible minority, use this as an example in your answer.

_____

_____

_____

_____

_____

REFERENCES

Centre for Criminal Justice Research. 2005. A 30-Year Analysis of Police Service Delivery and Costing: E Division. *British Columbia: Centre for Criminal Justice Research.*

Centre of Criminology, University of Toronto. 1996. A Preliminary Information Review and Gap Analysis of the Public Policing Sector in Canada. *Ottawa: Human Resources Development Canada.*

Civilian Review and Complaints Commission for the RCMP. 2014. Police Investigating Police: Final Public Report. *https://www.crcc-ccetp.gc.ca/en/police-investigating-police-final-public-report#dReview*

HayGroup, 2007. A National Diagnostic on Human Resources in Policing, Police Sector Council. *https://www.policecouncil.ca/wp-content/uploads/2013/03/National-Diagnostic-on-HR-in-Policing-2007.pdf*

Metropolitan Toronto Police. 1996. 1996 Environmental Scan and 1997–98 Service Goals and Objectives. *Toronto: Corporate Planning, Metropolitan Toronto Police, 9.*

Mitchell, A. 1997. "Face of Canada Changes." *Globe and Mail, 5 November, A1.*

Murphy, C. 2005. "Securitizing Community Policing: Towards a Canadian Public Policing Model." Canadian Review of Policing Research 1: 1–30.

Ontario. 1990. Police Services Act, *Revised Statutes of Ontario, Chapter P. 15.*

Ontario Provincial Police. 2015. Annual Report.

Public Safety Canada. 2016. Indigenous Policing: First Nations Policing Program. *https://www.publicsafety.gc.ca/cnt/cntrng-crm/plcng/brgnl-plcng/index-en.aspx*

R. v. McNeil [2009] SCC 3.

Statistics Canada. 2005. "Exploring Crime Patterns in Canada, 2005." Crime and Justice Research Paper Series. *Cat. no. 85-561-MIE2005005. Ottawa: Statistics Canada, Canadian Centre for Justice Statistics.*

—. 2008 Private Security and Public Policing, 2006. Cat. no. 85-002-X, 28(10). Ottawa: Statistics Canada, Canadian Centre for Justice Statistics.

—. 2010. Projections of the Diversity of the Canadian Population 2006 to 2031. Cat. no. 91-551-X. Ottawa.

—. 2011a. Annual Demographic Estimates: Canada, Provinces and Territories. Cat. no. 91-215-X. Ottawa.

—. 2011b. "Homicide in Canada." Juristat. Cat. no. 85-002-X. Ottawa.

—. 2011c. Police-Reported Crime Statistics in Canada, 2010. Cat. no. 85-002-X. Ottawa: Statistics Canada, Canadian Centre for Justice Statistics.

—. 2011d. *Police Resources in Canada, 2011.* Cat. no. 85-225-X. Ottawa: Statistics Canada, Canadian Centre for Justice Statistics.

—. 2012. *Police-Reported Crime in Canada, 2011.* Cat. no. 85-002-X. Ottawa: Statistics Canada, Canadian Centre for Justice Statistics.

—. 2013a. *Police Resources in Canada, 2012.* Cat. no. 85-225-X. Ottawa: Statistics Canada, Canadian Centre for Justice Statistics.

—, 2013b. *"Immigration and Ethnocultural Diversity in Canada." National Household Survey 2011.* Cat. no. 99-010-X2011001.

—. 2013c. *"Aboriginal Peoples in Canada: First Nations People, Métis and Inuit" National Household Survey, 2011.* Cat. no. 99-011-X2011001. Ottawa.

—. 2015. *Police Resources in Canada, 2014.* Cat. no. 85-002-X. Ottawa: Statistics Canada, Canadian Centre for Justice Statistics.

—. 2016a. *Police Resources in Canada, 2015.* Cat. no. 85-002-X. Ottawa: Statistics Canada, Canadian Centre for Justice Statistics.

—. 2016b. *Police-Reported Crime in Canada, 2015.* Cat. no. 85-002-X. Ottawa: Statistics Canada. Canadian Centre for Justice Statistics.

—. 2017a. *Police Resources in Canada, 2016.* Cat. no. 85-002-X. Ottawa: Statistics Canada, Canadian Centre for Justice Statistics.

—. 2017b. *Police-Reported Crime Statistics in Canada, 2016.* Cat. no. 85-002-X. Ottawa: Statistics Canada, Canadian Centre for Justice Statistics.

Toronto Police Service. 2011. "Planning for the Future: Scanning the Toronto Environment." http://www.torontopolice.on.ca/publications/files/reports/2011envscan.pdf

UNIT 2

Gail Shotlander/Moment/Getty Images

Understanding Community Policing

What Is Community Policing?

3

CHAPTER

Community policing is a philosophy, an attitude, and an organizational strategy that promotes a partnership between the people in the community and their police service. Together, as equal partners, the police and the community must work toward solving neighbourhood problems related to crime, fear of crime, and social and physical disorder—looking beyond differences and improving the overall quality of life in the community.

Source: Courtesy of Corunna Community Police Committee

Learning Objectives

After completing this chapter, you should be able to:

- Describe the traditional model of police work,
- Discuss measures of police effectiveness,
- Define and identify the principles of community policing,
- Compare the key features of traditional police practice and community policing,
- Describe community-based strategic policing,
- Discuss the evolution of community policing in Ontario,
- Discuss the key sections of Ontario's Police Services Act related to community policing, and
- Identify the key players in community policing.

INTRODUCTION

To maintain at all times relationship with the public that gives reality to the historic tradition that the police are the public and the public are the police; the police being only members of the public who are paid to give full-time attention to duties which are incumbent upon every citizen, in the interest of community welfare and existence.

—Sir Robert Peel, First Commissioner of the Metropolitan
Police in London, England, 1829

Community policing has become one of the most widely used catchphrases in the criminal justice system and in policing circles. Hundreds of books, articles, and reports have been written on the topic by university scholars and government agencies, and by police services themselves.

A primary objective of this chapter is to sort through the tangle of materials that exist about community policing and to identify what community policing is—and, as importantly, what it is not. We will consider the principles of community policing and see how police services implement strategies and programs that increase police–community collaboration while at the same time enhancing traditional approaches. We will also identify the key partners in the community policing model and provide background information on each. This will be important information to keep in mind because we will be examining these partners throughout the rest of the text. We will conclude the chapter with an explanation of how and why community policing is evolving to a higher stage, which we introduced in Chapter 2, called community-based strategic policing.

At the outset of our discussion, it is helpful to consider the **traditional or professional model of policing**, from which community policing has evolved.

THE TRADITIONAL OR PROFESSIONAL MODEL OF POLICING

The traditional, or professional, model of police work is based on several key principles. These include the following:

- Police officers are the professionals who have sole responsibility for crime control.
- The objectives of police work are legally defined and involve responding to calls that involve criminal incidents.
- The role of the police officer is to control crime, and this role is carried out by way of preventative patrol and rapid response times.
- The police tend not to work in conjunction with community residents or other agencies.
- Police services are centralized.
- Decision-making occurs through a hierarchical command and control structure (Kelling and Moore 1988; Murphy 1995).

Traditional Patrol Practice: The Three Rs

Traditional models of patrol practice are premised on the **three Rs**: random patrol, rapid response, and reactive investigation. The central premise of random patrol, also known as the **watch system**, is that the mere presence of patrol cars serves as a deterrent to crime and increases citizens' feelings of safety. Patrol officers spend their shifts responding to calls, and their remaining time is spent patrolling randomly, waiting for the next call for service. This traditional approach to police work is:

- *incident oriented*: the primary focus is on responding to specific incidents, calls, cases, or events;

- *response oriented*: police management and operations are oriented towards responding to events as they arise, response capacity and capability are emphasized, and little time and few resources are devoted to proactive intervention or prevention activities;
- *focused on limited analysis*: as rapid response and the availability of resources are top priority, information gathering is limited to specific situations and does not include analysis of the causes of events; and
- *focused on the means rather than the end*: the emphasis on response efficiency means that little significance is placed on the impact of police strategies of preventing, reducing, or eliminating problems (Oppal 1994).

Traditionally, police officers have been deployed in teams, platoons, and watches. This has meant that:

- patrol officers work the same shift rotation;
- patrol operations are based on a hierarchical and centralized "military" model of policing;
- there is an emphasis on command and control principles; and
- there is a narrow range of police response options.

Although this approach provides for better supervision of field patrol officers, it has a number of problems, including:

- insensitivity to community needs: officers deployed to one neighbourhood during a shift rotation are not redeployed to the same neighbourhood on the next rotation;
- creativity is stifled among front-line police officers; and
- policing becomes internally focused rather than having an external community focus.

In the words of retired Edmonton police inspector Chris Braiden, "traditional police work becomes an unknown police officer patrolling familiar buildings and unfamiliar faces."

Traditional Police Practice: How Effective Is It?

The reactive battle against crime and other community needs has been soundly lost.
—*Chief J. Harding, Halton Regional Police Service (Ret.)*

Within the traditional model of police work, effectiveness is determined by response times and the **clearance rate**. This rate is the percentage of cases in which an offence has been committed and a suspect identified, regardless of whether the suspect is ultimately convicted of the crime.

Another measure often used to assess the effectiveness of the police is the crime rate. However, a rising crime rate can reflect either good or poor police performance: when the official crime rate goes down, the police are generally credited with doing a good job; when the crime rate goes up, the police are seen as doing a poor job. However, an increase in the official crime rate could indicate good police performance, both in terms of more calls being reported by a supportive public and more criminals being apprehended. This is a bit confusing, to say the least, and it's one more reason why police performance should not be based solely on crime control measures.

Clearance Rates as a Measure of Police Effectiveness

There are a number of reasons why clearance rates should not be used as the only indicator of **police effectiveness**. These include the following:

- *Police officers do not spend most of their time chasing criminals.* Most of their time is spent on nonenforcement situations revolving around maintaining order, providing services, and preventing crime. Today, the movement towards restorative justice approaches, which we will talk about later, places less weight on laying charges.

- *The crime rate should be interpreted carefully to determine the effectiveness of the police.* If there is an increase in the official rate of crime in a community, does that mean that the police are (a) ineffective, which is why the crime rate went up, or (b) effective, with the official crime rate being an indicator that the police are catching more criminals? A number of research studies have found that the police have very little impact on the crime rate.
- *Not all police officers serve in the same types of communities.* While some officers are assigned to remote and rural areas, others work in suburban and urban areas. The specific levels and types of crime in these areas vary as well, which means that police officers are confronted with different types of problems and situations.
- *Not all police officers are engaged in the same type of police work.* Some officers work out of community police stations; others work in specialty units such as the gang squad and the auto theft task force. This makes it even more unrealistic to use only a single measure of police effectiveness.

Because the police play a variety of roles in the community and engage in a wide range of activities, we need to consider other ways of measuring their effectiveness. This is particularly important when adopting a community policing model, which pays a considerable amount of attention to preventing crimes rather than merely reacting to them.

The Effectiveness of Random, Reactive Patrol

Research studies over the past decade have continued to cast doubt on the effectiveness of random patrol, which is the cornerstone of traditional models of policing and remains at the core of most police services today. Similarly, questions have been raised about the effectiveness of rapid response and the preventive value of reactive arrests. One critic of random patrol suggested it makes as much sense as firefighters patrolling for fires. Check out Critical Perspectives 3.1 for an assessment of the three Rs of the traditional service delivery model.

It is important that the traditional model of police work not be set up as a "straw man" for the discussion of community policing. The material presented in Unit 4 will reveal that many of the strategies and programs implemented within the community policing framework have either proven to be less effective than originally anticipated or have not been adequately evaluated to determine their effectiveness. This suggests that the challenges facing Canadian police are varied and that no single approach to crime and social disorder is effective.

The Persistence of Traditional Police Attitudes and Practices

Many police officers still carry out their duties within a traditional model of patrol practice. In many respects, this is a product of the calls for service faced by modern police officers, leading some observers to refer to officers as "9-1-1 cops." Officers and senior personnel in many police services complain that they are too busy responding to calls to shift their focus to a problem-solving, community-based approach, despite the fact that random, preventive patrol does not contribute to the reduction of crime and disorder or foster partnerships with the community. Indeed, the persistence of this model of patrol may also be a major contributor to low officer morale and high levels of career dissatisfaction; police officers do not see positive results from their work.

The deterrent value of random patrol is limited; even so, communities often complain about the lack of visible police presence. This is a difficult issue for police services to resolve.

Later in this chapter, we will see that the implementation of community policing may have a positive effect on officer morale and levels of job satisfaction. However, as noted, we will also see that many community policing strategies have not produced the positive

> ## CRITICAL PERSPECTIVES 3.1
>
> ### THE EFFECTIVENESS OF TRADITIONAL PATROL PRACTICE
>
> **Question:** Does an increase in random police patrols have an impact on crime levels?
>
> **Answer:** Probably not.
>
> - Although the studies that have assessed this dimension of police crime prevention have many methodological problems, research generally has recorded no appreciable impact from an increase in random patrol.
> - Directed or targeted patrol is effective.
>
> **Question:** Is the response time of the police related to reductions in the level of crime?
>
> **Answer:** Not likely.
>
> - Reduced response time appears to have very little impact on the crime rate, due in large measure to the delays in initial reporting of crimes to the police.
>
> **Question:** Is there any relationship between the number of arrests that the police make and the crime rate? In other words, do reactive arrests serve as a general deterrent to crime?
>
> **Answer:** No.
>
> - Reactive police arrests do not serve as a general deterrent to criminal activity. The exception may be in communities of under 10,000 residents, but even here the research findings are inconsistent.
>
> **Question:** Is there any relationship between the reactive arrest of specific individuals and the crime rate? In other words, do reactive arrests function as a specific deterrent to crime?
>
> **Answer:** Generally not, with a few possible exceptions.
>
> - For many individuals, arrest increases subsequent reoffending.
> - Targeting prolific offenders does prevent them from reoffending if they are held in custody.
> - The impact of arrest varies with employment status: unemployed people who are arrested tend to reoffend; however, arrest appears to act as a deterrent for people who are employed.
>
> **Source:** Sherman, L. et al., 1997. *Preventing Crime: What Works, What Doesn't, What's Promising.* Washington, DC: United States Department of Justice, National Institute of Justice.

outcomes that had been anticipated and that the shift back to increasing contact with the community is more of an evolution of police work than a separate model of police work.

OTHER WAYS TO MEASURE POLICE PERFORMANCE AND EFFECTIVENESS

Besides the clearance rate, a number of other measures can be used to assess the effectiveness of a police service and to more accurately reflect the broad range of activities that officers are involved in when doing police work. These include:

- the extent to which a police service has succeeded in developing partnerships with the community;

- the experiences with and attitudes towards the police held by community residents. In this regard, many members of cultural and ethnic minorities come from countries where police are distrusted and feared;
- the experiences and attitudes towards the police held by crime victims;
- the ability of the police service to solve serious crimes that involve violence, have multiple victims, and create fear in the community;
- the extent to which senior police administrators use contemporary management practices, are familiar with the research and current techniques of policy formulation and application, and are able to provide leadership;
- the morale and attitudes of line police officers, who are the core of the police organization;
- the success of particular individual police officers or a particular unit in meeting specific goals and objectives, which in turn are defined by the specific nature of their work; and
- how the police service defines its core values, mission statement, vision and its ability to achieve organizational goals and objectives.

Can you think of others?

These performance indicators are far broader and include much more than just a focus on crime levels and "catch" rates. In fact, these are the very types of indicators that are used in community policing. Community policing focuses on the community's role in identifying, preventing, and responding to crime and disorder, so the extent to which local residents are effective in fulfilling their part of the police–community partnership is equally important (see Chapter 10 for more discussion on this matter). So, although community policing is not the opposite of the traditional model of police practice, it does broaden the role the police are asked to play. It also expands the measures that are used to assess their effectiveness and efficiency.

WHAT IS COMMUNITY POLICING?

The "new" approach to policing that has recently begun to sweep through North America, Europe, and the major common law countries is community policing. Rather than being a new approach, however, it is more correctly a renewal or re-emergence of the old approach developed in Metropolitan London.*

—*A. Normandeau and B. Leighton (1990)*

Defining community policing is one thing; attempting to determine whether a police service is *doing* community policing, whether a policy or program falls within the framework of community policing, and, importantly, whether the community's participation with the police constitutes a true partnership is often much more difficult. The term "community policing" has been used (and misused) to such an extent that there is a considerable amount of confusion on the part of both the public and the police as to what it actually means.

Over the past decade, the term has come to refer to both a philosophy of police work and an operational practice. So what exactly is it? And how do we know whether a police service is engaged in community policing? How do we know that the involvement of the community is substantive rather than superficial? What are the requirements of a true

*NORMANDEAU, A., & LEIGHTON, B. (1990). *A vision of the future of policing in Canada: police-challenge 2000: background document.* [Ottawa], Police and Security Branch, Ministry Secretariat, Solicitor, Library and Archives Canada.

Source: City of Côte Saint-Luc.

Côte-Saint-Luc is the first city in Quebec to implement the **Volunteer Citizens on Patrol (vCOP)** program. Working in collaboration with Côte-Saint-Luc Public Security, Emergency Medical Services (EMS), and the Montreal Police Department, vCOP members patrol the city, observing and reporting any suspicious activities or problems.

police–community partnership? One way we will address these questions is through a Community Policing Implementation Checklist, which is discussed below.

It is important to view community policing as more than what traditional policing is not. In other words, the definition of community policing must acknowledge that this model of police work incorporates many elements of traditional police practice, while at the same time extending and expanding the role, activities, and objectives of police services and patrol officers.

Let's see if we can get our heads around the philosophy and practice of community policing. Remember, at this point we are identifying some of the key components of community policing—in subsequent chapters we will be examining them in more detail. At the risk of sounding repetitive, a number of different explanations of community policing will be presented. Taken together, these should provide a good idea of the principles and practices of community policing. Keep in mind, however, that police services will implement the principles of community policing in a variety of ways and that community policing represents an evolution of the police role to address the increasingly complex issues of modern society. Ironically, as we have noted before, the principles set out by Sir Robert Peel in 1829 reflect the principles of community policing that are being set out nearly 200 years later. We are seeing today the re-emergence of community policing.

Community Policing Defined

For the purposes of this text, we will use the following definition of **community policing**:

Community policing is a philosophy, management style, and organizational strategy centred on police–community partnerships and problem solving to address problems of crime and social disorder in communities.

Trojanowicz and Bucqueroux (1997, 6) have broken the term "community policing" into three interrelated parts:

1. Community policing is a philosophy and an organizational strategy that promotes a new partnership between people and their police. It is based on the premise that both the police and the community must work together as equal partners to identify, prioritize, and solve contemporary problems such as crime, drugs, fear of crime, social and physical disorder, and overall neighbourhood decay with the goal of improving the overall quality of life in the area.

2. Community policing requires a department-wide commitment from everyone—sworn and civilian—to the community policing philosophy. It challenges all personnel to find ways to express this new philosophy in their jobs, thereby balancing the need to maintain an immediate and effective police response to individual crime incidents and emergencies with the goal of exploring new proactive initiatives aimed at solving problems before they occur or escalate.

3. Community policing rests on decentralizing and personalizing police service, so that line officers have the opportunity, freedom, and mandate to focus on community building and community-based problem-solving, and so that each and every neighbourhood can become a better place in which to live and work.

These dimensions are reflected in the operational definition of community policing provided by the Halton Regional Police Service:

Community policing in Halton is a philosophy based on the concept that police officers and private citizens work together, in partnership, resulting in creative ways to solve community problems related to crime, fear of crime, social and physical order, and neighbourhood decay.

Let's take a closer look.

The Principles of Community Policing: The Three Ps

Community policing requires patrol officers to take a proactive, interventionist, problem-solving approach. This is captured in the "**three Ps**":

- prevention;
- problem-solving; and
- partnership with the community.

We will explore each of these three building blocks of community policing throughout this book. At this point, however, the important point to note is that the three Ps are the building blocks on which community policing is built. Check out the 12 elements of community policing as identified by the Ministry of the Solicitor General in A Closer Look 3.1.

A CLOSER LOOK 3.1

THE ELEMENTS OF COMMUNITY POLICING

1. Police officers are *peace* officers rather than just law enforcement officers. Police organizations are a *service* to the community for crime and social disorder problems, rather than a force focused primarily on crime.

2. **Community consultation** is a key strategy designed to identify short-term priorities for addressing crime and social disorder and to secure, in the longer term, a reaffirmation of the police mandate from the public.

3. There is a **proactive approach** to policing, whereby the police can anticipate demands for service by identifying local problems of crime and social disorder. This is accomplished by the use of techniques such as scanning and forecasting (to be discussed in Chapter 5).

4. A **problem-oriented policing strategy** combines reactive, proactive, and coactive approaches to address the underlying causes of crime and social disorder.

5. Crime prevention initiatives focus on **responding to underlying causes of problems**.

---

6. **Interagency cooperation** involves the police developing strategic partnerships with social service agencies and community organizations.

7. Police personnel function as **information managers** and engage in interactive policing by routinely exchanging information with community members.

8. Strategies are used to **reduce unfounded fears of victimization**, particularly among children, the elderly, and vulnerable groups in the community.

9. Police officers are permitted to become career **generalists** rather than specialists and are responsible for a broader range of activities than was permitted under the professional model of police work.

10. Front-line police officers are given **greater responsibility and autonomy** to identify and address problems of crime and social disorder.

11. The **changed organizational structure** of a flat structure with front-line officers assuming primary importance replaces the traditional hierarchical, paramilitary organizational model.

12. There is increased **accountability to the community** through ongoing public consultation and structures and through procedures for reviewing police officer conduct.

Source: NORMANDEAU, A., & LEIGHTON, B. (1990). *A vision of the future of policing in Canada: police-challenge 2000: background document.* [Ottawa], Police and Security Branch, Ministry Secretariat, Solicitor, pp. 43–46, Library and Archives Canada.

The Policy and Practice of Community Policing

In principle, policy, and practice, community policing is reactive, proactive, and coactive. Coactive refers to the police–community partnerships that are developed within the community police framework. More specifically, community policing:

- *reassesses who is responsible for public safety and redefines the roles and relationships between the police and the community.* The community is identified as both the source of problems of crime and disorder and as having a key role to play in preventing and responding to these problems.
- *requires shared ownership, decision-making, and accountability, as well as a sustained commitment from both the police and the community.* The police must acknowledge that they cannot solve community problems on their own, and the community must become empowered to take responsibility for community safety and well-being.
- *establishes new public expectations of and measurement standards for police effectiveness.* Community policing focuses the attention and efforts of the police on developing partnerships to facilitate collaborative intervention, rather than merely reacting to incidents. Measures of police performance are expanded beyond crime control indices, such as 9-1-1 statistics and arrest/crime statistics, to include quality of service, customer (community) satisfaction, responsiveness to issues identified by the community, and cultural sensitivity.
- *increases understanding and trust between police and community leaders.* Police services become directed towards community needs and concerns, and officers are assigned to specific geographic zones, which provides them with the opportunity to develop relationships with the business and residential communities.
- *empowers and strengthens community-based efforts.* Community organizations and residents are provided the opportunity to develop substantive partnerships with the police, centred on solving problems.
- *requires constant flexibility to respond to all emerging issues.* This includes the expansion of alternatives for prevention and intervention available to the police, including restorative and community justice.

- *requires an ongoing commitment to developing long-term and proactive strategies and programs to address the underlying conditions that cause community problems.* This commitment, on the part of the police and the community, involves an assessment of community needs, the participation of all sectors of the community in formulating response strategies, and the redirection of available police and community resources to support the problem-solving strategy.
- *requires knowledge of available community resources and how to access and mobilize them, as well as the ability to develop new resources within the community.* This ensures that there will not be duplication of effort between the police, other agencies, and community organizations and that maximum use will be made of available resources.
- *requires a commitment from the top management of the police and other local government agencies, as well as a sustained personal commitment from all levels of management and other key personnel.* Skills of police leaders that are important include the ability to maintain a vision and manage through values rather than rules, to focus on teamwork, to seek widespread input prior to making decisions, and to solicit feedback from officers and the community on how policies and programs can be improved.
- *decentralizes the operations and management of police services, relaxes the traditional "chain of command," and encourages innovation and creative problem-solving.* In contrast to traditional policing, community policing and problem-solving are based on decentralized, community-based services driven from the bottom up, making full use of the knowledge, skills, and expertise found throughout the organization.
- *shifts the focus of police work from responding to individual incidents to addressing problems identified by the community as well as by the police.* Problems, rather than incidents, are the central focus of community policing, and careful analysis of the problem precedes the development of specific responses.
- *requires a commitment to developing new skills through training.* This training is provided at all levels of the police organization, from senior police leaders to line officers. Police managers must learn new styles of leadership, based on consensus management, while line officers must be taught skills in problem analysis and problem-solving, facilitation, community organization, communication, mediation and conflict resolution, and networking, to name a few (Community Oriented Policing and Problem Solving [COPPS] Advisory Committee 1995, 4–11).

What Community Policing Is Not

As we have noted, considerable confusion surrounds discussions of community policing. Often, community policing is offered as a polar opposite to traditional police practice. In fact, community policing incorporates many elements of traditional police work that are considered effective. One way to help clear this up is to address what community policing it is *not*. Among other things, community policing is not:

- a panacea for solving all of a community's problems of crime and disorder;
- a replacement for many traditional police services and crime prevention strategies, including reactive police response and serious crime investigation;
- a single police initiative, although specific programs can be developed within a community policing strategy;
- solely the responsibility of the police—rather, it requires a true (not symbolic) police–community partnership;
- a generic, "one size fits all" policing model that can be applied without adaptation to the specific needs of all individual communities across the country;
- a program or series of initiatives that can be added onto existing police organizational structures; or
- a policing strategy appropriate for addressing all types of criminal activity.

- Community policing is best viewed as the most recent phase in the evolution of police work that, ironically, has resulted in police services returning to the original roots of policing as set forth by Sir Robert Peel early in the 19th century. In fact, many police services and their officers, especially in smaller communities, have always pursued a "no call too small" approach to policing. This approach has allowed officers to develop close relations with the community, to collaborate with residents in identifying and responding to problems of crime and social disorder, and to respond to the needs and concerns of residents. Unfortunately, as we shall see later, the "no call too small" full-service model of policing has become increasingly difficult to sustain, and it is now necessary to look for more strategic ways to deliver police service and ensure vital community–police partnerships.

It is important to point out, however, that the increasing sophistication and globalization of crime requires that the police have access to the latest technologies as well as to officers who are technology-literate. The strategies for combating crimes committed over the Internet, for example, are considerably different from those required to implement community policing at the neighbourhood level. This suggests that over the next decade, urban police services will have to develop tactics and strategies that are responsive to community problems yet effective at responding to sophisticated criminal activity. Community policing is not a substitute for having the capability in a police service to fight the more sophisticated types of criminal activity.

TURNING PRINCIPLES INTO PRACTICE

Now that we have a good understanding of what community policing is (and, as importantly, what it is not), the next step is to examine how the principles of community policing actually play out.

- Within the framework of community policing:
    - citizens are actively responsible for policing their own neighbourhoods and communities;
    - the community is a source of operational information, crime control knowledge, and strategic operations for the police;
    - the police are more directly accountable to the community;
    - police have a more proactive and preventive role in the community that goes beyond traditional law enforcement;
    - the cultural and gender composition of a police agency reflects the community it serves; and
    - the organizational structure of the police agency facilitates broad consultation on strategic and policing issues.
- The objectives of community policing are:
    - greater police legitimacy and public acceptance: more responsive, less authoritarian, more inclusive;
    - increased police accountability: more open communication, consultation, and collaboration with the community;
    - more efficient use of police resources: new styles of police management, working relationships with the community, and use of community resources;
    - increased police effectiveness through innovative strategies: problem-oriented policing, intelligence-led policing, and preventive and proactive strategies;

- decreased fear of crime and enhanced public safety: foot patrols, community police stations, and increased police presence and visibility;
- increased job satisfaction and improved officer productivity: broadening operational responsibilities, reducing bureaucracy, and increasing autonomy of line officers; and
- a reduction in the number of public complaints against the police.

- In terms of operations, community policing is:
  - customer oriented;
  - responsive to community needs;
  - open to input from citizens;
  - visible in the community;
  - available on the streets;
  - knowledgeable and interested in the neighbourhoods and their problems;
  - proactive in its approach; and
  - accountable for its actions (Oppal 1994, C-3, C-6, C-8).

Check back to Chapter 1, A Closer Look 1.1. Note the close resemblance between the principles of modern policing first identified by Sir Robert Peel in the early 1800s and the basic principles of community policing. Both are premised on the philosophy advocated by Peel: "The police are the public, the public are the police." Yet it is clear that community-based policing represents an expansion of the role and activities of the police beyond merely focusing on law enforcement.

Although community policing incorporates key elements of traditional police practice, there are points of comparison that can be made between the two. These are set out in Table 3.1.

Table 3.1 Comparison of Traditional Policing and Community Policing

Question	Traditional	Community Policing
1. Who are the police?	A government agency principally responsible for law enforcement	Police are the public and the public are the police; police officers are those who are paid to give full-time attention to the duties of every citizen
2. What is the relationship between the police and other public service departments?	Priorities often conflict	The police are only one department among many responsible for improving the quality of life
3. What is the role of the police?	To solve crimes	To take a broader problem-solving approach
4. How is police efficiency measured?	By detection and arrest rates and by the absence of crime and disorder	By the absence of crime and disorder
5. What are the highest priorities?	Crimes that are high value, e.g., bank robberies and those involving violence	Whatever problems disturb the community the most
6. What, specifically, do the police deal with?	Incidents	Citizens' problems and concerns

7. What determines the effectiveness of the police?	Response times	Public co-operation
8. What view do police take of service calls?	Deal with them only if there is no real police work to do	Vital function and great opportunity
9. What is police professionalism?	Swift and effective response to serious crime	Keeping close to the community
10. What is the essential nature of police accountability?	Highly centralized; governed by rules, regulations, and policy directives; accountable to law	Emphasis on local accountability to community needs

Source: Malcolm K. Sparrow, "Implementing Community Policing", Perspectives on Policing, No. 9, National Institute of Justice, U.S. Department of Justice, Washington, D.C. (December 1988), pp. 8-9.

The concept and principles of community policing are thus perhaps best viewed as constituting a philosophy based on improving the effectiveness and efficiency of police services and establishing partnerships in the communities to address problems of crime and disorder. How to implement the principles of community policing, how to measure whether the objectives have been achieved, and what specific initiatives are required on the part of the police and the community remain to be determined. This determination is best accomplished on a community-by-community basis, depending on the needs and requirements of the community in question and the outcomes of the dialogue between the police and community residents.

Of course, the particular strategies that a police service develops to implement community policing will vary depending on the specific attributes of the community being policed, the demands made on the police, and the community's interest in and capacity for substantive involvement. As well, the strategies employed by a community to become an equal partner in preventing and responding to crime and disorder will depend on the capacities and fiscal resources that a community can commit to the endeavour, as well as on the levels of interest that exist among different segments of the community—often referred to as "community readiness."

COMMUNITY POLICING: ALL THINGS TO ALL PEOPLE?

Community policing holds considerable promise as a way to increase the effectiveness of the police, to involve the community significantly in the identification of and response to problems of crime and disorder, and to maximize police and community resources in times of fiscal restraint. It is important to acknowledge, however, that police organizations and their officers cannot be all things to all people. Priorities must be set. Police services must decide—ideally in consultation with communities, the private sector, and other governmental agencies—what they can do best and how they can assist governments and the community in developing alternative arrangements to deal with areas that are beyond the sole proprietorship of the police.

Communities must be made aware of the numerous challenges that confront police services and understand that choices must be made about the core role of the police. One fundamental question that must be addressed, for example, is whether the police are the most appropriate agency for resolving problems of disorder in the community or, given what we know about the multifaceted causes of crime, whether that task is best left to other agencies with a mandate to do community development (Findley and Taylor 1990, 76). In the words of one chief of police: "It is ludicrous to relegate the police to the role, responsibility, and accountability for urban renewal and social reform" (Fantino 1996, 21). This is certainly an issue that must be addressed as we enter a new era in policing.

Criticisms of Community Policing

Beyond the assertion that the police may not be the most appropriate agency to address social problems in the community, there are a number of additional criticisms that have been levelled against community policing. These include the following:

- *Community policing is too soft an approach to the prevention of and response to crime.* This statement reflects the view that community police officers are social workers in uniform, a view that conflicts with the traditional image of police as crime fighters.
- *Police services become beholden to communities.* This is the view that, if communities are provided the opportunity to participate as partners in preventing and responding to crime, the integrity and activities of the police will be compromised.
- *Community policing is not real policing.* This belief represents the clash between the traditional occupational subculture of the police and the new culture of community policing.
- *Community policing is nothing new—we have always done it.* There is considerable diversity in the size of police forces and in the specific organizational arrangements for carrying out police work across Canada. Many police officers—either out of necessity or because of their own personal style of policing—have always had close contacts with the community and have, as a result, solicited community participation. Police officers assigned to inner-city neighbourhoods with high rates of crime and social disorder as well as officers posted to remote areas must rely on both their professional skills and their individual resourcefulness to be effective in their work. These officers, while members of a highly centralized, hierarchical police service that has clear lines of command and control, are very far removed from their organization. However, community policing represents a systematic approach to crime prevention and response that goes beyond the efforts of individual officers who embrace the ideals of being close to the communities they police.
- *It is too difficult to determine who and what the community is.* The community of the 21st century is different from its counterparts in earlier centuries—more diverse, more mobile, more tech-savvy, more focused on accumulating wealth, and less interested in taking time to be part of a police–community partnership.

The successful development and implementation of community policing requires that the police and communities acknowledge and address these criticisms.

STRATEGIC PARTNERSHIPS AND COMMUNITY POLICING

A core component of community policing is the development of strategic partnerships. Transferring community policing from an abstract notion to actual practice requires a concerted effort on the part of a number of key players. Whereas under the traditional model of police practice, it was the police who assumed the primary role in the design and delivery of police services, community policing involves a partnership between the police and the community.

A Partnership of the Key Players

The **key players in community policing** include elected officials, social and government agencies, managers, police officers, their unions and associations, and the community at large. Our discussion will focus on the managers and chief constables (Chapters 6 and 7), police officers (Chapter 8), and the community (Chapter 10). See A Closer Look 3.2 for a description of the key players.

A Partnership of Public Services

Community policing also provides the opportunity for partnerships between public services that traditionally have not collaborated with one another and that have pursued their own organizational goals and objectives. Public service partnerships are able to develop a more integrated approach to addressing the underlying causes of crime and

A CLOSER LOOK 3.2

THE KEY PLAYERS IN COMMUNITY POLICING PARTNERSHIPS

I. Community Interest Groups

- Citizen, taxpayer, voter
- Media
- Associations
- Nongovernmental organizations
- Consultative committees
- Colleges, universities
- Volunteers
- Victims of crime
- Families, schools, churches
- Workplace
- Leisure milieux

II. Police Managers

- Police chiefs
- Police managers
- Public safety, private security

III. Police Officers

- Police unions or associations
- Rank-and-file police constables
- Public safety, private security

IV. Elected Officials

A. Municipal–Regional Government

- Mayors, municipal councillors
- Local boards of police commissioners

B. Provincial Government

- Ministers and provincial departments in charter of provincial police acts
- Police directorates in provincial departments (policy, program, research)
- Provincial police commissions

C. Federal Government

- Ministry of Public Safety Canada (formerly the Solicitor General of Canada), which oversees the Canada Border Services Agency (CBSA), the Canadian Security Intelligence Service (CSIS), Correctional Service Canada (CSC), the National Parole Board (NPB), and the Royal Canadian Mounted Police (RCMP)

- Department of Justice of Canada (minister and ministry) in charge of some dossiers: crime prevention, victims of crime, gun control, etc.

Source: NORMANDEAU, A., & LEIGHTON, B. (1990). *A vision of the future of policing in Canada: police-challenge 2000: background document.* [Ottawa], Police and Security Branch, Ministry Secretariat, Solicitor, pp. 81-82, Library and Archives Canada.

social disorder than the police acting alone. This is particularly true in the areas of unemployment, job training, housing, and the strengthening of social cohesion in communities. This approach is most commonly referred to as "crime prevention through social development" (CPSD) and will be considered later in the text.

Figure 3.1 depicts the partnerships that can be developed between public services within the framework of community policing, while A Closer Look 3.3 sets out the participants in each public service area.

Figure 3.1 Community Policing: A New Partnership between Public Services

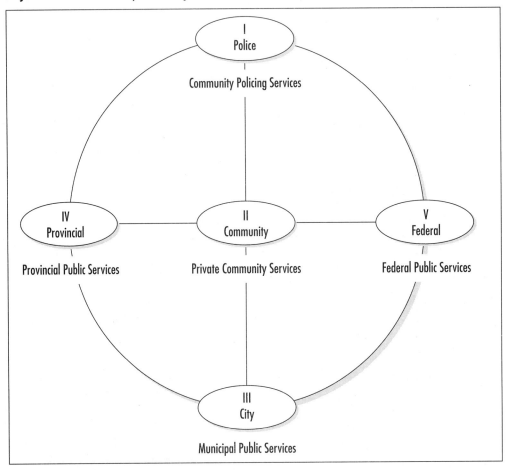

Source: NORMANDEAU, A., & LEIGHTON, B. (1990). *A vision of the future of policing in Canada: police-challenge 2000: background document.* [Ottawa], Police and Security Branch, Ministry Secretariat, Solicitor, p. 85, Library and Archives Canada.

A CLOSER LOOK 3.3

THE PUBLIC-SERVICE PARTNERS

I. Community Policing Services

- Consultative committees: citizens–police

- Neighbourhood watch

- Business watch

- Victims' services

- Special projects

II. Private Community Services

- Families, schools, churches
- Workplace
- Leisure milieux
- Media
- Associations
- Victims' and community release services
- Special projects

III. Municipal Public Services

- Employment, housing, health
- Social services
- Parks, sports, leisure
- Cultural equipment (libraries, theatres, etc.)
- Environmental design
- Special projects

IV. Provincial Public Services

- Employment, housing, health
- Social services, education
- Justice and Solicitor General
- Courts and corrections
- Special projects

V. Federal Public Services

- Employment, housing, health
- Family allowances, unemployment insurance
- Justice and Ministry of Public Safety and Emergency Preparedness Canada
- Courts and corrections
- Special projects

Source: NORMANDEAU, A., & LEIGHTON, B. (1990). *A vision of the future of policing in Canada: police-challenge 2000: background document.* [Ottawa], Police and Security Branch, Ministry Secretariat, Solicitor, pp. 86-87, Library and Archives Canada.

COMMUNITY POLICING IN ONTARIO

Many police services across the country have struggled with how to alter the organization, administration, and delivery of policing services to incorporate the philosophy and principles of community policing. Individual police services have often been left on their own to develop the capacity for community policing and to develop partnerships with the community. The Province of Ontario has established a legislated requirement for community policing, which is the focus of this section.

Ontario can be considered a leader in community policing, in that it provides a supportive environment for municipal and regional police services and the Ontario Provincial Police (OPP) to implement the principles of community policing. Let's take a brief look at how community policing evolved in Ontario and the framework within which police services across the province operate today. This will provide us with a good case study of how community policing has evolved (and continues to evolve) from the traditional or professional model of police work.

The Evolution of Community Policing in Ontario

The commitment to modern-day, community-based policing in Ontario can be traced back more than 30 years. In the early 1970s, a task force examined the impact of technology on policing and found that it had tended to widen the gap between the police and the community (Task Force on Policing in Ontario 1974). Police dispatch centres, reliance on radios, and the police patrol vehicle had all contributed to reduced contact between the police and the public. For example, although radios allowed officers to be dispatched more quickly to telephone requests for service, officers' attention shifted to cases that required immediate resolution. Traditionally, officers on foot patrol had spent a considerable portion of their time becoming familiar with the citizens and problems in the geographic areas they patrolled (Task Force 1974, 25).

The task force also noted that policing in Ontario was heavily influenced by military personalities and military structures. The organization and management of police services was based on a military model, and included centralized command and control, a top-down model of management, and rank structures. Centralized command and control are effective in emergency situations where clear lines of authority and communication are important; however, this structure is a key obstacle to the implementation of the principles of community policing. Rank structures may set out clear lines of accountability and function and thus increase stability within the organization, but that stability is achieved at the expense of flexibility to adapt to demands from the community.

A number of developments provided the impetus for the move towards community-based policing in Ontario. In the early 1970s, questions were raised about the effectiveness of conventional policing strategies and tactics. Random, motorized patrol appeared to be having little impact on rates of crime and social disorder in communities. This required police services to extend their attention beyond responding to incidents to consider public fear of crime and quality-of-life issues in the community.

A second development was the restructuring of Ontario policing that had begun in 1957, with the consolidation of 13 municipal police forces into the Metropolitan Toronto Police (now the Toronto Police Service). This resulted in nine regional police forces, including the Halton Regional Police and the Peel Regional Police, which were established between 1971 and 1974 in conjunction with the initiative to create regional governments across the province. The OPP began to adapt to incorporate the principles of community policing during the 1980s.

Community Policing Today in Ontario

Two key pieces of legislation relate to Ontario's police forces, both of which focus heavily on community policing. These are the Police Services Act (Revised Statutes of Ontario 1990, Chapter P.15) and the Adequacy and Effectiveness of Police Services Regulation(Ontario Regulation 3/99, commonly referred to as the **Adequacy Standards**).

The Police Services Act contains a number of provisions designed to integrate community policing into all aspects of policing. Furthermore, the act requires that the performance of police services be monitored and allows for intervention to correct any perceived deficiencies in service delivery, if necessary. The key sections of the act and the provisions relating to community policing are summarized in A Closer Look 3.4.

A CLOSER LOOK 3.4

ONTARIO'S POLICE SERVICES ACT: KEY PROVISIONS FOR COMMUNITY POLICING

Section 1. Declaration of Principles. Identifies the need for co-operation between the police and communities, the importance of police sensitivity to the multicultural diversity of communities, and the need to ensure that police services are representative of the communities they serve.

Section 3. The Solicitor General. Sets out the duties and powers of the Solicitor General, which include ensuring that adequate and effective police services are provided, that police service boards comply with the prescribed standards of service, and that the development and promotion of community policing programs are pursued.

Section 5(2). Same-Different Methods in One Municipality. Authorizes policing to be delivered differently in communities where two or more communities are widely dispersed or police services have historically been provided to one or more discrete areas of the municipality in a way that is different from the way police services are provided in the rest of the municipality.

Section 5.1(4). Community Policing Advisory Committees. Authorizes municipalities policed by the OPP to establish community policing advisory committees to advise OPP detachment commanders of community priorities and concerns.

Sections 21–26. The Ontario Civilian Commission on Police Services. Sets out duties including investigating police services not in compliance with prescribed standards of service and hearing public complaints against police services and officers.

Sections 27–40. Municipal Police Services Boards. Describes responsibilities including the provision of adequate and effective policing services in the municipality and determining priorities for police services.

Section 41(1). Chiefs of Police. Sets out duties including ensuring that policing services are provided in a manner that reflects the needs of the community; ensuring that the police force provides community-oriented police services.

Section 42(1). Police Officers. Sets out duties including preventing crimes and other offences and providing assistance and encouragement to other persons in their prevention.

Section 135(1). Regulations created by the Lieutenant Governor in Council. Sets out duties including proscribing standards for police service and creating provisions for monitoring the extent to which these standards are met by police services.

Source: Police Services Act, ONTARIO REGULATION 3/99 ADEQUACY AND EFFECTIVENESS OF POLICE SERVICES found at https://www.ontario.ca/laws/statute/90p15

As well, the Adequacy Standards that have been developed in conjunction with the Police Services Act set out specific guidelines for police services in relation to community policing. The most relevant sections are listed in Critical Perspectives 3.2.

There are several additional sources of support for Ontario police services in their efforts to develop and implement community policing policies, programs, and strategies. This includes the Program Development Section organized under the Ministry of Community Safety and Correctional Services, Policing Services Division.

The Policing Services Division is responsible for the ongoing development and improvement of policing throughout the province. The division seeks to ensure a world-class law enforcement network protects Ontario by providing effective training, professional standards and policies, systematic inspections and reviews, and advisory support to police services. The division also supports the development of community safety and crime prevention initiatives, operates Criminal Intelligence Services Ontario, and licenses the private security industry. As of 2007, the Ontario Private Security and Investigative Services Act requires all security companies and their personnel be licensed. This represents a significant step forward in regulating and professionalizing the private security

CRITICAL PERSPECTIVES 3.2

THE ADEQUACY AND EFFECTIVENESS OF POLICE SERVICES REGULATION: KEY PROVISIONS FOR COMMUNITY POLICING

Section 1(1). Police forces shall provide community-based crime prevention initiatives.

Section 2(1). A police force may use members of the police force, auxiliary members of the police force, special constables, and volunteers in community-based crime prevention initiatives.

Section 3. Every chief of police shall establish procedures and processes on problem-oriented policing and crime prevention initiatives, whether the police force provides community-based crime prevention initiatives or whether crime prevention initiatives are provided by another police force or on a combined or regional or cooperative basis or by another organization.

Section 13(2). Every police services board shall establish a policy on sharing data on crime, calls, and public disorder and information on crime trends with its municipal council and with the school boards, community organizations and groups, businesses, and members of the public it serves.

Section 30(1). Every police services board shall prepare a business plan for its police force at least once every three years.

Section 30(2). The business plan shall address:

    a. the objectives, core business, and functions of the police force, including how it will provide adequate and effective police services;

    b. quantitative and qualitative performance objectives and indicators relating to:

        —the police force's provision of community-based crime prevention initiatives, community patrol, and criminal investigation services;

        —community satisfaction with police services.

Section 35. Every board and chief of police shall implement a quality assurance process relating to the delivery of adequate and effective police services, and compliance with the act and its regulations.

Source: *Police Services Act, ONTARIO REGULATION 3/99 ADEQUACY AND EFFECTIVENESS OF POLICE SERVICES found at https://www.ontario.ca/laws/regulation/990003*

industry. Similar regulation of the security industry occurred in the provinces of Alberta and Nova Scotia in 2010.

The Program Development Section works in partnership with police and community agencies to develop and coordinate the planning, implementation, and evaluation of crime prevention and community safety initiatives. The section also provides input into policy and legislative amendments that affect policing, crime prevention, and road safety initiatives. The section liaises with other ministries, participates in the federal/provincial/territorial working group on crime prevention and community safety, and supports other related initiatives.

LEGISLATIVE REQUIREMENTS FOR COMMUNITY POLICING ACROSS CANADA

Ontario was profiled in the last section because it has adopted a strong commitment to community policing. The enactment of legislation has established a statutory framework for community-based policing, and this has greatly assisted police organizations to become community-based in their orientation and practices. Most other provinces, while committed to the concept of community policing, have not taken the same steps as the Ontario government. The Police Acts of other provinces include the following:

- In British Columbia, Part 6 of the British Columbia Police Act authorizes the creation of local police committees to foster positive relationships between the police and local residents and to raise issues concerning the adequacy of policing and law enforcement.
- In Alberta, the Alberta Police Act (Section 38) establishes police officer duties, which include helping the community prevent crime and establishing cooperative relationships between the police service and the community. Throughout 2007 and 2008, the Alberta Solicitor General and Ministry of Public Security finalized policing standards for all police services in the province except the RCMP. In addition, the ministry established a Law Enforcement Framework for the province in 2011, which incorporated community peace officers and sheriffs. In 2011, the ministry moved forward with the regulation of the private security industry, requiring mandatory training for in-house and contract security personnel, alarm responders, and loss prevention personnel.
- Nearly all police legislation across Canada establishes duties for the police to assist with crime prevention and to work with the community.
- Some police departments across Canada, such as the Edmonton Police Service and the Peel Regional Police, are also members of the Commission on Accreditation for Law Enforcement Agencies (CALEA), an American organization committed to the improvement of law-enforcement service delivery that offers a body of standards on a wide range of up-to-date policing topics. Edmonton was the first Canadian police service in Canada designated to receive the CALEA accreditation in 1988. This organization recognizes policing excellence and requires police agencies to maintain the standards established by CALEA. In jurisdictions that do not have a strong legislative foundation for community policing, voluntary membership to CALEA can help establish community-policing organizations. If you are interested in this initiative, check out CALEA's website at www.calea.org.

THE COMMUNITY POLICING CHECKLIST

Because a primary objective of this text is to provide you with a "how to" for community policing, a **Community Policing Implementation Checklist** is given for each of the major areas covered. This checklist will appear in the sections titled "Situations and Strategies" and will list the types of indicators used to determine the extent to which a community policing strategy and the key players are involved in the activities required by a community policing framework. This is particularly important in view of the fact that many police administrators and police officers "talk the talk" about community policing, but on further inspection do not "walk the walk" (i.e., they do not do it).

COMMUNITY-BASED STRATEGIC POLICING

Modern democratic countries like the United States, Britain and Canada have reached a watershed in the evolution of their systems of crime control and law enforcement. Future generations will look back on our era when one system of policing ended and another took its place.

— David Bailey and Clifford Shearing (1994)

So far we have been examining what community policing is. If you recall, we said it is a full-service model of policing, focused not just on law enforcement and crime control but also more broadly on social disorder and community quality-of-life concerns. Beginning in the mid-1990s, and particularly after 9/11, the mandate of the police has grown considerably to include a strong focus aimed at protecting Canada from threats of terrorism and extremism. The problem is that it has become increasingly more difficult for police organizations to sustain current levels of police service to the community. Police officers are feeling overwhelmed with community demands for service, and citizens question the basic ability of their police to fulfill their mandate. As a result, police departments across Canada are looking for better ways to deliver their service.

The factors that are shaping the evolving model of police service delivery (refer back to the trends in the previous chapter) require a more strategic approach to policing than has existed in the past. This approach is called **intelligence-led policing** and can be described as follows:

Intelligence-led policing is a collaborative enterprise based on improved intelligence operations and community-oriented policing and problem solving ... To implement intelligence-led policing, police organizations need to re-evaluate their current policies and protocols. Intelligence must be incorporated into the planning process to reflect community problems and issues. Information sharing must become a policy, not an informal practice. Most important, intelligence must be contingent on quality analysis of data. The development of analytical techniques, training, and technical assistance needs to be supported.

—*Bureau of Justice Assistance [US] (2005)*

The evolving model of community-based strategic policing incorporates intelligence-led policing along with the following elements:

- Policing activities must continue to forge strong relationships with diverse communities, particularly ethnic ones, which account for the majority of population growth in Canada. Trust, respect, and accountability must be at the forefront when building community relationships and partnerships.
- Policing people, places, and crime requires a high level of crime data analysis and evidence-based research with the goal that crime and disorder be predictable and therefore preventable.
- Policing utilizes technologies to improve crime prevention and detection as well as crime-solving ability. Part of this process involves engaging the public with an exchange of information through the Internet and social media. Smart phones, apps, and other evolving technologies serve as a means for the public and police to gather and distribute information in a timely manner for the purpose of community safety.
- Policing is delivered not just by public police but also by a variety of public safety service providers, including private security personnel, private investigators, special constables, sheriffs, and auxiliary constables.
- Better use of crime and disorder reduction strategies such as problem-solving policing (Chapter 5), crime prevention through environmental design or social development (Chapter 4), and broken windows policing (Chapter 4) produce measurable results.
- Changed organizational structures and strategies including integrated service delivery improve the capacity of the police to respond to the broadened mandate of policing.

As community-based policing continues to evolve, the key challenge and priority is to ensure the community remains an integral partner in the management of crime and disorder within society. To achieve this goal, new strategies and tactics need to be evaluated with the goal of enhancing the role of the community beyond simply acting as the "eyes and ears" of the police (the watchman role). While a number of technologies are available to strengthen the crime-solving abilities of the police, it is essential that these

Table 3.2 Community-Based Strategic Policing versus Other Policing Models

	Traditional	Community	Strategic
Administrative approach (locus of control)	Centralized	Decentralized	Integrated control
Authority	Statute	Community	Community/statute
Community role	Report violations of the law	Partnered with police to address crime, disorder, and quality of life	Strategic community partnerships, formalized by protocols and agreements, which integrate into police operations
Operational focus	Crime and disorder	Crime, disorder, quality of life, fear of crime, and disorder	Crime, disorder, security, quality of life, fear of crime, and disorder
Operational strategies	Random patrol, reactive investigation, rapid response	Targeted patrol partnerships, problem solving, proactive or preventative policing, geographic-based deployment of personnel	Target management focused on "hot spots, hot people and hot crimes," strategic partnerships, resource sharing and integrated service delivery; greater reliance on analysis and technology

Source: Whitelaw (2004).

technologies not distance the police from the communities and re-establish the criticisms of the earlier "professional" era of policing.

Table 3.2 summarizes some of the key differences between traditional policing and community-based strategic policing. It is still too early to determine whether community-based strategic policing represents an altogether new model of police service delivery or, rather, a more evolved form of community policing, shaped by the change agents we have described. The critical idea is that a "smarter" model of policing is developing.

CHAPTER SUMMARY

This chapter provided a general orientation to the philosophy, principles, and practice of community policing. Community policing was compared to the traditional, professional model of police practice, and it was noted that community policing represents an expansion of the traditional or professional model of police practice rather than a replacement of it. The emergence of community policing in Ontario was discussed, and the key players in police–community partnerships were identified.

The discussion also examined the evolution of community policing in Ontario. The move towards community policing began during the 1970s, when questions were raised about the effectiveness of traditional police practices. At that time, the restructuring of Ontario police services also began, with the creation of a number of regional police services.

Today in Ontario, the Police Services Act contains a number of provisions designed to ensure that community policing is central to all police services; also, the Adequacy and Effectiveness of Police Service Regulation sets out specific guidelines that police services must follow in implementing the core principles of community policing.

In Chapter 7, we will examine the attributes of police services that have built the principles of community policing into the organization and delivery of policing services. You will see that these police services are organized differently from traditional, hierarchical police services and that the delivery of policing services is centred on the development of police–community partnerships. In Chapter 8, we will present a number of case studies to illustrate how several police services across Canada have attempted to alter their organizational structure, service delivery, and planning process to incorporate the principles of community policing. These case studies provide important insights into the significant changes that community policing requires and reaffirm the point that such changes do not occur overnight but can take a decade or longer.

Chapter Review

Key Terms

- Adequacy Standards, p. 70
- clearance rate, p. 55
- community policing, p. 59
- Community Policing Implementation Checklist, p. 73
- intelligence-led policing, p. 74
- key players in community policing, p. 66
- police effectiveness, p. 55
- the three Ps—prevention, problem solving, partnership, p. 60
- the three Rs—random patrol, rapid response, reactive investigation, p. 54
- traditional or professional model of policing, p. 54
- watch system, p. 54

Key Points

- The "three Rs" of traditional policing—random patrol, rapid response, and reactive investigation—are not generally effective in preventing or responding to crime.
- Clearance rates alone are not an accurate measure of police effectiveness.
- Community policing is based on the "three Ps": prevention, problem-solving, and partnership with the community.
- Community policing is most accurately viewed as an evolution of the police role rather than as a completely different model from traditional policing.
- Community policing includes law enforcement and reactive response to crime and disorder.
- There are key differences between community policing and traditional policing in terms of the role of the police, how the effectiveness of the police is assessed, the priorities of the police, and accountability of the police.
- The specific needs and demands of a community will determine how community policing is implemented.
- Community policing has been criticized for being soft on crime, as not "real" police work, and as nothing new.
- The move towards community policing began in Ontario during the 1970s, when the effectiveness of traditional police practice began to be questioned and when regionalization of police services began in earnest.
- Ontario can be considered a leading jurisdiction in the implementation of community policing.
- The Police Services Act provides the framework within which community policing operates in Ontario.
- The Adequacy and Effectiveness of Police Services Regulation(more commonly referred to as the "Adequacy Standards") sets out guidelines for police services in relation to community policing.

- The key players in community policing are the police service, the police officers, criminal justice agencies and organizations, volunteers, and the community.
- A smarter approach to police service delivery is being developed called "community-based strategic policing."

Self-Evaluation

QUESTIONS

1. What do research studies indicate about the effectiveness of **traditional patrol practice**?
2. What is a **clearance rate** and why might it not be a good measure of police effectiveness?
3. Within the framework of community policing, what would be good measures of **police effectiveness**?
4. What are the **three Rs** of traditional policing?
5. Define the term **community policing** and identify its components.
6. What are the **three Ps** of community policing?
7. What are the key provisions of the Ontario **Police Services Act** that relate to community policing?
8. What are the key provisions in the Ontario **Adequacy Standards** that relate to community policing?
9. Who are the **key players in community policing**?
10. What is **intelligence-led** policing?
11. Explain how **community-based strategic policing** represents an enhanced level of community policing.
12. Contrast and compare **traditional policing** with community policing. What are the key differences?

KEY IDEAS

1. In policing, what are "the three Rs"?
   a. random patrol, rapid response, and reactive investigation
   b. random patrol, reconnaissance, and review of investigation
   c. rapid response, rescue, and reworking investigation
   d. random patrol, reactive call delivery, and response investigation

2. Which of the following best defines clearance rate?
   a. A measure of police effectiveness in a community policing model.
   b. A measure of police effectiveness no longer used by police services.
   c. The percentage of cases where an offence has been committed and a suspect identified.
   d. The percentage of cases where an offence has been committed and a suspect convicted.

3. Which of the following has been indicated in studies of police services?
   a. Most police services have implemented community policing.
   b. Although provincial police forces have adopted community policing, municipal police services still rely on traditional police practice.
   c. The majority of police officers in Canada still carry out their duties within a traditional model of patrol practice.
   d. The RCMP has achieved the highest level of community policing implementation due to their federal role.

4. What has been revealed by research studies on traditional patrol practice?
   a. Increasing random patrols has a significant impact on the levels of crime.
   b. The response time of the police is not related to levels of crime.
   c. The number of arrests made by the police reduces the levels of crime.
   d. The number of female police officers in an agency reduces the levels of crime.

5. Which of the following is *not* a characteristic of the traditional model of police work?
   a. Patrol officers working the same shift rotation.
   b. An emphasis on centralized command and control.
   c. Partnerships with the community.
   d. A highly centralized, hierarchical organizational structure.

6. How is community policing best described?
   a. As a series of crime prevention programs.
   b. As an approach to policing based on prevention, problem-solving, and partnership.
   c. As a series of traditional police practices that have been renamed.
   d. As an approach to policing largely abandoned by Canadian police services.

7. In community policing, what are "the three Ps"?
   a. protection, privacy, and perfection
   b. prevention, problem-solving, and partnership
   c. police, pistols, and pretence
   d. politics, perseverance, and protection

8. Which of the following does *not* define community policing?
   a. It incorporates many elements of traditional policing.
   b. It is a strategy that involves partnering with the community.
   c. It is an appropriate policing strategy for all types of criminal activity.
   d. It is the responsibility of the police and community.

9. What was found in research studies that assessed the impact of community policing?
   a. People tend to dislike community policing as it is time consuming.
   b. With a few exceptions, community policing reduces the levels of crime.
   c. Officers involved in community policing tend to have higher levels of job satisfaction.
   d. Community policing reduces the fear of crime among residents.

10. Which provincial legislation establishes the framework for police agencies in Ontario?
    a. Police Services Act
    b. Criminal Code
    c. Criminal Apprehension Act
    d. Police Enforcement Act

11. 11. In which decade did the move towards community policing in Ontario begin?
    a. 1960s
    b. 1970s
    c. 1980s
    d. 1990s

12. In the 1970s a task force examined policing and technology in Ontario. What did its report find?
    a. The increasing use of technology was facilitating the implementation of community policing.
    b. There was a need for more up-to-date technology for police services.
    c. Technology was widening the gap between the police and the public.
    d. Most police services made very little use of technology.

13. What provided the impetus for the move towards community policing in Ontario?
    a. Increasing concerns about the effectiveness of traditional police practice.
    b. Increasing demands by community residents that the police change.
    c. Increasing concerns by the government to hold the police more accountable.
    d. Increasing demands by civil libertarians for the community to shape the police services that are provided.

14. Ontario's Police Services Act contains sections relating to which one of the following?
    a. A declaration of principles for public partnerships.
    b. The role of provincial police service boards.
    c. The duties of community police practitioners.
    d. The Ontario Civilian Commission on Police Services.

15. In 2003, which body replaced the Solicitor General of Canada?
    a. Department of Justice
    b. Director of Homeland Security
    c. Public Safety Canada
    d. Prime Minister's Office

16. What are the organizational characteristics of the traditional police organization?
    a. flexible working conditions
    b. private sector managerialism
    c. decentralized operations
    d. centralized command and control

17. Which performance measure is *not* a contemporary performance measure?
    a. quality of police work
    b. number of arrests
    c. quality of victim's experiences with police
    d. number of community partnerships

18. Which police service in Canada was the first to receive the Commission on Accreditation for Law Enforcement Agencies (CALEA) designation?
    a. Peel Regional Police
    b. Edmonton Police Service
    c. Vancouver Police Department
    d. Toronto Police Service

Community Policing: Situations and Strategies

Case Studies

Police Reform in Alberta

Over the past eight years, Alberta has conducted a complete and thorough review of policing. A number of reports were prepared, including "Policing Alberta—A Discussion Paper" (2000), "Report of the MLA Policing Review Committee" (2004), and, finally, "Keeping Communities Safe: Report and Recommendations" (2007). Each report examined the effectiveness and efficiency of police service delivery in Alberta; taken together, the reports identify a number of deficiencies and make a number of key recommendations.

In response to the uneven distribution of policing resources, the Solicitor General of Alberta created provincial sheriffs and peace officers through the passage of new legislation called the Peace Officer Act (Alberta). Public Safety Peace Officers have limited powers and authorities. As of 2008 there were more than 3,000 PSPOs in Alberta, working for some 284 different agencies, with provincial government offices being the largest employer. The role of sheriffs includes traffic enforcement, investigative support including surveillance, and fugitive apprehension. These new sheriffs allow police officers to focus on more serious crime in the communities they serve and supplement police when required.

The Government of Alberta also created the Alberta Policing Secretariat to implement recommendations of the Crime Reduction and Safe Communities Task Force. In keeping with these recommendations, more Crown prosecutors and support positions had been authorized, file ownership policies have been instituted to ensure better prosecutorial file management, a comprehensive bail application process has been developed to better respond to repeat offenders, and the province has examined the development of specialized courts designed to tailor better response options (e.g., drug and addiction courts).

Additional initiatives include the establishment of organized crime investigation funding through an arm's-length body headed by a CEO. Furthermore, additional policing oversight has been established through the creation of Alberta Serious Incident Response Teams (ASIRTs), whose mandate is to investigate incidents or complaints involving serious injury or death of any person and matters of a serious or sensitive nature that may have resulted from the actions of a police officer. Finally, provincial policing standards have been instituted.

The steps taken to date have strengthened the overall response to crime and community disorder by increasing police visibility and improving overall capacity to investigate, and have strengthened overall deterrence by reducing gaps in investigation and enforcement.

Can you think of any other options available to increase visibility without significantly increasing spending? What other options are available? Are any of these options available in your local police service?

Exercises: Knowledge into Practice

Exercise 1. Your Hometown

Recalling the community where you spent most of your childhood, complete the following:

Population: _____	**Remote rural/Rural/Suburban/Urban**		
Ethnic diversity:	High	Medium	Low
Police Service:	Provincial	Regional	City/Municipal Independent
Level of Crime:	High	Medium	Low

The most common types of crime:

_____

_____

_____

_____

The most common social problems:

_____

_____

_____

Your perceptions of the sources of problems in the community:

_____

_____

_____

	Positive				Negative
Your perceptions of the police:	1	2	3	4	5
Your contacts with the police:	Positive/Negative				

The major challenges that the police in your community faced:

_____

_____

_____

	Highly Effective				Not Effective
Were the police effective in meetings these challenges?	1	2	3	4	5

The Challenge   Effectiveness of Response

1. _____

2. _____

3. _____

4. _____

5. _____

For those challenges you feel the police were effective in addressing, list the reasons why you feel they were effective.

1. _____

2. _____

3. _____

4. _____

5. _____

For those challenges you feel the police were less effective in addressing, list the reasons why.

1. _____

2. _____

3. _____

4. _____

5. _____

Compare your responses to those of your classmates.

Exercise 2. Measuring What Counts in Policing

Critical Idea: The performance measures listed earlier in this chapter assess the quality of a police service. Traditional measures of police performance tend to be quantitative—concerned more with measurable data such as number of arrests, calls responded to, and response times. If you were to develop a "report card" for your local police service, what would the advantages and disadvantages of qualitative and quantitative performance measures be? If you were the chief of police, how might you use each of these measures when (a) crime rates are increasing and City Hall is very concerned, and (b) crime rates are decreasing and the police chief wants to hire more personnel?

REFERENCES

Bureau of Justice Assistance. 2005. Intelligence-led Policing: The New Intelligence Architecture. *Washington, DC.*

Community Oriented Policing and Problem Solving Advisory Committee. 1995. Community Oriented Policing and Problem Solving. *Sacramento: Attorney General's Office, California Department of Justice.*

Fantino, J. 1996. "Community Policing: The Myth and the Reality!" Blue Line Magazine *8(5): 20–23.*

Findley, K.W., and R.W. Taylor. 1990. "Re-Thinking Neighborhood Policing." Journal of Contemporary Criminal Justice *6(2): 70–78.*

Government of Alberta. 2000. "Policing Alberta: A Discussion Paper." Edmonton: Alberta Justice.

—. 2004. "Report of the MLA Policing Review Committee." Edmonton: Alberta Justice.

—. 2007. "Keeping Communities Safe: Report and Recommendations." Edmonton: Alberta's Crime Reduction and Safe Communities Task Force.

Kelling, G.L., and M.L. Moore. 1998. "From Political to Reform to Community: The Evolving Strategy of Police." In Community Policing: Rhetoric or Reality?, *ed. J.R. Green and S.D. Mastrofski. 3–25. Mastrofski. New York: Praeger.*

Murphy, C. 1995. "Community Policing and Police Leadership." Unpublished manuscript. Halifax: Henson College, Dalhousie University.

Normandeau, A., and B. Leighton. 1990. A Vision of the Future of Policing in Canada: Police—Challenge 2000. *Ottawa: Police and Security Branch, Solicitor General Canada.*

Ontario. Regulation 3/99—Adequacy and Effectiveness of Police Services (1999). Toronto: Queen's Park.

—. Police Services Act (2009). Toronto: Queen's Park.

Oppal, W.T. (Commissioner). 1994. Closing the Gap: Policing and the Community. *Policing in British Columbia Commission of Inquiry Final Report, vol. 1. Victoria: Attorney General of British Columbia.*

Sherman, L., et al. 1997. Preventing Crime: What Works, What Doesn't, What's Promising. *Washington, DC: National Institute of Justice.*

Sparrow, M.K. 1988. Implementing Community Policing. *Washington, DC: National Institute of Justice.*

Task Force on Policing in Ontario. 1974. The Task Force on Policing in Ontario: Report to the Solicitor General. *Toronto: Ministry of the Attorney General.*

Trojanowicz, R., and B. Bucqueroux. 1997. Community Policing: How To Get Started, *2nd ed. Cincinnati: Anderson Publishing.*

Whitelaw, B. 2004. Policing the Modern Community. *Halifax: Henson College, Dalhousie University.*

UNIT 3

REUTERS/Mathieu Belanger

Crime Prevention and Crime Response within a Community Policing Framework

Responding to and Preventing Crime within a Community Policing Framework

Source: THE CANADIAN PRESS/Dave Chidley

Learning Objectives

After completing this chapter, you should be able to:

- Define targeting strategies, community service approaches, and crime prevention programs,

- Provide examples of primary prevention programs, secondary prevention programs, and tertiary prevention programs,

- Describe how environmental design can prevent crime,

- Provide examples of the strategies for reducing opportunities for crime and social disorder,

- Discuss the effectiveness of and limits on crime prevention programs, and

- Discuss the mediation and conflict resolution strategies used by patrol officers.

INTRODUCTION

What actions do you believe will be the most effective in reducing the level of crime?

1. Tougher sentencing
2. Increasing social programs, for example, education, job training, drug treatment, recreation, job creation
3. Providing more police and correctional officers
4. Increasing crime prevention
5. Public/community awareness and neighbours watching out for one another

—Top five responses to an Environics public opinion poll in 1997

Preventing and reducing levels of crime is a high priority for community residents and for police services across the country. This is because of the economic, social, and human costs of crime. It has been estimated that reacting to crime—apprehending, sentencing, incarcerating, and rehabilitating offenders—costs Canadian taxpayers around $31 billion annually, or about $943 per person. This figure is, in fact, only a small portion of the actual cost of crime. It does not include the costs of property loss, security services, insurance fraud, and crime-related hospitalization. Nor does it include the human costs—the impact of crime on victims and their families; the loss of a sense of personal and community well-being, security, and safety; and the fear of crime. When these impacts are factored in, the cost of crime in Canada is estimated to be as high as $70 billion per year (National Crime Prevention Centre 2008).

In Chapter 3 we noted that community policing involves three types of police work: proactive, reactive, and coactive. Over the past decade there has been a rapid expansion of community-based programs designed to respond to a variety of problems and issues. Many of these developments are in response to the 1993 Report of the Standing Committee on Justice and the Solicitor General that outlined the Safer Communities Strategy, commonly referred to as the **safer communities approach to crime prevention**.

The four principles of the safer communities approach are:

1. The community is the focal point of effective crime prevention.
2. The community must identify and respond to both short- and long-term needs.
3. Crime prevention efforts should bring together individuals from a range of sectors to tackle crime.
4. Strategies for preventing crime should be supported by the entire community.

Another major initiative is the Safer Communities Initiative, which was launched in 1998 as part of the federal government's National Strategy on Community Safety and Crime Prevention. This initiative, which is administered by the National Crime Prevention Centre, promotes integrated action between governmental and nongovernmental partners and assists communities in developing and implementing community-based solutions to crime, with a particular emphasis on children, youth, Indigenous people, and women. It also provides funding to assist communities in developing partnerships and programs that address the underlying causes of crime. The National Crime Prevention Strategy (NCPS), as it is called today, is administered through Public Safety Canada's National Crime Prevention Centre (NCPC). For further information, visit http://www.publicsafety.gc.ca/index-eng.aspx.

Across Canada, police services are engaged in a wide variety of activities designed to prevent and respond to crime, as well as to increase the likelihood that people involved in criminal activity will be detected and apprehended. Programs include community police stations, police storefronts, and foot patrols. School-based programs include school liaison officers, safety presentations to students in primary grades, the DARE program to fight drug abuse at the middle and high school levels, anti-bullying programs, and various recreational and sports programs that bring police officers together with students in nonconfrontational activities. These programs and strategies depend on front-line patrol officers who, within the model of community policing, are empowered to work with community residents to identify and resolve problems and issues.

These various programs and activities can generally be grouped into *proactive targeted strategies*, *community service approaches*, and *crime prevention programs*; each of these is discussed below. An element common to all of these approaches is the central role played by patrol officers. The implementation of the principles of community policing has resulted in a fundamental shift in the roles and activities of line patrol officers. This has been accomplished by decentralizing the traditional command and control hierarchy. Assigning officers responsibility for crime and disorder prevention at the neighbourhood level has created opportunities to take a more proactive approach and to broaden the role and activities of police officers beyond merely responding to calls for service. We will explore this in greater detail in our discussion of community police officers in Chapter 8.

PROACTIVE TARGETED STRATEGIES

Proactive targeted strategies rely on the use of patrol to apprehend, deter, and incapacitate criminal offenders. Among the strategies used are:

- cover patrol,
- repeat offender targeting,
- saturation patrol,
- roadblocks, and
- repeat complaint address policing. (Mastrofski 1990, 34)

In contrast to traditional patrol, which is random and incident-driven, patrol within a targeted strategy is undertaken for three related reasons:

- *To achieve visibility*. The presence of an officer may eliminate the opportunity for someone to commit a crime, besides allowing the officer to investigate leads and observe infractions of the law.
- *To pursue proactive policing*. Patrolling allows the officer to be proactive by determining the opportunities for criminal behaviour and initiating appropriate preventive strategies. This maintains contact with the community and encourages cooperation and trust between officers and citizens.
- *To provide for rapid response*. Patrolling provides the officer with an opportunity to respond or react quickly to calls for service.

Addressing Crime: Tactical or Directed Patrol

Tactical or directed patrol involves saturating high-crime areas, called "hot spots," with police officers or targeting individuals involved in specific types of criminal activity. Hot spots are operationally defined as small clusters of addresses with frequent **hard crime calls** (hold-up alarms, shootings, stabbings, auto thefts, thefts from autos, assaults, and sexual assaults) as well as substantial **soft crime calls** for service (audible break-in alarms, disturbances, drunks, noise, unwanted persons, vandalism, prowlers, fights, and physical injuries).

Tactical or directed patrol projects have four common characteristics:

1. Patrol is based on a thorough analysis of crime data.
2. Officers use uncommitted time to engage in purposeful activity.
3. Officers have specific instructions directing their activities.
4. Officers are proactive and, as a result, may seem aggressive.

Directed forms of patrol are usually either location- or person-oriented. Police resources are focused in areas identified as hot spots of crime and disorder, or they target offenders. Directed patrol may also be event-oriented, especially at large public gatherings where violence is anticipated. In contrast to random, reactive strategies, tactical or directed patrol strategies give police managers greater control over their most valuable resource—the time and activities of patrol officers. Police services may also make use of citizen volunteer groups to conduct static or mobile surveillance in hot spots.

The Effectiveness of Tactical or Directed Patrol

The proactive approach of tactical or directed patrol produces positive results in terms of crime prevention and intervention (see Critical Perspectives 4.1).

It is essential, however, that tactical patrol strategies be implemented on the basis of a careful analysis and evaluation of crime data if the objectives of the specific project are to be achieved. Since aggressive patrol may involve car stops, person checks, zero tolerance enforcement, and other crackdowns, officers must ensure that their actions do not

---

CRITICAL PERSPECTIVES 4.1

THE EFFECTIVENESS OF PROACTIVE STRATEGIES

Question: Does the number of police officers have an impact on levels of crime?

Answer: In certain situations, yes.

- There is some evidence that crime rates increase during police strikes. During a police strike in Montreal in 1969, for example, the rate of bank robberies increased 50 times and the number of burglaries of commercial establishments was 14 times the average.

- Increases in the numbers of police officers appear to reduce the levels of crime in urban areas and to have a preventive effect as well; this is most likely due to increased police visibility.

Question: Do proactive police arrests that focus on high-risk individuals and offences reduce the levels of serious, violent crime?

Answer: Yes, for certain types of offences.

- Police drug crackdowns appear not to affect the levels of violent crime.

- Police campaigns against impaired driving have an impact and reduce death rates.

- "Zero tolerance" arrest policies directed towards street activity can reduce serious crime, particularly if the needs of those persons arrested are addressed.

Question: Do directed preventive patrols that target hot spots and that are directed at peak times of criminal activity affect levels of crime?

Answer: In many instances, yes.

- Increasing the numbers of uniformed police officers in patrol cars in hot spots and during "hot times" (crime peaks) may significantly reduce levels of criminal activity.

(continues)

Question: Is there an optimal time that officers should remain at a hot spot in order to be effective?

Answer: Yes.

- Patrol stops must reach a threshold dosage of about 10 minutes in order to generate significantly longer "survival" or time spans without disorder, as opposed to simply driving through a hot spot.
- The optimal length for patrol stops appears to be 11 to 15 minutes, after which continued police presence brings diminishing returns.
- Increasing the number of patrols may not be as important as time spent at a hot spot targeting specific individuals.

Question: Does tactical or directed patrol result in the displacement of criminal activity to other areas?

Answer: Potentially, yes.

- Recent research finds little evidence to support the "belief" that geographic displacement occurs due to location based directed patrol.

Source: Koper, C.S., 1995. "Just Enough Police Presence: Reducing Crime and Disorderly Behavior by Optimizing Patrol Time in Crime Hot Spots." Justice Quarterly 12(4): 649–72; Sherman, L.W., and D. Weisburd, 1995. "General Deterrent Effects of Police Patrol in Crime 'Hot Spots': A Randomized, Controlled Trial." Justice Quarterly 12(4): 625–48. Sherman, L.W., et al., 1997. Preventing Crime: What Works, What Doesn't, What's Promising. Washington, DC: Office of Justice Programs, U.S. Department of Justice.

violate the citizens' rights guaranteed in the Canadian Charter of Rights and Freedoms. Furthermore, strategies that combine tactical patrol with longer-term problem-solving approaches may be more effective and have more impact in the long run.

The Problems of Tactical or Directed Patrol

While there is conclusive evidence that tactical or directed patrol produces more positive outcomes than does random, reactive patrol, the success of this approach to police work requires that police services resolve a number of issues. For example, they must:

- develop strategies to alter the role and attitude of police officers from reactive to proactive;
- convince patrol officers that their current call loads do not preclude carrying out tactical or directed patrol projects;
- analyze crime patterns, trends, and patrol officer workloads and activities (time and tasks); and
- deal with diminished police resources, which inhibit the ability to implement tactical or directed patrol.

COMMUNITY SERVICE APPROACHES

The shift towards community policing as the model of police service delivery has resulted in significant changes in the role of community residents: from passive consumers of policing services to active participants in the prevention of and response to crime and disorder. **Community service approaches** "focus on protecting, aiding, and mobilizing members of the community in dealing with crime, disorders and the underlying factors contributing to these problems" (Mastrofski 1990, 33). These strategies include foot patrols, community police stations, and organizing the community to become involved in addressing problems of crime and disorder. The objective of these initiatives is to "shift the focus of police-citizen contacts toward the 'good' people, the victims, and the potential victims in the community" (36).

Foot Patrol: Back to the Beat

Foot patrols, or **beats**, are prevalent among many Canadian police departments and predate the use of automobiles in patrol work. Organized foot patrols were first instituted in 1829 in London, when Robert Peel hired officers for the Metropolitan Police, yet since the 1990s they have been heralded as a breakthrough and as a major component of community policing.

Foot patrols address the major criticism that patrol cars—equipped with computers, cellphones, video cameras, and police radios—distance officers from the community and discourage them from interacting with residents. Foot patrols are often found in urban centres where the population density is much higher and concentrated vertically (e.g., in high-rise apartments), unlike the horizontal distribution found in suburban communities. In urban areas across North America, foot patrol has produced some interesting results that suggest it holds great potential.

But with a few exceptions (the city of Edmonton being one), there is no evidence that foot patrols directly affect the levels of crime in neighbourhoods. Field research studies do, however, indicate that foot patrols:

- reduce citizens' fear of crime;
- increase feelings of personal safety among community residents;
- reduce calls for service;
- increase officer familiarity with neighbourhoods; and
- increase officers' feelings of safety on the job, which results in greater job satisfaction and a higher level of morale than is experienced by those in patrol cars.

Foot patrols generally receive high marks from community residents, who appreciate the increased visibility and accessibility of police officers. In fact, community residents often equate beat officers with community policing.

Although foot patrols may provide an opportunity for officers to focus on common reoccurring problems that tax police resources, such patrols can be difficult to implement, for many front-line supervisors would prefer to have patrol units available to deal with calls for service, especially during peak service times.

Bicycle Patrols

Officers on mountain bikes are often deployed into areas of high crime and social disorder. On bicycles, officers are able to deploy and manoeuvre where patrol cars are unable to travel. Bicycles have the additional feature of being silent. In addition, the health benefits to officers and the environmental "friendliness" of bicycle patrols are significant. The first urban uniformed mountain bike patrol was established by the Seattle Police Department in 1987; since then, many Canadian police services have implemented year-round bike patrols modelled after the successful Seattle program.

An evaluation of the Seattle bike patrol program identified the following advantages:

- Bicycle patrol officers made more arrests in a shorter period of time over a larger beat area.
- The Seattle bike patrol averaged four times more arrests than foot patrols and were able to extend their patrol area over several square kilometres.
- Bicycle officers arrived sooner than the patrol cars to most of the calls for service in the downtown core. In addition, mountain bikes had greater mobility than patrol cars in serious snowfalls.
- Bicycle patrol units are much less expensive to operate and maintain than patrol cars (Grady 1990).
- The findings of a recent study noted that bicycle patrols result in over twice as much contact with the public compared to automobile patrols. The same study documented the clear tactical advantages of bicycle patrols over other methods (Menton, 2008).

RCMP citizen volunteer bike patrol.

Source: Reproduced with the permission of the RCMP.

IN YOUR COMMUNITY 4.1

THE MAPLE RIDGE VOLUNTEER BICYCLE PATROL PROGRAM

In Metro Vancouver, the Maple Ridge Volunteer Bicycle Patrol Program was launched in August 2003. It serves as a crime deterrent, with rides occurring in local neighbourhoods. The program serves as the eyes and ears of the local RCMP Detachment; it reports all suspicious, criminal, and nuisance behaviour observed. Team patrols maintain contact with the program dispatcher and with the RCMP dispatcher, as needed. Volunteer bicycle patrol members also assist with stolen auto recovery, community events, bicycle safety training, and security assessments.

The benefits of becoming a volunteer bicycle patrol member include:

- Belonging to a team of community volunteers
- Interaction with the public
- Learning and practising crime prevention techniques
- Enjoying the benefits of outdoor physical activity

To become a volunteer bicycle patrol member you must:

- Be 19 years of age or older
- Be a resident of Maple Ridge or Pitt Meadows
- Successfully pass a criminal record check
- Be committed to the program for at least one year
- Successfully complete the training required for the Volunteer Bike Patrol Program

Source: *Ridge Meadows RCMP, Citizens Volunteer Bike Patrol. Found at http://ridgemeadows. rcmp-grc.gc.ca/ViewPage.action?siteNodeId=353&languageId=1&contentId=18084 Reproduced with the permission of the RCMP.*

In Canada, the success of police officers patrolling on bikes has resulted in several police services enlisting the support of volunteers to provide additional bike patrols within the community. Citizen bike patrol programs exist in various forms, serving as the "eyes and ears" of the police in preventing and detecting criminal activity. Comprised of trained and equipped volunteers, the citizen bike patrols enhance community–police relations; they also add valuable resources to the police service by enhancing the deployment advantages associated with bikes (see In Your Community 4.1).

So far we have examined only two dominant modes of patrol. There are others, including helicopters, snowmobiles, motorcycles, boats, and mounted patrol.

Deployment of Police Personnel

The effective use of police resources requires the deployment of personnel in a manner that is responsive to a number of factors, including:

- predicted call load and call volumes;
- police collective agreements that specify the length of police shifts or the deployment of one- or two-person patrol units;
- specific crime and disorder problems; and
- community concerns regarding dedicated police personnel.

The goal is to develop deployment models that do not over- or under-deploy police officers, that allow police to get to know communities, and that are flexible enough to respond to developing crime and disorder trends. We now examine some of these models.

Team Policing

Team policing or platoon/squad policing originated in the late 1940s in Aberdeen, Scotland, and appeared, albeit briefly, in a number of Canadian and US police services during the 1970s. The ideal attributes of team policing include:

- the same group of police officers work the same set of shifts on a continuous basis;
- geographic stability of patrol through permanent assignment of teams of police to small neighbourhood areas;
- maximized communication among team members assigned to a specific area around the clock, seven days a week; and
- maximum interaction and communication between team members and the community.
- capitalizing on the strengths of individual team members;
- improved police–community relations;
- reduced crime and disorder problems;
- improved police officer morale; and
- improved officer productivity.

The objectives of team policing include:

A number of Canadian police agencies have implemented team-based deployment models, including the Calgary Police Service (see Critical Perspectives 4.2). Team policing models share the following characteristics:

- Teams of 8 to 12 officers work the same rotating shift schedule, under a decentralized system of policing.
- Officers are assigned to geographic areas or zones, which allows the development and retention of ties with the community.
- Community liaison officers work strategically and tactically with communities, ensuring the exchange of information between communities and teams.
- Teams are supervised by a sergeant, who works alongside team personnel on a rotating shift schedule.

CRITICAL PERSPECTIVES 4.2

ATTRIBUTES OF AN EFFECTIVE POLICE DEPLOYMENT MODEL

Based on sound research and experience, all Canadian police services attempt to incorporate the following elements into their deployment of front-line police officers.

1. Police officers are assigned to specific geographic areas.

2. Police officers are encouraged to work with communities to identify problems.

3. Communities have a say in how police services are delivered.

4. Crime analysis combined with community consultation enables a more targeted deployment approach.

5. Officer workload is taken into account in an effort to ensure staffing levels that will allow police officers to work on proactive policing activities.

6. Citizen access to police service is available in a number of formats, including telephone-based service delivery, Web-based crime reporting (typing and texting), access to police stations, and police dispatch to calls.

7. Supervision of personnel, often called "span of control," sees 7 to 10 officers assigned to every supervisor. This is essential in police organizations where there is considerable inexperience among police officers having front-line responsibilities (remember our discussion of demographic trends in Chapter 2).

In terms of current leadership theory, the deployment of police personnel as teams makes sense; however, the following implementation problems have been observed:

- Teams develop an inward focus, as opposed to an external, community-based focus.
- Community liaison officers work directly with communities, leaving line officers for reactive patrol duties; this inhibits rather than enhances whole-team interaction with the community.
- Workload demands on supervisors create difficulties in supervision.
- Entire teams would respond to incidents of crime and disorder, fostering a "mob" policing mentality.
- Without adequate supervisory/leadership training, team leaders may have difficulty performing their role.

Other service delivery deployment models include the following:

- *Zone or geopolicing*, in which police officers are assigned to geographic-based communities typically for periods of one to two years. Personnel start at different times throughout a 24-hour period and are all responsible for policing the same area.
- *Problem-based policing*, in which police are deployed according to the zone policing model. However, resources are mobilized to target prioritized problems, requiring officers to police outside geographic "zone" assignments. This is a sophisticated deployment model consistent with community-based strategic policing.

COMMUNITY POLICE STATIONS AND STOREFRONTS

Community or storefront police stations have become very popular in Canada and are often staffed by a mixture of uniformed police personnel, civilian staff, and volunteers. There is considerable variation in the activities of these police stations. There is some evidence that community police stations may result in more positive evaluations of the police by community residents. However, these facilities appear to have little impact on crime rates.

Among the difficulties experienced by community police stations are staffing concerns, limited hours of operation, a lack of awareness among motorized patrol officers about community police stations and their activities, and a lack of coordination between officers assigned to community police stations and patrol (Graham 1997). To be effective, community police stations must be part of a much larger process of decentralizing police services and must involve empowering officers to work with community residents to address problems of crime and disorder.

CRIME PREVENTION PROGRAMS

The emphasis on crime prevention is not a recent phenomenon. At the same time that Sir Robert Peel proposed his Nine Principles of Policing, Sir Richard Mayne, a London Chief Commissioner, stated that "the primary object of an efficient police [service] is the prevention of crime" (1829).

Any discussion of the effectiveness of crime prevention initiatives must be tempered with the following observation: the causes of crime and disorder in any community are varied and complex. It is unrealistic to expect that the police alone, or even the police acting in concert with dedicated community residents, can reduce or eliminate all of society's problems. This is particularly true for crimes that are international in scope and that involve large criminal syndicates, and for those offenders who are the products or victims of the emerging technological society. With this caveat in mind, we can proceed.

Canadian police services are involved in a variety of **crime prevention programs**. Many were developed within the general framework of community policing; others existed before community policing became fashionable. Today, policing efforts fall within the **National Crime Prevention Strategy (NCPS)**, which aims to reduce crime and victimization by tackling crime before it happens and is an integral part of the Government of Canada's continued efforts to tackle crime in order to build stronger, healthier communities. The National Strategy is based on the principle that the surest way to reduce crime is to focus on the factors that put individuals at risk, such as family violence, school problems, and drug abuse. The NCPS provides a policy framework for implementing crime prevention interventions in Canada. The program is administered by the National Crime Prevention Centre (NCPC) in the Community Safety and Partnerships Branch of Public Safety Cnada, and managed in collaboration with the provinces and territories.* Crime prevention news releases and crime prevention publications and reports can be found on the NCPS website. For more information, visit https://www.publicsafety.gc.ca/cnt/cntrng-crm/crm-prvntn/strtg-en.aspx.

Crime prevention programs can be classified into two broad groups:

1. situational crime prevention strategies, which seek to reduce the availability and attractiveness of opportunities to commit criminal activity; and
2. crime prevention through social development, which focuses on addressing the root causes of crime and disorder.

While there is considerable diversity in the scope and objectives of these programs, the primary objective is to prevent crime and reduce levels of criminal activity. Underpinning crime prevention efforts are a number of theories that serve to guide prevention efforts. Let's look briefly at two dominant theories.

• *Rational choice theory.* This theory focuses on the decision-making of potential offenders. Offenders are viewed as acting rationally and as making decisions based on the information they have at hand about costs and benefits, without thinking through alternative

*Public Safety Canada, National Crime Prevention Strategy (2017-04-28) found at https://www.publicsafety.gc.ca/cnt/cntrng-crm/crm-prvntn/strtg-en.aspx

courses of action. This theory forms the foundation for a number of situational crime prevention strategies (Cornish and Clarke 1986; Newman, Clarke, and Shoham 1997).

- *Routine activities theory.* This theory, which is one of the main theories of "environmental criminology," falls under rational choice theory, because offenders are involved in a rational and calculated assessment of criminal opportunities, risks, and potential rewards. The routine activities theory requires three elements to be present for a crime to take place—a suitable target, a motivated offender, and the absence of a safeguard to protect the victim or deter the offender (Cohen and Felson 1979; Felson 1994). To prevent crime, at least one of these elements needs to be altered (see Critical Perspectives 4.3). In Chapter 5, we will examine this idea further when we describe the "problem analysis triangle."

Traditionally, crime prevention initiatives fall into three categories: primary, secondary, and tertiary.

Primary Prevention Programs

Primary prevention programs are the most common type of crime prevention initiative and are most often directed towards property offences. They are designed to identify opportunities for criminal offences and to alter these conditions in an attempt to reduce the likelihood of crimes being committed. Primary prevention programs include both

---

CRITICAL PERSPECTIVES 4.3

PREVENTING CRIME USING ROUTINE ACTIVITY AND RATIONAL CHOICE THEORY

Criminologists Lawrence Cohen and Marcus Felson developed "routine activity theory" to assist in developing crime prevention approaches. Their theory posits that for crime to occur, three conditions must be present:

- a suitable target;
- the lack of a suitable guardian to prevent the crime from happening; and
- the presence of a motivated offender.

Altering any of the above factors will reduce the likelihood of a crime occurring.

A "target" might include a person, location, or object. Suitable guardians are typically people; however, a guardian may also include technology such as CCTV systems. Guardians include:

- police patrol;
- security guards;
- Neighbourhood Watch programs;
- door staff;
- vigilant staff and co-workers;
- friends;
- neighbours; and
- closed-circuit television (CCTV) systems.

An offender may be motivated to commit a crime if, based on their situational assessment of risk and reward, the likelihood of gain exceeds the risk of being caught (rational choice theory). For additional information, the UK's Home Office website at www.crimereduction. homeoffice.gov.uk is very useful.

Source: *Adapted from Gerald Maxwell, American Sociological Review, American Sociological Association, American Sociological Society. Copyright 1979.*

general approaches to crime prevention and specific crime prevention initiatives. The more common primary crime prevention programs are discussed below.

Operation Identification

Citizens mark their property with identification numbers for two purposes: (1) to make the disposal of stolen goods more difficult, and (2) to assist in the recovery of items by the police. A similar program for businesses is called Operation Provident.

Neighbourhood Watch

Neighbourhood Watch is the oldest and best-known of all crime prevention programs. It involves raising residents' awareness of strangers and criminal activities—particularly break and enters—in their neighbourhoods. "This Is a Neighbourhood Watch Community" signs are a common sight across Canada. Variations of this concept appear as Apartment Watch, Block Watch, Rural Crime Watch, and, in rural Ontario, Cottage Watch.

Citizen Patrols

In many communities there are citizens' crime watch programs, which involve foot and vehicle patrols by trained volunteers under the supervision of police officers. The primary function of these patrols is to observe and report. Volunteers do not become involved with suspects or leave their vehicles without explicit instructions from their police supervisors. The primary responsibility of citizen patrols is to observe, not to intervene (Harman 1996). The Edmonton Mill Woods Community Patrol and Halton Regional Police Service Communities on Phone Patrol (COPPS) are good examples of citizen patrol initiatives. You can check out both these programs online at http://seedmonton.ca/about-mwpc/mill-woods-community-patrol and https://www.haltonpolice.ca/community/safetyeducation/copp.php.

Media-Based Programs

Media-based programs include those designed to educate the public about crime, as well as "crime time" programs that solicit the public's assistance in locating known criminals. Perhaps the best known programs of this sort are the television programs *America's Most Wanted* and *Unsolved Mysteries*, which, unfortunately for criminal offenders from the United States who slip across the border, are also watched by Canadians. In addition, many police services have developed "hot tip" lines and televised re-enactment programs such as Crime Stoppers, which offer cash rewards for information leading to the arrest and conviction of offenders. In 2016, Crime Stoppers turned 40 years old. Remember our discussion of trends in Chapter 2, in which we identified social media as a powerful tool for crime-solving—for example, suspect identification and communicating with social networks for preventive purposes. The use of social media within community policing is expanding rapidly; there are immense opportunities for development. The Edmonton Police Service provides up-to-date information on various social media sites, including news releases, success stories, and crime files. Along with corporate social media accounts, the EPS utilizes front-line officer Twitter accounts. This latter platform allows the public to interact directly with EPS officers and provide information about real-time events occurring in the community.* For more information, visit http://www.edmontonpolice.ca/resources/socialmedia.aspx.

Preventing Crime at Places: Crime Prevention through Environmental Design

Proper design and effective use of the built environment can lead to a reduction in the incidence and fear of crime and an improvement in the quality of life.
—*Crowe (2000)*

*Edmonton Police Service, Social Media, found at http://www.edmontonpolice.ca/resources/socialmedia.aspx

Police services have developed a wide range of initiatives in an attempt to prevent crime in specific types of places, such as in apartment complexes, subway and transit stations, stores, and homes. A common element of these approaches is that they attempt to "block" criminal opportunities, making it difficult and risky for potential offenders. One of the better-known approaches is **crime prevention through environmental design (CPTED)**, which sets out to reduce criminal opportunities by altering the physical environment of structures and places. These changes may include improving lighting and altering access routes for pedestrians and vehicles. Another tactic, target hardening, involves proactive measures such as installing locks and improving property security to reduce break and enters. Property marking and the use of closed-circuit television(CCTV)are also often employed. A number of opportunity-reducing techniques are presented in Table 4.1.

Table 4.1 Sixteen Crime Opportunity-Reducing Techniques

1.	**Target Hardening**
	Install strengthened coin boxes in telephone kiosks
	Use steering column locks on cars
	Install anti-robbery screens in banks
2.	**Control of Access to Crime Targets in Multiple-Unit Dwellings**
	Install fencing around buildings to reduce vandalism
	Install entry phones
	Employ caretakers
3.	**Deflection of Offenders from Targets**
	Segregate fans at sporting events
	Pay attention to pub locations
	Alter streets to stop cruising for prostitutes
4.	**Control of Crime Facilitators**
	Include photographs on credit cards
	Use toughened glasses and bottles in pubs
	Require passwords for mobile phones
5.	**Entrance and Exit Screening**
	Install automatic ticket gates at stations
	Screen baggage at airports
	Use merchandise tags in shops
6.	**Formal Surveillance**
	Install speeding and red light cameras
	Install burglar alarms
	Employ guards
7.	**Surveillance by Employees**
	Locate pay phones where employees can see them
	Employ park attendants
	Install closed-circuit television systems

(continues)

8.	**Natural Surveillance**
	Use "defensible space" environmental design
	Improve street lighting
	Promote Neighbourhood Watch
9.	**Target Removal**
	Install removable car radios
	Open women's refuges
	Install public telephones that require phone cards instead of change
10.	**Property Identification**
	Implement property-marking programs
	Require vehicle licensing
11.	**Temptation Reduction**
	Encourage gender-neutral phone listings
	Create well-lit, attended off-street parking
	Promote rapid repair
12.	**Crime "Benefits" Removal**
	Use ink merchandise tags (that mark shoplifters)
	Clean graffiti promptly
	Disable stolen mobile phones promptly
13.	**Rule Setting**
	Require customs declarations
	Establish harassment codes
	Require hotel registration
14.	**Conscience Raising**
	Install roadside speedometers
	Post "shoplifting is stealing" signs
	Post "Idiots drink and drive" signs
15.	**Control of Factors that Undermine Constraint**
	Pass a law controlling drinking age
	Install V-chip in TVs to block violent programs
	Control alcohol at public events
16.	**Ease of Compliance**
	Make easy library checkouts to discourage book theft
	Install public lavatories
	Install litter bins

Source: Adapted from Goldblatt and Lewis (1998), 24

CPTED assumes that many criminal acts are the result of a cost/benefit decision by the offender and that such offences are less likely to occur when there is a high risk of apprehension and a corresponding lack of potential gain from committing the act (see Critical Perspectives 4.4). CPTED has been incorporated into local government crime prevention plans (Ottawa, Toronto, and Edmonton), into police mandates (in Peel Region, Ontario), and into the design of towns (Fort McMurray, Alberta, and Tumbler Ridge, BC). It is also part of efforts to encourage resident interaction and to foster social cohesion (in Montreal). Today, CPTED principles are being incorporated as part of the overall urban planning process, especially with regard to the development of public transit. A study conducted for the Ottawa Police Service found that the application of CPTED principles resulted in crime and fear reduction both in planned communities and in crime-prone locations. In locations where CPTED was not applied, crime and disorder problems either continued or occurred as predicted. To learn more about CPTED principles and practices, visit http://www.cptedontario.ca.

Problem-Oriented Policing

Problem-oriented policing (POP) is often cited as a primary component of community policing and as an alternative to the traditional, reactive model of policing. This strategy focuses on preventing criminal activity rather than merely responding to it. It involves the community as a partner in identifying and resolving community problems. There are several clearly defined stages, usually referred to as SARA:

- *Scanning*: identifying the problem;
- *Analysis*: determining the cause, scope, and effect of the problem;
- *Response*: developing a plan to address and solve the problem; and
- *Assessment*: determining whether the response was effective.

The particular problem to be addressed may be community-wide and require a long-term plan of action, or it may involve a single individual and a situation that can be addressed in relatively short order.

Given the central role of problem-oriented policing in the framework of community policing, we will consider POP in greater detail in Chapter 5.

Emergency phone services, such as the blue emergency phone shown here at the University of Western Ontario, help create a safe environment. There are 22 emergency phones located strategically on the campus that provide a direct link to the police should a situation arise where assistance is required.

Source: Courtesy the University of Western Ontario.

CRITICAL PERSPECTIVES 4.4

USING CPTED TO REDUCE CRIME AND FEAR OF CRIME

CPTED is an appropriate crime reduction strategy that can reduce crime and fear through:

- **Territoriality:** fostering residents' interaction, vigilance, and control over their neighbourhood

- **Surveillance:** maximizing the ability to spot suspicious people and activities

- **Activity support:** encouraging the intended use of public space by residents

- **Hierarchy of space:** identifying ownership by delineating private space from public space through real or symbolic boundaries

- **Access control/target hardening:** using physical barriers, security devices, and tamper-resistant materials to restrict entrance

- **Environment:** a design or location decision that takes into account the surrounding environment and that minimizes the use of space by conflicting groups

- **Image/Maintenance:** ensuring that a building or area is clean, well maintained, and graffiti-free

Source: *Royal Canadian Mounted Police, Crime Prevention through Environmental Design, (1998). Found at http://nvan.bc.rcmp-grc.gc.ca/ViewPage.action?siteNodeId=429&languageId=1&contentId=4814 Reproduced with the permission of the RCMP.*

School-based programs such as this "safety village" operated by the Waterloo Regional Police are one example of a police secondary prevention program.

Courtesy of Waterloo Regional Police Service

Secondary Prevention Programs

Secondary prevention programs focus on areas that produce crime and other types of disorder. They seek to identify high-risk offenders and are often based on crime-area analysis. Strategies include neighbourhood dispute resolution and the diversion of offenders, as well as various school-based crime prevention initiatives and intervention programs for youth.

School Programs

Residential school programs involve assigning police officers full-time to a school campus. These school liaison officers, as they are commonly called, participate as fully as possible in all facets of school life. The objectives include developing positive relations with teens, improving youth attitudes towards the police, and providing security for the school and its students. Nonresidential school programs most often involve officers periodically making presentations on various topics. At the elementary school level, for example, these presentations tend to focus on safety issues, including "stranger-danger" and bicycle safety.

An innovative program conducted by the Halton Regional Police Service is the Safety Village. Operated with the assistance of the Optimist Clubs of Halton, the village consists of 12 miniature replica buildings in a community setting. Students in kindergarten and grades two and three are taught traffic safety in the village and are exposed to traffic simulations with bicycles and battery-operated cars. At the middle school and high school levels, presentations may focus on such topics as drug and alcohol abuse and gangs.

Tertiary Prevention Programs

Tertiary prevention programs are designed to deter, incapacitate, and rehabilitate offenders. The focus is on intervening with youth and adult offenders in an attempt to reduce the likelihood of further criminal behaviour. Most tertiary prevention programs are conducted within the criminal justice system and generally do not involve police.

OTHER APPROACHES TO PREVENTING AND REDUCING CRIME
Crime Prevention through Social Development

Crime prevention through social development(CPSD) attempts to eliminate some of the underlying factors that contribute to crime. These approaches include initiatives to reduce poverty, improve childhood nutrition, and increase the availability of proper housing, employment, educational opportunities, and adequate play and recreational facilities. Some of the factors that place people at risk for criminal activity include:

- child poverty;
- inadequate living conditions;
- inconsistent and uncaring parenting;
- childhood trauma, such as physical and sexual abuse;
- family breakdown;
- racism and other forms of discrimination;

- difficulties in school;
- friends who engage in criminal behaviour; and
- living situations involving alcohol, drugs, and other kinds of substance abuse.

Among the prevention and intervention programs designed to prevent and respond to these underlying conditions are family-based programs, school-based programs, and peer-group-based programs.

Early intervention with children at risk has become a particular focus of attention. Preschool or "Head Start" programs, aimed at improving the intellectual and social skills of high-risk children, operate in many parts of the country.

A prominent US study of child development that followed children into adulthood found that children born into poverty who attended a targeted daycare program had fewer arrests, depended less on welfare, were more likely to complete high school, and had higher earnings than those who did not participate in this type of program. Furthermore, taxpayers saved $7.16 for each dollar invested in the program. Preschool participants consumed fewer resources because they were less likely to come into conflict with the law (Schweinhart, Barnes, and Wiekhart 1993). Patrol officers are increasingly involved in these programs, often in collaboration with other agencies and community groups.

In 2005 the Canadian Association of Chiefs of Police (CACP) received funding from Canada's National Crime Prevention Centre to develop a coalition of national organizations not traditionally involved in community safety, to promote the concept of crime prevention through social development. The Federation of Canadian Municipalities, the Canadian Association of Police Boards, and the Canadian Professional Police Association formally supported this objective.

From 2005 to 2007, the CACP developed and implemented a public awareness strategy to help build support for community-owned approaches to crime prevention through social development. The CACP is demonstrating police leadership by including strategic partners in its efforts to strengthen public safety. Its website provides important details on strategic crime prevention initiatives across Canada; visit http://www.cacp.ca.

Increasing Police Legitimacy

One strategy that is generally not included in discussions of crime prevention is **police legitimacy**. This approach, which holds considerable promise, refers to the collective efforts by a police service to ensure that citizens are treated fairly, and to the initiatives taken by police to explain their role and activities through personal contact.

Two of the more common strategies to increase police legitimacy are police–community meetings and door-to-door visits by police officers. Police–community meetings include community consultative committees that provide a forum for identifying the problems and concerns of community residents as well as strategies for addressing them (see Chapter 10). Police–community meetings also help break down stereotypes and open lines of communication between the police and the community.

Door-to-door visits by police officers provide officers with the opportunity to seek information from residents on specific persons and criminal activities. They also provide an opportunity for police officers to distribute information to residents and to introduce themselves.

One of the more innovative approaches to enhancing police legitimacy is the Coffee with a Cop program that emerged in the United States in 2011 and has now spread across Canada. The program's mission is to "break down barriers between police officers and the citizens they serve." In 2014, the Quebec version—*Café avec un policier*—was introduced in Blainville, Mirabel, St-Eustache, Deux-Montagnes, and St-Jérôme and with the Sûreté

Source: Courtesy of Coffee with a Cop.

du Québec. Since then, over 12 police services in Québec have promoted this program, including the Service de police de la Ville de Montréal (SPVM).

The Coffee with a Cop program provides yet another venue for front-line police officers to speak face-to-face with the public about their concerns, expectations, and ideas. In Montreal, the *Café avec un policier* program also allows the SPVM to make contact with certain groups that may be reluctant to approach an officer in the street or make contact with their neighbourhood police station. This new and evolving program is allowing police services across Canada to reach out to their local communities and build relationships with a focus on identifying concerns and working towards solutions.

These methods of contact are among the many ways that police services and officers try to legitimize their role and activities and create the perception among community residents that the police behave in a fair, impartial, and professional manner.

There is some evidence from the United States that this strategy for increasing police legitimacy produces positive outcomes, including reduced fear of the police, a reduced crime rate, lower recidivism among offenders, and increased obedience of the law (Sherman et al. 1997).

In Canada, a 2013 General Social Survey on Social Identity found that 76 per-cent of individuals have some or a great deal of confidence in the police, making it the institution with the highest level of public confidence in Canada. Clearly, the policy enjoy some measure of legitimacy. The next-highest Canadian institutions were the school system (61 percent), banks (59 percent), and the justice system and courts (57 percent). In contrast, fewer than half of Canadians expressed confidence in the media (40 percent), the federal Parliament (38 percent), or major corporations (30 percent). For further details, visit Statistics Canada and the spotlight on Canadian Institutions at http://www.statcan.gc.ca/pub/89-652-x/89-652-x2015007-eng.htm.

The "Broken Windows" Approach

Closed-circuit television (CCTV) systems are monitored by operators who are able to contact the police should an event occur. CCTVs are positioned in "hot spots" to deter crime and to identify the individuals responsible for criminal activities.

Source: Deborah Baic/The Globe and Mail

In the early 1980s, two US criminologists, James Q. Wilson and George L. Kelling (1982), wrote an article titled "Broken Windows: The Police and Neighbourhood Safety." **Broken windows** was a metaphor for neighbourhood deterioration based on the observations of patrol officers that if a window was broken in a building and not repaired, in very short order all the windows would be broken. A broken window that remains unrepaired is a statement that no one cares enough about the quality of life in the neighbourhood to bother fixing the little things that are wrong. While a broken window is a small thing, it triggers further neglect and results in the progressive deterioration of the entire neighbourhood. Wilson and Kelling argued that police services had neglected little things—the law enforcement equivalent of broken windows—and that there was a need to reorient the efforts of police work. "Broken windows" policing addresses minor nuisances and offences, based on the assumption that if these offences are left unchecked they will lead to more serious crime and disorder.

The "broken windows" approach to policing was implemented in New York City during the 1990s, and while it is difficult to isolate the effects of any one particular intervention, one study generally credits the approach with a significant and consistent decline in violent crime. Kelling and Sousa (2001) credit "broken windows" policing with the prevention of more than 60,000 violent crimes in New York City between 1989 to 1998.

High Technology in Crime Prevention: CCTVs—Big Help or Big Brother?

One technology that is being applied to crime prevention is closed-circuit television (CCTV). CCTV systems, which have been adopted by many cities worldwide, use cameras that can be monitored by operators, who are able to contact the police if an event occurs. CCTVs are deployed in many businesses such as banks and shopping malls as well as in public spaces such as streets and transit systems. Some CCTVs are monitored by private security personnel, who are contracted to summon the police if an incident occurs. In other instances, CCTVs are not monitored but have been installed to provide visual and audio recordings should a crime or incident occur. The police are then able to investigate potential leads. Street-focused systems typically target property crimes, such as theft, break and enters, and suspicious activities. CCTVs have also provided valuable information to the police with regard to more serious incidents such as assaults, shootings, and terrorist activities.

Research on CCTV systems suggests that they may be effective in reducing some types of criminal behaviour. However, the following observations have been made:

- CCTVs help police solve crimes after the fact.
- CCTVs do little to deter public disorder offences.
- CCTVs should be utilized as part of an overall crime reduction strategy and tailored to community needs.
- Evaluations conducted in the United States and United Kingdom found that CCTVs had a deterrent effect in car parks in terms of theft from and of vehicles.
- CCTVs enhance the perception of personal safety and may help reduce citizens' fear of crime and disorder.
- The deterrence effects of CCTV are mixed, and well-designed evaluations are necessary to ensure that they are deployed correctly (Deisman 2003; Gill and Spriggs 2005).

CRITICAL PERSPECTIVES 4.5

TECHNOLOGY VERSUS PRIVACY RIGHTS: WALKING A SLIPPERY SLOPE

Proponents of CCTV argue that law-abiding citizens have nothing to fear from being monitored by CCTV cameras. Opponents fear that the technological monitoring of public spaces represents an unjustified intrusion on a citizen's right to privacy. What do you think? If technology could prevent all crime or identify all offenders, would it be worth the investment? Now think about other forms of current technology that can track our every movement—from biometric scanning devices such as facial recognition software in Heathrow Airport to gunshot detection systems in Chicago, from so-called black boxes in motor vehicles to global positioning systems (GPSs). Another technological system is a photo-radar grid system that calculates the speed and distance travelled by a motor vehicle between several points. If the motor vehicle passes another camera located in the grid earlier than predicted, then a speeding ticket is issued. All of these examples of technology are in use around the world. In Canada, provincial and federal privacy bodies (i.e., Ontario Office of the Information and the Privacy Commissioner) recommend that all public bodies, including the police, prepare Privacy Impact Assessments in order to achieve a balance between intrusive technology and privacy rights.

Many Canadian municipalities have wrestled with whether to add CCTVs to their crime prevention arsenals. Unlike in other parts of the world, Canadians continue to resist the widespread implementation of CCTVs in cities and communities. There are some concerns regarding the infringement of Charter rights; also, there are substantial costs associated with establishing and monitoring CCTV systems. Kelowna, BC, Sudbury, Ontario, and Calgary, Alberta, have installed CCTV cameras to monitor public spaces. The Toronto Police Service (TPS) has developed a very good CCTV program that uses mobile CCTVs that can be moved into an area and deployed for a short period of time until a specific problem has been addressed. (The TPS program is profiled as a case study at the end of this chapter.) Civil libertarians have raised concerns that these "electronic spies" have the potential to violate expectations of privacy, which would outweigh potential crime prevention benefits (see Critical Perspectives 4.5). Advances in CCTV technology, such as facial recognition software, will likely increase concerns about privacy. With technology growing more sophisticated, it is likely that there will be increased pressure to use CCTVs and other devices in an attempt to prevent crime and to detect criminal activities such as terrorism. A comprehensive evaluation of CCTVs has been conducted in the United Kingdom. The evaluation report and other publications related to CCTVs can be found at the Home Office website, http://www.homeoffice.gov.uk.

THE EFFECTIVENESS OF CRIME PREVENTION PROGRAMS

Assessing the effectiveness of a particular police strategy or program is difficult under the best of circumstances (see Critical Perspectives 4.6). Among the obstacles are the following:

- Research studies vary in their methodologies, in the types of data gathered, and in the outcomes measured.
- How a specific program or strategy is implemented is influenced by the priorities and resources of the police service, the enthusiasm and commitment of the police officers and community residents involved, and the specific attributes of the community itself.
- Most of the research studies have been done in the United States, not Canada.
- There is the slippery issue of **crime displacement**—the possibility that offenders and their activities have merely relocated. Canadian criminologist Kim Rossmo (1995, 5–6) has identified five forms of crime displacement:

  - *geographic,* which involves offenders relocating their criminal activities to another area;
  - *temporal,* where criminals alter the times they commit offences;
  - *tactical,* where offenders develop different strategies to commit crimes;
  - *target,* which involves offenders selecting different places to commit crimes or different persons to victimize; and
  - *functional,* where changes in technology reduce criminal opportunity in some areas (e.g., bank robberies decline as we move towards a cashless society, but new criminal opportunities such as wire fraud are created).

There is increasing evidence that the police can indeed affect crime levels if police services manage and deploy their resources wisely and address problems systematically and comprehensively. It should also be remembered that a reduced crime rate is not the only indicator of program success. There are other important considerations, such as the quality of police–community relationships, the fear of crime and related perceptions of personal safety, the experiences of crime victims and their attitudes towards the police, and the extent to which the specific initiative was successful in securing the participation of community residents over the long term. Do not forget that a reactive model of policing has very little impact on the crime rate.

CRITICAL PERSPECTIVES 4.6

THE EFFECTIVENESS OF SELECTED CRIME PREVENTION STRATEGIES

Operation Identification/Operation Provident: Impact on property crimes unclear. Studies on similar programs in the United States found that they do not reduce break and enters or property loss. The programs do increase police–citizen interaction and citizen awareness of crime prevention activities. They may function to displace crime to neighbouring areas not participating in the program.

Neighbourhood Watch: Does not prevent crime. Areas of high crime have less involvement, while the strategy is most successful in middle-class communities that have little crime. May increase the fear of crime among community residents. The anonymity of most neighbourhoods and apartment complexes—the fact that people do not get to know their neighbours—is a primary obstacle to the success of Neighbourhood Watch. Typically, most community residents hesitate to become involved with their neighbourhoods, even if such involvement is limited to being watchful for suspicious behaviour.

Community meetings: Have little impact on the crime rate. Exceptions include a program in Chicago where community meetings focus specifically on crime patterns in the neighbourhood and on developing ideas to address them. Although it is not certain that crime rates have been reduced, the project has been successful in involving residents in high-crime areas in meetings and specific projects.

Door-to-door visits: Some evidence that visits may reduce the rates of crime victimization. In addition, visits increase police legitimacy; this may in turn relate to a number of police outcomes (see below).

Citizen patrols: No published evaluations in Canada. Findings from US and European research indicate that such patrols may reduce property crime, levels of violence, and residents' fear of crime.

Problem-oriented policing: No formal evaluations of POP in Canada. Results from studies that have examined the application of POP to specific problems by several US police departments have been mixed: some have indicated reduced levels of certain types of crime, improved police–community relationships, and the acquisition of problem-solving skills by police officers. At other sites, POP initiatives have had no apparent impact.

Crime prevention through environmental design: Target hardening, property marking, improving security (including the installation of CCTV), and altering building design and pedestrian routes have, in some jurisdictions, reduced levels of residential break and enters, robberies, and assaults. Closing or selling properties used for drug abuse has, in some jurisdictions, reduced calls for service. Some evidence suggests that using CCTV and employing multiple clerks in stores that are open late hours may reduce the rates of robbery and property theft.

Source: *Polowek 1995; Sherman et al. 1997.*

Factors Limiting Program Effectiveness

At the very worst, the findings as to the "noneffectiveness" of many community policing initiatives might lead one into deep depression; at the very least, they suggest that there are a number of obstacles—in police organizations, among line officers, in other community agencies, and in the community itself—that may undermine the objectives of crime prevention programs.

Promoting change among the rank-and-file subculture has been described as being as easy as "bending granite" (Guyot 1979). This is especially evident any time a police organization implements new procedures, as in the case of police response to domestic violence. Because of increasing demands on police organizations and the explosion in information, we require police who are flexible and adaptable and who are excellent information managers. Contemporary police officers must be able to process information quickly (e.g., new laws, new procedures, new case decisions) and incorporate them into policing responses. This requires effective change management strategies both organizationally and individually. In Chapter 8, we will see that even in progressive police services there are obstacles and sources of resistance to the implementation of community policing, including:

- apathy towards and lack of participation in crime prevention programs by residents;
- the frequent absence of a clearly defined role for the community; and
- the fact that communities afflicted by high rates of crime and disorder are often those where it is most difficult to interest community residents.

CRIME PREVENTION IN INDIGENOUS COMMUNITIES

Developing and implementing effective crime prevention programs in Indigenous communities has proven to be a challenge both for police services (Indigenous and non-Indigenous) and for the communities themselves. The crime prevention initiatives that have been developed fall into two categories:

1. Programs that are part of an overall crime prevention strategy developed by senior police administrators and implemented in both Indigenous and non-Indigenous communities.
2. Programs developed by police officers at the local community level in collaboration with chiefs, band councils, and community residents. Needless to say, these latter programs have been the most effective.

Crime prevention initiatives that have been established in Indigenous communities across Canada include the following:

- *Outreach Support Worker Project.* The Winnipeg Native Alliance developed this project to help youths leaving gangs or institutions reintegrate into society.
- *Stl'atl'imx Citizens on Patrol (COPS).* In BC, the Stl'atl'imx Tribal Police received funding to establish a Citizens on Patrol (COPS) network in 10 communities of the Stl'atl'imx Nation. Through the COPS network, volunteer citizens are trained to patrol their communities, recognize suspicious activities, and report them to police. This initiative helped build the community's capacity to prevent crime.
- *Atikamekw Community-Based Training on Suicide Intervention/Recognition.* Funding was provided to the Conseil de la Nation Atikamekw to support the delivery of two training sessions on suicide intervention to 24 Atikamekw community professionals who work with at-risk youth. The program takes a community-based approach to suicide intervention by linking existing national training resources to people and organizations at the community level. The program included the following elements:

  – two days of suicide intervention training;

  – a one-day Healing Circle;

– a component on Indigenous spirituality;

– training in critical incident stress debriefing; and

– training in community building.

• *Home Repairs Fraud Prevention Program.* This program was developed in response to incidents in which elders on Six Nations Territory were victimized by home repair fraud. Working with the Ohsweken Branch of the Royal Bank, located on Six Nations Territory, the police developed a plan to warn the elders about different ways they could be victimized by fraudulent contractors. This involved producing and distributing a brochure, and meetings with the territory's elders' clubs (Lewis et al. 1995).

Public Safety Canada has established the Northern and Aboriginal Crime Prevention Fund (NACPF) to assist communities experiencing multiple risk factors and other challenges that affect the community's ability to respond to crime issues due to remote geographical location and limited capacity. The funding facilitates culturally sensitive initiatives that foster the development and implementation of crime prevention approaches in Indigenous communities, both on-and off-reserve and in the North. The funding program also builds the knowledge and capacity that is required to develop or adapt culturally sensitive, effective ways to prevent crime.

• the adaptation, development, and implementation of innovative and promising culturally sensitive crime prevention practices that address known risk and protective factors to reduce offending among at-risk children and youth, as well as high-risk offenders in communities;
• the dissemination of knowledge and the development of tools and resources for Indigenous and northern populations;
• capacity building as a means to explore ways to develop or implement culturally sensitive crime prevention practices among Indigenous and northern populations. (Public Safety Canada, 2015)

The NACPF will support:

The greatest potential lies in the development of culturally sensitive community-focused crime prevention, to ensure that program initiatives are adapted to the specific needs of individual Indigenous communities and, furthermore, that community residents play an integral part in identifying the problems to be addressed and then participate in the programs.

CRIME PREVENTION IN THE CYBER WORLD

Internet crime is a new aspect of community policing. Social media and the Internet continue to evolve as significant elements of contemporary society that need to be secure and safe. *Canada's Cyber Security Strategy* was developed in 2010 to protect Canadian governments, businesses, and critical infrastructure, as well as the public, from cyberthreats.

A cybercrime can be defined as a criminal offence involving a computer as the object of the crime (e.g., spamming, phishing, hacking), or as the tool used to commit a material component of the offence (e.g., child pornography, hate crimes, computer fraud). In addition, individuals can use computers to commit crimes associated with communications and document or data storage. The RCMP considers there to be two broad categories of cybercrime:

• *technology-as-target*: criminal offences targeting computers and other information technologies, such as those involving the unauthorized use of computers or mischief in relation to data; and
• *technology-as-instrument*: criminal offences where the Internet and information technologies are instrumental in the commission of a crime, such as those involving fraud, identity theft, intellectual property infringement, money laundering, drug trafficking, human trafficking, organized crime or terrorist activities, child sexual exploitation, or cyberbullying (RCMP 2015).

Cybercrimes require a new approach to policing. Across Canada, police services are taking steps to prevent crime in the cyber world by the creating specialty units trained and equipped to deal with computer-related crimes. For example, the Ottawa Police Service (OPS) has established a Computer Forensics Unit that provides support to various sections and units within the OPS by:

- analyzing forensic data on computers and cellphones;
- tracing e-mails;
- executing search warrants related to electronic material;
- assisting in the investigation of online threats of violence or suicide and • cyberbullying;
- identifying IP addresses;
- recovering stolen property;
- providing expert technical assistance; and
- providing education to the public and high-tech sectors (Ottawa Police Service, 2017).

While cybercrime specialty units evolve, police services across Canada continue to face challenges associated with resources, capacity, and knowledge. For example, the Calgary Police Service created the Cybercrime Support Team (CST) in 2013. The team was made up of seven individuals assigned to roughly 200 cyber-related cases ranging from murders to international fraud schemes. By 2014, the number of cases assigned to the CST had doubled to roughly 400. In response, Calgary's Police Chief Rick Hanson stated: "Our cyber-crime area is already stretched to the limit because the use of technology to commit crimes—everything from bullying to identity theft to trafficking and child pornography, to the multitude of frauds committed—is continuing to grow" (Nolais 2015).

The challenges posed by the growing problem of cybercrime remind us of the need for the police to partner with post-secondary institutions and private corporations. When these bodies work together to use their resources and expertise in the most effective ways, partnerships can develop with the goal of devising comprehensive strategies for preventing and responding to cybercrimes. It is also important to underscore that most cybercrimes are preventable. Public education and the use of security measures to protect electronic devices are key aspects of cybercrime prevention. Police services across Canada will need to continue recruiting and training individuals to respond to cybercrime issues and educating the community on how to stay safe while online.

Public Notification

In the traditional model of police work, police involvement in the prevention of and response to crime ended when suspects were arrested. Increasingly, police involvement is being extended to the post-sentencing and post-incarceration stages of the justice system. Whenever an offender is released back into the community, either through a decision of a parole board or after having served most or all of the sentence, one critical question is whether the public should be notified. In Ontario, for example, Christopher's Law (Sex Offender Registry), passed in 2000, sets out the statutory framework for the registration of sex offenders in the province. The practice of **public notification** raises a moral dilemma, as offenders who have served their time in jail are deemed suitable for return to the community. The debate can be characterized as one between the rights of society and the rights of the individual.

The pressure on politicians and the police to notify the community when certain offenders are released from correctional institutions originated in various victims' groups across the country. Most jurisdictions have passed, or are in the process of passing, legislation that provides for notification. In Ontario, for example, the Community Safety Act was designed to increase the amount of information about offenders available to victims and the community and to supplement the Victim's Bill of Rights. Under the act, police and corrections authorities may provide victims and the community at large with personal information about an offender who is being released and who may pose a risk to public safety. The act also includes provisions for tracking name changes by offenders—a first in Canada. In Saskatchewan, the government operates a website that provides alerts about high-risk individuals, disclosing the offender's name and including a recent photograph and background information. The disclosure encourages members of the public to take reasonable steps to ensure their safety, and offers suggestions how.

There are also programs that target offenders who have been released from confinement. These include the OPP's Repeat Offender Parole Enforcement Squad (ROPE) and the High Risk Offender Units in Vancouver, Edmonton, and Calgary. Correctional Service Canada works with various agencies and police services to provide assistance with regard to the supervision, education, and surveillance of offenders who return to the community after completing their sentence.

ASSESSING EFFECTIVENESS

Even within a community policing framework, police services continue to assume the primary role in the control of crime in the community. It is vital that crime prevention and crime reduction strategies be evaluated in order to determine their overall effectiveness. This is increasingly becoming a requirement to obtain funding. For example, the National Crime Prevention Centre requires program evaluations for continued funding. There are a number of standard measures for assessing the effectiveness of the police in controlling crime and social disorder (see Table 4.2).

Table 4.2 Measures of Crime Control Effectiveness

Objective	Quality Characteristic	Specific Measure	Data Collection Procedure
Prevention of crime	Reported crime rates	Number of reported crimes per 100,000 population, total and by type of crime	Incident reports
	Victimization rates	Number of reported plus unreported crimes per 1,000 households (or residents or businesses), by type of crime	Household survey, such as the General Social Survey conducted during each federal census
	Victimization of households and businesses	Percentage of (a) households, (b) businesses victimized	Household survey, business survey
	Physical casualties	Number and rate of persons (a) physically injured, (b) killed in course of crimes or nontraffic, crime-related police work including victims and the police	Incident reports
		Percentage of domestic disputes and other disturbance calls with no arrest and no second call within x number of hours	Dispatch records, incident reports

(continues)

Objective	Quality Characteristic	Specific Measure	Data Collection Procedure
	Peacekeeping in domestic disputes	Number of injuries to (a) citizens (after police arrival), (b) police per 100 domestic quarrel calls	Incident reports
Apprehension of offenders	Crimes "solved" at least in part	Percentage of reported crimes cleared, by type of crime and whether cleared by arrest or by "exception"	Incident reports
	Completeness of apprehension	Percentage of "person-crimes" cleared, by type of crime	Incident reports, arrest reports
	Quality/effective-ness of arrest	Percentage of arrests that survive preliminary court hearing and percentage dropped for police-related reasons, by type of crime	Arrest and court records
		Percentage of arrests resulting in conviction or treatment (a) on at least one charge, (b) on highest initial charge, by type of crime	Arrest and court records
	Stolen property recovery	Percentage of (a) stolen vehicles, (b) other stolen property subsequently recovered	Incident reports, arrest or special property records
Responsiveness of police	Response time	Percentage of emergency or high-priority calls responded to within x minutes and percentage of nonemergency calls responded to within six minutes	Dispatch records
	Perceived responsiveness	Percentage of (a) citizens, (b) businesses that feel police respond fast enough when called	Household survey, business survey, complainant survey
Feeling of security	Perceived safety	Percentage of (a) citizens, (b) business persons who feel safe (or unsafe) walking in their neighbourhoods at night	Household survey, business survey

Objective	Quality Characteristic	Specific Measure	Data Collection Procedure
Fairness, courtesy, helpfulness/co-operativeness, honesty	Fairness	Percentage of (a) citizens, (b) businesses that feel police are generally fair in dealing with them	Household survey, business survey, complainant survey
	Courtesy	Percentage of (a) citizens, (b) businesses that feel police are generally courteous in dealing with them	Household survey, business survey, complainant survey
	Helpfulness/ co-operativeness	Percentage of (a) citizens, (b) businesses that feel police are generally helpful, cooperative and sensitive to their concerns	Household survey, business survey, complainant survey
		Number of reported incidents or complaints of police misbehaviour, and the number resulting in judgment against the local government or employee (by type of complaint civil charge, criminal charge, other service complaints), per 100 police	Police and mayor's office records
	Honesty	Percentage of citizens who feel police are in general honest and can be trusted	Household survey, complainant survey
	Citizen satisfaction with police handling of miscellaneous incidents	Percentage of persons requesting assistance for other than serious crimes who are satisfied (or dissatisfied) with police handling of their problems, categorized by reason for dissatisfaction and by type of call	Complainant survey
	Citizen satisfaction with overall performance	Percentage of (a) citizens, (b) businesses that rate police performance as excellent or good (or fair or poor), by reason for satisfaction (or dissatisfaction)	Household survey, business survey, complainant survey
	Police safety	Number of injuries to police officers (a) per 100 officers, (b) per 100 calls	Police injury reports

Source: Hatry et al., 1992, pp.72-73. Reprinted with permission of The International City/County Management Association, 777 North Capital Street, NE, Suite 500, Washington, DC 20002. All Rights Reserved.

Chapter Summary

This chapter has focused on how police services, often in collaboration with the community, respond to crime and social disorder. Within the framework of community policing, a variety of strategies can be used, including proactive strategies, community service approaches, and crime prevention programs. This variety reflects the key point that community policing involves police work that is reactive, proactive, and coactive (with the community).

In recent years, police services have also adopted additional approaches to crime prevention and response, including preventing crime through social development, creating programs that increase police legitimacy, supporting the increased deployment of CCTVs, and developing strategies to fight cybercrime. A critical issue that must be addressed in determining the effectiveness of crime prevention initiatives is that of crime displacement—the possibility that offenders and their activities have merely been relocated, rather than crime having been eliminated. Among the obstacles that often limit the effectiveness of crime prevention are resistance on the part of police services and disinterest on the part of the community in becoming involved.

Chapter Review

Key Terms

- broken windows approach, p. 104
- community service approaches, p. 91
- crime displacement, p. 106
- crime prevention programs, p. 96
- crime prevention through environmental design (CPTED), p. 99
- crime prevention through social development (CPSD), p. 102
- foot patrols or beats, p. 92
- hard crime calls, p. 89
- National Crime Prevention Strategy, p. 96
- police legitimacy, p. 103
- primary prevention programs, p. 97
- proactive targeted strategies, p. 89
- problem-oriented policing (POP), p. 101
- public notification, p. 110
- safer communities approach to crime prevention, p. 88
- secondary prevention programs, p. 102
- soft crime calls, p. 89
- tactical or directed patrol, p. 89
- team policing or platoon/squad policing, p. 94
- tertiary prevention programs, p. 102

Key Points

- The strategies used to prevent and respond to crime can be generally grouped into proactive targeting strategies, community service approaches, and crime prevention programs.
- Although foot patrols do not appear to reduce overall levels of crime, they do function to reduce citizen fear of crime and create favourable community perceptions of the police.
- The three categories of crime prevention programs are primary, secondary, and tertiary. Strategies in each of these areas may be situational or focus on social development.
- Crime prevention through environmental design (CPTED) attempts to reduce criminal opportunities by altering the physical environment of structures and places.

- Problem-oriented policing (POP) is a primary component of community policing and focuses on the identification and resolution of community problems.
- Crime displacement—the relocation of offenders and their activities—makes it difficult to determine the effectiveness of many crime prevention programs.
- There are a number of factors that may limit the potential effectiveness of crime prevention strategies.
- Public notification, a strategy to inform communities when certain offenders are released from custody, raises the issue of individual rights versus the rights of society.

Self-Evaluation

QUESTIONS

1. What is the safer communities approach to crime prevention?
2. What is meant by proactive targeted strategies?
3. What are community service approaches to preventing crime?
4. What are crime prevention programs and how do they differ from proactive targeted strategies and community service approaches?
5. What is tactical or directed patrol and how is it carried out?
6. Compare hard crime calls and soft crime calls.
7. What is team policing and what role does it play in community policing?
8. Compare primary prevention programs, secondary prevention programs, and tertiary prevention programs.
9. Provide an example of a situational crime prevention program and one that seeks to prevent crime through social development.
10. What is crime prevention through environmental design (CPTED)?
11. What is meant by increasing policing legitimacy?
12. What is the broken windows approach to crime prevention?
13. What is crime displacement and what are the various forms it may take?
14. Why is public notification the subject of controversy?

KEY IDEAS

1. Which of the following relies on police patrols for the apprehension, deterrence, and incapacitation of criminal offenders?
   a. proactive targeting strategy
   b. community service approach
   c. crime prevention
   d. team policing

2. Which kind of calls are hold-up alarms, shootings, stabbings, auto thefts, and assaults examples of?
   a. community-initiated crime calls
   b. hard crime calls
   c. soft crime calls
   d. victim-precipitated crime calls

3. What is suggested by research studies on crime attack strategies?
   a. The number of police officers does not significantly reduce the levels of crime.
   b. Proactive police arrests, focusing on high-risk persons and offences, may reduce levels of serious violent crime.
   c. Random police patrols may reduce levels of crime.
   d. Nonviolent crimes continue to increase but at a modest level.

4. Foot patrols, bicycle patrols, team policing, and community police stations and storefronts are examples of which of the following categories?
   a. crime prevention programs
   b. proactive targeting strategies
   c. community service approaches
   d. crime prevention strategies that do not work

5. According to research studies, which of the following is a result of foot patrols?
   a. decreased fear of crime among citizens
   b. increased calls for service
   c. increased reports of patrol officer misconduct
   d. decreased job satisfaction for patrol officers due to fatigue

6. What type of crime prevention programs identify opportunities for criminal offences and alter these conditions in order to reduce the likelihood of crimes being committed?
   a. tertiary crime prevention programs
   b. secondary crime prevention programs
   c. primary crime prevention programs
   d. ancillary crime prevention programs

7. What is the intended purpose of door-to-door visits by police officers and police–community meetings?
   a. increasing police information and intelligence
   b. increasing community awareness of police programs
   c. increasing crime prevention through environmental design (CPTED)
   d. increasing police legitimacy

8. One approach to crime prevention attempts to alleviate the conditions that contribute to crime, such as poverty, poor housing, unemployment, and lack of educational opportunities. What is this approach called?
   a. crime prevention through opportunity
   b. tertiary crime prevention
   c. the broken windows approach
   d. crime prevention through social development

9. In one type of crime displacement, offenders develop different strategies to commit crimes. What does this refer to?
   a. tertiary crime displacement
   b. temporal crime displacement
   c. target crime displacement
   d. tactical crime displacement

10. Which of the following statements has been suggested by research studies?
    a. Operation Identification significantly reduces the levels of property crime.
    b. Neighbourhood Watch is an effective approach to crime prevention.
    c. Citizen patrols may reduce property crimes and citizens' fear of crime.
    d. Crime prevention through environmental design (CPTED) is generally ineffective in reducing property crimes.

Responding to and Preventing Crime: Situations and Strategies

Case Studies

Case Study 1. Indigenous Community Involvement in Crime Prevention through Community Development

A successful program in Alberta is the First Nations Crime Prevention Program in association with Alberta Justice. First Nations people have expressed a strong desire to create and deliver crime prevention programs appropriate to their unique culture and local needs. Through funding provided to the First Nations Crime Prevention Program, four crime prevention coordinator positions have been established to serve nine reserves located throughout the province. Coordinators are responsible for developing local initiatives, particularly for youth, in the areas of recreation, employment, social care, and family violence, and for monitoring crime trends on reserves, designing programs to address the needs of the residents, and collaborating with groups such as the local police service, community agencies, elders, and schools in addressing the particular crime-related problems of the reserves.

Case Study 2. Problem-Oriented Policing in Action

In Antigonish, Nova Scotia, the community and local RCMP were concerned with increasing disorder related to alcohol consumption, crowds, violence, traffic congestion, property damage, and noise in relation to an identified "hot spot"—Pipers Pub. The RCMP coordinated an approach with the bar owners, patrons, neighbours, and business community and developed the following interventions:

- CPTED approaches included adding extra lighting to the street outside the pub, removing seating that encouraged crowds to gather, adding a crosswalk, landscaping areas for safety, and installing a camera to monitor activity;

- including campus security to control crowds;

- preventing alcohol sales to minors and intoxicated parties;

- moving fast-food stands away from crowd areas to discourage gathering;

- creating a taxi stand for better traffic flow;

- generating town council participation and support;

- attending town meetings that include business owners, students, the university, taxi drivers, town council, and the Detachment; and

- conducting an ongoing evaluation of the impact of each intervention.

As a result of the partnerships and the response, the town saw a 40 percent decrease in assaults, a significant reduction in property damage, fewer crowds and fights, and a safer nightlife environment. Campus security developed a better working relationship with the detachment. Students offered positive feedback through newspaper articles, citing increased safety in the pub area.

Case Study 3. Crime Prevention through Environmental Design: Planned Design Changes

Design can involve a single building, a single park, a single school, or a large multi-building development. In this case, a police constable used the principles of CPTED to reduce the calls for service and levels of criminal activity around a video arcade in a shopping mall. An assessment was made of all of the problems associated with the arcade, both inside the store and in the area. In addition, other arcades in the municipality and in neighbouring municipalities were studied. The design features associated with low-problem video arcades were noted and incorporated into a plan to address the problem arcade.

Among the recommended changes, which were presented to the municipal council and to the owner of the arcade, were internal alterations that included the placement of the video machines (against the walls only, and not in the centre of the floor, to ensure good sight lines for the on-duty cashier) and ample inside lighting. External changes involved limiting the number of parking spaces to prevent overcrowding in the arcade. In addition, changes were made in the management of the arcade, including restricting the hours of operation to those of other businesses in the mall, enforcing age restrictions, and controlling access to the washrooms. Implementation of these changes resulted in a steep reduction in crime and calls for service during the first year and a further 5 percent reduction the following year. The project provided the basis for developing model bylaws for video arcades that have been adopted by a number of municipalities across Canada and the United States.

From Griffiths/Whitelaw/Parent. *Canadian Police Work*, 4E, p. 214. © 1999 Nelson Education Ltd. Reproduced by permission. www.cengage.com/permissions

Case Study 4. The OPP Cottage Watch Program: A Partnership of the Police and the Community

The Cottage Watch program was initiated in 1993 by the Ontario Provincial Police in an effort to address cottage break-ins, theft, and vandalism. The program operates as a partnership between the OPP and the Federation of Ontario Cottagers' Associations (FOCA) and is run by local community groups.

Some of the program's objectives are to organize effective cottage watch groups from among local cottagers; involve the community in crime prevention and detection and fire safety by assisting police and through self-help initiatives; reduce break-ins, theft, and vandalism; and improve communications between cottagers and policing authorities. Participants in the program carry out these objectives through various initiatives such as watching for, and recording, details of suspicious vehicles or strangers; installing Cottage Watch street signs; and distributing information to raise awareness of community safety.

Cottage Watch does not include citizen patrols, nor are participants expected to pursue or confront suspicious individuals—only police authorities are responsible for apprehending or arresting individuals.

Sources: Federation of Ontario Cottages' Association, "Cottage Watch Manual" (2010) found at http://www.bennettandfaganlakes.com/index_htm_files/Cottage%20Watch%20Manual_2010_1; Mississippi Mills, Cottage Watch Brochure, found at http://www.mississippimills.ca/en/live/resources/Cottage_Watch_General_Brochure.pdf.

Case Study 5. Conflict Resolution at 4:00 a.m.: A Case of Unpaid Taxi Fare

In the early morning hours, a two-officer unit in an urban police service is sent to a scene where two young adults, after having been driven by taxi, are unable to pay the fare of approximately $50. One of the passengers had run from the scene, leaving the other passenger in the back seat. Upon arrival, the officers question both the driver and the passenger. Satisfied that the passenger has no money with which to pay, the driver, passenger, and the officers proceed to the passenger's home several blocks away. The officers instruct the passenger to secure the funds to pay the driver or else provide property as collateral.

Source: Griffiths, Whitelaw, and Parent(1999), 190.

Case Study 6: Public Surveillance: Closed Circuit Television (CCTV) in Cornwall, Ontario

In November 2009, the Cornwall Community Police Service submitted a grant application through the Civil Remedies Grant Program to secure funding for the purchase and installation of a public surveillance CCTV network in the City of Cornwall. The grant application was approved and the CCPS received over $100,000 in July 2010 from the Ministry of the Attorney General for this initiative.

> *It is proposed that, in support of the vision statement of the Cornwall Community Police Service, "A Safer Cornwall, reducing crime always" that 6 cameras be purchased and installed within the city on a three-year pilot period. It is further proposed that the effectiveness of the CCTV Public Surveillance Project be measured during this time period to determine the effect on enhancing a sense of safety among the public who use Cornwall's downtown areas, and further to measure its deterrent effect on the commission of crime in the areas under surveillance.*

Purpose and Principles of Monitoring

The key purpose of the Cornwall Public Surveillance CCTV Project is to promote public safety in the downtown areas of the City of Cornwall.

The goals of the Cornwall Public Surveillance CCTV Project are:

- to contribute to the safe environment of the downtown areas;
- to assist as one of the components of the downtown areas revitalization efforts; and,
- to improve the ability of the Cornwall Community Police Service and community to respond to crime and anti-social behaviour occurring in Cornwall's downtown areas.

The objectives of the Cornwall Public Surveillance CCTV Project are:

- to deter crime and anti-social behaviour;
- to increase the perception of safety; and,
- to use camera images as evidence to identify suspects involved in criminal activities.

Many Business Owners Support Cameras

In Toronto, many business owners have been particularly supportive of the police installing CCTV cameras. Some have even offered to help pay for the pilot program, although it's $2 million cost is being picked up by the province. "If you're not doing anything wrong, you've got nothing to worry about," John Kiru of the Toronto Area Business Improvement Association told the *Globe and Mail*. "I'm of the view that this (CCTV program) is the right thing to do."

Law enforcement officials say that video surveillance can be both a deterrent to crime and a valuable forensic tool. Cameras are highly visible and might stop a mugger or a rapist. If an offence is committed within view of police cameras, investigators can pore over video images to find clues and suspects. (As in the case of the June 2011 Stanley Cup riot in Vancouver and the subsequent police investigation, which utilized public CCTV images and those held by private retail stores, in addition to cellphone images provided by the public.)

Statistics from US cities that use video surveillance point to reductions in crime in areas where cameras are installed. Civil libertarians have counter-arguments to these and other points made by those in favour of video surveillance, but the fact remains that the public in

Canada and elsewhere wants crime deterred, and offenders caught. High-profile cases like the London Underground bombings and the Creba slaying in Toronto tend to ramp up support for police CCTV programs. Canadians may not be sleepwalking to British levels of video surveillance, but life in Canadian cities is definitely becoming more camera-friendly.

© Cornwall Community Police. http://www.cornwallpolice.com/en/our-programs/public-surveillance-cctv.html"

Case Study 7. Abducted Baby Now with Family after Facebook Spurs Search

Day-old Victoria is back with her family this morning, thanks to four friends who went hunting for the baby after they saw a Facebook alert about her abduction last night from a hospital in Trois-Rivières, Que.

In a Facebook post also thanking the three women and one man for their help, Victoria's mother, Mélissa McMahon, on Tuesday expressed the family's horror of having the newborn taken from the maternity ward at the Sainte-Marie pavillion of the Centre hospitalier régional de Trois-Rivières (CHRTR) the night before.

"Yesterday we experienced the worst time of our lives. It was a feeling that nobody should have to live through. The helplessness in this situation was difficult to accept," wrote McMahon.

Quebec provincial police said that just before 7 p.m. ET Monday, a woman dressed as a nurse showed up at the hospital and entered the maternity ward.

Police said the woman took the baby from the mother, and left the room with the newborn wrapped in a blue blanket.

"She walked calmly down the hall, wearing a nurse's uniform. No one asked any questions about who she was," a hospital employee told Radio-Canada.

Amber Alert

Police issued an Amber Alert around 7 p.m., looking for a red Toyota Yaris hatchback with a "Bébé à bord" ("Baby on Board") sticker.

Sgt. Martine Asselin with provincial police says many people were contacting police with tips after the Amber Alert went out.

"The media really helped us put out the picture and the description fast. We could see on the TV, on the media, on Facebook, everything we needed and very fast ... the public was able to call us and give us information," said Asselin.

The baby was found three hours later after the four young adults learned of the abduction through Facebook. Police had shared a photo on social networks of the woman police were seeking.

The four say they went looking for the vehicle of the woman at the centre of the hunt, and found one that fit the description—then called police.

"We saw [the alert] on Facebook, and decided to go looking for red cars, and we saw the woman. We recognized her," said 20-year-old Mélizanne Bergeron.

21-Year-Old Suspect Arrested

Police say they arrested a 21-year-old woman at her home. They found baby Victoria, and returned her to hospital. On Tuesday, Victoria was taken home to her family. McMahon said in her Facebook post that it was social media that helped save the baby:

"Thousands of people shared the photo of the woman on social networks," McMahon wrote. "Know that this is what has saved our little Victoria. Each click, each share made the difference. Four wonderful people, who we had the chance to meet, identified the woman through Facebook."

The 21-year-old woman picked up by police is in hospital for a psychiatric evaluation, they say. She may appear in court later Tuesday.

Asselin said it is not yet known if there was any previous connection between the baby's mother and the suspect.

Security Protocols

The head of health services in the region says the hospital is cooperating with the police investigation and will also conduct its own internal review.

Health Minister Gaétan Barrette says he has sent letters to all Quebec hospitals with obstetrics units, asking them to review security protocols.

> CBC News, "Abducted baby now with family after Facebook spurs search," (May 27, 2014). Found at http://www.cbc.ca/news/canada/montreal/abducted-baby-now-with-family-after-facebook-spurs-search-1.2655252

EXERCISES: KNOWLEDGE INTO PRACTICE

Exercise 1. Developing and Implementing Crime Prevention Programs

The development and implementation of crime prevention programs in unique environments presents challenges to police officers. Consider each of the following "task environments." Then, for each environment, (1) identify the types of challenges that might confront police officers developing partnerships with the community, and(2) note how each of these challenges might be successfully met and resolved.

Task Environment 1. Inner-City Neighbourhood with a High Population of Recent Immigrants
A community is populated by recent immigrants to Canada who come from countries where the police are feared and avoided. Many of the immigrants speak English as a second language and are still adjusting to life in Canada. There have been several high-profile incidents involving the police and allegations of excessive use of force. Community residents are fearful of being victimized by gangs of youth in the neighbourhood but are reluctant to involve the police.

Challenge   Meeting the Challenge

_____

_____

_____

_____

Task Environment 2. Suburban Bedroom Community
This upper-middle-class community is adjacent to a large urban centre and is largely residential. During the day, most residents are away from their homes working in the city. Although break-ins have been occurring with increasing frequency, to date residents have been generally unresponsive to police efforts to become involved in crime prevention initiatives. In the words of one resident: "I'd rather play golf during my free time. Let the police and the insurance companies figure it out."

Challenge   Meeting the Challenge

_____

_____

_____

_____

Task Environment 3. Cottage Country

An increase in property vandalism, theft, and break and enters—particularly during the off-season—has accompanied the explosive growth of cottage country. Most cottage owners are residents in the area during the summer months, and there is a small population of residents who live in the region year-round. Cottages on some lakes are accessible during the winter months, while others are not because of snowfall and unploughed roadways.

Challenge   Meeting the Challenge

_____

_____

_____

_____

Task Environment 4. A Remote Community in Northwestern Ontario

This community has a population of 450. It is accessible by air and, during several months of the year, by road. It has one resident police officer, and other services, such as the courts, are provided on a "fly in" basis. There is an active band council. The community follows a traditional way of life, centred on hunting and fishing, although in recent years there have been increasing problems with youth misbehaviour, including solvent and alcohol abuse.

Challenge   Meeting the Challenge

_____

_____

_____

_____

Exercise 2. CCTVs: Effective Crime Prevention or Big Brother?

The municipal council in your community is considering a proposal by the police to install CCTVs to reduce crime and disorder in an area of restaurants and nightclubs. The proposal is supported by local business owners as well as by the police officers assigned to the area. Opposition has come from a citizens' group that feels the CCTVs infringe on rights of privacy and mark the beginning of "Big Brother" society.

Consider the issues related to CCTVs generally and then specifically in this context.

a. Would you support the installation of CCTVs in the area as a member of the municipal council?

_____

_____

_____

_____

b. Would you support the installation of CCTVs in the area as a resident of the community not residing in the area to be placed under CCTVs?

_____

_____

_____

_____

c. Would you support the installation of CCTVs in the area as a resident of the community residing in the area to be placed under CCTVs?

_____

_____

_____

_____

d. Would you support the installation of CCTVs in the area as a patron of the restaurants and nightclubs in the area?

_____

_____

_____

_____

e. Would you support the installation of CCTVs in your neighbourhood?

Yes _____ No _____

f. Why?

_____

_____

_____

_____

Exercise 3. Social Media Task

In Chapter 2, we discussed how social media can help the police—or undermine them. Social media are leading to changes in a variety of factors, from crime detection and crime solving to community mobilization. Using YouTube, Facebook, and Twitter, find examples related to crime. Perhaps the police or members of social networks are seeking assistance from social networks to identify criminals, to find new evidence about a crime, or to alert people to developing issues.

What have you discovered? Should the government be involved in regulating citizen uploads to social networks? How might social networks help prevent crime? Are you concerned about the proliferation of this type of information on the Internet? When you have thought this through, visit the Toronto police chief's discussion of the Toronto Police Service Social Media Strategy at http://www.youtube.com/watch?v=LTuKGOuvfVk and the International Association of Chiefs of Police Center for Social Media at http://www.iacpsocialmedia.org.

REFERENCES

Cohen, L., and M. Felson. 1979. "Social Change and Crime Rate Trends: A Routine Activity Approach." American Sociological Review 44: 588–608.

Cornish, D., and R. Clarke, eds. 1986. The Reasoning Criminal: Rational Choice Perspectives on Offending. New York: Springer-Verlag.

Crowe, T.D. 2000. Crime Prevention through Environmental Design, 2nd ed. Washington, DC: National Crime Prevention Institute.

Deisman, W. 2003. CCTV: Literature Review and Bibliography. Royal Canadian Mounted Police, Research and Evaluation Branch. http://www.rcmp-grc.gc.ca/ccaps/cctv_e.htm

Felson, M. 1994. Crime and Everyday Life. Thousand Oaks: Pine Forge Press.

Gill, M., and A. Spriggs. 2005. Assessing the Impact of CCTV: Home Office Research Study 292. London: Home Office Research, Development, and Statistics Directorate.

Goldblatt, P., and C. Lewis. 1998. Reducing Offending: An Assessment of Research Evidence on Ways of Dealing with Offending Behaviour. London: Home Office Research and Statistics Directorate, Home Office.

Grady, P. 1990. Policing by Mountain Bike. Seattle: PDG Enterprises.

Graham, K.L. 1997. An Evaluation of the Strathcona Neighbourhood Police Office. Vancouver: Strathcona Neighbourhood Police Office Advisory Committee.

Griffiths, C.T., B. Whitelaw, and R. Parent. 1999. Canadian Police Work. Toronto: ITP Nelson.

Guyot, D. 1979. "Bending Granite: Attempts to Change the Rank Structure of American Police Departments." Journal of Police Science and Administration 7(3): 253–84.

Harman, A. 1996. "Citizens' Crime Watch." Law and Order 44(12): 41–44.

Hatry, H.P., et al. 1992. How Effective Are Your Community Services? Procedures for Measuring Their Quality, 2nd ed. Washington, DC: International City/County Management Association (ICMA).

Kelling, G.L., and W.H. Sousa. 2001. "Do Police Matter? An Analysis of the Impact of New York City's Police Reforms." *Civic Report no. 22. New York: Centre for Civic Innovation.*

Koper, C.S. 1995. "Just Enough Police Presence: Reducing Crime and Disorderly Behavior by Optimizing Patrol Time in Crime Hot Spots." Justice Quarterly *12(4): 649–72.*

Lewis, P., K. Roberts, C.T. Griffiths, and D.S. Wood. 1995. Crime Prevention in Rural Aboriginal Communities. *Ottawa: Aboriginal Policing Directorate, Solicitor General Canada.*

Mastrofski, S.D. 1990. "The Prospects of Change in Police Patrol: A Decade in Review." American Journal of Police *9(3): 1–79.*

Menton, Chris. 2008. "Bicycle Patrols: An Underutilized Resource." Policing: An International Journal of Police Strategies and Management *31(1): 93–108.*

National Crime Prevention Centre. 2008. Safer Communities: A Parliamentarian's Crime Prevention Handbook. *Ottawa: Department of Justice Canada.*

National Crime Prevention Strategy. 2004. Risk Factors and Protective Factors Fact Sheet. *Ottawa: National Crime Prevention Centre. Department of Justice Canada.*

Newman, G., R. Clarke, and S. Shoham, eds. 1997. Rational Choice and Situational Crime Prevention. *Aldershot: Dartmouth.*

Nolais, J. 2015. "Calgary Police Cyber-Crime Team 'Already Stretched to the Limit.'" Metro News, 16 January 2015.www.metronews.ca/news/calgary/2015/01/16/calgary-police-cyber-crime-team-already-stretched-to-the-limit.html

Ontario Provincial Police. 1999. "Cottage Watch: A Community Crime Prevention Program." *CPDC News 5 (April).*

Ottawa Police Service. 2017. Computer Forensics Unit. *https://www.ottawapolice.ca/en/about-us/computer-forensics-unit.asp*

Polowek, K. 1995. Community Policing: Is It Working and How Do We Know? An Introductory Guide for Police Managers and Police Boards. Victoria: British Columbia Ministry of the Attorney General.

Public Safety Canada. 2015. "Northern and Aboriginal Crime Prevention Fund (NACPF)." *https://www.publicsafety.gc.ca/cnt/cntrng-crm/crm-prvntn/fndng-prgrms/nrthrn-brgnl-crm-prvntn-fnd-en.aspx*

RCMP. 1998. Building Safer Communities: An Introduction to Crime Prevention through Environmental Design for Architects, Planners, and Builders. *http://www.rcmp-grc.gc.ca/ccaps/safecomm_e.htm.*

—. 2015. "Royal Canadian Mounted Police Cybercrime Strategy." *http://www. rcmp-grc.gc.ca/en/royal-canadian-mounted-police-cybercrime-strategy*

Rossmo, D.K. 1995. "Strategic Crime Patterning: Problem-Oriented Policing and Displacement." In Crime Analysis through Computer Mapping, *ed. C. Block, M. Dabdob, and S. Fregly. 1–14. Washington, DC: Police Executive Research Forum.*

Schweinhart, L.J., H.V. Barnes, and D.P. Weikart. 1993. Significant Benefits: The High/Scope Perry Preschool Study through Age 27. *Ypsilanti: High/Scope.*

Sherman, L.W., and D. Weisburd. 1995. "General Deterrent Effects of Police Patrol in Crime 'Hot Spots': A Randomized, Controlled Trial." Justice Quarterly *12(4):* 625–48.

Sherman, L.W., et al. 1997. Preventing Crime: What Works, What Doesn't, What's Promising. Washington, DC: Office of Justice Programs, US Department of Justice.

Toronto Police Service. 2006. "Closed Circuit Television." *http://www.torontopolice. on.ca/media/text/20061214-tps_cctv_project.pdf*

Wilson, J.Q., and G.L. Kelling. 1982. "Broken Windows: The Police and Neighborhood Safety." Atlantic Monthly *249: 29–38.*

Problem-Oriented Policing

Problem-oriented policing (POP) involves the police taking a proactive approach to address the underlying causes of a problem in the community and a formulated response designed to alleviate the problem. For example, a community may be facing a series of property crimes that are linked to illicit drug use—individuals are committing thefts in order to fuel their drug dependency. A POP response would direct police resources towards drug enforcement and harm reduction as well as the overt property crimes.

Source: © Janine Wiedel Photolibrary/Alamy

Learning Objectives

After completing this chapter, you should be able to:

- Define problem-oriented policing and discuss its importance to community policing,
- Explain the steps of problem-solving,
- Describe what is meant by the problem analysis triangle,
- Differentiate between the expert model and collaborative model of problem-solving,
- Identify the conditions for successful problem-solving, and
- Explain the relationship of intelligence-led policing to problem oriented policing.

INTRODUCTION

Police work generally consists of responding to problems. When patrol officers arrive at a call for service, the matter is seldom clear. The officer must listen to the complainant to determine whether an offence has occurred or whether the person is seeking information. In fact, for most officers, enforcing the law comprises only about 25 percent of their activities. All incidents require officers to assess the best way to address the situation, but in a reactive model of police work, they would respond to the situation at hand with little thought to the underlying causes of the incident or its long-term solution.

The advent of community policing has had a significant impact on how officers respond to the situations and incidents in which they become involved. One of the primary response strategies within the framework of community policing is problem-oriented policing, or POP. Problem-oriented policing involves the police taking a proactive approach to addressing the underlying causes of a particular problem as well as formulating a response designed to solve or alleviate the problem. It is a more efficient approach to policing than traditional reactive approaches. POP is the focus of our discussion in this chapter.

The Situations and Strategies section of the chapter contains a checklist for carrying out problem-oriented policing, along with case studies that illustrate how POP has been applied. As well, there are a number of exercises that provide you with the opportunity to apply problem-oriented policing to various situations.

WHAT IS PROBLEM-SOLVING?

When implemented properly, problem-solving is the very essence of community-based policing. That essence is the collaboration of the police with the community in dealing with issues of concern.

Problem-solving attempts to address the root causes of crime and social disorder. Research studies on crime and the police response to it have revealed the following important facts:

- Simply applying additional resources in response to individual crimes appears to have little real impact.
- Few incidents or crimes are isolated. Most are symptoms of underlying problems, which means that many will recur predictably.
- Since the causes of crime are multifaceted, the most effective responses should be those that coordinate police, government, and private citizens and businesses (Eck and Spelman 1987a).

WHAT IS A PROBLEM AND WHOSE IS IT?

Surprisingly, defining the problem that will be the focus of attention by the police and the community can be the most difficult part of the problem-solving process. A problem can be:

- a cluster of similar, related, or recurring incidents or a single incident;
- a substantive community concern; or
- a unit of police business.

For the purposes of our discussion, a **problem** is defined as a group or pattern of crimes, cases, calls, or incidents that are of concern to the public or police, or both, and that require a solution. This definition is broad enough to allow for a wide variety of situations. In community policing, a "problem" is the basic unit of police work; in contrast, traditional police work focused on single crimes, cases, calls, or incidents.

The second question is "Whose problem is it?" Community residents and the police may have different views about what is and what is not a problem. In the traditional model of police work, the police defined who and what was a problem and assumed full ownership of it.

If the problem is defined only as a police problem, then either there is no role for the community in addressing it or, as important, the community does not see a role to play. For example, the police may be very concerned about a trend in night-time break and enters along a commercial strip. The identification of this as a problem would result in the allocation of police resources through targeted saturation techniques of police patrol. The community, on the other hand, may identify problems such as speeders on residential streets, or constant pedestrian and vehicle traffic around a suspected drug house. Collaborative problem-solving requires a willingness to work together once there is agreement that a problem exists and how it can best be addressed.

Collaborative Problem-Solving

Community policing has altered the process of defining a problem and has extended the responsibility for problems to include the community and human service agencies and organizations. This has created a framework for collaborative problem-solving, which involves the police and the community agreeing that a problem exists and what the dimensions of the problem are, then formulating and implementing a strategy to address it. Problem-solving is a more effective use of community and police resources and is a good illustration of the evolving model of community policing we have described as "community-based strategic policing" (see Chapter 3 if you need to review this concept).

The number of situations that qualify as problems is limitless. Among those that might be identified by police and communities are:

- house break and enters in rural cottage areas;
- speeding and vehicle collisions;
- youth drag racing;
- groups of youth trespassing on private land or congregating in public places;
- suspected drug activity in private residences;
- vagrants or street people;
- street prostitution and related robberies;
- houses used for prostitution;
- false alarm complaints;
- graffiti; and
- repeat domestic violence calls to certain addresses.

Not All Problems Are Law Enforcement Problems

Television portrays the activities of police as primarily conducting investigations and arresting criminals; however, in reality this work consumes only an estimated 10 to 25 percent of an officer's time. Today, a large amount of police work tends to be focused on "social disorder" behaviours, which are not crimes but nevertheless impact the quality of life for residents in a community. Such behaviours include chronic drug use, public intoxication, aggressive panhandling, and behaviours that disturb peaceful living conditions. Most police work is characterized by non–law enforcement responses related to maintaining order and providing service. Clearly, not all community problems involve violations of the law.

In the evolving model of community policing, community residents are often more concerned about quality-of-life issues than violations of law. These issues may include the visible presence of prostitutes in a neighbourhood, discarded hypodermic needles and condoms, noise from stereos, or the presence of street people or people suffering mental disabilities wandering through the neighbourhood. One of the most common problems in urban areas is speeders and dangerous drivers.

PROBLEM-ORIENTED POLICING

Although the two concepts are complementary, **problem-oriented policing** (**POP**) and community policing are grounded in slightly different principles. The least confusing way to distinguish the two is to view POP as a strategy that puts the community-oriented policing philosophy into practice. It calls for police to examine the underlying or root causes of recurring incidents of crime and disorder. The problem-solving model helps officers identify problems, analyze them thoroughly, develop response strategies, and assess the results.

The principal architect of POP is the criminologist **Herman Goldstein**, who published the book *Problem-Oriented Policing* in 1990. Central to his argument is that police work is problem-oriented. Put another way, police officers responding to calls for service are presented with a problem and must find a solution to that problem. The type of analysis the patrol officer uses is much more detailed and in-depth than the assessment of whether a formal law has been broken.

Problem-oriented policing goes beyond assessing whether a law has been violated to examine the underlying causes of crime and disorder in the community and to tailor solutions that address those causes. Often, the violation of the law itself is the tip of the iceberg. This is known as the **iceberg or 80/20 rule:** like an iceberg, no matter how large the part above water is, 80 percent of the iceberg—or problem—is below the surface. So to eliminate a problem, the 80 percent that is not visible must be attacked. Those are the underlying causes or conditions that expose the remaining 20 percent. In addressing problems of crime and social disorder, the police and the community must consider not only the crime or incidents (the 20 percent), but also the broader community, social, and economic contexts in which the incidents occur. This approach represents a major shift in police work, from a focus on isolated incidents to a consideration of the factors that contributed to those incidents. POP is consistent with contemporary police management approaches that strive to empower front-line police officers and encourage creativity and risk-taking.

Table 5.1 sets out several of the basic principles of problem-oriented policing. As you review them, think about how they differ from the principles of traditional police work.

Table 5.1 Doing Problem-Oriented Policing: A Guide for Police Departments

• Focus on problems of concern to the public	• Avoid using overly broad labels in grouping incidents so separate problems can be identified
• Zero in on effectiveness as the primary concern	
• Be proactive	
• Be committed to systematic inquiry as the first step in solving substantive problems	• Encourage a broad, uninhibited search for solutions
• Encourage the use of rigorous methods in making inquiries	
• Make full use of data in police files and the experience of police personnel	• Acknowledge the limits of the criminal justice system as a response to problems
• Group like incidents together so they can be addressed as a common problem	• Identify multiple interests in any one problem and weigh them when analyzing the value of different responses
• Be committed to taking some risks in responding to problems	

Source: J.E. Eck and W. Spelman, "Doing Problem-Oriented Policing: A Guide for Police Departments," *Problem-Solving: Problem-Oriented Policing in Newport News,* Police Executive Research Forum (1987).

Components of the Basic Problem-Solving Model

The process of problem-solving has four components, usually referred to as **SARA**:

- **S**canning
- **A**nalysis
- **R**esponse
- **A**ssessment

The SARA model is depicted in Figure 5.1. Below, we examine the components of the basic problem-solving model and consider how the RCMP has developed that model as a framework for problem-solving with the community and as part of an internally focused approach to improved service delivery.

Scanning

During the scanning stage, a preliminary inquiry is conducted to determine whether a problem really exists and whether further analysis is required. Police have a number of resources available to them to assist with this inquiry, including data on calls for service, victim surveys, citizen complaints, census data, data available from other government agencies, media reports of citizens' concerns, officer observations, and community surveys. Each source provides useful information in problem identification.

The police can use other methods to determine the existence of problems, including:

- crime analyses;
- letters of complaint;
- input from elected officials, business groups, and neighbourhood organizations;
- data on fluctuations in the market value of property;
- data on cases treated in emergency rooms;
- probation and parole records; and
- the insights of social agencies and other public institutions, such as schools, that have responsibility for problems that are also of concern to the police, such as runaways, the homeless, victims of sexual assault, and the mentally ill (Eck and Spelman 1987b).

Analysis

During the analysis stage, there is an effort to determine the cause, scope, and impact of the problem. This is the most critical stage of the problem-solving process, and it may require considerable time and attention. The results will be used to allocate resources and mobilize the community.

Figure 5.1 Components of the Basic Problem-Solving Model

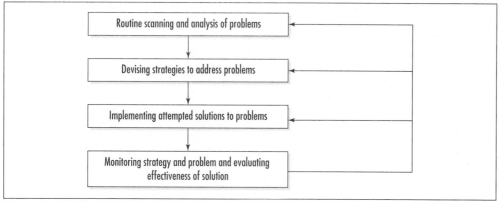

Source: Hough, M. and N. Tilley, *Getting the Grease to the Squeak: Research Lessons for Crime Prevention.* London, UK: Police Research Group, Home Office (1998), p. 8.

It is important to identify the following:

- Who is being harmed by the problem? Is the harm inflicted on specific persons or groups, or does the problem detract from the quality of life in the area and increase the fear of crime?
- Can the problem be broken into specific elements or subsets of problems such that progress can be achieved on each subset until a positive result is obtained for the overall problem?

A useful method for understanding the dimensions of a problem involves understanding it in relation to the victim, the accused, and the location. These are represented in a **problem analysis triangle** (see Critical Perspectives 5.1).

Response

The analysis is used to develop an appropriate response tailored to the problem. While arrest is often the primary response option in traditional police work, in problem-solving within a community policing framework it is only one of many options. Other possible responses include:

- *concentrating attention on the individuals responsible for a disproportionate share of the problem*. This approach, often described as "targeting," involves tactical or directed patrol aimed at individuals involved in a specific type of criminal activity. It is also known as perpetrator-oriented patrol.

CRITICAL PERSPECTIVES 5.1

THE PROBLEM ANALYSIS TRIANGLE

For a problem to exist, there must be three elements: an offender, a victim, and a location. We can think of this as a "problem analysis triangle" that helps us understand the relationships among those three elements and that may indicate areas where further information is required.

There may be a potential victim in an area that is prone to crime, but if there is no offender present, then there is no crime. Similarly, if there is an offender in a crime-prone area but no potential victim, then no crime will occur. Furthermore, the location may be an area that is relatively unsafe, but without the presence of both a potential victim and a potential offender, no crime will occur. The key point is that if any of the triangle's sides are missing, there is no problem. This is similar to the crime triangle we discussed in Chapter 4, in which there is a target, a lack of a suitable guardian, and a motivated offender.

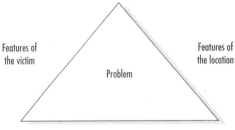

Features of the victim

Features of the location

Problem

Features of the offender

Applying the problem-solving triangle allows front-line officers to develop appropriate intervention strategies. Patrol strategies, which are the most common form of police-initiated strategy, have proven successful in the short term when directed at a specific problem. Targeted or directed patrol strategies commonly focus on offenders (offender-specific patrol) or locations (location-specific patrol [LSP]). Victim-oriented strategies often require a combination of situational (SCP) and social development (CPSD) strategies to effectively address the problem.

Source: Hough, M. and N. Tilley, *Getting the Grease to the Squeak: Research Lessons for Crime Prevention.* London, UK: Police Research Group, Home Office (1998), p. 23.

- *connecting with other government and private agencies.* A thorough analysis often indicates the need for:

  —more effective referrals to existing governmental and private services;

  —improved coordination with agencies that exert control over some of the problems or individuals involved in the incidents; and

  —initiatives that respond to deficiencies identified in existing municipal services or to the fact that services do not exist.

- *using mediation and negotiation skills* rather than the traditional police responses of arrest or aggressive targeted patrol.
- *conveying information.* Surprisingly, conveying sound and accurate information is one of the least used responses. Open communication can foster the attainment of a number of goals, including:

  —reducing anxiety and fear;

  —enabling citizens to solve their own problems;

  —obtaining conformity with laws and regulations that are not known or well understood;

  —warning potential victims about their vulnerability and advising them how to protect themselves;

  —demonstrating to people how they unwittingly contribute to problems;

  —developing support for addressing a problem; and

  —acquainting the community with the limitations on government agencies and defining what can be realistically expected of those agencies.

- *mobilizing the community.* This is essential and can result in more sustainable outcomes. Mobilization may occur through various strategies, including:

  —establishing neighbourhood watches;

  —identifying abandoned vehicles;

  —promoting community interaction to reduce fear, mistrust, or tension;

  —installing telephone notification systems to alert potential victims;

  —forming citizen patrols; and

  —soliciting information on criminal activity.

- *making use of existing forms of social control.* This involves solving problems by applying specific forms of social control inherent in existing relationships, such as the influence of a parent, teacher, employer, or church.
- *altering the physical environment to reduce opportunities for problems to recur.* In other words, adopting the principles of crime prevention through environmental design (CPTED) and situational crime prevention (SCP).
- *using civil law to control public nuisances, offensive behaviour, and conditions contributing to crime.* This means initiating a number of other legal proceedings, including those related to:

  —licensing;

  —zoning;

  —property confiscation;

  —nuisance abatement; and

  —injunctions.

Assessment

In this stage of the problem-solving process, the police and the community examine the outcomes that have occurred as a result of the problem-solving response. The intent is to measure the effectiveness of the response, which can be a very difficult task. Scott (2000), who evaluated 20 years of POP in the United States, found that this stage often receives the least attention, although it is critical from the standpoint of resources being utilized effectively.

Expert versus Collaborative Approaches to Problem-Solving

There are two models of problem-solving that can be implemented by the police. These are known as the expert model and the collaborative model. The **expert model of problem-solving** involves an outside person—the "expert"—going to the location (community, neighbourhood, school) where the problem is occurring, identifying and analyzing the problem, and developing a solution. In contrast, the **collaborative model of problem-solving** emphasizes shared responsibility between an expert and those in the neighbourhood, area, or setting where the problem is being experienced. In this model, the expert helps the community members identify and analyze the problem, brainstorm possible solutions, and select and implement an appropriate plan. The expert here serves as a facilitator, posing questions and leading the other participants in the development of a solution.

Degrees of Impact on the Problem

The police and the community may have varying degrees of success in solving the problem, including:

- eliminating the problem;
- reducing the number of incidents created by the problem;
- reducing the seriousness of the incidents created by the problem;
- designing methods for better handling the incidents created by the problem; and
- removing the problem from police consideration (Eck and Spelman 1987a, 5–6).

CAPRA: THE PROBLEM-SOLVING MODEL USED BY THE RCMP

While the problem-solving process varies among police services, the basic process is fundamentally the same. For example, the RCMP has developed a problem-solving model called CAPRA, which stands for:

- **C**lients
- **A**cquire/Analyze information
- **P**artnerships
- **R**esponse
- **A**ssessment

The CAPRA problem-solving model is taught to new police officers and is applied throughout the RCMP to a number of internal and external problems. The CAPRA model draws attention to important stakeholders, whether it is the community itself (clients) or agencies that may contribute to problem-solving efforts (partnerships). The communities policed by the RCMP across Canada are highly diverse; the CAPRA problem-solving model provides a method of inquiry that an RCMP officer in any community can use to improve quality of life in that community—indeed, it can improve service delivery overall. The key is to develop strong partnerships in which each partner or client shares in the development of a solution. In Your Community 5.1 provides an excellent example of problem-oriented policing in an Indigenous community.

PROBLEM-SOLVING PROCESS

Since the introduction of the problem-oriented policing model, most, if not all, social agencies have conducted problem-solving activities. Health care services, corrections facilities, probation offices, youth services, and local governments all have a vested interest in

IN YOUR COMMUNITY 5.1

PROBLEM-ORIENTED POLICING IN ELSIPOGTOG, NEW BRUNSWICK

Reproduced with the permission of the RCMP.

Constable Adam Peter-Paul during the Elsipogtog
moose hunting training camp for youth.

New RCMP officers must demonstrate the application of CAPRA problem-solving in their new postings. When Constable Jason Gauthier arrived at the New Brunswick RCMP Detachment of Elsipogtog in July 2015 he examined problems impacting the community. He observed there was a lack of communication between youth and adults, resulting in a lack of positive engagement opportunities. He noted that some youth were becoming involved in criminal activity. He found there were very few opportunities to bring both age groups together. To improve relations between the generations, he and Constable Peter-Paul approached the band chief and manager. This discussion resulted in the RCMP participating in a moose hunting training camp for youth, led by community adults. This improved communications between all participants; it also provided an opportunity for youth to learn traditional hunting methods and safety practices. It also facilitated RCMP officers being able to spend time with band members of varying ages in a casual, natural environment. By observing principles of sensitivity and respecting diversity, the RCMP participated as a member of the community; this fostered positive relations and built community trust.

Six youths and seven adults attended the inaugural moose hunting camp in October 2015. Ethical hunting skills and respect for both animals and the environment were some of the knowledge shared during the camp.

Source: Adapted from RCMP in New Brunswick Annual Report 2015 found at http://www.rcmp-grc. gc.ca/en/nb/rcmp-new-brunswick-annual-report-2015, p.19. Reproduced with the permission of the RCMP.

building stronger, healthier communities, and this has resulted in partnerships in which local police share their expertise in the development of more holistic and sustainable solutions. While the police often perform a strong leadership role in initiating problem-oriented responses, it is typically the community and other social agencies that support and sustain ongoing community improvement efforts. In Chapter 10 we examine this in greater detail in our discussion of the Ontario Mobilization and Engagement Model of Community Policing.

Adapting a model of problem-solving developed by the Ontario Provincial Police, we now walk you through the steps involved in problem-solving.

Problem Identification

Identifying the problem is perhaps the most important stage of the entire process. It involves a number of steps:

1. *List* everyone's perceptions of the problem.
2. *Identify* the perceived problem(s) and ask the question: "Is this the real problem or just a symptom or indication of a bigger or different problem?"
3. *Examine* the problem using the five Ws—Who, What, When, Where, and Why.
4. *Consider* the information available on the victim, the offender, and the situation to understand what has contributed to the problem.

Analysis

The objective of the analysis stage is to generate information on the underlying causes or conditions of the problem. More specifically, at this stage there is an attempt to answer the five Ws: Who, What, When, Where, and Why. A number of strategies may be used to gather this information, including:

- calls for service;
- community meetings;
- incident analysis;
- direct observation;
- focus groups;
- interviews;
- library research;
- meetings with other agencies; and
- surveys and questionnaires administered to community residents and other stakeholder groups.

Information must be gathered on the victim, the offender, and the situation—the three "sides" of the problem analysis triangle.

To assist patrol officers and communities in screening, prioritizing, and ranking problems, four **problem analysis filters** have been developed. These filters include the following:

- Impact of the problem:
   —How big is it?
   —Who is affected by it?
   —What other problems are affected by the situation?
   —Who are the stakeholders?
- Seriousness of the problem:
   —How much danger or damage would there be if it were left unchecked?
   —How much public concern is there on the issue?
   —What is the police priority or status regarding the issue?

- Complexity of the problem:
    - —How complex or deep-rooted is it?
    - —Are resources available to handle it (police, community, government, social agencies, etc.)?
    - —Who owns it?
- Solvability of the problem:
    - —To what degree can individuals or teams affect it?

It is important to remember that considerable time and human resources can be expended on a problem to very little effect. Conversely, quality-of-life improvements can be obtained with considerably less effort and expense. Also, if the information gathered during the analysis stage indicates that there is, in fact, no verifiable problem, then the problem-solving process is terminated.

Prioritizing Problems: A Scoring System

During the analysis stage, it is not uncommon to discover related problems, so it may become necessary to prioritize. The problem-solving model offers a mechanism for assigning a numeric value to each of the problem analysis filters to help set priorities. This technique is illustrated in the following example:

- Impact
- Seriousness
- Complexity
- Solvability

- 1 (least) to 5 (most)
- 1 (least) to 5 (most)
- 1 (very) to 5 (little)
- 1 (difficult) to 5 (easy)

Note: For complexity and solvability, the scale is designed to ensure that the least complex and easiest to solve are the higher priority (OPP 1997, 7–11).

After the scores are totalled up and the results are compared, the problems with the highest scores can be ranked highest in terms of priority.

Strategic Response

During this stage the police team develops a strategic response in collaboration with the community and partner agencies. The strategies are limited only by the imagination and resourcefulness of the partnership.

Objectives of the Response

The objectives of the problem-solving process may include one or several of the following:

- *Eliminate the problem.* This response often works when the problem is small, relatively simple, and involves few people and policing resources.
- *Reduce the size of the problem.* An effort is made to reduce or eliminate parts of the problem, recognizing that it may be too deep-rooted or persistent to be entirely eliminated (e.g., prostitution).
- *Reduce the harm or impact.* If the problem is too difficult to reduce or eliminate, an attempt is made to reduce the impact on the immediate victim, the broader community, or indirect or secondary victims (e.g., children who witness domestic violence). Harm reduction strategies include victim assistance initiatives and domestic violence assistance programs.
- *Improve the response to the problem.* For complex, societal problems, improvements in services to crime victims or to the broader community may be the only realistic goal.

- *Redefine responsibility for the problem.* An important requirement of the problem-solving process is to assess not only which individuals and agencies are affected by a problem but also who should assume the primary role in terms of a strategic response. As we have noted, the police are often called upon to address problems that would be handled better by another organization. Relative to other organizations, they may be limited in their ability to bring about long-term progress. Often, the appropriate strategic response for police is to shed the "expert" role—that is, to recognize other agencies with mutually vested interests in a problem and to defer authority to those groups.

Response Options

Depending on the goals and objectives of the problem-solving process, a number of response options are available:

- *Traditional response strategies and investigation.* Traditional strategies are used, such as targeted saturation techniques and increased patrol, including foot patrol. These approaches often combine investigation with enforcement. Generally, the benefits of this approach are limited and the problem returns once traditional strategies have been exhausted. For this reason, it is preferable to consider alternative strategies that may be used in combination with traditional strategies, such as the others described here.
- *Interagency strategies.* This involves collaboration between the police and other agencies that share mutual concerns in relation to a problem. For example, many police services have response teams for youth at risk that pair a police officer with a social worker, mental health worker, or youth worker, thus providing a more comprehensive approach. Interagency strategies may be formal or informal depending on the specific problem and the level of response required.
- *Use of noncriminal laws and regulations.* This approach recognizes that the enforcement of private and public laws, regulations, and statutes, such as building codes, noise bylaws, and health regulations, can affect many problems. It may be more effective to enforce these laws and regulations than to apply the criminal law or statutes that would typically require enforcement by the police.
- *More discriminate use of law enforcement.* The police service examines past approaches and determines possible improvements to the problem-solving process itself. For example, neighbourhood programs to eradicate prostitution may simply displace the problem to another community. These programs could instead focus on preventing the problem from migrating to another community or neighbourhood.
- *Information, communication, and education strategies.* Information campaigns are directed at educating the community, with the goal of preventing or reducing further victimization.
- *Community mobilization.* This approach involves mobilizing the community residents and any community resources that can be brought to bear on the problem.
- *Focused strategies.* These strategies focus on individuals and locations that are prone to crime. The assumption is that a relatively small number of individuals or locations are responsible for a disproportionate number of problems. Strategies then focus on the individual or location.
- *Crime prevention strategies and programs.* Crime prevention strategies and programs include initiatives such as the Cottage Watch Program, profiled in our discussion of crime prevention programs in Chapter 4. Such strategies and programs are considered only after a careful analysis of the problem has been undertaken; once these programs are selected, continuous evaluation and monitoring is required to ensure that they remain effective and meet their stated objectives.
- *Mediation strategies.* Mediating community problems and disputes may be a more effective approach than legal responses when there is no clear dividing line between wrong and right. Police tend not to get involved in formal mediation, although part of an appropriate police response is referral to mediation agencies.

- *Environmental design.* This involves participating in community development, including the planning and design of features such as roadways, parks, parking lots, greenery, and street lighting. Such changes can be an immediate response to an identified concern, or they can be part of long-range community planning.
- *Social development.* This addresses improvements to quality of life through community and social development initiatives, which may address deep social problems relating to the decaying family structure, child poverty, substance abuse, domestic violence, unemployment, illiteracy, inadequate housing, mental illness, and so on.
- *Community control.* The police must attempt to establish meaningful collaboration with the community so that they do not become solely responsible for solving problems. Public safety becomes the responsibility of the community as well as the police (Osborne and Gaebler 1993).

Individual police officers, problem-solving teams, and specific government and social service agencies, as well as community residents, organizations, and groups, may participate in these response options. Many of the problems that are identified in communities require a collaborative response that involves police officers and the community. Some can be addressed by individual police officers on their own.

The Intervention Plan

Once response options are selected according to the objectives of the specific problem-solving process, the team develops its intervention plan. The intervention plan should follow **SMART** guidelines; that is, it should involve tasks that are:

- **S**pecific, identifying individual/agency and community responsibilities;
- **M**easurable (quantitatively, qualitatively, or both);
- **A**ttainable—for example, reducing the severity or prevalence of a problem;
- **R**ealistic and related to previously established goals and objectives; and
- **T**imely (bound to a schedule for implementation).

Gathering Information on the Response

In order to evaluate the effectiveness of the response, it is important to gather information specifically related to the problem. For example, if the objective is to reduce or eliminate a problem, quantifiable measures, such as a decrease in the number of house break and enters over a specified period, are easily obtained. If the objective is to reduce harm or impact or to improve responses to the problem, then qualitative measures are required. This information can be obtained from victim and citizen surveys designed to measure levels of satisfaction and reduced perceptions of fear.

Evaluation

At this stage, the police team assesses whether the response options were effective and whether the goals and objectives were achieved. Both process evaluation and impact evaluation should be used.

Process Evaluation

The first step in **process evaluation** is to analyze the implementation of the strategies by asking such questions as:

- Were the strategies easy to implement?
- If the team has to implement the process again, are there any factors that would act as barriers to success?
- Are there steps that would facilitate implementation?
- What should others be aware of if attempting to implement a similar plan?

Impact Evaluation

Impact evaluation involves assessing the qualitative and quantitative outcomes or consequences of problem-solving strategies. Not all outcomes may have been positive. An honest assessment is made to determine whether the strategies worked and what steps could be taken to improve them.

Once the process of evaluation is complete, there should be ongoing maintenance and monitoring of the problem to ensure that it does not appear again. Often the immediate symptoms of a problem disappear, only to emerge again.

Furthermore, records of problem-solving plans must be kept. Keeping a history allows the process to be shared with community policing committees, operational planning forums, and other officers facing similar problems.

THE PROBLEM-SOLVING PROCESS IN ACTION

To illustrate the problem-solving process in action, we examine a number of real-life problems impacting our communities today. It is important to recognize that modern problems are complex and often deeply embedded in broader societal forces such as homelessness, or the opioid crisis. For this reason, problem-solving efforts may need to address smaller problems first, with the eventual goal of addressing the root causes of the problems. Let's begin with an assessment of common community problems.

Problem Identification

At a monthly meeting of the Community Policing Committee, the OPP officers and the committee members perceived that the following problems existed in their small town:

- Dump trucks speeding on a residential street that connects the highway to a stone quarry.
- Problems in the town park caused by youths, including vandalism, drinking parties, and fear among older residents who use the park.
- Lack of recreational opportunities for youths.
- Business break and enters.
- A lack of police patrols.

Identify the Perceived Problems

By discussing the perceptions and asking "Why," the group identified three problems:

- Speeding dump trucks on 5th Street, a residential area.
- Youths with nothing to do causing problems in the park.
- Business breaks and enters.

Analysis

Examine the Problem (the Five Ws)

The problems were assessed (Who, What, Where, When, and Why) by gathering information about the victims, the offenders, and the situation. This information was applied in considering the impact, seriousness, complexity, and solvability of the problems. The police provided statistical information on all of the perceived problems, including:

- the number of automobile accidents on 5th Street, the number of business break and enters, and the number of offences that occurred in the park in the last year;
- the hours of patrol and radar enforcement in the area, the number of complaints received related to the perceived issues, and the types of charges laid;
- where and when offences and complaints occurred;
- the ages of the accused;

- information on the victims and complainants (age, sex, driver, passenger, etc.); and
- the number of complaints from senior citizens.

The community provided the following information:

- Demographics on the number of youth and senior citizens in the community.
- The number of organized activities for youth.
- The current physical characteristics and environment of the park, 5th Street, and the downtown.

Consider the Victim, Offender, and Situation

From this information, the following picture emerged of the perceived problems:

- *Speeding dump trucks.* There were no accidents related to speeding dump trucks in the town in the past year. Police radar enforcement in response to calls revealed very few charges, and in fact, most of the trucks were travelling within the speed limit. Several homes on 5th Street were situated very close to the road, and it was from them that most of the complaints originated.
- *Youths causing problems in the park.* The park had poor lighting, and people could easily hide from sight. The seniors and youths were not communicating. There was a lack of recreational facilities, and as a consequence the youths were congregating in the park, where they committed various offences. The police had investigated a number of vandalism and liquor complaints during the past few months involving youths.
- *Business break and enters.* There had been only three break-ins in the preceding six months. The businesses targeted could benefit from some crime-proofing, as they were found to be vulnerable to this type of crime. The break-ins involved minor thefts of no greater than $500.

Prioritize the Problems

Each problem was assigned a numeric classification:

- **Problem 1:**   **Speeding dump trucks on 5th Street**

Impact	3
Seriousness	3
Complexity	3
Solvability	2
	11

- **Problem 2:**   **Youths causing problems in the park**

Impact	4
Seriousness	4
Complexity	3
Solvability	4
	15

- **Problem 3:**   **Business break and enters**

Impact	1
Seriousness	1
Complexity	5
Solvability	5
	12

Outcome: Based on a prioritization of the problems, the first priority was the problem of youth in the park, followed by business break and enters and speeding dump trucks.

Problem Identification

During the past year there had been 80 offences in the park, largely related to youths drinking and damaging park equipment. The youths had nothing to do and congregated in the park on weekends to drink, set campfires, and party. The park's poor lighting concealed the offenders. Older residents felt intimidated when walking in the area.

The Goal

To reduce the number of offences being committed by youths in the town park by 50 percent during the next 12 months as compared to the previous 12-month period.

The Response

- Identify strategies
- Assess and select strategies

After reviewing each available response strategy, the partners decided on strategies to achieve their goals; these are listed in Table 5.2.

After an assessment of the strategies, those selected were incorporated into an action plan with assigned tasks.

Write and Implement Action Plans

Let's consider one of the strategies in the action plan.

One of the strategies was to improve the town park environment by installing additional lighting and basketball and tennis courts by the end of December. The tasks identified to accomplish this strategy were as follows:

Table 5.2 Strategies to Deal with Youth in the Park

Strategy	Strategy type	Advantage	Disadvantage
• Increase police patrols of park	• Visibility	• Increases enforcement • Deters youth violations • Reduces senior citizens' fear	• Unable to commit police resources consistently
• Improve park environment with additional lighting, and basketball and tennis courts	• Environmental design	• Improves visibility • Encourages youth activities • Encourages adult attendance	• Cost to install facilities and equipment
• Meet with youth to discuss concerns and seek solutions	• Mediation	• Involves youth in the solution • Encourages youth to take ownership of the problem	• Youth perceiving they are the problem • Reluctance of youth to participate
• Alternative youth sentencing to community service in the park	• Interagency/ stakeholder	• Encourages youth to take responsibility for their actions	• Needs youth agreement to participate in alternative measures

Source: J.E. Eck and W. Spelman, "Strategies to Deal with Youth in the Park," in *Problem-Solving: Problem-Oriented Policing in Newport News* (Washington, DC: Police Executive Research Forum, 1987), p. 3.

1. The Community Policing Committee (CPC) chair would approach the town's parks maintenance supervisor by the end of June and identify the need for three more light standards in designated areas in the park.
2. A CPC subcommittee would be formed immediately to develop a proposal by the end of July considering the costs, possible funding sources, and possibility of installing two tennis courts and a basketball court in the park.
3. The CPC subcommittee chair would present the park environment proposal to council by the end of September, for its consideration and acceptance.
4. The OPP detachment commander would forward a letter of support to the CPC sub-committee chair for the installation of lighting and sporting facilities.
5. The CPC subcommittee chair would report to the CPC at each regular meeting on the progress of tasks 1 to 4.

Plan and strategy results were recorded upon completion. The Community Policing team leader was responsible for completing a template, for making sure that the required activities were monitored at the local level, and for forwarding any recommended "best strategies" to the OPP.

CONDITIONS FOR SUCCESSFUL PROBLEM-SOLVING

Police services that have successfully made problem-solving a core component of their services within a community policing framework share a number of characteristics. From an organizational perspective, they have recognized the following principles.

- Policing involves addressing a wide range of problems, not just crime.
- These problems are interrelated and the priority given them must be constantly reassessed rather than ranked in traditional ways.
- Each problem requires a unique response rather than a generic "one size fits all" response.
- The criminal law is only one of several response options.
- Police services can succeed by working to prevent problems, rather than simply by responding to incidents that are only symptoms of underlying problems.
- Developing an effective response to a problem requires prior analysis rather than simply invoking traditional police practices.
- Contrary to the traditional image of the police—held by both the police and the public—the capacity of the police to solve problems is extremely limited.
- The role of the police is best viewed as one of strengthening the community's problem-solving capacity, rather than assuming full responsibility for identifying and responding to problems (Goldstein 1990, 179).

Herman Goldstein (1990, 179) contends that police agencies that have embraced these notions develop a "new honesty" about the role of the police, their relationship with the community, and their capacity and role limitations vis-à-vis problem-solving. Ultimately, these police services are better positioned to respond to community problems and to create organizations that focus on community problem-solving.

Police Management's Role in Creating a Problem-Solving Police Organization

If problem-solving is to succeed organizationally, there must be a significant commitment from police management. This is necessary in order to provide direction to the effort, communicate vision, and ensure that problem-solving helps the organization achieve its broader goals and purposes.

There are a number of specific practices that police executives must adopt in order to ensure that the entire police service becomes involved in problem-solving. These include:

- communicating to all department members why responding to and solving problems is more effective than responding to incidents, and why police services and patrol officers should engage in problem-solving;
- providing incentives to those members who engage in problem-solving;
- reducing the barriers to officers engaging in the process, such as by making more time available and eliminating administrative practices that hinder initiative and creativity; and
- providing examples of what constitutes good problem-solving (Eck and Spelman 1987a, 100–1).

Police managers must "walk the talk"; that is, they must lead and manage in ways that are consistent with the vision and values of the organization. This requires principle-centred leadership on the part of front-line supervisors and managers to ensure that an "entrepreneurial" atmosphere exists that encourages officers to create, develop, and test their intellectual and creative capacities and to take risks without fear of being punished for unintentional mistakes and failures.

Barriers to Effective Problem-Solving

There are a number of potential barriers to effective problem-solving, some of which are discussed below.

- *Failing to plan is planning to fail.* One of the most common barriers is simply not examining a problem in sufficient detail. Where only a surface understanding exists, what often results is a superficial response to a problem. This, again, sensitizes us to the fact that the problem identification stage is perhaps the most important phase of the entire problem-solving process.
- *Failure to conduct a thorough analysis of the problem or working on the wrong problem.* Failure to conduct a thorough diagnosis of the problem results in a response that does not address the real issue. The problem-solving process may be ineffective so that valuable resources are wasted.
- *Failure to dedicate resources to the problem, leaving officers feeling ill-equipped and under-supported.* A major impediment to success is the incident-driven policing environment. Patrol officers may be too busy responding to calls to engage in problem-solving. Patrol sergeants are often caught between ensuring that dispatched calls are answered promptly and trying to free up resources to deal with the underlying issues that place demands on police resources in the first place. This often represents an organizational "Catch-22" for the police service and illustrates the significant tension that often exists between the dispatch function and priorities of a police service and community expectations.
- *Failure to follow up in the assessment stage.* As noted earlier in the discussion, the assessment stage is often the weakest link in the entire problem-solving process. This is due, in part, to the fact that patrol officers may rotate to new assignments before a thorough assessment of the intervention can be carried out. In addition, the resources allocated to the original problem may end after some of the objectives relating to the original problem have been achieved. Little time or attention may be given to issues such as the displacement of the problem to another area of the community.
- *Failure to initiate a process or to take ownership of problem.* In this case, neither the police nor the community recognizes that a problem exists, or a problem is acknowledged to

exist but neither the community nor the police will take responsibility for addressing it. This effectively prevents the development of a collaborative effort.

- *Problems in implementing an agency-wide program.* The agency charged with lead responsibility for a problem is unable to establish implementation plans that translate into plans for operational action.
- *The police take an expert role as opposed to a collaborative one.* The police fail to develop an effective collaborative response and end up assuming an expert role in relation to the problem. The expert approach is much more resource-intensive and difficult to implement and sustain.
- *Failure to communicate successes and results.* It is essential to establish a level of problem-solving memory of what works and what does not work. This can occur only through effective documentation and sharing of lessons learned about the problem-solving process with other patrol officers and with the communities.
- *Difference in definitions between the community's perception and the police service's perception.* There may be a lack of agreement that a problem exists, or there may be a disagreement between the police and the community about the nature of the problem.
- *Problems in implementation at the organizational, front-line, or community level.* Problems in implementation may relate to lack of buy-in from involved police personnel or from stakeholders. It is important that responses be developed through consensus. The assessment stage then evaluates the effectiveness of the problem-solving efforts.
- *Failure of police technology to identify problems beyond the police service.* A balance must be achieved between using technology-based crime analysis for identifying problems and seeking community input. There is a risk that the increasing use of computer technology to analyze patterns of crime will overshadow community participation and undermine community collaboration.

In light of the economics of policing today, it is more critical than ever that police efforts have a measurable effect on the outcome of a problem. For example, simply attending community meetings, while informative for community residents, may have little bearing on the outcome of a problem. Ideally, the intervention can be measured in some way. In A Closer Look 5.1 we examine a range of responses available for addressing pharmacy robberies. Clearly a reduction in this type of robbery would be an important outcome. We will examine this in greater detail in Chapter 6, where we discuss results-based accountability (RBA), which involves carefully measuring outcomes of community problems in order to ensure that policing efforts are both effective and efficient.

A CLOSER LOOK 5.1

RESPONDING TO PHARMACY ROBBERIES

Pharmacies are often the targets of criminals seeking to obtain prescription drugs, and many of these robberies are very violent (see, for example, Report to the Minister of Justice and Attorney General, "Public fatality inquiry: Arthur George Provencal," https://open.alberta.ca/publications/fatality-inquiry-2002-07-05#detailed).

The increasing abuse of opioids in society increases the risk of pharmacy robberies. While police investigations focus on the criminals themselves, the problem-solving process looks for interventions that will deter robberies in the first instance, with the overall goal of improving public safety.

(continues)

Contributing Factors

1. Misuse of prescription drugs and opioid abuse (fentanyl, OxyContin).

2. Pharmacy management practices, including location of the pharmacy.

3. The robbery is typically motivated to obtain drugs and not money.

Stakeholders

Police, health care professionals, substance abuse treatment professionals, pharmacists, parents, and educators.

Specific Responses

Increase the Risk of Detection

1. Informing pharmacy employees about robbery trends.

2. Providing prevention guidance to pharmacy employees.

3. Managing risk factors including urban planning/geographic location.

4. Install a panic alarm.

5. Install CCTV surveillance system.

6. Tracking the stolen drugs and offenders using GPS and DNA spray.

7. Use of deterrent signage.

Increase the Effort Required to Commit Pharmacy Robbery

8. Employ security measures

    a. Increase pharmacy lighting.

    b. Lock up drugs.

    c. Install physical barriers.

    d. Ensure front windows are clear.

Decrease Susceptibility to Robberies

9. Limit the drugs available.

10. Limit the amount of drug information given over the phone.

Responses with Limited Effectiveness

11. Conducting focused surveillance and enforcement.

12. Increasing penalties for pharmacy robbery.

Measuring Effectiveness

Process Measures

• Changes in arrest patterns for drug possession and sales in your and neighbouring jurisdictions.

• Changes in types of prescription drug diversion (e.g., if you prevent pharmacy robberies, would burglaries increase).

• Changes in locations of pharmacy robberies.

• Changes in types of drugs obtained through robberies and other forms of prescription drug diversion.

• Changes in the number of prescriptions filled for certain target drugs such as OxyContin.

• Increased adoption by pharmacies of robbery-prevention good practices.

(continues)

Outcome Measures

- Reduced number of reported pharmacy robbery cases.

- Reduced number and severity of injuries related to pharmacy robberies.

- Reduced value/dollar loss related to pharmacy robberies.

- Reduced number of arrests of possession of the types of pharmaceuticals typically taken in pharmacy robberies.

Sources: Adapted from Nancy LaVigne and Julie Wartell, *Robbery of Pharmacies: Problem-Oriented Guides for Police, Problem-Specific Guide No. 73.* Washington, DC: Office of Community Oriented Policing Services (2015).

CHAPTER SUMMARY

This chapter has focused on problem-oriented policing (POP), which is one of the core components of community policing. Our overview began with a discussion of what constitutes a problem and of the importance of the community and the police being involved in defining problems. We then turned to examine problem-oriented policing, a term coined by the criminologist Herman Goldstein three decades ago. A key element of POP is the 80/20 rule, which holds that crime and other problems in a community or neighbourhood are only the tip of the iceberg and that the underlying conditions or causes of the problem lie beneath the surface. It is these underlying conditions that are the focus of POP.

The problem-solving process, based on SARA (scanning, analysis, response, and assessment) was outlined, followed by a brief examination of the RCMP's CAPRA problem-solving model. A case study was presented to illustrate how patrol officers working in collaboration with the community apply the POP model. Finally, the conditions for the successful implementation of POP, as well as the barriers that hinder problem-solving, were discussed.

If you would like to learn more about any of the information described in this unit, we would highly recommend you visit the websites for the Ontario Provincial Police (www.opp.ca) and the RCMP (www.rcmp.ca). For detailed examples of POP, go to popcenter.org, where you will find numerous POP guides. You will also find the RCMP CAPRA Problem-Solving Model.

CHAPTER REVIEW

Key Terms

- collaborative model of problem-solving, p. 134
- expert model of problem-solving, p. 134
- Herman Goldstein, p. 130
- iceberg or 80/20 rule, p. 130
- impact evaluation, p. 140
- problem, p. 128
- problem analysis filters, p. 136
- problem analysis triangle, p. 132
- problem-solving, p. 128
- problem-oriented policing (POP), p. 130
- process evaluation, p. 139
- SARA, p. 131
- SMART, p. 139

Key Points

- Problem-solving is a key element of community policing. It attempts to address the underlying causes of crime and social disorder.
- It is important that problems be appropriately identified and that the responsibility for the problem be established.
- Collaborative policing involves the police and the community agreeing that a problem exists, identifying the dimensions of the problem, and formulating and then implementing a strategy to address the problem.
- Problem-oriented policing (POP) puts the community-oriented policing strategy into practice.
- The iceberg or 80/20 rule holds that only a small portion of a problem is visible and that in order to eliminate a problem the root causes must be attacked.
- The problem-solving process is captured in the term SARA—scanning, analysis, response, and assessment.
- Problem analysis filters are used by the police and community to prioritize problems.
- A number of conditions must exist in police services for problem-solving to succeed.
- A number of barriers in police services may undermine problem-solving efforts including insufficient analysis and assessment.
- Problem-oriented policing incorporates all modern principles of policing, including intelligence-led police work and community engagement and mobilization.
- Problem-oriented policing strategies include approaches based on crime prevention through environmental design and crime prevention through social development.

Self-Evaluation

QUESTIONS

1. What is meant by **problem-solving** and what role does it play in community policing?
2. What is meant by a **problem**?
3. What is **collaborative problem-solving**, and why is it important in any discussion of problem-oriented policing?
4. Who was **Herman Goldstein** and what was his contribution to the field of problem-oriented policing?
5. Define and discuss the key elements of **problem-oriented policing (POP)**.
6. What is the **iceberg** or **80/20 rule**, and why is it important in our study of community policing and problem-oriented policing?
7. What is **SARA**?
8. Discuss what is meant by the **problem analysis triangle** and what its role is in problem-oriented policing.
9. Compare the **expert model of problem-solving** to the **collaborative model of problem-solving**.
10. What are **problem analysis filters** and what role do they play in problem-oriented policing? Provide an example.
11. Compare **process evaluation** and **impact evaluation**.

KEY IDEAS

1. Problem-solving attempts to address the underlying causes of crime and social disorder. How is problem-solving best described?
   a. As one element of community policing.
   b. As a new and emerging model of community policing.
   c. As a technique no longer used in contemporary policing.
   d. As a method of policing with minimal community involvement.

2. During the strategic response stage, the police team develops a response in collaboration with the community. What is the only limit on the strategies used?
   a. The funding amount allocated to the project.
   b. The size of the police agency and community facilities.
   c. The tax base and budget of the community.
   d. The imagination and resourcefulness of the partnership.

3. What is problem-oriented policing (POP)?
   a. An approach to policing used primarily in the United States.
   b. A strategy that puts community policing into practice.
   c. A strategy most often used for identifying high-risk offenders.
   d. An approach that has largely been abandoned due to costs.

4. Who was Herman Goldstein?
   a. The first police chief in Ontario to implement problem-oriented policing.
   b. The author of a book that was critical of problem-oriented policing.
   c. The principal architect of problem-oriented policing.
   d. The chief proponent of traditional policing.

5. What does the acronym SARA stand for?
   a. scanning, analysis, response, assessment
   b. safety, alertness, readiness, awareness
   c. security, awareness, review, analysis
   d. sensing, arming, reacting, activating

6. Which statement describes the collaborative model of problem-solving?
   a. It involves patrol officers and the community working together.
   b. It emphasizes shared responsibility between the police and the community.
   c. It uses experts to assist in the identification and response to problems.
   d. It emphasizes multi-police agencies working together on a major crime.

7. Which of the following is most often of concern to community residents?
   a. Quality of life issues rather than violations of law.
   b. White-collar and corporate crime.
   c. Police response times as well as dress and deportment.
   d. Allegations of police misconduct including excessive force.

8. What are problem analysis filters?
   a. Statistical methods used in calculating the number of crimes in a community.
   b. Tools used by police services that have not adopted community policing.
   c. Tools used in the analysis phase of problem-oriented policing to prioritize problems.
   d. Methods of preventing the displacement of a problem.

9. In the evaluation stage of PARE, the process of asking questions such as "Were the strategies easy to implement?" and "What should others be aware of if attempting to implement a similar plan?" is known by which term?
   a. impact evaluation
   b. process evaluation
   c. assessment evaluation
   d. inquiry evaluation

10. The RCMP has developed a problem-solving model called CAPRA. What does the acronym stand for?
   a. customer, agents/ability, people, respond, assess
   b. crime, answers/actions, police, react, allow
   c. clients, acquire/analyze information, partnerships, response, assessment
   d. capability, allow/answer information, persistence, readiness, action

Problem-Oriented Policing: Situations and Strategies

Problem-Solving Process Checklist

Problem-solving is a key component of community policing, and there are specific questions and issues that must be asked and addressed at each of the scanning, analysis, response, and assessment stages of SARA.

Scanning

- Has the problem been described by all affected persons or groups?

- Has the problem been scrutinized for unforeseen elements?

- Has the problem been identified by more than one person or group? How do others describe the problem?

- Does your description contain all of the observed elements or components?

- After reviewing the problem from a variety of viewpoints, what are the common elements that can be used to develop a collective (community) description of the problem?

Analysis

- Who are the people involved or affected by the problem? Who are the victims? Who are the offenders? Who should respond to the problem?

- What is the scope of the problem? How large is it? Why did it develop?

- How did the problem develop? What actions or events constitute the problem?

- What is the sequence of events that produced the problem?

- When and where does the problem occur?

- What is the physical setting in which the problem is taking place? Does the location contribute to the problem?

- Has all of the available information or data on the problem been collected and analyzed?

- What underlying conditions precipitated the problem? Has the problem's causal relationship to agency or government policies, procedures, or practices been examined?

- What is the current community and governmental response to the problem? How do individuals and agencies react to the actions or problem? What have they done about the problem? What results have they had?

Response

- Have those individuals involved or affected by the problem (including residents) participated in a brainstorming session to identify potential responses?

- Has the response been tried before? If so, what were the results?

- What actions does the response include? What agencies need to be involved? Are representatives from those agencies present to discuss feasibility of action?

- What other resources are available for the response?

- What is the time frame for implementing the response?

- What barriers exist to implementing the response?

- What results can the stakeholders realistically expect?

- Can you reach consensus on a response, based on all the information you have gleaned?

- Have you developed an action plan for implementing the process?
- Have you set the response goals and objectives?
- Can you identify the steps necessary to implement the response?
- Can you identify the key stakeholders involved in or affected by each step?
- Have you assigned individual responsibilities for carrying out each step?
- Have you set time lines for completing each step?

Assessment

Process Evaluation

- Was the response implemented as intended? What problems were encountered, and how were they overcome?
- What specific steps were implemented? Were they all implemented? Were they implemented according to the timetable?
- Did these steps lead to the attainment of specific objectives? Were objectives revised? Were any additional objectives added?
- Were the overall goals achieved?
- To what extent were successes or failures a result of factors other than the response?
- What was the level of cooperation and participation among team members? Were the lines of communication between individuals and groups adequate?
- What changes in policies, procedures, or practices occurred or should have occurred during the implementation?

Impact Evaluation

- What were the expected results of the response?
- Were there any unintended effects?
- What will be measured and how? How long should the response remain operational to give a fair opportunity to show results or failure?
- How will data be collected? Did the response include a citizen survey, an examination of police statistics, or some other method?
- How will the data be analyzed? Was the response cost-effective? Did the response make a substantial difference?
- Will the response be replicated in other areas experiencing the same problem?

Case Studies in Problem-Solving

The following cases illustrate how police officers have applied a problem-solving approach to address a wide range of problems in the community.

For each case study, list what you consider to be the most important items of information at each stage of the SARA process.

Case Studies

Case Study 1. Robberies at a Major Transit Station

Scanning: Several robberies had taken place at a major transit station. A large amount of pedestrian traffic from the nearby shopping centre was creating a target-rich environment for criminals. The problem had been identified by local police, on-site security personnel, the public, and the transit police.

The most important items of information at this stage are:

1. _____

2. _____

3. _____

Analysis: The transit station had become a gathering place for young people travelling to the city core or suburban areas. The theatres and video arcades catered to youth populations in particular. Gangs and youth at risk in the area were preying on transit patrons in the form of "strong-arm" robberies. The station had become lucrative turf for groups of youths intent on exploiting the situation. They set up "offices" at this location. The sheer volume of patrons using the transit station (approximately 80,000 per day) made the usual surveillance techniques ineffective. Young victims hesitated to contact the police for fear of retribution from "gang types." In addition, the general public was intimidated by the number of young people loitering in and around the station. As a result, the number of incidents increased. The incidence of collateral crimes such as drug use, recruiting of juveniles for prostitution, and assaults also increased at the station.

Crime analysis found that strong-arm robberies occurred almost daily, with three or four incidents reported to the police per week. This pattern had been present for two years. Each robbery lasted approximately five minutes, and gang members had become so confident that they would not be caught that they took their time searching the victims' belongings (clothing, knapsacks, purses, etc.). Upon releasing their victims, the gang members even remained in the immediate area, confident their victims would not call the police.

The immediate impact was that young victims were traumatized. The public avoided the area due to fear. Local retailers lost business. The neighbourhood suffered a reputation for being a "hot spot" of crime activity.

The most important items of information in this stage are:

1. _____

2. _____

3. _____

Response: Police personnel in the specialized youth squad gathered additional information and increased the level of "perceived" police presence in the station area. The Crime Analysis Computer correlated the dates and locations of incidents and suspect information. Staff members also submitted a CPTED (crime prevention through environmental design) report to transit management that recommended removing benches in the area, cutting back shrubbery, and installing sodium lighting and CCTVs. Patrols by security personnel were also increased. Neighbourhood officers worked in tandem with the transit police to photograph and videotape loitering youth known to be involved in the strong-arm robberies. This "in your face" technique had two effects: (1) it helped to identify gang members, and (2) it created a type of "benign intimidation" that had a noticeable effect.

The goal of the response was to reduce the number of robberies and calls for service to the transit station. Vital partnerships were formed to share intelligence and surveillance equipment.

The most important items of information in this stage are:

1. _____

2. _____

3. _____

Evaluation (Assessment): There was a noticeable effect, but no data were provided about qualitative or quantitative results. No ongoing assessment measures were reported. *The most important items of information in this stage are:*

1. _____

2. _____

3. _____

Your Views: Using the SARA checklists presented above, assess whether you feel the problem-solving intervention was carried out well.

_____

_____

_____

_____

_____

What were the strengths of the approach?

_____

_____

_____

_____

_____

_____

What improvements would you suggest?

_____

_____

_____

_____

_____

Case Study 2. Trespassing at a High School

Scanning: A member of the regional police service received a letter from a local high school requesting advice on how to make the campus more secure from trespassers. The school had developed a reputation for not being safe. There had been 62 calls for service that year.

The most important items of information at this stage are:

1. _____

2. _____

3. _____

Analysis: There were 2,000 students at the school, and staff did not know every student. This allowed the problem of intruders to escalate. On any given day, the school received 20–25 trespassers, some travelling a distance of up to 25 kilometres to be with friends and acquaintances. Furthermore, by employing a CPTED approach, a number of deficiencies were identified, including: (1) a parking lot that divided the campus physically and psychologically into two halves, (2) a parking lot entrance characterized by an irregular border and multiple access points and escape routes, (3) an open and undifferentiated classroom and gymnasium area, (4) a lack of effective or well-placed signage, (5) a lack of walkways for people to move safely between school buildings, and (6) a complete lack of bus-loading facilities to address the loitering and congestion problems in the parking lot.

The problem had existed for less than a year and was creating a general nuisance and increasing fear, especially in relation to an incident when a handgun was brandished at a basketball game. School officials, students, and police were very concerned.

The most important items of information at this stage are:

1. _____

2. _____

3. _____

Response: A local officer developed a 64-page CPTED study illustrating a series of external changes to accomplish the following objectives:

1. Provide for the anticipated increase in pedestrian traffic between the soon-to-be-amalgamated schools.

2. Introduce regular natural surveillance opportunities into the parking lot and between school buildings.

3. Define the parking lot entrance better and develop clearly marked transitional zones between semi-public and private spaces.

4. Reduce parking-lot entry points from three to two while limiting escape routes by 50 percent.

5. Develop safe, raised concrete walkways and bus-loading areas complete with feeder sidewalks.

6. Establish a fire route.

7. Develop a sense of territoriality by effectively communicating campus rules, bolstering property rights, and reinforcing transitions from public to private space.

8. Slow traffic.

9. Distinguish undifferentiated corridors from more active hallways.

10. Establish out-of-bounds hallways and territorial feelings.

11. Provide the continued surveillance of problem corridors.

The plan also included reorienting the school's parking lot from an east–west bias to a north–south bias and strategically placing signs, speed bumps, and partitions throughout the campus and driveway areas. In addition, the plan recommended installing safety glass in problem corridors in order to increase surveillance. The document was presented to the principal and board of superintendents.

The goal of the plan was to reduce trespassing around the school. A broader objective was to develop an effective and efficient school environment.

The most important items of information at this stage are:

1. _____

2. _____

3. _____

Evaluation (Assessment): Construction began a few months after the presentation of the report. In the three years following the modifications, police occurrences at the 2,000-student high school dropped by an average of 87 percent, to between seven and nine occurrences per year. The environment became self-policing, and strong feelings of ownership developed. School officials, students, and police reported the positive effects of the new construction on the school.

The most important items of information at this stage are:

1. _____

2. _____

3. _____

Your Views: Using the SARA checklists presented above, assess whether you feel the problem-solving intervention was carried out well.

_____

_____

_____

_____

_____

_____

What were the strengths of the approach?

_____

_____

_____

_____

_____

What improvements would you suggest?

_____

_____

_____

_____

_____

Case Study 3. Traffic Accidents Involving Schoolchildren

Scanning: In 1990, there were 252 collisions involving pedestrians or cyclists under the age of 16. Eighty percent of the collisions involving children aged six to eight were "dart out" collisions resulting from children running out into traffic from between parked cars. The results were surprising because one of the seven rules first graders were routinely taught was not to play between parked cars. Records from 1985 to 1989 revealed the same statistics. In 1991, the Community Service Traffic Safety Branch of the local police service decided it was time to evaluate school traffic safety programs.

The most important items of information at this stage are:

1. _____

2. _____

3. _____

Analysis: Discussions of the Traffic Safety Advisory Committee revealed that several organizations were teaching completely different programs, which resulted in a scattered and inconsistent approach. Parents were identified as the best teachers because they had the most access to their children and were often willing to spend the time required for children to learn traffic safety. However, they often lacked the proper information or knowledge to take on this role. Moreover, in some family settings, traffic safety was not taught at all. Additional findings from a traffic safety research study confirmed the following conclusions:

1. Community agencies must work together to address traffic safety issues.

2. Police officers are not the best safety educators.

3. Dart-out collisions are a major cause for concern.

4. Parents often fail to become involved in teaching traffic safety.

5. Parents are an important part of any safety program.

Data analysis found that 250 collisions between cars and pedestrians or cyclists under the age of 16 occurred annually.

A previous traffic safety program—"Elmer's Safety Rules"—existed at the time the project was initiated. This 30-year-old program involved an elephant mascot who educated first graders on the seven rules to follow when around traffic.

Citizen representatives from city traffic departments, public health departments, early education organizations, and parents' groups participated in an advisory committee meeting in which they voiced their concerns about traffic safety education for children.

The most important items of information at this stage are:

1. _____

2. _____

3. _____

Response: Police collaborated with community members and organization representatives to adapt the "KIDestrian Book and Education Program," which was developed in Germany and consisted of simple and fun lessons that parents or other caregivers could teach their children. The program was then field-tested by parents at two local schools and by public health nurses. The officers then solicited corporations for sponsorship of the book. The team also sent letters and order forms to particular groups of people connected to the children. In addition, the police video training branch produced a promotional video. A media event was scheduled to launch the KIDestrian program. The goal of the project was to promote a consistent and effective form of traffic safety education in order to reduce the number of traffic accidents involving children.

To prepare, officers met with residents and various organization members to increase their knowledge of the problem and involve them in finding a solution to the problem of educating children on traffic safety. The advisory committee also obtained a copy of the original German program book and sought permission to use the material in order to develop a similar program.

Parents' groups, traffic engineers, health department officials, educators, and public health nurses provided available resources. Canadian Tire, an automotive, sporting goods, and hardware retailer, provided the finances to produce prototypes of the book in both English and French. Canada Post offered to package and distribute the materials at no cost, mailed out a fundraising request, provided a cash donation, purchased sidewalk chalk to accompany the books, and put advertising posters on postal trucks. *Today's Parent*, a national magazine, offered to print the books at a reduced cost and used their marketing expertise to enhance the book's layout. Finally, the video training branch of the police service contributed its resources as needed.

Citizen involvement occurred in the following manner. Two volunteer authors from the advisory committee worked with two police officers to develop the KIDestrian program and adapt the German book *Traffic Training: Parents Practise with Their Children* (English translation). Additional community members assisted in launching the program and in making further additions and revisions.

The most important items of information at this stage are:

1. _____
2. _____
3. _____

Evaluation (Assessment): At the time of this study, no quantifiable data existed to illustrate the impact of the program on reducing child traffic injuries. No correlation could be determined between the safety program and the number of child traffic accidents. However, qualitative measures found that the KIDestrian program reached the intended audience and that it was well received. As a result of feedback, the books were redesigned to include sections on rural and railroad-crossing safety. In addition, a new KIDestrian manual was developed to publicize the program.

The program was evaluated for approximately one year. Program evaluations were distributed to parents, day care workers, teachers, community groups, and the Canadian Association of Chiefs of Police.

The most important items of information at this stage are:

1. _____
2. _____
3. _____

Your Views: Using the SARA checklists presented above, assess whether you feel the problem-solving intervention was carried out well.

_____
_____
_____
_____
_____
_____

What were the strengths of the approach?

_____

_____

_____

_____

_____

_____

What improvements would you suggest?

_____

_____

_____

_____

_____

_____

_____

Case Study 4. Convenience Store Robberies

Scanning: An internal year-end report produced by the Police Service Robbery Unit identified one major convenience store chain as the target of 44 percent of total convenience store robberies. By February the following year, the same convenience store chain represented 49 percent of the total number of robberies for the year. The police service decided to initiate a community-based approach to resolving the problem.
The most important items of information at this stage are:

1. _____

2. _____

3. _____

Analysis: Through crime analysis it was found that several clerks had been victimized. Two clerks required hospital treatment after being slashed with knives. Three males had been identified as suspects in the robberies. The director of employee safety and training was consulted. Both the director and a detective attended all the high-risk and high-incident stores in the city, where physical security surveys and internal procedural reports were completed. The analysis showed that there were physical problems with security associated with the lighting and that there was a lack of adherence to cash-handling techniques and policies regarding cigarette lock-up and inventory control. The region became a first priority for security upgrading and store retrofitting.

The analysis concluded that the large numbers of robberies were consuming a significant percentage of police time. In addition, staff and customers at these stores were targets of violence. Moreover, the parent company was losing a great deal of money.
The most important items of information at this stage are:

1. _____

2. _____

3. _____

Response: Based on recommendations from the police and safety director, the company agreed to change the physical environment of the stores in order to discourage further robberies. Changes and upgrades included the following: a 24-hour time-lapse video recorder and camera; a video monitor to be displayed publicly near an entrance to educate the public that observation and recording were occurring; a locked cash-dispensing unit, cigarette safe, and locked safes for the counter area; additional alarms to be used in the event of personal threat or injury; computer upgrades to monitor entrances, exit tills, and storage areas; new, aggressive signage (large red and white signs placed in conspicuous areas alerting the public to video and security programs); upgraded levels of light; and revised robbery prevention manuals for all the dealers and stores.

Future outlined goals included corporate involvement in the Crime Stoppers program, corporate financing of additional projects undertaken by the robbery unit, public announcements highlighting the liaison with the police as well as crime prevention measures, and an improved cigarette disposal unit allowing removal of only a single package of cigarettes at a time, thus eliminating the "scoop and run" aspect of the robberies.

The goal of the community problem-solving plan was to reduce the number of armed robberies by increasing community, corporate, and police involvement and by educating community residents through media and corporate advertising. The police hoped to create a safer working environment for the convenience store employees and customers, and decrease the parent company's losses.

The most important items of information at this stage are:

1. _____

2. _____

3. _____

Evaluation (Assessment): Details of the evaluation have not been provided. Evaluate the problem-solving process. What outcomes are predictable? What impact do you think the problem-solving process would have in this case?

The most important items of information at this stage are:

1. _____

2. _____

3. _____

Your Views: Using the SARA checklists presented above, assess whether you feel the problem-solving intervention was carried out well.

_____

_____

_____

_____

_____

_____

What were the strengths of the approach?

_____

_____

_____

_____

_____

_____

What improvements would you suggest?

_____

_____

_____

_____

_____

Case Study 5. Dealing with a Person Suffering from a Mental Illness

Scanning: Over a period of eight months, a person dealing with a mental illness repeatedly escaped from a group home and broke into hair salons to satisfy a fetish for shaving his head and pubic hair. In addition, he would expose himself and masturbate in public without concern for others watching.
The most important items of information at this stage are:

1. _____

2. _____

3. _____

Analysis: A beat officer responded to a break-and-enter call still in progress at a hair salon. He later checked police records and found 22 files concerning the same individual. Each call tied up police resources. Property owners who were the victims of the break-and-enters suffered without any hope of compensation. The police met with the subject's parents, psychiatrist, and caseworkers, and executive members from Social Services, to understand the nature of the problem and possible response options. He learned that the subject posed a serious challenge for the caseworkers attempting to control his activities.

The goal was to identify strategies that would eliminate, or at least reduce, police response and public concern regarding the mischief to property and indecent exposure.
The most important items of information at this stage are:

1. _____

2. _____

3. _____

Response: Police met again with the subject's parents, psychiatrist, and caseworkers, as well as with executives from Social Services. All parties agreed to implement the following strategies: (1) a buzzer system was put in place to enable caseworkers to restrict the subject's comings and goings, (2) a plan was developed that would help the subject burn off excess energy by involving him in household chores and sporting events, and (3) the subject was permitted to use his own hair clippers to shave his head and pubic hair.
The most important items of information at this stage are:

1. _____

2. _____

3. _____

Evaluation (Assessment): As a result of the targeted response, there were no further calls in relation to this individual for the duration of the eight-month evaluation period. Following this period, the subject experienced several relapses in his behaviour and was charged with a mischief offence. Once police resumed their vigilance, however, there were only isolated incidents, and the subject did not appear on the police database for the following 12 months. The problem-solving process drastically reduced, though it did not eliminate, the subject's offensive behaviour.

The most important items of information at this stage are:

1. _____

2. _____

3. _____

Your Views: Using the SARA checklists presented above, assess whether you feel the problem-solving intervention was carried out well.

_____

_____

_____

_____

_____

_____

What were the strengths of the approach?

_____

_____

_____

_____

_____

_____

What improvements would you suggest?

_____

_____

_____

_____

_____

_____

Case Study 6. The Methamphetamine Lab

Scanning: The fire department responded to a call to extinguish a small fire at a fenced compound. Other workers from the neighbourhood had responded previously after the occupant set his clothing and footwear on fire while working with some chemicals. Emergency response found a fenced-in "fortress" that contained run-down buildings and a significant amount of toxic and volatile chemicals. Police involvement occurred when it became apparent that this was, in all probability, a clandestine methamphetamine laboratory. Several months later, neighbourhood residents reported unusual circumstances at this location. An ominous-looking, dense white cloud had formed over the compound. The occupant was reluctant to grant access to the emergency response team, but they entered nevertheless under the authority of the provincial Health Safety Act. The team quickly determined that the smoke resulted from another chemical experiment gone awry.

The most important items of information at this stage are:

1. _____

2. _____

3. _____

Analysis: Once the police concluded that the location was likely a meth lab, forensic experts were called in to examine the property. Unfortunately, they were unable to support this hypothesis. Various environmental agencies then assumed the case and served several control and access orders against the occupant. Because no charges were laid, all seized items had to be returned to the property owner.

Conversations with neighbourhood residents confirmed that the occupant had purchased an old abandoned house on an oversized city lot several years earlier. He had constructed a three-metre solid fence with a reinforced gate that blocked any view of the interior grounds. With his mysterious comings and goings at all hours of the night, the occupant had become known as the neighbourhood eccentric. Area residents had become accustomed to occasional clouds of smoke, colourful gaseous clouds, and strange noises. The police also learned that the science department at a local university had unknowingly supplied a good portion of the chemicals found at this location.

Among the agencies available to solve the problem were the environmental protection ministry and members of emergency response. Independent contractors from the Dangerous Goods Team of the Ministry of the Environment were also called in to clean up the location at a cost of nearly $100,000.

The most important items of information at this stage are:

1. _____

2. _____

3. _____

Response: The goal was to stop the occupant's experimentation with potentially hazardous materials and to ensure that the area was safe for local residents. To achieve this objective the following steps were taken.

A charge of common nuisance was laid against the occupant. The occupant remained silent throughout the entire investigation. The police began to work closely with the provincial Environmental Protection Ministry. Consultants to the ministry provided the expertise to conduct the safety investigation and to interpret the installation. Emergency response and their dangerous goods team dealt with the Safety Codes Act. A private company was assigned responsibility for the clean-up and the storage of unsafe substances. A multitude of city departments got involved as well, including water and sanitation, which used robotics to document the damage done to the drainage system downstream.

The most important items of information at this stage are:

1. _____

2. _____

3. _____

Evaluation (Assessment): The long-standing problem was brought to a halt. There is no longer a chemical laboratory at this location, and all noxious substances have been purged. Results were measured through direct observation, and no ongoing effort is required as there are no longer noxious chemicals on the site and utilities have been suspended.

The most important items of information at this stage are:

1. _____

2. _____

3. _____

Your Views: Using the SARA checklists presented above, assess whether you feel the problem-solving intervention was carried out well.

_____
_____
_____
_____
_____
_____
_____

What were the strengths of the approach?

_____
_____
_____
_____
_____
_____

What improvements would you suggest?

_____
_____
_____
_____
_____
_____

EXERCISES: KNOWLEDGE INTO PRACTICE

Exercise 1: When Is Problem-Solving an Appropriate Response? The Case of Doe v. the Metropolitan Toronto Board of Commissioners of Police

In 1986 a serial rapist attacked Jane Doe. She sued the chief of police, the Board of Commissioners of Police, and the two investigators, alleging that they were responsible for her injuries. Doe argued that she was part of a narrow and distinct group of potential victims. The victims were all single, white women who resided in second- or third-floor apartments with accessible balconies that had been used to gain access. The serial rapist confined his attacks to a small geographic area and an easily identifiable class of victims.

Doe claimed that the police were negligent in that they had failed to warn her of a danger that they knew (or ought to have known) existed or, in the absence of such a warning, that they had failed to adequately protect her against the danger.

The Ontario Court ruled:

The police failed in their duty to protect these women and [Jane Doe] in particular from the serial rapist the police knew to be in their midst by failing to warn so that they may have had the opportunity to take steps to protect themselves.

It is no answer for the police to say women are always at risk and as an urban adult living in downtown Toronto they have an obligation to look out for themselves. Women generally do, every day of their lives, conduct themselves and their lives in such a way as to avoid the general pervasive threat of male violence which exists in our society. Here the police were aware of a specific threat or risk to a specific group of women and they did nothing to warn those women of the danger they were in, nor did they take any measures to protect them. (Ontario Court [General Division] 1998, 61, quoted in Ceyssens and Childs 1998, 103).

It is important to note that during this investigation, there was another investigation going on in another part of the city involving more violent attacks, regarding which the police from the same department had issued a series of effective public warnings.

Questions
1. How would you have handled this investigation?
2. Would your response have been different if you knew who the offender was but did not have reasonable evidence on which to base an arrest? If so, how would it have been different?
3. Would the problem-solving process have been useful in this investigation? If so, what problems would it have addressed? If not, why not?
4. Which segments of the community were affected by this problem? What would have been an appropriate role for those communities?
5. Was there an appropriate role for the police to play in this investigation? What arguments would they have made for not informing the public?

Exercise 2. Identify a Problem in Your Community

1. Identify a current problem in your community.
2. Apply the problem-solving process to it.
3. Identify who is affected by the problem. What are the consequences related to the problem?
4. Make a detailed list of agencies and stakeholders that have an interest in resolving the problem. This may involve contacting the agency to determine whether it has a specific mandate to be involved in the problem.
5. Which groups have a mutual interest in improving the problem?

6. What are the objectives of your problem-solving process? If there are several aspects to the problem, what are the priorities, and why?
7. Where would you look to find more information about the problem?
8. In the assessment stage, what are the probable outcomes of your response (e.g., displacement, new problem)?
9. What steps or actions would you take to ensure that the problem does not appear again or manifest itself in a different way?

Exercise 3. The Criminal Apartment Building

Complete the SARA form for the following scenario. In your area, there is a rundown apartment building housing a mix of welfare tenants, new immigrants, elderly citizens, and criminals. Patrol officers have encountered several drug dealers, prostitutes, and other offenders with extensive backgrounds involving both property and violent crime. Over the last six months, you have noticed a dramatic increase in calls for service to or near this building, many of them coming through the 911 system as disturbances. The situation has now reached a point where the problems have spilled over into the surrounding area and nearby residents are becoming extremely frustrated and are complaining to the police chief and the mayor's office. You are directed to deal with this situation.

What approach would you take to address this problem, and what measures would you initiate? What difficulties might be encountered? How would you measure the effectiveness of your efforts?

The Problem-Solving Process

Scanning

Describe the problem (be specific):

_____

_____

_____

_____

_____

List the person(s) and/or groups affected by the problem:

_____

_____

_____

_____

_____

_____

Analysis

List the questions you have about this problem and the sources you would go to for the answers:

Question   Source

1. _____

2. _____

_____

3. _____

_____

4. _____

_____

5. _____

_____

6. _____

_____

Goals (Short and Long Term)

Short Term   Long Term

_____

_____

_____

_____

Responses

What strategies would you apply to solve this problem?

_____

_____

_____

_____

_____

Assessment

How would you measure the effectiveness of your problem-solving effort?

_____

_____

_____

_____

_____

Additional Notes on the Case

_____

_____

_____

_____

Exercise 4. Drug Trafficking in the Park

Complete the SARA form for the following scenario. The unemployed, the homeless, and new immigrants are more heavily frequenting a large public park. Drug dealing, public drinking, littering, and the occasional disturbance have resulted in several complaints to the police. Some elderly people who have traditionally used the park are now too frightened to enter it, and a local newspaper has started publicizing their concerns, exacerbating already high levels of fear in the neighbourhood. Park officials and community activists have asked for more police attention, but aggressive patrol tactics have led to complaints from political minority groups and street workers, who say that the park is for everyone. Summer is approaching, and the resulting increased use of the park holds the potential for even greater problems. This park is located within your zone of responsibility. Design a plan to address the problem.

What approach would you take to address this problem, and what measures would you initiate? What difficulties might be encountered? How would you measure the effectiveness of your efforts?

The Problem-Solving Process

Scanning

Describe the problem (be specific):

_____

_____

_____

_____

_____

List the person(s) and/or groups affected by the problem:

_____

_____

_____

_____

_____

Analysis

List the questions you have about this problem and the sources you would go to for the answers:

Question	Source
1.	
2.	
3.	
4.	
5.	
6.	

Goals (Short and Long Term)

Short Term	Long Term

Responses

What strategies would you apply to solve this problem?

_____

_____

_____

_____

_____

Assessment

How would you measure the effectiveness of your problem-solving effort?

_____

_____

_____

_____

_____

Additional Notes on the Case

_____

_____

_____

_____

Exercise 5. Trouble in the Nightclub District

Complete the SARA form for the following scenario. A trendy nightclub district has created many problems for the police in the last few months. Residents of a nearby exclusive downtown apartment complex have phoned in numerous complaints about drunks on the street and frequent fights, and police checks of the premises have found problems with overcrowding and serving liquor to minors. Patrol officers in the area have been so busy processing the large number of impaired drivers in club parking lots that they have lacked the time to give sufficient attention to the street disturbances that have been occurring.

After bar closing time the supply of taxis is very limited and there is no public transit service at this time either. Concerns exist that unless the situation is brought under control, it will become totally and permanently unmanageable. You are the team sergeant of the zone in which these incidents are occurring. Devise a plan to respond to and solve this problem.

What approach would you take to address this problem, and what measures would you initiate? What difficulties might be encountered? How would you measure the effectiveness of your efforts?

The Problem-Solving Process

Scanning

Describe the problem (be specific):

_____

_____

_____

_____

_____

_____

List the person(s) and/or groups affected by the problem:

_____

_____

_____

_____

_____

Analysis

List the questions you have about this problem and the sources you would go to for the answers:

Question	Source
1. _____	_____
2. _____	_____
3. _____	_____
4. _____	_____
5. _____	_____
6. _____	_____

Why the discrepancy?

Goals (Short and Long Term)

Short Term	Long Term
_____	_____
_____	_____
_____	_____
_____	_____

Responses

What strategies would you apply to solve this problem?

_____

_____

_____

_____

_____

Assessment

How would you measure the effectiveness of your problem-solving effort?

_____

_____

_____

_____

_____

Additional Notes on the Case

_____

_____

_____

_____

Exercise 6. Loitering Youths

A local convenience store has become a hangout for youths in the area. The shopping complex in which the store is situated also contains a fast-food restaurant and a gas station. The complex is within two blocks of a high school, and all of these services are open until midnight. Serious crimes in the complex are rare, but there are an increasing number of calls related to disturbances, shoplifting, and fights. On most occasions, by the time police officers arrive on the scene, the youths have fled. Both the convenience store and the fast-food outlet have expressed an interest in solving the problem, as the situation is affecting their business. The gas station owner has stated that he is not concerned about the issue because the youths do not frequent his station, and he does not believe they detrimentally affect his business.

What approach would you take to address this problem, and what measures would you initiate? What difficulties might be encountered? How would you measure the effectiveness of your efforts?

The Problem-Solving Process

Scanning

Describe the problem (be specific):

_____

_____

_____

_____

_____

_____

List the person(s) and/or groups affected by the problem:

_____

_____

_____

_____

_____

Analysis

List the questions you have about this problem and the sources you would go to for the answers:

Question	Source
1. _____	_____
2. _____	_____
3. _____	_____
4. _____	_____
5. _____	_____
6. _____	_____

Goals (Short and Long Term)

Short Term	Long Term
_____	_____
_____	_____
_____	_____
_____	_____

Responses

What strategies would you apply to solve this problem?

_____

_____

_____

_____

_____

Assessment

How would you measure the effectiveness of your problem-solving effort?

_____

_____

_____

_____

_____

Additional Notes on the Case

_____

_____

_____

_____

Exercise 7. Social Disorder in a Remote Community

Complete the SARA form for the following scenario. A remote northwestern Ontario community is experiencing a high rate of solvent abuse among teenagers. This includes sniffing "white-out" correction fluid stolen from the school and gasoline siphoned from snowmobiles and other equipment in the community. Within the past year, three teenagers have committed suicide while under the influence of solvents and two others have been evacuated for medical treatment.

Except during the summer months, this community is accessible only by air. Although the population is around 200, there is widespread crime, and there are other social problems. The community has acknowledged that problems exist among the teenagers and that action is required. A new chief and council have indicated an interest in addressing the solvent abuse problem among the teenagers.

You have recently been posted to this community for a two-year tour of duty. What approach would you take to address this problem, and what measures would you initiate? What difficulties might be encountered? How would you measure the effectiveness of your efforts?

The Problem-Solving Process

Scanning

Describe the problem (be specific):

_____

_____

_____

_____

_____

_____

List the person(s) and/or groups affected by the problem:

_____

_____

_____

_____

_____

Analysis

List the questions you have about this problem and the sources you would go to for the answers:

	Question	Source
1.	_____	_____
2.	_____	_____
3.	_____	_____
4.	_____	_____
5.	_____	_____
6.	_____	_____

Goals (Short and Long Term)

Short Term	Long Term
_____	_____
_____	_____

_____

_____

Responses

What strategies would you apply to solve this problem?

_____

_____

_____

_____

_____

Assessment

How would you measure the effectiveness of your problem-solving effort?

_____

_____

_____

_____

_____

Additional Notes on the Case

_____

_____

_____

_____

REFERENCES

Ceyssens, P., and S. Childs. 1998. "*Doe v. Metropolitan Toronto Board of Commissioners of Police* and the Status of Public Oversight of the Police in Canada." *Alberta Law Review* 36(4): 1000.

Eck, J.E., and W. Spelman. 1987. "Who Ya Gonna Call? The Police as Problem-Busters." *Crime and Delinquency* 33(1): 31–52.

Eck, J.E., and W. Spelman. 1987a. *Problem-Solving: Problem-Oriented Policing in Newport News*. Washington, DC: Police Executive Research Forum.

Goldstein, H. 1987. "Toward Community-Oriented Policing: Potential, Basic Requirements, and Threshold Questions." *Crime and Delinquency* 3: 6–30.

—. 1990. *Problem-Oriented Policing*. New York: McGraw-Hill.

Hough, M., and N. Tilley. 1998. *Getting the Grease to the Squeak: Research Lessons for Crime Prevention*. London: Police Research Group, Home Office.

LaVigne, N., and Wartell, J. 2015. *Robbery of Pharmacies*. Problem-Oriented Guides for Police, Problem-Specific Guide no. 73. Washington, DC: Office of Community Oriented Policing Services.

Ontario Police College. 2016. "Emerging Practices in Ontario Policing." https://www.opcva.ca/learning; https://www.mcscs.jus.gov.on.ca/english/police_serv/OPC/OPCVA/opc_opcva.html.

Ontario Provincial Police. 1997. *The "How Do We Do It" Manual*. Orillia: Community Policing Development Centre.

Osborne, D., and T. Gaebler. 1993. *Reinventing Government: How the Entrepreneurial Spirit Is Transforming the Public Sector*. New York: Penguin.

RCMP. 2015. RCMP in New Brunswick Annual Report 2015, *Building a Safer New Brunswick*. http://www.rcmp-grc.gc.ca/en/nb/rcmp-znew-brunswick-annual-report-2015.

Scott, M. 2000. *Problem-Oriented Policing: Reflections on the First 20 Years*. Washington, DC: US Department of Justice, Office of Community-Oriented Policing Services.

The Canadian Press Images/Francis Vachon

The Key Players in Community Policing

The Community Policing Police Service

Learning Objectives

After completing this chapter, you should be able to:

- Discuss how community policing has affected the way police services are organized,
- Discuss the role of mission, value, and vision statements in policing,
- Describe the techniques of environmental scans, bench-marking, best practices, growth positions, and performance indicators,
- Discuss what is meant by the police service as a learning organization,
- Describe the Policing for Results Survey used by the Ontario Provincial Police,
- Discuss the role of teams in community policing,
- Describe the role of strategic planning and business plans in community policing, and
- Discuss the Ontario Provincial Police's customized approach and delivery process.

Community Policing: providing community-oriented police services in a manner that reflects the needs of the community. A community policing approach involves partnering with other members of the community to gain their assistance in reducing crime, maintaining peace and order, and promoting safety.

Source: Photo by Peter Power/Toronto Star via Getty Images

INTRODUCTION

Community policing requires both a philosophical shift in the way that police departments think about their mission, as well as a commitment to structural changes this new form of policing demands.

—*Trojanowicz and Bucqueroux (1990)*

Police services across the country have often struggled with the question of how to redesign the organization and delivery of police services in order to incorporate the philosophy and principles of community policing. Many of those principles require rethinking how police services are organized. Community policing is about much more than merely introducing new programs in the community; it involves a substantial shift in organization and delivery as well as an expansion of the roles and responsibilities of line officers.

In reviewing the experience of many Canadian police services with community policing, there has often been a "cart before the horse" problem. Initiatives have been undertaken without a clear understanding of the organizational and operational changes required to institutionalize this new model of service delivery. In the absence of a blueprint for implementing these principles, individual police leaders and police organizations have been left on their own to craft the structural, policy, and program changes required to "do" community policing (Rosenbaum, Yeh, and Wilkinson 1994). This has resulted in considerable diversity across the country in how the concept of community policing has been interpreted and implemented. A key element of community policing is recording the lessons of the past so that future efforts make substantive improvements rather than simply "reinvent the wheel" or even make the same mistakes again.

In this chapter, we examine the organizational and institutional changes required by community policing as well as the tools and techniques used by police services to deliver services within a community policing framework.

ORGANIZATIONAL REQUIREMENTS FOR COMMUNITY POLICING

The perfect community policing department does not exist. No department is a paragon of the values represented by the concept of community policing, nor is there one model of community policing.

—*Hartmann, Brown, and Stephens (1988)*

Organizational change is difficult under the best of circumstances. Community policing requires police services to re-examine all aspects of the organization, administration, and delivery of policing services. This requires time, vision, commitment, planning, and an ability to question and assess outcomes constantly. In this chapter, we examine the key organizational requirements for implementing the principles of community policing.

In the words of R.D. Hunter and T. Barker (1993), two US police scholars, discussions of community policing tend to be afflicted by a considerable amount of "BS and buzzwords." Trendy terms are applied to traditional practices, and new programs are developed in the absence of any framework for delivering policing services. To fulfill the philosophy and the principles of community policing, police services must make a number of significant changes in how they organize, administer, and deliver their services. This is easier said than done.

A number of ingredients are required in any effort to implement community policing. Many of these are discussed throughout this chapter.

Table 6.1 presents a matrix used by the Seattle Police Department that can be used to determine the particular stage of development in the process of moving towards adopting and implementing the principles of community policing. As an organization evolves

Table 6.1 Community Policing Stage Assessment Matrix: Development Stages

Development Stage	Program Components/Elements	
Stage 1: Awareness/discovery	Problem-solving approach	Program evaluation
Initial interest in the new style of policing from magazine articles/conferences/exchange of information with other police personnel; take action to learn more about new community policing approach; discuss use of new programs in meetings and formulate tentative new program ideas.	General discussions about how projects are selected held between police and citizens; concerns about involvement of citizens and security issues addressed; concerns about police workload and limited resources addressed; little or no interaction with public about problems.	No specific evaluation questions considered relevant at this stage; basic process evaluations of planning and information-gathering timeliness (if formal project designation) considered.
Stage 2: Experimental/exploratory	Problem-solving approach	Program evaluation
Police agency and/or city identify potential applications of community policing model; acquire more information about specific programs and plan/implement pilot efforts; begin limited discussions with other city personnel to familiarize them with new problem-solving approach; evaluate pilot projects.	Initial problem-solving meetings on how to set agendas/select problems and procedures; solution approaches reflect little creativity or involvement of other (non-police) resources; feedback on outcomes requested by citizens but viewed as time consuming by police.	Process evaluations and tracking of activities; report actions/successes of problem-solving projects; initial use of customer surveys to identify needs/priorities.
Stage 3: Commitment/understanding	Problem-Solving approach	Program evaluation
More in-depth analysis of information about community policing programs and requirements; review results of pilot programs; establish open communications links with other city departments and provide educational materials; develop and conduct extensive training programs; expand involvement of citizens/business groups and build trust; police agency, city officials, and other departments analyze required organizational and managerial changes; commit resources and begin coordinated implementation.	Working relationships among police/citizens/other city departments built on trust and respect; problem targets selected by community; long-term problems addressed; level of creative and innovative solutions increases; amount and quality of analysis increase.	Develop outcome/impact measures for performance evaluations tied to goals; use customer surveys to assess priorities and satisfaction with results of city/police efforts.
Stage 4: Proficiency/renewal	Problem-solving approach	Program evaluation
The new approach to police service delivery and community/business partnership becomes ingrained in police agency operations and management style; most city departments focus on coordinated service delivery; ongoing and automatic processes for service improvement and innovation are operational; innovative managerial approaches and structural changes to the organization completed (and revised as necessary) based on the new mission and vision.	Joint city-wide problem-solving program involves regular meetings and open communications process; private sector and regional resources are part of process; coordinated service delivery is city-wide standard.	Continuous process, impact, and project monitoring part of normal operations; constant "fine tuning" of performance measures with focus on service improvement.

Source: D. W. Fleissner, *Community Policing Stage Assessment Model for Implementation Planning and Organizational Measurement*. Seattle: Seattle Police Department and National Institute of Justice (1997), p. 62.

through each stage, the principles and practices of community-based policing become more embedded in the organization. By the time a police organization has evolved to the fourth stage (and many, if not most, do not get this far!), the organization is practising community policing in a strategic way.

History has proven it can be quite difficult for police organizations to advance the basic model of community policing to one that represents a high degree of strategic integration in which the community is able to resolve many deeply embedded issues. One of the difficulties in implementing community policing is moving from concept to implementation. Too often, well-intentioned efforts are applied to a problem, but the intervention has very little chance of succeeding because it does not match the level of community development. For example, a community that requires a high level of reactive response from the police is unlikely to successfully implement a Community Watch program. In Ontario, the Community Mobilization and Engagement Model of Community Policing is taught to all police officers in the province through an online learning program called the "*Emerging Practices in Ontario Policing*" course, brought to you by the Ontario Police College (OPC) and Laurier's Centre for Public Safety and Well-Being. The "*Emerging Practices in Ontario Policing*" modules were developed through a partnership among the Sault Ste. Marie Police Service (SSMPS), the OPC, and Wilfrid Laurier University.

The training helps police officers assess the stage of community development—that is, the underlying supports that contribute to community well-being. This allows a better assessment of the degree of community intervention required from the police. Strategies can be customized to fit the communities' overall state of readiness.

These modules are designed in such a way that the SSMPS and community partners can use them as a guide when considering collaborating to increase safety and well-being for everyone in Sault Ste. Marie. These practices all stem from a growing awareness that community safety and well-being is not just a police matter, but a responsibility to be shared among police, social agencies and organizations, the municipal government, and the community itself. The modules will provide you with an overview of three transformative practices in policing that have emerged in recent years throughout Ontario.

The Police Leader and Community Policing

The task facing modern police leadership oriented to CPB [community-based policing] is obviously daunting. Added to the typical leadership responsibilities is the challenge of effecting major organizational transformation.

—*D. Clairmont (1996)*

There is little doubt that police leaders are in the spotlight as never before. They must be oriented towards action and results rather than towards merely maintaining the status quo. Police leaders must be educated, be creative, have vision (as well as the ability to communicate that vision), and be willing to take risks and break with tradition. Moreover, they must apply all of these qualities at a time when increasing demands are being placed upon the police, including demands arising from significant human resource and financial pressures and a broadened security policing mandate. The priorities and challenges of contemporary police leaders can be summarized as needing to be focused on three Cs: cost of policing, conduct of police officers, and crime control.

Police chiefs and chief constables play a critical role in implementing the principles of community policing and building the organizational capacity to facilitate community-based policing. Section 41(1) of the Ontario Police Services Act lists the duties of the chief of police, two of which are ensuring that members of the police force carry out their duties in accordance with the act in a manner that reflects the needs of the community, and ensuring that the police force provides community-oriented police services.

A CLOSER LOOK 6.1

TOOLS FOR IMPROVING POLICE LEADERSHIP

While there are many community roads into a police service, the nature and structure of Canadian policing, and the statutory framework for delivering police service, can expose a police chief to "tipping point" events signifying that long-standing issues have not been adequately resolved and that crisis management is required. None of this bodes well for the police chief. To avoid this situation, a number of resources are on the "must read" list for those chiefs. These include:

- *2013 Summit on the Economics of Policing: Strengthening Canada's Policing Advantage*
- *Tyler's Troubled Life: The Story of One Young Man's Life Towards a Life of Crime (Research Report)*
- *Policing Canada in the 21st Century: New Policing for New Challenges (2014)*
- *Missing and Murdered Aboriginal Women: A National Operations Review*
- *The Police and Community Engagement Review (PACER report)*
- *Framework for Planning: Community Safety and Wellbeing (Ontario)*
- *Braidwood Commission on the Death of Robert Dziekanski*
- *RCMP Mental Health Strategy (2014–2019)* and *Mental Health Action Plan*

The Canadian Association of Chiefs of Police and the provincial Association of Chiefs of Police actively develop initiatives to improve the quality of police leadership across Canada.

Implementing community policing presents police leaders with a formidable management challenge. Police leaders must abandon traditional command and control practices and decentralize power in order to create a much more participatory organizational environment; within that environment, it must be possible to incorporate the ideas and requirements of line officers. Table 6.2 illustrates some of the changes in management that are required for community policing.

The task for senior police leadership is to create a framework within which the role of the line officer can be transformed from one of reacting to incidents and "crime fighting" to one of actively solving problems and understanding the needs and issues of the community, and working in partnership with the community to address these issues.

There are key differences between *managing* a police service and *leading* a police service:

- The manager administers; the leader innovates.
- The manager is a copy; the leader is an original.
- The manager maintains; the leader develops.

Table 6.2 Changes in Management Required for Community Policing

From	To
Bureaucratic management	Strategic management
Administrative management	People management
Maintenance management	Change management

Source: C. Murphy, and C.T. Griffiths, "Community Based Policing—A Review of the Issues, Research, and Development of a Provincial Policy," Unpublished research report prepared for the Commission of Inquiry, Policing in British Columbia. Victoria: Ministry of Attorney General. (1994), p. 8. Copyright © Province of British Columbia. All rights reserved. Reproduced with permission of the Province of British Columbia.

- The manager focuses on systems and structures; the leader focuses on people.
- The manager relies on control; the leader inspires trust.
- The manager has a short-range view; the leader has a long-range perspective.
- The manager asks how and when; the leader asks what and why.
- The manager has an eye on the bottom line; the leader has an eye on the horizon. (Bennis 1989, 44)

In describing the transition required to implement a management philosophy of total integrated policing in the Halton Regional Police Service, the chief of police stated: "Our managers will become coaches and team leaders rather than drivers and bosses and will help contribute to the team building and problem solving at lower levels … Our success and real solutions to everyday problems will only come from staff involvement" (Halton Regional Police Service 2000).

Implementing Community Policing

Contemporary policing has become very complex, and the manner in which police services are structured across the country makes it very difficult for chiefs of police to lead progressive change in police organizations. Those organizations must plan for both the long term and the near term. All of the trends we identified in Chapter 2 have combined to make police work more complex than ever. And it is not just the police who are having to adapt to these challenges: *all* public services are increasingly being scrutinized to ensure that the services they provide, and the investments made to provide them, are actually producing tangible improvements in the community. This complexity of public service delivery is encompassed by the acronym "VUCA"—volatility, uncertainty, complexity, ambiguity. In Critical Perspectives 6.1, we describe the challenges that a police chief must manage effectively.

CRITICAL PERSPECTIVES 6.1

BEING A CHIEF IN THE VUCA WORLD!

It is not easy providing police services to Canada's diverse and remote communities. To be successful in policing modern communities, a police chief needs to deliver high-quality service in an environment characterized by the acronym VUCA (volatile, uncertain, complex, and ambiguous). Here are some of the issues that Canadian police chiefs are dealing with.

Volatility: The challenge is unexpected or unstable and may be of unknown duration, but it is not necessarily hard to understand; knowledge about it is often available.

Example: In the Toronto Pride Parade in 2016, the Black Lives Matter (BLM) movement (see Chapter 10) staged a protest and demanded that police not be a visible presence, such as marching in uniform or having floats, in future parades. Citing divisions in the LGBTQ community, the chief of the Toronto Police Service decided that the TPS would not participate in the parade in 2017.

Complexity: The situation has many interconnected parts and variables. Some information is available or can be predicted, but the volume or nature of it can overwhelm the process.

Example: Changes to federal drug laws with respect to the legalization of marijuana will impose many challenges on the police ranging from the enforcement of new laws to the management of critical human resource issues, including police officers using medically prescribed marijuana.

Ambiguity: Causal relationships are completely unclear. No precedents exist. You face unknown unknowns.

Example: In Ontario (and across Canada) police agencies have traditionally conducted "stop and talk" checks on people where police have encountered someone who they feel seems out of place at the time. This generalized suspicion results in a brief report submitted to the police database. This practice, referred to as "carding" in Ontario, is now illegal, and new procedures have been implemented in Ontario Regulation 58/16—Collection of Identifying Information in Certain Circumstances—Prohibition and Duties. Police officers and their respective agencies must adapt past practices to modern requirements.

Uncertainty: Despite a lack of other information, the event's basic cause and effect are known. Change is possible but not a given.

Example: Since the Supreme Court of Canada's decision in *R. v. Jordan* [2016] SCC 27, strict time limits have been placed on the time that can elapse before trials must be heard by a court. Due to the increasingly complex nature of police investigations, time has become an additional element for police to take into account.

Mission, Value, and Vision Statements

The right mission of an organization is not a fixed, permanent thing ... The challenge is to find the highest value use of an organization's capabilities in its existing environment, not to assume that its mission remains what it has always been.

—*Moore (2003)*

Police organizations today have developed **mission, value,** and **vision statements** that set out the general principles for providing policing services. These statements generally incorporate the basic tenets of community policing and reflect the general orientation of the police service. The mission of the York Regional Police Service is "We will ensure our citizens feel safe and secure through excellence in policing"; the mission of the Winnipeg Police Service is "Build safe and healthy communities across Winnipeg through excellence in law enforcement and leadership in crime prevention through social development." Check out the vision and value statements of the Royal Newfoundland Constabulary in In Your Community 6.1 and the mission statement of the Edmonton Police Service in A Closer Look 6.2. Do you notice any resemblance between these mission statements and Sir Robert Peel's principles? Now compare these mission statements to that of the Anishinabek Police Service, an Indigenous police service in Ontario, in A Closer Look 6.3.

IN YOUR COMMUNITY 6.1

THE ROYAL NEWFOUNDLAND CONSTABULARY: VISION AND VALUES

Vision

Safer communities through policing excellence.

Values

In accomplishing its vision the Royal Newfoundland Constabulary believes in:

- Foremost, protecting and helping people;
- Treating people with respect;
- Delivering police services compassionately, ethically and free of bias;
- Using police authority judiciously;

(continues)

- Seeking the truth;
- Working with the community to identify and resolve crime and disorder problems; and
- Being approachable, accessible, and of service to every individual.

Within the organization, the Royal Newfoundland Constabulary believes in:

- Embracing change;
- Approaching duty diligently and enthusiastically;
- Continuing the professional development of each individual through education and training;
- Being a team player—acting in harmony, being respectful and supportive of individuals; and
- Upholding the proud traditions of policing and the Royal Newfoundland Constabulary.

Source: *Used with permission of Royal Newfoundland Constabulary, https://www.rnc.gov.nl.ca/about-us/*

Redesigning the Organizational Structure

Community policing requires that police services make significant changes to their traditional, hierarchical organizational structures. These include decentralizing decision-making and giving line officers more authority and autonomy to work collaboratively with community residents; trimming the bureaucracy, which often hinders officer initiatives; reducing specialization in the police service and expanding the role of police constables as generalists; and "flattening" the organizational structure by reducing the levels of management and supervision. Over the past decade, police services across Canada have made a number of efforts to reorganize and restructure the delivery of police services and to improve the effectiveness of service delivery.

A CLOSER LOOK 6.2

MISSION AND VISION STATEMENT AND CORE VALUES OF THE EDMONTON POLICE SERVICE

Mission Statement

To increase public safety through excellence in the prevention, intervention and suppression of crime and disorder.

Vision

To make Edmonton the safest major city in Canada and for the Edmonton Police Service to be recognized as a leader in policing.

Core Values

Integrity—Doing the right things for the right reasons all the time.

Accountability—Responsible for our own decisions and actions.

Respect—Treating others as we would like to be treated.

Innovation—Pursuing excellence and creativity.

Courage—Maintain strength in the face of our greatest challenges.

Community—Respect and honour the diverse communities that we are Dedicated to Protect and Proud to Serve.

Sources: Used with permission of Edmonton Police Service, http://www.edmontonpolice.ca/AboutEPS.aspx

A CLOSER LOOK 6.3

ANISHINABEK POLICE SERVICES MISSION STATEMENT

The Anishinabek Police Service provides for the safety and well-being of our communities and our citizens through traditional peacekeeping efforts. We support victims of crime and are committed to the protection of inherent rights and freedoms.

We work cooperatively with our communities and our citizens to address their needs and priorities through the adhesion to community policing principles including, community involvement, public education, and unbiased enforcement strategies. We provide these services and supports with transparency and accountability.

Source: Used with permission of Anishinabek Police Service, http://www.apscops.org/?businessplan

Today, this reorganization often involves complex structures in which social agencies with related mandates work alongside police officers in the same facility. For example, while police typically use terms such as "crime prevention," school boards talk about "safe schools," and health care professionals focus on the "social determinants of health." What these sectors are all referring to is community safety and well-being. The shared conversation, now more than ever, is about preventing crime through social development; this is why police resources and services are increasingly being delivered through coordinated, integrated service delivery teams.

The impact of reorganization on police personnel should not be underestimated. It has the potential to be a major obstacle to implementing community policing. Flattening the organizational structure and increasing the emphasis on line-level police work has direct implications for the careers of many police personnel, particularly those officers in middle management. Reform often involves eliminating or reducing senior-level positions and streamlining the organizational hierarchy.

The management structure of a traditional police service is a hierarchical pyramid, reflecting a top-down system in which senior management issues directives to be carried out by line officers. A one-way flow of information—from senior officers to line officers—ensures obedience to the goals and objectives established by senior officers. Community policing turns the traditional pyramid on its head: now, senior police managers provide leadership and support for line officers, who implement the principles of community policing daily. The focus shifts from achieving the goals set by senior managers to building communities, keeping the peace, and solving problems. In short, implementing community policing requires police services to invert the traditional **police pyramid** (see Figure 6.1).

Figure 6.1 Inverting the Police Pyramid

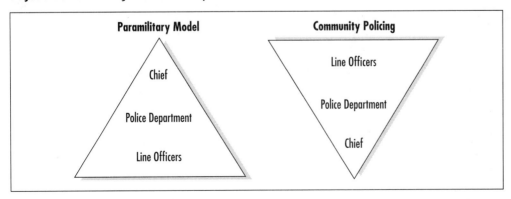

Source: Reprinted with permission from *Community Policing: How to Get Started,* 2nd Ed. Copyright 1997 Matthew Bender & Company Inc. a member of the LexisNexis Group. All Rights Reserved.

Across Canada, today's police agencies have organized themselves to maximize strategic partnerships with their communities. This is particularly evident in relation to front-line services that address the needs of vulnerable populations, including youth at risk, individuals living in poverty, and those suffering from addiction and mental health issues. Most Ontario police agencies, for example, have aligned their organizational structures to support the OACP's Community Mobilization and Engagement Model of Community Policing (see Chapter 10). In addition, the delivery of police services is increasingly being done through integrated units comprised of police officers from a number of police agencies. In BC Lower Mainland, a number of integrated Provincial Police Units operate, including the following:

- Combined Forces Special Enforcement Unit
- Integrated Road Safety Unit
- Integrated Child Exploitation Team
- Hate Crime Task Force
- Integrated Sexual Predator Observation Team
- Integrated Gang Task Force
- Integrated Technological Crime Unit

In short, community policing has evolved considerably since its adoption in Canada nearly 40 years ago.

What does the organizational structure of a community policing police service look like? Each municipal or regional force has taken a different approach to changing its organizational structure to incorporate the principles and practice of community policing. Figure 6.2 illustrates the organizational structure of the York Regional Police Service. Notice how the organization addresses contemporary demands for police service within its structure and how sections are grouped together to maximize organizational effectiveness. For example, York Regional Community Services incorporates the Community Mobilization Bureau.

Reorienting the Organization: The Police Service as a Learning Organization

For an organization to learn, its systems for learning from its own experiences and those of other organizations must be explicit as well as understood by all employees ... Organizations must value and recognize learning, be intentional about learning, or be ones that have discovered how to learn ... [This] will enable them to adapt quickly notwithstanding rapid technological, social and economic changes ... Learning also has to do with "unlearning" ... the ability to cast off those practices determined by experience to be redundant and counterproductive.

—*D.S. Campbell (1992)*

A key component in community policing is the concept of the **police service as a learning organization**. A learning organization is "an organization that is continually expanding its capacity to create its future" (Senge 1994, 14). This involves creating an organizational environment that interacts with its external environment rather than being isolated from it. The goal is greater organizational effectiveness through the use of a number of systems or processes, including:

- *generating a holistic view of the organization*: ensuring that police personnel understand the objectives of the organization and their role in achieving them;
- *obtaining and using information about the "external" environment*: developing networks with other agency personnel, such as social workers and community groups, and conducting research and incorporating research findings into operational policy and practice;
- *encouraging the development of new knowledge*: encouraging officers to think creatively and independently and to take risks, and ensuring that new recruits have an opportunity to contribute ideas;

Figure 6.2 York Regional Police Organizational Structure

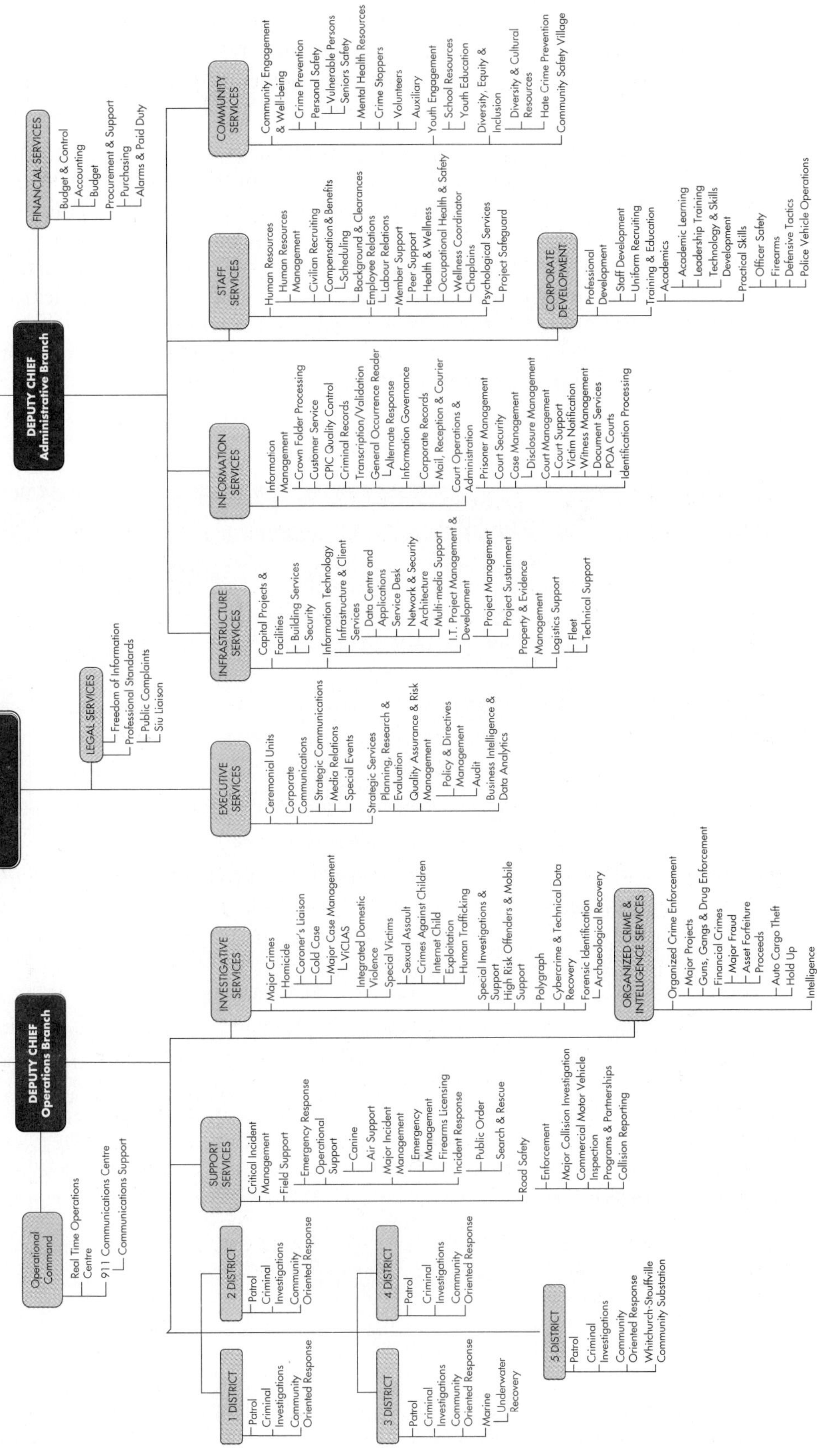

Source: Courtesy of York Regional Police.

- *learning from other organizations*: forging alliances with public and private sector organizations to facilitate sharing information;
- *providing feedback to officers about their performance*: considering the results from community surveys, using different criteria to assess officers' contributions to overall objectives, and using roll calls and debriefings effectively; and
- *questioning assumptions*: giving officers the opportunity to question longstanding policies and practices and the rationale for them. (Campbell 1992, 253–62)

In the learning organization, employees continually expand their knowledge base and improve their performance and the effectiveness of their activities. The Province of Ontario has given considerable attention to developing the capacity for police services to become learning organizations. The Police Learning System (PLS), implemented in 1995, redesigned the training, education, and development programs for police personnel. The PLS Advisory Committee is tasked with identifying new trends and strategies to enhance the learning capabilities of police services throughout the province.

Another key resource in Ontario is the Ontario Provincial Police Community Safety Services, described in In Your Community 6.2.

IN YOUR COMMUNITY 6.2

ONTARIO PROVINCIAL POLICE COMMUNITY SAFETY SERVICES

The Ontario Provincial Police Community Safety Services provides expertise to the OPP in the areas of crime prevention, community safety and well-being planning, risk analysis, and mitigation. In doing this the OPP has embraced Ontario's Mobilization and Engagement Model of Community Policing (see Chapter 10). Community Safety Officers serve in Ontario communities building relationships and working collaboratively with local community partners to support social development and increase community safety. CSOs work closely with communities to effectively mobilize and engage the community based on the degree of community supports in place. One of the goals is to develop sustainable strategic partnerships encouraging crime prevention through social development at the community level and results in the development of community capacity to build a safe community.

Community Safety Services takes a lead role in coordinating large crime prevention programs—such as Community Watch, Cottage Watch, and so on—to ensure that the delivery of these programs is consistent throughout the province and aligned with the communities' own abilities to become safer. The unit is designed to support the development of police–community partnerships, enhance the problem-solving capacities of line officers, and identify and encourage the use of best practices in preventing and responding to crime and disorder. Developing strategies to assist with community engagement is a key service provided by the Unit.

The development of resources such as the OPP's Community Safety Service increases the capacity of the OPP to support the organizational priorities of community safety and well-being and improve adaptability to emerging risks facing Ontario's communities. You can learn more about the OPP's Community Safety Services at www.opp.ca.

Source: OPP, Community Safety Services, found at https://www.opp.ca/index.php?id=115&entryid=5 6b79a118f94ace85c28d180

The creation of learning organizations is key to the success of a community-policing police service. At the heart of the learning organization is *continuous learning,* which helps an organization innovate, learn from past experience, and manage the change process rather than simply react to it. An organization that is capable of learning not only innovates but also can be much more strategic, and hence efficient, in applying resources where they can be most effective.

A concept related to the learning organization is called "intelligence-led policing." Intelligence-led policing (also referred to as evidence-based policing) can be defined as:

[A] collaborative enterprise based on improved intelligence operations and community-oriented policing and problem solving … To implement intelligence-led policing, police organizations need to re-evaluate their current policies and protocols. Intelligence must be incorporated into the planning process to reflect community problems and issues. Information sharing must become a policy, not an informal practice. Most important, intelligence must be contingent on quality analysis of data. The development of analytical techniques, training, and technical assistance needs to be supported.

—*Bureau of Justice Assistance [US] (2005)*

It is similar in the attempt to ensure that the organization learns in an institutional way from its experiences. It is dependent on technology and the IT resources of police services. You will recall that one trend is towards integrating databases in an effort to improve knowledge acquisition and make better decisions based on business intelligence. For this reason, we are seeing steps to do the following:

- Build the infrastructure for "smarter cities" in which police databases are integrated to share information between police services, in tandem with efforts to link public CCTV cameras through integrated public security networks.
- Integrate justice system databases to ensure more comprehensive decision-making throughout the justice system.

Adopting a Corporate Model: Strategies and Measures

Increasingly, police services are adopting strategies and measures traditionally found in the private sector. The language of modern policing includes terms such as *environmental scans, benchmarking, intelligence-led policing, best practices, results-based accountability, strategic planning, community surveying, performance metrics, performance indicators,* and *outcomes.* These efforts are designed to improve the efficiency, effectiveness, and accountability of police services while responding to increased public demands for service, despite budgetary constraints. This has become known as the **corporate model of policing,** and it complements the requirements of community policing besides meeting the needs of the municipal governments that allocate the funds for police services.

Within this framework, governments can often accomplish more by entering into strategic partnerships with private sector or not-for-profit organizations, or by reducing their role so as to allow other organizations to do things better. This trend is largely a response by government agencies in general to reduce the direct delivery of some services and to become facilitators rather than doers. In just about every urban centre in Canada today, there has been restructuring of services to better respond to very difficult community problems related to mental health, addictions, and the specific needs of vulnerable populations. This evolution will result in much more strategic and sophisticated service delivery models in which issues and services are funded as opposed to more traditional models of budgeting. Some key components of the corporate model are discussed below.

Strategic Planning

Strategic planning isn't an "event" or "exercise" in TPS [the Toronto Police Service]. It's a dynamic and continuous process that helps the organization and its units set objectives, develop programs to achieve them, and arrange its resources to make that happen.
—*Toronto Police Service (1999)*

As police services adopt the principles of community policing and make more effective and efficient use of their resources, the functions of planning and research assume even more importance. They provide the organization with the capacity not only to assess the effectiveness of specific policy and program initiatives but also to anticipate future demands that are likely to be made on the department.

A key component of the planning process is the **business plan**, also known as the **strategic plan**. In Ontario, the Adequacy and Effectiveness of Police Services standards (Sections 30(1) and 30(2)) require all police service boards to produce a business plan for their police force at least once every three years. This plan must set out the core business and function of the police force and include how it will provide adequate and effective police services. It must also establish quantitative and qualitative performance objectives and indicators relating to:

- the provision of community-based crime-prevention initiatives;
- community patrol;
- criminal investigation;
- community satisfaction with police services;
- emergency calls for service;
- violent crime and clearance rates for violent crime;
- property crime and clearance rates for property crime;
- youth crime and clearance rates for youth crime;
- police assistance to the victims of crime;
- revictimization rates;
- road safety;
- information technology;
- resource planning; and
- police facilities.

Note that several of the above-noted areas are most often associated with traditional police practice, again illustrating that the strategies and approaches in community policing are best viewed as an expansion of police activities rather than a replacement of them.

Taylor (1999, 14) has identified the requirements and benefits of strategic planning. The requirements include:

- an accurate assessment of the strengths and weaknesses of the service;
- the opportunities for improved service and the threats to its effectiveness;
- a comprehensive review of the operational environment, including incident statistics and demographic data;
- consideration of provincial standards;
- opportunities for collaborative efforts with other agencies or private industry;
- a thorough understanding of service parameters and of the extent to which the agency meets demands for service; and
- a clear understanding of the strategic direction of the agency.

As for benefits, a good strategic plan provides:

- a focus for the organizational framework that determines organization needs and practices;
- a basis for assessing the effectiveness and efficiency of organizational practices;
- a long-term perspective; and
- information from people in all parts of the organization (Taylor 1999, 15).

Taylor also notes that strategic plans have the potential for greatest impact when the plan and its performance measures are understood and applied by personnel at all levels of the organization. Check out the RCMP's strategies and priorities, which are highlighted in A Closer Look 6.4.

A CLOSER LOOK 6.4

ROYAL CANADIAN MOUNTED POLICE

The Canadian policing landscape is complex and multifaceted. As crime evolves, so does the RCMP's response, which includes numerous strategies designed to address complex operations faced on a daily basis. Two essential elements are at the core of the RCMP's contribution to a safe and secure Canada: getting results, and earning respect. The Results and Respect model is designed on four building blocks that guide the work of the RCMP: service, innovation, engagement, and accountability. Every year, the RCMP prepares a Departmental Plan and a Departmental Performance Report to account for progress made in its programs and priority areas.

Service

Through service to and collaboration with the public and partners, the RCMP will achieve tangible results that support operations. Under its five operational priorities, the RCMP will enhance the safety of Canadians.

- In support of Economic Integrity, work will continue on protecting Canadians and critical infrastructure from cyber threats.

- To further the Serious and Organized Crime priority, the RCMP will support efforts to take action to get handguns and assault weapons off our streets.

- Under the National Security priority, the organization will support the work being led by Public Safety Canada to develop anti-terrorism legislation that strengthens accountability while balancing collective security with rights and freedoms.

- In prioritizing service to Indigenous Communities, the RCMP will continue to develop strategies to address the long-term goals of the Government of Canada's National Inquiry into Missing and Murdered Indigenous Women and Girls and will deliver culturally competent services.

- The RCMP will also continue to prioritize the prevention of Youth crime and victimization through strategies that focus on engagement, awareness, and active intervention.

Innovation

The RCMP will support results through innovation that is reflective of a modern professional police service. Three areas will be the focus of innovation: Information Management, Information Technology, and Specialized Policing Services. Through the delivery and stewardship of National Police Services, the RCMP will continue to provide critical frontline operational and specialized services not only to its business lines, but to all Canadian law enforcement and criminal justice communities and international partners.

Engagement

A healthy and engaged workforce is essential to the RCMP's contributions to a safe and secure Canada. The RCMP will foster employee engagement and support its people by prioritizing its recruitment efforts to attract the most qualified candidates. It will identify and encourage strong, inclusive and promising leaders and continue to work on health modernization initiatives including the five-year Mental Health Strategy.

Accountability

The RCMP will show respect to the public, partners, stakeholders and to each other, through accountability. The organization will foster a professional environment where ethical standards are modeled and enforced. The RCMP will also continue to strive for greater diversity and will foster inclusion by creating a work environment where all employees feel valued and respected and are able to contribute to their full potential regardless of gender, ethnicity, language, disability, sexual orientation, age or any other personal attribute.

Source: From the *Royal Canadian Mounted Police 2017-18 Departmental Plan.* Reproduced with the permission of the RCMP.http://www.rcmp-grc.gc.ca/en/royal-canadian-mounted-police-2017-18-departmental-plan

The (Ontario) Adequacy Standards (Section 32(2)) also require each police service board to consult with the local municipal council, school boards, community organizations and groups, businesses, and community residents in developing its business plan. **Forecasting** involves using the information gathered to anticipate future demands on the police service and to identify the resources that will be required to meet these demands.

The increasing use of strategic planning and forecasting indicates that police organizations are adopting many of the techniques used by private sector companies and are becoming more corporate in their structure and activities. All of this is occurring against a backdrop of increasing fiscal accountability and a philosophy that what gets measured counts. Virtually all Canadian police agencies publish their strategic plans on their websites. For example, see the Ottawa Police Service's strategic plan at http://www.ottawapolice.ca under the "News and Media" link.

Audits

Audits provide a valuable barometer of the health of the organization. They identify areas of concern that may render the agency vulnerable. They monitor and maintain a balance between those tasks that contribute to agency objectives and those which meet the public demand for protection and reassurance. At the same time, they assure police managers and oversight bodies that the agency is acting in a fiscally responsible way and conforming to provincial or legislative guidelines.

—*Taylor (1999)*

Ontario's Adequacy Standards require that police services conduct audits of their administrative and operational activities as well as of specific programs and policing initiatives.

Environmental Scans

A key element of the planning process, **environmental scans** are studies that identify forces or change agents in the community (environment) that may affect the demands that will be made upon the police. A typical environmental scan involves gathering information, from a wide range of sources, on topics such as:

- demographic, social, and economic trends;
- crime and disorder trends;
- public perceptions of and satisfaction with the police;
- the impact of federal legislation, including the Youth Criminal Justice Act and Criminal Code, and changes to provincial legislation, including Police Acts;
- the impact of judicial decisions in relation to *Charter of Rights and Freedoms*;
- the impact of technology;
- human resources;
- finances;
- the goals and objectives of the police service; and
- a profile of police personnel.

Many police services conduct scans annually or semiannually in order to maintain a continual flow of information on critical issues that may require changes in policies and operational practice. Both the Ontario Provincial Police and Toronto Police Service have highly detailed environmental scans available on their respective websites.

Service Performance Indicators

The public expects the Police Service to provide quality service and to be accountable. Performance measures can both indicate how well we are doing in providing that service and provide a vehicle for accountability.

—*Toronto Police Service (2011)*

The move away from traditional styles of policing has necessitated the development of performance measures that more accurately measure the activities and accomplishments of the police service and its officers. **Performance indicators** are specific numerical measurements for each aspect of performance (i.e., output or outcome) under consideration.

In Toronto, where significant pressure has been placed on Toronto Police Service management to justify the number of personnel, the municipal government has identified and defined three types of performance indicators, as follows:

- *Condition/demand indicators*: These are indicators of environmental conditions and include the population served, the number of calls for service, traffic accident statistics, reported criminal victimization, and information volunteered to the police by community residents through programs such as Crime Stoppers.
- *Units of service*: These are measurable components that indicate how much service is provided and include the number of police and civilian members, the number of police officers per population, the ratio of constables to Criminal Code offences, the number of uniformed officers on the street, the proportion of plainclothes officers (detectives) to uniformed officers, the ratio of supervisors to police officers, and community participation in programs, including Neighbourhood Watch.
- *Effectiveness/efficiency measures*: These are indicators of how well the organization is doing in various areas, and include crime rates in the various divisions, number of arrests, clearance rates, response times to critical incidents, and the per capita costs of policing.

Media-based crime prevention programs such as Crime Stoppers offer cash rewards for information leading to the arrest and conviction of offenders. These programs also serve to educate the public about crimes occurring in their community.

Source: Neal/Wickware/Ciccocioppo/Tour. Reproduced with Permission of Crime Stoppers of Wellington County Inc.

Traditionally, the most commonly used performance indicators for police services were costs per capita, the number of citizens per sworn police officer, and the number of citizens per police employee (all employees). However, a police service that is cost-efficient is not necessarily an effective police service. Increasingly, police agencies are evaluated according to an framework called **"results-based accountability"** that evaluates programs and strategies against this fundamental question: "Is anyone better off?" (Friedman 2015). Innovative Canadian police services have begun to adopt a new management paradigm that focuses on the use of performance indicators to help (1) rethink what services are of highest priority; (2) generate improved outcomes; and (3) better control service delivery costs (Kiedrowski and Petrunik 2013). Community policing requires that police services expand the range of performance indicators for both the police service and individual officers. One such indicator is discussed in Critical Perspectives 6.2.

Best Practices and Benchmarking

Best practices refer to those organizational, administrative, and operational strategies that have proven successful in preventing and responding to crime and disorder. Many were first developed in the corporate sector and have been adapted for use in police services. Best practices are activities—implementing a philosophy, policy, strategy, program, process, and/or practice—that an organization does better than other organizations and that serve as models for other organizations that want to enhance their performance. The process of searching for best-practice organizations is called **benchmarking**.

CRITICAL PERSPECTIVES 6.2

IMPLEMENTING COMMUNITY POLICING BY "STAFFING TO WORKLOAD"

While "pop to cop" ratios tell us how many police officers there are per number of citizens, they tell us very little about the nature of the work or the need for more police. What does it mean if one community has 1 officer per 530 residents, while another community has 1 officer for every 425 residents? Does it mean the community with more police per capita receives better police service or has a lower crime rate? Several Canadian municipalities have established service-level targets as a better approach to delivering community police service. The Calgary and Edmonton police services, for example, try to ensure there are enough police officers to provide the following patrol performance targets:

1. Seven-minute average response time to high-priority calls.

2. Forty percent of a police officer's shift is available for problem-solving activities.

3. One two-person unit is available in each specified geographic location to provide back-up.

Staffing to workload assesses the work demands placed upon officers and then redistributes them so that all officers have essentially the same amount of reactive workload as well as time available to engage in proactive, preventive activities. The Durham Regional Police Service, the Vancouver Police Department, and the Edmonton and Calgary Police Services have all moved to patrol performance deployment models, which staff according to workload.

Benchmarking is a tool for improving performance. It is a process whereby an organization continually measures and compares its activities and performance with other organizations in order to improve its effectiveness.

In Canada, the International Centre for the Prevention of Crime (ICPC) performs important crime prevention benchmarking both nationally and internationally. You can see their work at http://www.crime-prevention-intl.org.

Community Surveys

A valuable tool for defining police priorities within a community policing framework is the community survey. **Community surveys** generally seek information in relation to the following three areas:

• Overall citizen satisfaction with the police;
• Policing problems in the community; and
• Questions related to criminal victimization, including the fear of crime.

In Chapter 7, we will see how the corporate model used by the police services in Guelph and Calgary improves the effectiveness and efficiency of those services. In our discussion in Chapter 10, we will also see that community surveys can be used to determine the concerns and perceptions of the residents of a particular neighbourhood or area. If you are interested in community surveys, you can find actual surveys at most Canadian police websites or, alternatively, on the websites of their governing police boards and commissions. The OPP has a community survey based on a province-wide sample of Ontario residents, posted on their website at http://www.opp.ca

Police services also gain important information from **victimization surveys**; these serve to identify rates of self-reported victimization, which are typically higher than rates of reported crime. For example, the rate of reported domestic violence in a community will be lower than the self-reported victimization rate; the difference is one indicator of how well police and community initiatives are addressing this critical issue. During every federal census, Statistics Canada administers the General Social Survey (GSS) to determine victim reporting rates for numerous criminal offences. Results for the most recent survey, conducted in 2014, can be found at the Statistics Canada website, http://statcan.gc.ca (search for the document *Criminal Victimization in Canada, 2014*).

ORGANIZATION FOR SERVICE DELIVERY

The adoption of community policing has changed how service delivery is organized.

Community Policing Teams

In contrast to the traditional model of police work, officers in community policing police services are assigned a geographically designed zone or sector. This geographic assignment of officers is often referred to as **geopolicing**. The term is relatively new to Canada, but you can learn more about it through the Seattle Police Service's Micro Community Policing Plans at http://www.seattle.gov/police/community-policing/about-mcpp. It is the responsibility of officers to work together in **community policing teams** to develop partnerships with the community, to engage in problem-solving, and to respond to incidents that occur within the zone. The Edmonton Police Service implemented a new patrol service delivery model in 2007 that incorporated community policing teams with geographic assignments; today it uses the Geographical Deployment Model. We will examine this initiative in greater detail in Chapter 7.

Community policing teams are a departure from the structure of police platoons in traditional police work. Under traditional models of deployment, police often deployed from a central headquarters to an assigned area where the role they performed was essentially a reactive one. Today the objective is to assign police officers to geographic locations for extended periods of time; in this way, the police officer gains a thorough understanding of the crime and quality-of-life conditions impacting the community in that geographic area. This also allows the police to interact with the community in more strategic ways to sustain longer-term quality-of-life improvements in the community. At the same time police officers are deployed geographically, the model for service delivery is organized by teams. Each member of a team works the same rotating shift schedule, with the same days off; this enables the team itself to learn and to increase overall team performance and effectiveness. The principles are the same as they are with sports teams.

The sergeants in charge of the community policing teams have two primary sets of relationships: to their specific platoon or shift, and to members of other platoons that are responsible for the zone or area being policed. The sergeants are also responsible for initiating and maintaining contact with community groups, participating in setting goals and objectives for the zone, and evaluating the performance of individual officers and the entire team. As well, the sergeants are accountable for the successes and the shortcomings of the community policing team.

While this model of service delivery deployment has proven quite effective, it is not without its challenges. Highly effective supervision is required to ensure that the team does not develop an inward focus—that is, to ensure that the needs of the team do not become more important than those of the community. In addition, in many geographic locations calls for service limit the ability of front-line police officers to work with the community in proactive, strategic ways that would lead to improvements in community quality of life. Sustaining progress can be difficult for this reason, and also because human resource practices in police services tend to move personnel around frequently. To counter these issues, many police agencies assign "community policing specialists" to police teams. Most often, these are constables who work directly with communities without having to respond to calls for service. Community safety officers in the OPP and community liaison officers in the Calgary Police Service perform these important supportive roles.

Community policing teams provide an opportunity for officers to work both individually and collectively to set goals and objectives for the zone, to identify community resources and establish partnerships with the community, and to address community priorities and concerns within a problem-solving framework.

Community Policing in Prince Albert, Saskatchewan: The HUB Model

Over the past five years, Canadian police services have become key players in the establishment of multi–social agency teams, which have been assembled to address chronic community problems that lead to crime and serious disorder. While there are variations in the organization and work of these multi-agency teams, they all apply principles that result in crime prevention through social development (see Chapter 7).

Like many Canadian communities, Prince Albert, Saskatchewan, recognized it had many social problems that were contributing to crime and reducing quality of life for residents. Consequently, it wanted to "change the conversation about an old problem" (McFee and Taylor 2014). Saskatchewan had a high crime severity rate, and in Prince Albert, alcohol abuse was very high. Significant social problems impacting the community included:

- a high mortality rate of young persons that was 15 percent above the national average;
- Hepatitis C rates higher than the rest of the province;
- HIV rates that were increasing drastically;
- intravenous drug use as the main risk factor for the spread of disease;
- lower school completion and higher truancy and absenteeism rates in local schools and in many feeder areas;
- inadequate housing; and
- changing demographics placing more and more young people in harm's way.

The chief of the Prince Albert Police wanted to mobilize the community in an effort to bring substantive change to these community issues. A consultant hired to assess community conditions commented that "it would take more than the policing system to reverse the disturbing trends of high crime and violence in Saskatchewan" (McFee and Taylor 2014, 5).

The chief of the Prince Albert Police recognized that the police service was well-positioned to take a leadership role in building a team of agencies, all having a mandate to address the same community problems albeit from their respective agency-specific lenses. Rather than debate "who owned the problem," the chief sought more permanent and lasting solutions to common problems affecting all communities.

The chief along with community partners recognized that the people generating significant demand for police resources were the same people straining the health care system and all other human services in the province. This led to the creation of the Prince Albert Hub.

The Prince Albert Hub is not a traditional or contemporary policing model as much as it is a community safety model, designed to improve a much broader set of social outcomes, including reducing crime, violence, and victimization.

The Prince Albert Hub meets twice a week for 90 minutes to engage in a "purposeful discussion" about individuals who are at acutely elevated risk that is recognized across multiple disciplines. The Hub considers cases that meet the following four criteria:

1. There is significant community interest at stake;
2. There is a clear probability of harm occurring;
3. Severe harm is predicted; and
4. There is a multi-disciplinary nature to the elevated risk factors.

If these criteria are met, then there is a rapid deployment of collaborative interventions aimed at connecting those at risk to the services they need most at that point in time. The strengths of the Hub include the following:

- It allows for efficient case management and timely response;
- Privacy issues (e.g., health care records) are addressed and taken into account;
- Powerful new forms of analysis are available for problem identification and tailored intervention; and
- The Hub model is easily replicable to other jurisdictions.

The Prince Albert Hub is an example of how policing and the entire human services sector can benefit by working more strategically to bring about positive change in people's lives and to improve to overall community safety. While not every jurisdiction will experience the same results, it is worth noting that violent crime in Prince Albert decreased by 37 percent between 2010 and 2013 (the evaluation period). This model can be applied to any community in Canada, and its importance to problem-oriented policing should not be underestimated. See In Your Community 6.3 for more examples of how the Hub is applied across Canada.

IN YOUR COMMUNITY 6.3

COLLABORATIONS THAT ARE MAKING A DIFFERENCE

The Toronto Police Service in partnership with the United Way and the City of Toronto established "FOCUS Rexdale" (FOCUS is an acronym for Furthering Our Communities—Uniting Services). For two hours, once a week, 20 to 30 human service workers meet to identify and intervene on situations of acutely elevated risk in the neighbourhoods of Rexdale.

In 2013 the Greater Sudbury Police Service (GSPS) invited human services agencies to support a local CRISIS table (Collaborative Risk-Identified Situation, Intervention Strategy) which led to the hiring of an executive director.

Waterloo Region, through the leadership of the Waterloo Regional Police Service, and partnering with health and social service partners, launched a "Connectivity Table" that brought acute care workers together regularly to identify and intervene on situations of imminent risk of harm.

Peel Regional Police (PRPS) undertook a training initiative for themselves and partners on how to collaborate effectively across sectors. A "situation table" was created in 2013 to address risk factors in a Mississauga housing development.

The Hamilton Police Service, in partnership with the City of Hamilton's Neighbourhood Development Strategies, Urban Renewal Section of Economic Development, and Hamilton Paramedic Service developed the Social Navigator Project to refer "at risk" people and those who have had repeat interactions with the Hamilton Police Service, to the appropriate agencies. The program is part of the anti-violence ACTION strategy. This initiative won the 2013 Cisco International Association of Chiefs of Police Community Policing Award.

The Sault Ste. Marie Police Service undertook a thorough examination of calls for service throughout its policing area and identified one area that constituted the most disadvantaged area in terms of available supports and services. With a relatively small investment in start-up costs, the Sault Ste. Marie police set up a storefront *Neighbourhood Resource Centre*. Supported by the private sector, this initiative has grown from 8 agencies to more than 30. This initiative has won a number of awards and was a finalist in the 2016 International Association of Chiefs of Police Community Policing Awards.

Source: *Hugh C. Russell and Norman E. Taylor, New Directions in Community Safety Consolidating Lessons Learned about Risk and Collaboration, Ontario Association of Chiefs of Police (April 2014), found at http://www.oacp.on.ca/Userfiles/StandingCommittees/CommunityPolicing/ResourceDocs/OWG%20New%20Directions%20in%20Community%20Safety.pdf Used with permission. Hamilton Police Service, Social Navigator Project. Used with permission. Found at https://hamiltonpolice.on.ca/about/sections-units/crisis-response-unit/social-navigator-project*

Community Policing in Winnipeg

The Winnipeg Police Service deploys community support foot patrol officers to provide proactive policing services that involve solving problems rather than simply reporting incidents. The police officer provides a service that is community-based rather than criminal justice–based, acting as a community team leader in identifying problems. The officer then works through community resources, identifying and applying solutions to the problems.

Objectives

In Winnipeg, the goal of community support foot patrols is:
- to reduce the number of repeat calls for service;
- to solve community problems;
- to improve the public's satisfaction with the police;
- to increase the job satisfaction of constables; and
- to increase the reporting of intelligence and sharing of information.

Strategies

Winnipeg's foot patrols apply the following strategies:
- target police services to "hot spots";
- decentralize the service;
- increase constables' autonomy and problem-solving abilities;
- involve the community in defining and solving problems;
- increase constables' knowledge of the community; and
- increase police visibility.

How Does It Work?

An analysis of calls for service is completed, to identify small geographical areas that require additional police resources. A constable is assigned to patrol this area; this encourages accessibility and community involvement. The constable is encouraged to form community liaison committees, which are organized to identify community ownership problems. Together, the police officer and the community use innovative problem-solving strategies to address the concerns of the particular community.

Community Mobilization and Engagement in Ontario

One difficulty in implementing community policing has been figuring out how to effectively engage a community so that improvements to community well-being can be sustained over time, resulting in improved quality of life for all residents. In Ontario, OACP and the Ministry of Community Safety and Correctional Services collaborated to develop the Community Mobilization and Engagement Model of Community Policing. The model outlines the roles and responsibilities for both police services and community members in addressing safety and crime. When community partners engage with police, the level of safety, security, and well-being in Ontario neighbourhoods is enhanced and victimization is reduced.

This model holds considerable promise for improving community safety. Its reliance on the principles of community policing, incorporating the many elements we have examined in this chapter such as business plans, environmental scans, and citizen surveys, results in a much more strategic model of police service delivery. Most Ontario police services have included in their organizational structures community mobilization sections. For example, the Chatham–Kent Police Service recently created the Community Mobilization Section, and the York Regional Police have a Community Mobilization Bureau.

A CLOSER LOOK 6.5

ONTARIO PROVINCIAL POLICE CRIME PREVENTION SECTION

During 2014, the Ontario Provincial Police's Crime Prevention Section was restructured under Community Safety Services to:

- Provide community safety expertise in support of frontline policing;

- Identify best practices through evidence-based research;

- Promote public messaging with a focus on social media and web-based messaging; and

- Forecast and develop responses to emerging crime trends through crime and risk-based analysis.

Regional Community Safety Committees reporting to a centralized provincial committee were established to facilitate information sharing and best practice recommendations and to develop crime prevention plans and accountability frameworks to ensure a coordinated approach across the organization.

Source: OPP, *2014 Ontario Provincial Police Annual Report*, p. 21. Found at https://www.opp.ca/index.php?id=115&entryid=56c22aac8f94acff6aa009d0 © Queen's Printer for Ontario, 2014. Reproduced with permission.

A key component of the Ontario Community Mobilization Model is **Situation Tables**. These are meetings organized much like the Prince Albert Hub described earlier. They bring together professionals on a regular basis to explore ways to reduce risk in the community. They include human service professionals from many agencies and sectors, who work together to identify individuals, families, groups, or locations that present acutely elevated risk (AER) and to customize multidisciplinary interventions that serve mitigate or lessen those risks.

Like the Hub Model, AER can be summarized as a situation that:

- involves multiple risk factors;
- exceeds an agency's ability to deal with the risk factors alone;
- will result in imminent harms or victimization if these risks are not reduced; and
- requires multiple agencies to reduce risks.

During a Situation Table, participants work together to reduce the likelihood of anyone in a community facing harms that increase the likelihood of imminent victimization. The OACP defines risk factors as negative characteristics or conditions in individuals, families, communities or society that may increase social disorder, crime or fear of crime, or the likelihood of harms or victimization to persons or property (Ontario Association of Chiefs of Police 2016).

The Ontario Community Mobilization and Engagement Model of Community Policing and its use of Situation Tables builds on early models of community policing. It recognizes that community problems can be very complex and that the police are typically only part of the solution. When agencies combine their respective knowledge and energies, better and more sustainable solutions can be found that contribute to improved community safety and well-being.

CHAPTER SUMMARY

Our discussion in this chapter has focused on issues related to the police organization and community policing. For police services to translate the model of community policing successfully from an idea or philosophy to the operational level requires a number of changes, including modifying how police services are organized, administered, and delivered. A promising approach is the adoption of a corporate model of police work and the use of a number of key tools, including mission, value, and vision statements, strategic planning, benchmarking, and environmental scans. Using these strategies, police services can assess the effectiveness of their current practices, discard those approaches that are not effective, and adopt best practices whenever possible.

However, it is important to note the discrepancy between how police organizations are structured to deliver services and the ever increasing and changing demands that are being placed on them. This includes the increasing sophistication and globalization of crime, which requires the police to have access to the latest technologies as well as officers who are comfortable with that technology. The strategies for combating transnational fraud, for example, are considerably different from those required to implement community policing at the neighbourhood level, yet the community can be overlooked when solutions to these issues are sought. This suggests that over the next decade, urban police services will be required to re-examine whether the generalist model is effective or whether greater specialization may be required to meet the complex demands of many calls for service.

CHAPTER REVIEW

Key Terms

- benchmarking, p. 195
- best practices, p. 195
- business or strategic plan, p. 192
- community policing teams, p. 197
- community surveys, p. 196
- corporate model of policing, p. 191
- environmental scans, p. 194
- forecasting, p. 194
- geopolicing, p. 197
- mission, value, and vision statements, p. 185
- performance indicators, p. 195
- police pyramid, p. 187
- police service as a learning organization, p. 188
- results-based accountability, p. 195
- Situation Tables, p. 201
- victimization surveys, p. 196

Key Points

- Adoption of the community policing model requires significant changes to all facets of the police organization.
- Police chiefs and chief constables play a critical role in community policing, although one that is much different from the traditional model of police work.
- Mission, value, and vision statements are a core component of the community policing police service.
- Key changes required for community policing include inverting the police pyramid, decentralizing command and control functions, and adopting appropriate organizational strategies from the private sector.
- Community policing police services are learning organizations that have the capacity to continually gather and analyze information, assess performance, and make the adjustments required in order to deliver effective police services.
- Business or strategic plans are a core component of the community policing police service.

- Environmental scans are used by police services to gather information that can be used in planning and in developing police–community partnerships.
- Community policing teams are a primary way to deliver community-based policing.
- The Ontario Community Mobilization and Community Engagement Model provides an effective and efficient model for community-based policing.
- Situation Tables or Hubs are effective for organizing the response to community problems.

Self-Evaluation

QUESTIONS

1. What are **mission**, **value**, and **vision statements** in policing, and what role do they play in community policing?
2. What is the **police pyramid** and how is it affected by the community policing model?
3. Describe what it means for a police service to be a **learning organization**, and identify the characteristics of a police service that is a learning organization.
4. What is a **business** or **strategic plan**, and what role does it play in community policing?
5. What is an **environmental scan**, and what role does it play in community policing?
6. Identify and discuss the types of **performance indicators** used by community police services.
7. Define and describe the role of the following in community policing: **benchmarking**, **best practices**, **forecasting**, **audits**, and **community policing teams**.
8. Define and describe what is meant by the term **geopolicing** and explain its importance to community-based service delivery.
9. Explain why **staffing to workload** is a better method for calculating police resources than "pop-to-cop" ratios.
10. Why is it said that the OPP delivers **customized policing services**?

KEY IDEAS

1. Which of the following is a characteristic of police leadership within a community policing model?
   a. Change management
   b. Bureaucratic management
   c. Administrative management
   d. Maintenance management

2. Where are words such as "honesty," "integrity," "respect," and "fairness" most often found within the administrative components of a community policing service?
   a. In audits
   b. In core value statements
   c. In emergency response guidelines
   d. In forecasting scans

3. Which of the following does *not* occur when a police service alters its organizational structure to incorporate the principles of community policing?
   a. Decentralization of command and control.
   b. More autonomy and discretion to line police officers.
   c. Flattening of the organizational structure.
   d. Increased specialization of line police officers.

4. Which documents typically provide general principles for providing policing services?
   a. Legislation provided by the provincial government.
   b. The mission, value, and vision statements of the police agency.
   c. The policy and procedures manuals of the police agency.
   d. The Criminal Code of Canada.

5. What is Ontario's Police Learning System?
   a. A pre-training program for police recruits.
   b. A system of teaching the community about community policing.
   c. A program of training and education for police personnel.
   d. A system for identifying potential trouble spots in the community.

6. What is the term for the community policing strategy designed to identify forces in the community that may have an impact on police services?
   a. Environmental scan
   b. Benchmarking
   c. Auditing
   d. Best practices

7. Which of the following is typically given to officers in community policing police services?
   a. A partner to coordinate activities in the community.
   b. Police motor vehicles that display community decals and have the ability to transport several volunteers.
   c. Training in a second language that is reflective of what is spoken in the community.
   d. A geographic assignment known as a zone or turf.

8. In the context of community policing, what are performance indicators?
   a. The criteria used for promoting officers from one rank to another.
   b. The criteria used to determine the effectiveness of police technology.
   c. The criteria used to compare the effectiveness of the police with other components of the criminal justice system.
   d. The criteria used to measure the activities and accomplishments of a police service and its officers.

9. Which of the following is an accurate statement about the current state of policing in Ontario in terms of the requirements of community policing?
   a. Only a very few police services in Ontario have redesigned the organization and delivery of policing services.
   b. The Police Services Act and the Adequacy Standards have had a major impact on Ontario police services.
   c. Attempts to legislate change in Ontario police services have not been very successful.
   d. There have been modest changes in the organization of police services and in how police services are delivered.

The Police Organization: Situations and Strategies

Community Policing Implementation Checklist

There are a number of key questions that can be asked to determine whether a police service has adopted the principles of community policing. Note that these are general points and that more specific questions should be asked, depending on the particular police service and the community it polices.

Mission and Value Statements

- Does the police service have a current mission statement?

- Does the mission statement refer to a police–community partnership?

- Is the mission statement widely published in the community, both on the police service's website and in print material?

- Is there a value statement that indicates the priorities and focus of the police service?
- Does the value statement refer to community involvement?
- Does the value statement indicate support for officers?

Decentralization of Command and Control

- Has the police service decentralized its command and decision-making authority?
- Are line officers given the discretion and autonomy to solve problems?
- Are officers assigned to specific zones or turfs for an extended period of time?
- Are the principles of community policing reflected in the organization, administration, and delivery of police services?
- Have lines of communication between line officers and their superiors been created so that information from the community can flow upward?

Building Organizational Capacity to Do Community Policing

- Has the police service developed the capacity to be a learning organization?
- Does the police service conduct environmental scans and use this information in the planning process?
- Does the police service use a corporate model for planning and for implementing goals and objectives?
- Does the police service use growth positions and performance indicators in its planning process and in annual evaluations of organizational effectiveness?
- Is there an attempt to integrate best practices into the administration and delivery of police services?

Partnering with the Community

- Is the police service successful in communicating its goals and objectives to the community?
- Does the police service have a media strategy to promote police–community partnerships and highlight program successes, as well as to respond to criticisms and incidents involving officers?

EXERCISES: KNOWLEDGE INTO PRACTICE

Exercise 1. The Mission Statement

Develop a mission statement for the police service in the community where you spent the most time while growing up. Address the following:

- What is the purpose of the mission statement?
- How does the mission statement reflect the unique attributes of your community, the demands made on the police service, and the current and potential role of the community?
- How will the extent to which the mission statement is reflected in the policies, strategies, and operational delivery of policing services be assessed?
- Take a look at the Ontario Provincial Police's Promise (http://www.opp.ca/ecms/index.php?id=20). Would your community benefit from a similar statement? Why or why not?

Exercise 2. Using the World Wide Web

Select four police departments, one each in the United States, Canada, Asia, and Europe.

1. Print out and read through the website materials for each service.
2. Then, for each police service, consider what the materials on the website tell you about:
   - how the particular police service is organized;
   - what its goals and objectives are;
   - what its orientation is;
   - how it recruits and trains officers;
   - how it deploys its resources;
   - the community it polices, and the demands made upon it by the community; and
   - how it carries out patrol and general duty.
3. Assess each police service as to whether it is a community policing organization, noting the reasons why or why not.

Exercise 3. Providing Policing Services under Contract: The RCMP and the OPP

When a municipality in Ontario considers having the OPP as the local police service, a request for costing of police services is made to the Ministry of Community Safety and Correctional Services.

This initiates a process of community profiling, workload analysis, and community consultations to build a picture of the community and its specific needs. The primary objective is to develop a policing contract tailored to the community. This process is referred to as *Customized* or *Community First Policing*. In Ontario, a reference manual called *Restructuring Police Services in Ontario: A Guidebook and Resource Kit for Municipalities from Ontario's Police Community* provides guidance on disbanding police services and contracting with the OPP.

The RCMP also contract its service to communities. Contract policing is authorized under the federal RCMP Act. The current Provincial Police Services Agreement (PPSA) is the umbrella under which the RCMP provides contract policing services to three territories and all provinces except Ontario and Quebec. This amounts to approximately 198 municipalities and, under 172 agreements, to 192 First Nations communities. The RCMP, in contrast, applies a standard agreement to all communities, although in the past several years, the RCMP process has incorporated a more community-based approach.

The approach taken by the OPP is due in large measure to the fact that the OPP is establishing many first-time contracts, whereas the RCMP tends to be involved primarily in the renewal of existing contracts.

List what you consider to be the advantages and disadvantages associated with the process by which the RCMP and OPP create a contract for a municipality.

Exercise 4. Contract Policing versus Independent Municipal Police Service

Consider the following scenario: The former Town of New Liskeard established a municipal police service on 1 July 1963. That service was renamed the Temiskaming Shores Police Service following amalgamation. It polices the portion of the city that was the Town of New Liskeard. Under current policing arrangements, the former town of New Liskeard is policed by a municipal service, while the rest of the city is policed by the OPP from the Temiskaming OPP Detachment Temiskaming Shores. Like many communities in Northern Ontario, New Liskeard is faced with economic setbacks including declines in traditional resource-based industries and economic indicators such as housing demand, while the proportion of seniors is expected to double from 16 percent (2006) to 34 percent (2026). Faced with these challenges, and the requirement for a significant expenditure of funds to bring the current police facility up to standard, council has been considering policing options for some time. The municipal council of New Liskeard is considering disbanding the Temiskaming Shores Police Service to bring it under a policing contract with the OPP. This has many residents of New Liskeard feeling that they will not receive the same level of policing service as they did in the past and that they will not have control over local policing decisions. They have formed an advocacy group called "Keep Our Police Service (KOPS)." A consultant has been hired to advise this group on practical and technical matters.

You are a member of New Liskeard Municipal Council, and the mayor has asked you to prepare a short paper outlining the benefits, limitations, and implications of dismantling the independent municipal force in favour of a contractual policing arrangement with the OPP, with specific reference to the implications for community policing. Once you have considered the issues, check your responses to the real-life scenario available on the Ontario Civilian Commission on Police Services website at www.occps.on.ca, where you will find the actual Temiskaming Shores Police integration application.

Exercise 5. Selecting a Detachment Commander in the RCMP and OPP

One of the concerns a community has when it opts to have the RCMP or OPP deliver policing services is whether the community will have a say in the selection of the detachment commander. The process for identifying a detachment commander in the RCMP has traditionally been an internal process carried out by senior management at RCMP headquarters in Ottawa. That process has begun to change; now, internal processes identify two or three potential candidates for a detachment posting. These candidates are then presented to the town council or municipal government for their input. In Yukon, the RCMP recently developed a process that formalizes community participation in the selection of a detachment commander (Sharing Common Ground 2011). Similarly, the OPP provides an opportunity for the municipality to state a preference between potential candidates. The OPP thus provides some opportunity for the municipality to participate in selecting the detachment commander and to maintain a degree of control over who will in effect become the next police chief (even though the list of candidates is provided by the OPP). This is set out by statute in the Police Services Act, Section 10(9). Similarly with independent municipal police departments, local police commissions and police boards use a process of community consultation to identify and select police chiefs (Police Services Act, Section 31(1)(d)).

Identify advantages and disadvantages to having the OPP or RMCP select a detachment commander. What could be a disadvantage of inviting community participation in the selection of a detachment commander?

Advantages   Disadvantages

_____

_____

_____

_____

_____

In your view, which process best exemplifies the principles and practices of community policing? Provide reasons for your response.

_____

_____

_____

_____

_____

Exercise 6. Selecting a Police Leader

Place yourself in the position of a member of a municipal police board that has the authority to hire and fire the chief of police in the municipality. Your committee has been charged with developing a set of criteria for hiring the next chief of police. The goal is to hire a person with strong leadership skills who will implement the principles of community policing.

List the criteria that should be used in recruiting the new police chief. Then list the criteria that should be used to assess the performance of the chief of police in the annual performance review conducted by the municipal police board.

_____

_____

_____

_____

_____

When you are finished, search online and check an actual posting for police chief.

REFERENCES

Anishinabek Police Service. 2017. "Mission Statement." *http://www.apscops.org*

Arnold, S., P. Clark, and D. Cooley. 2011. Sharing Common Ground: Review of Yukon's Police Force—Final Report. *Yukon: Government of Yukon, 2011.*

Bennis, W. 1989. On Becoming a Leader. *New York: Addison-Wesley.*

Black, L., D. Brown, R. Drouin, N. Inkster, and L. Murray. 2007. Rebuilding the Trust: Task Force on Governance and Cultural Change in the RCMP. *Cat. no.: PS4-53/2007E-PDF. Ottawa: Public Safety Canada. http://www.publicsafety.gc.ca/ rcmp-grc/_fl/Task_Force_Report-English.pdf*

Bureau of Justice Assistance. 2005. Intelligence-Led Policing—The New Policing Architecture. *Washington, DC: US Department of Justice.*

Calgary Police Service. 2012. 2012–2014 Strategic Plan. *Calgary.*

Campbell, D.S. (chair). 1992. A Police Learning System for Ontario: Final Report and Recommendations. *Toronto: Strategic Planning Committee on Police Training and Education, Ministry of the Solicitor General.*

Canadian Press. "Toronto Police Won't Participate in Pride Parade, Black Lives Matter Responds." *10 February 2017. citynew.ca.*

Clairmont, D. 1996. Community-Based Policing at Halton Regional: The Years 1980 to 1995. *Ottawa: Solicitor General Canada.*

Fleissner, D.W. 1997. Community Policing Stage Assessment Model for Implementation Planning and Organizational Measurement. *Seattle: Seattle Police Department.*

Friedman, Mark. 2015. Trying Hard Is Not Good Enough. *Charleston: BookSurge Publishing, 2009.*

Halton Regional Police Service. 2000. "Team Policing." http://www.hrps.on.ca/teampol.htm

—. 2011. "Corporate Business Plan 2011–2013." http://hrps.on.ca

Hartmann, Francis X., Lee Brown, and Darrel Stephens. 1988. Community Policing: Would You Know It If You Saw It? Community Policing Series no. 16. East Lansing: National Neighborhood Foot Patrol Center.

Hunter, R.D., and T. Barker. 1993. "BS and Buzzwords: The New Police Operational Style." American Journal of Police 12(3): 157–68.

Kiedrowski, John, Michael Petrunik, Todd Macdonald, and Ron Melchers. 2013. "Compliance Strategy Group Canadian Police Board Reviews on the Use of Police Performance Metrics." https://www.publicsafety.gc.ca/cnt/rsrcs/pblctns/plc-vws-prfrmnc-mtrcs/plc-vws-prfrmnc-mtrcs-eng.pdf

McFee, D., and N. Taylor. 2014. "The Prince Albert Hub and the Emergence of Collaborative Risk Driven Community Safety." CPC Discussion Paper, Ottawa: Canadian Police College.

Moore, M. 2003. "The Bottom Line of Policing: What Citizens Should Value and Measure in Police Performance." Boston: Police Executive Research Forum.

Murphy, C., and C.T. Griffiths. 1994. "Community Based Policing—A Review of the Issues, Research, and Development of a Provincial Policy." Unpublished research report prepared for the Commission of Inquiry, Policing in British Columbia. Victoria: Attorney General.

Murphy, C., and P. McKenna. 2007. "Rethinking Police Governance, Culture, and Management: A Summary Review of the Literature." http://www.publicsafety.gc.ca/rcmp-grc/_fl/eng/rethinkingpolice.pdf

Ontario Provincial Police. 1997a. "What's a Community Policing Team?" CPDC News 1 (June): 4–5.

—. 1997b. Community Policing "How Do We Do It" Manual. Orillia: Ontario Provincial Police Community Policing Development Centre.

—. 1997c. "Civilian Governance: Is There a Difference?" Ontario Provincial Police Focus: A Police Service to Call Your Own, November.

—. 1998. "Customizing Your Police Service Delivery." CPDC News 3 (June).

—. 2004. Ontario Provincial Police Focus: A Police Service to Call Your Own. October.

—. 2011a. 2010 Annual Report. Orillia.

—. 2011b. Environmental Scan. Orillia.

—. 2011c. Strategic Plan 2011–2013. Orillia.

RCMP. 2004. The Canada We Want—Speech from the Throne. *http://www. rcmp-grc.gc.ca/rpp/rpp_2003_b_e.htm*

—. 2012. "Report on Plans and Priorities 2012–2013." *http://publications.gc.ca/ collections/collection_2012/grc-rcmp/PS61-20-2012-eng.pdf*

Rosenbaum, D.P., S. Yeh, and D.L. Wilkinson. 1994. *"Impact of Community Policing on Police Personnel: A Quasi-Experimental Test."* Crime and Delinquency 40(3): 331–53.

Royal Newfoundland Constabulary. 2011. "Corporate Plan 2011–2014." *http://www. www.rnc.gov.nl.ca*

Russell, Hugh C., and Norman E. Taylor. 2014. "New Directions in Community Safety: The Ontario Working Group on Collaborative Risk-Driven Community Safety." *http://www.oacp.on.ca/Userfiles/StandingCommittees/Community-Policing/ResourceDocs/OWG%20The%20Ontario%20Working%20Group_6.pdf*

Senge, P.M. 1994. The Fifth Discipline: The Art and Practice of the Learning Organization. *New York: Doubleday.*

Taylor, K. 1999. Bringing into Focus—Policing in Halton Region: The Executive Summary. *Oakville: Halton Regional Police Service.*

Toronto Police Service. 2011. Environmental Scan.

Trojanowicz, R., and B. Bucqueroux. 1990. Community Policing: A Contemporary Perspective. *Cincinnati: Anderson Publishing.*

—. 1998. Community Policing: How to Get Started, *2nd ed. Cincinnati: Anderson Publishing Company.*

Winnipeg Police Service. 2004. "What Is Community Policing? Neighbourhood Foot Patrol." *http://www.city.winnipeg.mb.ca/police/About The Service/neighbour-hood foot patrol.htm*

York Regional Police. 1999. "Strategic Plan." *Newmarket: York Regional Police.*

Implementing Community Policing

A decentralized community policing centre is designed to improve community access to police services and allow police to be informed about local conditions of crime and disorder.

Source: Dundas Star News/Hamilton Community News

Learning Objectives

After completing this chapter, you should be able to:

- Describe the key stages of transforming a traditional policing service into one centred on community policing,

- Discuss how the Edmonton Police Service, the City of Montreal Police Service, and the Surrey (B.C.) RCMP altered the organization and delivery of their police services to implement the principles of community policing,

- Describe the Edmonton Police Service's transformation to community policing,

- Identify the phases the Halton Regional Police Service went through in implementing community policing,

- Identify the difficulties encountered and the lessons learned by the Halton Regional Police Service in implementing community policing,

- Discuss the role of police leaders and patrol officers in the Halton Regional Police Service transformation to community policing,

- Discuss the Organizational Renewal Project of the Durham Regional Police,

- Identify issues relating to regional police services and community policing,

- Discuss the ways in which the Ottawa Police Service addressed the issue of community policing when the service was created, and

- Describe how the Guelph Police Service and the Vancouver Police Department use a corporate model to organize, deliver, and assess the effectiveness and efficiency of policing services.

INTRODUCTION

Across Canada there are a number of excellent examples of police services undertaking the organizational and operational reforms required to implement the principles of community policing. Often, when a department hires a new chief of police, that chief launches an intensive examination of the department's overall effectiveness and efficiency. In this chapter, we examine how several departments have restructured the delivery of their police services. Among the case studies are an independent municipal police service, regional police services, and an RCMP detachment.

We will then consider how two police services—the Guelph Police Service and the Vancouver Police Department—use a corporate model to improve the effectiveness and efficiency of policing services. All of the police services examined demonstrate a high level of commitment to the principles of community-based policing. You will also notice that each department uses research and evaluation to provide a more strategic approach to the delivery of police service.

As you read each case study, keep in mind that these police services are presented only for illustrative purposes. The nature and extent of organizational reform required by a given police service will depend greatly on the types of demands that are placed on the service, the community it serves, and the level of interest among community residents. These case illustrations do, however, provide insights into the types of organizational initiatives that are involved as a police service moves towards an operational model of community policing.

WHY A CORPORATE MODEL?

Why do many Canadian police services adopt a corporate model? In Chapter 6, we examined how some police services have tried to become learning organizations—a corporate model borrowed from Dr. Peter Senge, author of *The Fifth Discipline: The Art and Practice of the Learning Organization*. Other corporate models are also being applied to police operations, including total quality management (TQM), Six Sigma, the balanced scorecard, and SWOT analysis, (which stands for strengths, weaknesses, opportunities, and threats).

Corporate models are being adopted because they provide a framework for police organizations to:

- manage costs and resources more effectively and efficiently;
- demonstrate organizational effectiveness and efficiency;
- model the practices put in place by the local government, (which ultimately funds policing in the jurisdiction);
- foster a highly motivated and empowered work environment; and
- empower police personnel.

All of these objectives help make police officers' careers much more satisfying. If you listen to a manager or police executive, you will hear the buzzwords and catchphrases that illustrate the adoption of these models.

Adoption of corporate models is not unique to policing. The entire public sector, including the Canadian civil service, has undergone significant change, with a number of parallels to policing. The public service has developed a model called **new public management**. Table 7.1 reflects the priorities and principles of new public management. This shift in the management of police organizations away from a paramilitary system towards a bureaucratic, corporate model has established the framework for modern police service delivery. The evolving community-based policing model is being shaped by the management principles and practices of the corporate model.

Table 7.1 Comparison of New Public Management and Traditional Public Administration

Components	New Public Management	Traditional Public Administration
Focus	Clients	Citizens and communities
Principal means	Management	Policy making
Characteristics of public servants	Entrepreneur (acting)	Analyst (thinking)
Values	Entrepreneurship, freedom for managers, flexibility, creativity, enthusiasm, risk taking	Ministerial responsibility, prudence, stability, ethics, probity, fairness, transparency
Vocabulary	Service to clients, quality skills, managerialism, empowerment, privatization	Public interest, democracy, social equity, due process
Culture	Private sector, innovation, business management, accountability by results, politics/administration dichotomy	Bureaucratic (hierarchical), functionalism stability, process accountability, politics–administration continuum
Structures	Civil service as organizational units, simple and frugal government, introduction to quasi-market mechanism, decentralization	Civil service as an institution, large departments, government-wide systems, central authority resource allocation

Source: M. Charih, and L. Rouillard, "The New Public Management" in M. Charih, and A. Daniels (eds.), *New Public Management*. Reprinted with permission of The Institute of Public Administration of Canada, d'Administration Publique du Canada. (1997), p.31.

Before examining specific examples, an important point needs to be addressed. Many elements of police work do not easily fit the corporate model. Notably, people who access police services are not necessarily consumers or customers; generating revenue and profits is not a police service goal; and many performance indicators are considerably different in public organizations than in private organizations. There are essential differences between public and private sector management models that should not get lost in the rhetoric.

THE TRANSFORMATION OF THE EDMONTON POLICE SERVICE

In our discussion of community policing in Chapter 3, we noted that police services often experience difficulties translating the philosophy and principles of community policing into practice. The transformation of the Edmonton Police Service from a traditional, reactive police service to a community-policing police service helps us understand the many challenges that police services encounter and the strategies that can be used to overcome these challenges.

The EPS took its first cautious steps towards reform in 1988, at a time when demands on the police service were increasing and available resources were declining. It was not unusual for the service to receive 500 calls per day, and the response time for nonemergency calls often exceeded three hours.

Table 7.2 provides an overview of the types of demands that were being made on the EPS from 1980 to 1990. In the years since these figures were compiled, demands on the EPS have become even more severe, especially in relation to the decline in available police resources. Overall demands for police service have grown, and actual calls for service have been increasing as well.

A further indication of the pressures on the EPS and the inadequacy of the police response is illustrated by the fact that in 1991, 60,000 callers to the police complaint line

Table 7.2 Demands on the Edmonton Police Service, 1980–1990

Subject	Indicator	Outcome
Demographics	Population	19 percent increase
Reported crime	Annual criminal occurrences	44 percent increase
Communications division workload	Complaint-line calls answered Calls dispatched	No change 16 percent increase
Police service strength	Crime reports taken over phone	67 percent increase
Authorized civilian strength	Authorized sworn strength	2 percent decrease
	Authorized patrol constables	1 percent decrease
		12.4 percent increase
Self-initiated work	Impaired driving charges	101 percent increase
	Drug charges	51 percent decrease
Budget	Portion of operating budget allocated to communications and patrol divisions	41 percent of budget
Time-oriented measures of effectiveness	Consumed time and response (on scene) time	15 percent increase to April 1990

Source: D. Veitch, *Community Policing in Edmonton*, 3rd edition. Edmonton: Community and Organizational Support. D., (1995), pg.18. © Edmonton Police Services

hung up before being answered. Many would then call the 911 emergency line, tying up this emergency system.

Responding to the Challenge: The Development of a New Model of Service Delivery

These pressures were the catalyst for the EPS to examine new ways of delivering police services. Like many police organizations, the EPS had traditionally been hierarchical and was characterized by a high degree of specialization. In 1969, there were 64 different units in the department; by 1991, the number of units had grown to 120.

As part of its restructuring, EPS conducted a thorough review of all units in the organization, asking five basic questions:

1. What is the unit intended to do?
2. What is it actually doing at this time?
3. Should it be doing what it is actually doing?
4. What should it be doing?
5. How should it do what it should be doing?

The EPS then identified 21 "hot spots" in the city. It was discovered that 81 percent of calls in these areas were to "repeat" locations. Twenty-one members of the newly formed Neighbourhood Foot Patrol Program (NFPP) began walking the beat in these areas, becoming familiar with the residents and solving their problems. The success of this initial approach resulted in the development of a core value that would guide the entire service: "Committed to Community Needs."

Organizational changes were structured using a modified **differential response model**, supported by decentralized reporting outlets, face-to-face interactions when reporting crimes, problem-solving, and public involvement in policing (see Figure 7.1).

Figure 7.1 Edmonton Police Service Differential Response Model

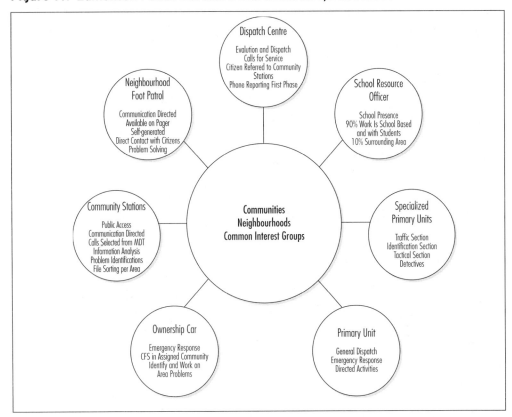

Source: D. Veitch, *Community Policing in Edmonton,* 3rd edition. Edmonton: Community and Organizational Support. (1995), pg.18. © Edmonton Police Services

In addition, police officers were given "ownership" of areas and problems, decision-making was decentralized, and efforts were made to "despecialize" officers' activities. Calls for service that were not resolved at the initial stages by the dispatch centre or at the community police station were referred to officers with knowledge of the area or issue. These policies maximized police resources while increasing the likelihood that a solution would be found to the problem at hand.

In 2004, the EPS established the Community Advisory Council (CAC) to engage in a dialogue with diverse communities with the aim of fostering mutual trust, sharing information, and building relationships. (For this, the EPS received the 2006 International Association of Chief's of Police Civil Rights Award.) In 2017, this dialogue focused on eight diverse Community Liaison Committees, including Indigenous, Black, Muslim, and Sexual Minorities Committees (Edmonton Police Service 2017, http://www.edmonton-police.ca/AboutEPS/CommunityInitiatives/ChiefsCAC.aspx).

Also in 2004, the EPS underwent a second wave of organizational renewal. An organizational review was conducted in 2004 and 2005, which led to the release of the document *Agenda for Change,* which made 123 recommendations for organizational improvement based on the findings of extensive research and the examination of best practices from the public and private sectors. In 2006, after a series of scandals, including allegations of police corruption, infiltration of the EPS by organized crime, and improper use of authority, the EPS released its Professional Committee Report, which made 58 recommendations aimed at increasing public trust and confidence in the service by enhancing ethics and professionalism.

Later in 2006, after an extensive search, the Edmonton Police Commission hired a new chief of police, Mike Boyd. He needed to strengthen public confidence in the EPS, and shortly after taking office, he released a 100-Day Plan as a first step towards rebuilding trust with citizens. The plan involved extensive consultation with the "Big 5" (residential and business community, social and government agencies, political leaders, media, and police), and identified 57 recommendations to enhance service and to move the organization forward.

After the extensive consultation, the following five strategic directions for 2006 to 2008 were established:

1. Reduce victimization;
2. Improve service;
3. Improve effectiveness, efficiency, and innovative business processes;
4. Improve financial investment, sustainability, and accountability; and
5. Enhance professionalism.

Under these five strategic directions, 27 priorities were identified that would provide the framework for prioritizing those needs and ideas that stemmed from the 100-Day Plan, as well as past needs outlined in the 2004 organizational review and the 2005 Professionalism Committee. In the end, the EPS and Police Commission created a working document with 143 recommendations charting the course for future policing in the City of Edmonton.

Today the EPS operates a number of full-service community police stations, each staffed by uniformed officers who are assisted by community volunteers. EPS ran a marketing campaign to encourage community residents to report incidents and problems directly to the community police stations. At all times, the focus was on the community and its needs rather than the needs of the police organization. There are also neighbourhood foot patrol officers who staff offices located throughout the city.

Empowerment and Ownership: A New Role for Patrol Officers

Two critical components of the model of community policing developed by the EPS are **empowerment** and **ownership**. Approximately 75 percent of officers in the service have been given ownership responsibilities in communities, regardless of whether community is defined by specific geographic boundaries or by other attributes, such as residents who are members of a visible or cultural minority. Ownership members, including foot patrol officers, are responsible for developing contacts with the community and working with community residents (including businesses) to identify, address, and solve problems. Ownership officers are given the authority and discretion to address issues and to respond to calls for service that arise in their area. The remaining EPS officers are considered primary response officers, answering emergency calls. All officers in the EPS are encouraged to be innovative, to take risks, and to work with community residents.

For the reorganization to succeed, both police officers of the EPS and community residents had to understand the changes that were occurring. This required internal and external communication strategies. The **internal communication strategy** exposed police officers to the principles of community policing, and their participation in redesigning the model of service delivery was solicited. In recent years, the EPS has also partnered with local post-secondary institutions to provide advanced education opportunities for students to learn about community policing. In addition, the process of recruiting and training new officers was altered. The **external communication strategy** was designed to inform the general public about the changes in how police services would be delivered and to solicit public's participation and involvement as active partners in the process and in the new policing model.

Outcomes and Effectiveness of the EPS Model of Service Delivery

Over the past decade, the EPS has assessed the effectiveness of the new model of service delivery. These assessments have been carried out by the EPS itself, by the Edmonton Police Commission, and by external researchers. The results of the studies that have been conducted to date indicate conclusively that the reforms have produced positive outcomes on a number of measures. These include:

- *Increased citizen satisfaction with the police.* The results of annual surveys of community residents, covering a wide range of issues from fear of crime to attitudes towards the police, reveal that citizens support the police and have a high level of confidence in the EPS. In addition, there is widespread support for community policing as practised by EPS: a survey conducted in 2016 by the EPS indicated that 89 percent of those residents surveyed rated the overall performance as average to excellent. In addition, 12 percent of residents said their confidence in the EPS had gone up in the previous year—a slight decrease from the year before. This is an important measure of trust and support for the EPS.
- *Improved officer morale, motivation, and job satisfaction.* Community police officers and foot patrol officers have responded favourably to being empowered to address and resolve issues and problems in the areas in which they work.
- *Reduction in levels of crime.* The City of Edmonton, in sharp contrast to other western urban centres, has recorded reductions in the total number of Criminal Code occurrences as well as in the levels of person-related offences and property crime in recent years. Key crime indicators have for the most part seen decreases; however, there have been marginal increases in auto theft and violent youth crime.
- *Increases in clearance rates.* In 1995, the clearance rate for person and violent crimes was 66 percent, a 12.5 percent improvement over 1991. For property-related crimes, (which traditionally have a very low clearance rate), the clearance rate in 1995 was 27 percent, an improvement of nearly 39 percent from 1991. The overall clearance rate for all crime in 2010 was 39 percent, and there was a 7 percent decrease in reported crime compared to 2005. From 1997 to 2007, the crime rate (measured as reported crime per 100,000 population) increased by 12 percent. Nationally, clearance rates have been improving since 2004, and while violent crime clearance rates have followed the same upward shorter-term trend, they have decreased since the mid-1990s.
- *Reductions in complaint-line calls and decreases in dispatches.* Between 1991 and 1993, dispatched calls declined 18 percent while at the same time the number of contacts with community citizens rose dramatically. More specifically, from 1991 to 1995, there were the following reductions related to calls to the communications centre: 911 police (−37 percent), calls answered (−40 percent), abandoned calls (−70 percent), average speed of answer of calls (−69 percent), total calls (−44 percent), and dispatched calls (−32 percent). In recent years, the EPS has created **specialty units** such as the Derelict Housing Unit to target specific crimes and disorder that would typically result in numerous complaints to the police communication centre requesting police attendance. By adopting a broader, problem-solving approach, the EPS has reduced the demand on its communication section to dispatch units to repeat calls for service to the same address.

Previously, the primary ways of assessing the effectiveness of the police were the levels of criminal activity and the clearance rates. It is interesting to note that the implementation of a service delivery model based on community policing has had a significant impact on these two factors and has resulted in positive outcomes on a number of other measures.

The EPS and Organizational Reform

Identifying the principles of community policing and paying them "lip service" is easy. Making the organizational changes required to implement community policing is the most difficult part.

The EPS passed through several identifiable stages in developing and implementing its model of community policing. In each stage, senior police administrators in the department played a critical role in launching the reform effort, but line officers participated actively in the process.

Stage 1: Recognition of a Performance Gap

Senior administrators acknowledged that the department, as it was traditionally structured, was not effectively meeting the demands and expectations being placed on it. This performance gap was evident in the volume of calls on the complaint line, the high percentage of abandoned calls, the slow response time to requests for service, and the apparent ineffectiveness of the police in reducing levels of crime. Added to this was a crisis in confidence in the EPS among many citizens.

Stage 2: Recognition of a Need for Organizational Change

The inability of a police service to respond effectively to demands does not automatically result in senior administrators undertaking reform. Rather, there is often a tendency to rely on traditional responses, such as increasing police personnel or seeking additional fiscal resources. For the reform process to begin, senior police leaders must recognize that fundamental changes are required in the structure and delivery of policing services. The EPS conducted a thorough review of all facets of the police service, and the results provided impetus to the reform movement.

Stage 3: Creating an Organizational Climate Receptive to Reform

It is the responsibility of the senior police leadership in a department to create an atmosphere conducive to change. Since the implementation of the principles of community policing requires change at all levels of the organization, a commitment to change (or, at the very minimum, a receptiveness to change) must be secured from senior administrators, middle managers, and line officers. Significantly, the EPS's senior administration used the findings of a complete organizational review to flatten and decentralize the organizational structure and to reduce or eliminate the traditional boundaries between the different levels and units of the EPS.

The EPS's internal communication strategy informed police members at all levels of the organization of the principles of community policing and solicited their participation in the development of a new model of service delivery. According to the results of surveys on job satisfaction and morale among EPS officers, it is clear that the senior administration succeeded in creating a positive environment in which officers made use of the new model of service delivery. This success is also reflected in the other positive outcomes produced by evaluations and assessments.

Stage 4: Creating a Community Climate Receptive to Reform

Given the importance of the community in any model of community policing, residents must be told about the reforms and their impact on the delivery of policing services. In addition, community residents must be educated about the role of the community in the new model of service delivery. To accomplish this, the EPS's designed an external communication strategy to promote the idea of community policing and the new service delivery model among the citizens of Edmonton.

Stage 5: Creating a New Model of Service Delivery and Call Response

If the well-entrenched, reactive model of police service delivery is to be replaced, it is essential that the organization develop a viable alternative. The EPS model of service delivery provides for line officers to assume ownership of problems in the areas they police and thus empowers them to work with community residents to solve those problems. In short, new roles and responsibilities have been created for line officers, and these have resulted in greater autonomy being vested in officers on the street.

The model also identifies a key role for the community and highlights the importance of community police stations and neighbourhood foot patrol as strategies for service delivery.

You will also recall from Chapter 6 that the Edmonton Police Service changed the way it deploys its resources by implementing a "staffing to workload" model that attempts to match resourcing requirements to predicted call volumes and tasks and to evenly distribute the workload. This is part of an effort to free up time for police officers to work on preventative initiatives.

Stage 6: Conducting Ongoing Analyses and Evaluations of the Service Delivery Model

To ensure that organizational reforms and the model of service delivery are effective in meeting the demands placed on the police service, ongoing analyses and evaluations are essential. In recognition of this, the EPS has a substantial in-house capacity to conduct surveys and studies. These include assessments of the impact of various policing strategies on the rates of criminal activity in Edmonton, and surveys of police members to record their levels of job satisfaction and issues of concern, as well as surveys to determine the levels of citizen satisfaction with the police. In 2002, the EPS committed itself to becoming an **intelligence-led police organization**, taking its commitment to research and evaluation to a new level. While we will examine this idea in more detail in Chapter 10, the EPS defines "intelligence-led policing" as follows:

Intelligence-led policing involves the collection and analysis of information to produce an intelligence product designed to inform police decision making at both the tactical and strategic levels. In this model, intelligence serves as a guide to operations, rather than the reverse. It begins with the notion that a principal task of the police is to prevent and detect crime rather than simply react to it.

(Edmonton Police Service 2002)

The EPS has also been supportive of external evaluations conducted by university-based scholars and by representatives of internationally recognized organizations such as the Police Executive Research Forum, located in Washington, DC. Rather than viewing these external evaluations and assessments as a threat, the EPS sees such studies and reviews as part of its continuing efforts to excel in the provision of police services to the City of Edmonton.

Final Thoughts on the EPS and Community Policing

The experience of the EPS illustrates conclusively that it is possible for police services to reform their organizational and operational structures and to adopt new models of service delivery based on the principles of community policing. The EPS's reform was undertaken very deliberately and with considerable planning, and its experience provides an example for police services and communities across the country as to what is possible. Particularly significant for our focus in this text is that line officers were involved in all phases of the reform process and that the new model of service delivery resulted in a major transformation of the role of police members.

Furthermore, both internal and external assessments of the effectiveness of the activities and initiatives of the EPS, using a variety of performance indicators, provide strong and consistent evidence that service delivery based on community policing is a "win–win" situation—for the community, which experiences reduced levels of criminal activity and positive relationships with and perceptions of the police, and for police officers, who are given the autonomy and authority to use their skills and imagination to address and solve problems at the neighbourhood level.

It is important to note that the EPS continues to evolve to meet the changing demands and needs of the communities it serves. In 2011, soaring numbers of homicides in Edmonton required the organization to adapt its processes and capacities, something it was capable of doing based on the foundation of trust it had built with its communities. Although the experiences of this police service may serve as an example of what is possible in the realm of policing, each police service must chart its own course, depending on the demands placed on it, the capabilities of its personnel, and the interests and abilities of the citizens it serves.

THE CITY OF MONTREAL POLICE SERVICE NEIGHBOURHOOD POLICING PROJECT: REORGANIZATION FOR COMMUNITY POLICING

In December 1996, after five years of analysis, debate, and union negotiations, the *Service de police de la Ville de Montréal (SPVM) (*Montreal Police Service [MPS]) implemented the first phase of a major reform of the organization and delivery of policing services in the Montreal Urban Community region. The reform included the following changes:

- *Organizational decentralization*: a shift from a traditional, centralized command and control structure with 24 precincts to a decentralized service delivery structure with 49 precincts.
- *The creation of 49 neighbourhood police stations*: "mini stations" staffed by a small number of civilian employees and a uniformed officer complement ranging from 30 to 98, depending on the size of the population served.
- *Four operations centres, one in each region*: centres containing prisoner cells, detectives' offices, and specialized units such as SWAT teams.

Planning for the reorganization involved recruiting, selecting, and training commanders for the neighbourhood police stations and for the operations centres; reviewing and evaluating potential locations for the neighbourhood stations and two of the operations centres; restructuring the call-response procedures; and training police constables and their supervisors in community policing methods. Extensive improvements were also made to the telecommunications systems; this included providing patrol officers with cellular telephones and pagers.

The external marketing strategy involved a promotional campaign featuring posters placed on buses and in other public places. In addition, a newsletter on neighbourhood policing was mailed to 900 to 1,000 homes and businesses in the region (Communauté urbaine de Montréal 1997).

The changes put officers in closer contact with the community, with the goal of increasing the involvement of community residents in identifying and responding to crime and disorder, and, by having citizens use the neighbourhood police station to complete reports, of reducing the amount of paperwork for officers. In addition, each station has an advisory committee that meets monthly to discuss community concerns.

The neighbourhood stations provide basic police services, while case investigations and specialized police services such as crime-scene analysis and traffic control are delivered by the four operations centres, which are situated in each of the police regions. The mini-stations are situated mainly in shopping districts and in areas of heavy pedestrian traffic.

For cases that are not urgent, community residents file a report at the neighbourhood station. At least one officer at each station serves as a liaison with the local community, providing citizens with the opportunity to express their concerns and problems. Emergency calls are still handled by MPS dispatch, which forwards them to the appropriate police district.

Since the inception of the Neighbourhood Policing Project there has been ongoing evaluation. In 2003, a significant review of the project established a number of priorities for the years ahead. These priorities, determined through an extensive consultative process with the community and the municipal government, identified six areas of focus: (1) meeting residents' expectations, (2) establishing closer ties between the constabulary and investigations, (3) strengthening neighbourhood stations, (4) valuing individuals and integrating culture, (5) optimizing processes, and (6) structure and management.

Today, the SPVM operates 32 local police stations (PDQs). Each PDQ reports to one of the four community services: North, South, East, and West divisions. The four management areas have full authority to customize their service delivery to local needs. As a result, services provided by PDQs may vary from station to station or across regions. In carrying out their activities and meeting their mandate, the PDQs may rely on support from the Specialized Investigation Service (SES) as well as a number of administrative departments.

THE EVOLUTION OF COMMUNITY POLICING IN SURREY, BC

Surrey is very culturally, socio-economically, and geographically diverse. By decentralizing our operations to five district policing offices, our members can better meet the needs and concerns of each unique community, while still maintaining a consistent quality of service throughout Surrey.
—*Chief Superintendent T. Smith, former Surrey RCMP (1997)*

The Surrey RCMP community policing project in BC began in 1997, focusing on the decentralization of policing services. The Surrey Detachment is the largest RCMP detachment in Canada, with 1,000 personnel (police officers, civilian members, and volunteers) (RCMP 2017). As the largest and busiest RCMP detachment in Canada (in 2011, Surrey's population was over 468,251, of which 191,000 were visible minorities [40.5 percent] [Statistics Canada 2012]), the municipality has been divided into five districts, based on an analysis of call levels. Each district office is under the command of a district commander, who has the authority to arrange shift schedules and officer assignments to respond to the policing needs of each district. Taking a page out of the EPS approach to service delivery, patrol officers are assigned to one of the five district offices and work with their colleagues and community residents to address the specific needs and concerns of each area.

The original main detachment remains open to the public and continues to house all plainclothes units, including the drug and break and enter sections, as well as victim services and administrative offices. In addition, patrol strategies have been adapted to the requirements of each district. For example, unique to District 1 is the RCMP's only full-time "Footbeat Section," which deals with a number of special community concerns, including a needle exchange and drop-in centre, prostitution, welfare offices, methadone clinics, and drug recovery houses. The 11-person, full-time foot patrol section represents a return to strategic street-level community policing with zero tolerance for crime. Through increased visibility and an "up close and personal" policing style, the Footbeat Section is attempting to restore the community's sense of safety within the area. In 2006, a community storefront station was added to District 1.

In 2006, a delegation consisting of representatives from the RCMP, the BC attorney general, the BC solicitor general, the school board, the fire department, and social service agencies, travelled to the UK to learn first-hand how their crime rates had dropped by as much as 44 percent in some jurisdictions. They also went to New York City to study community courts. Based on their observations, which focused on root causes of crime, the Municipality of Surrey established the Mayor's Task Force on Public Safety and Crime Reduction. More than 100 individuals representing over 50 different organizations, including the RCMP, not-for-profits, provincial and federal governments, the Parole Office, the Crown Counsel, the school board, the Board of Trade, and numerous community organizations, brought their expertise and resources to the creation of the **Surrey Crime Reduction Strategy**.

The Crime Reduction Strategy has four components:

1. Prevent and Deter Crime
2. Apprehend and Prosecute Offenders
3. Rehabilitate and Reintegrate Offenders
4. Reality and Perceptions of Crime

Under each component are a number of strategies and recommendations that arose from meetings of the Mayor's Task Force on Public Safety and Crime Reduction.

1. Prevent and Deter Crime

- Community safety officers
- Skytrain and transit safety
- Education and awareness programs
- CRS website in the three most common languages in Surrey
- Community drug action teams
- CCTV pilot program
- Crime-free multi-housing
- Parenting orders
- Youth intervention programs

2. Apprehend and Prosecute Offenders

- Identifying prolific offenders and crime hot spots
- Dismantling grow-op and drug houses
- Community court model
- Night court
- Stiffer penalties for priority crimes
- Prolific offender management teams
- Enhanced treatment in provincial corrections facilities

3. Rehabilitate and Reintegrate Offenders

- Expanded treatment through the private sector
- Regional approach to treatment
- Recovery house accreditation
- Homelessness and housing foundation ($8.4 million)
- Sobering centre
- Transitional housing
- Full-time homelessness outreach workers
- Education and job training
- Community support teams

4. Reality and Perceptions of Crime

- Communications strategy
- Community action groups
- Working with seniors and the most vulnerable
- Leaflet drops in neighbourhoods after drug houses are taken down (City of Surrey 2006)

Implementation of the crime reduction strategy has produced some promising results, including reductions in auto theft (by 22 percent in 2006) and business break and enters in the Whalley area (by 45 percent).

Community policing in Surrey has evolved. It was the first RCMP detachment to decentralize its service delivery model; it is now creating and implementing a crime reduction strategy that incorporates a number of community partnerships designed to address underlying causes of crime and disorder. Many RCMP detachments are too small for this type of reorganization; however, there are a number of large detachments in urban areas where similar changes have been made, including the creation of specialized units to better address the community's needs.

You will recall from our discussion of community policing that it is the particular relationship between the police and the community that gives the model of policing its own distinct character, and that accounts for why some strategies work and others do not. Surrey is no exception, and it is worth keeping up to date with policing developments in BC, particularly in relation to evaluations of the crime reduction strategy.

The three fundamental policing philosophies of the Surrey RCMP are listed below. Its service delivery model is depicted in Figure 7.2.

- *Community policing*: Based on the belief that the community plays an integral role in crime reduction and that through collaborative working relationships the underlying causes of crime and disorder can be addressed.

Figure 7.2 Surrey RCMP Service Delivery Model

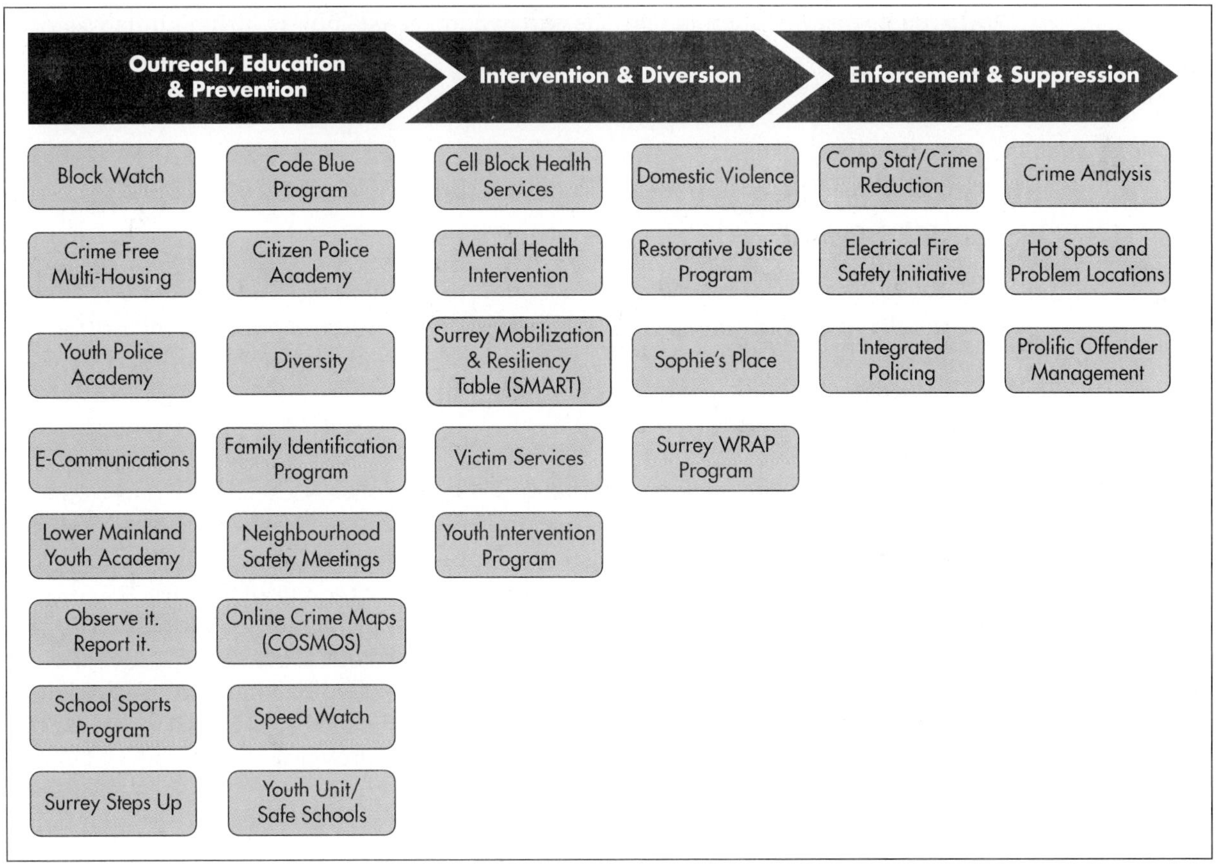

Source: Reproduced with the permission of the RCMP. http://surrey.rcmp-grc.gc.ca/digitalAssets/51/51378_Service_Delivery_English.pdf

- *Intelligence-led policing*: Acknowledges that research, analysis, and evidence-based decision-making are critical to effective and efficient policing and that reliable and timely crime analysis is critical for the utilization of both police and community resources (i.e., enforcement, as well as investigation and prevention measures proactively targeting habitual offenders, high-crime areas, and crime causation factors).
- *Integrated policing*: Recognizes that success in crime reduction can better be achieved by partnering with other organizations that also contribute to public safety, either directly or indirectly; combined efforts are better equipped to address complex community problems.*

In November 2015, the Surrey RCMP implemented the Surrey Mobilization and Resiliency Table (SMART). Modelled after the Hub model from Prince Albert, Saskatchewan, and the Situation Tables in Ontario (see Chapter 6), the Surrey Hub was the 56th Hub in Canada (Bhayani and Thompson 2016). In establishing the Hub, the Surrey RCMP adopted a "slow and steady" tactic. The goal was to turn over control of the process and to employ a truly participatory method, wherein community agencies and organizations would be engaged and involved as equal partners at every stage of selection, design, and implementation of a collaborative risk-driven model in the neighbourhood of Whalley. In keeping with the overarching goal, the model would transition from being police-initiated to becoming a truly community driven and controlled initiative.

By July 2016, 83 situations had been addressed by Hub participants, with the following results: 40 percent of referred persons had been successfully connected to services that lowered their overall risk of harm; information and response "silos" between service delivery partners had been reduced; and demands for emergency service response had also been reduced.

In addition, there was some evidence that the Hub had increased collaboration between diverse community partners and had increased "buy-in" from human services providers. It is likely the Hub model will continue to develop across Canada as a best practice leading to substantive improvements to community safety.

THE EVOLUTION OF COMMUNITY POLICING IN THE HALTON REGIONAL POLICE SERVICE

To transform an organization from one that is traditionally oriented, quasi-militaristically managed and relatively impermeable to external policy collaboration, to one that can fully embody the community-based policing philosophy is clearly a formidable task.

—Clairmont (1996)

The changes that were made in the Halton Regional Police Service (HRPS) as it moved from a traditional police service to one centred on community-based policing are another good illustration of the various stages of adopting and implementing the principles of community policing. The Halton Regional Police Service was one of the earliest and most comprehensive community policing programs to be implemented in North America and is considered to be a leading-edge police service (Clairmont 1996, 6).

As fate would have it, there have been a number of studies conducted on the HRPS covering the period from the 1970s to 2000. A composite picture of the phases the HRPS went through in implementing community policing is provided by the work of Donald

---

*RCMP in Surrey, Service Delivery model, found at http://bc.rcmp-grc.gc.ca/ViewPage.action?siteNodeId=70&languageId=1&contentId=675 Reproduced with the permission of the RCMP.

Loree of the Canadian Police College (1988), Don Clairmont of the Atlantic Institute of Criminology in Halifax (1996), Lori Cooke-Scott (1998), and K. Taylor (1999). Taken together, the studies provide unique insight into the evolution of a police service. These investigations make it clear that the HRPS is one of the most, if not *the* most, studied police services in Canada.

Among the highlights of the evolution of community policing in the HRPS are the following:

The 1970s

- *1974–1980*: Following the creation of the HRPS in 1974, team policing and other components of what was to become known as "community policing" are used.
- *1975*: HRPS establishes a team-policing program in Burlington. Teams of 10 officers work together in designated areas. Police administrators support the approach, which is viewed as a way to increase police–community contact and to improve officer awareness and understanding of community problems. A year later, the *Burlington Post* writes: "This system gets people closer to the people they serve by giving constables more of a chance to leave their cars and mingle with the public, getting to know them and their problems on a less formal basis" (1976, 3, 5). The project collapses several years later due to a lack of resources.
- *1979*: James Harding becomes chief of police and announces a commitment to crime prevention and community policing, a proactive approach to policing, and the adoption of a participatory management style. Although reception to this approach among officers appears to be mixed, Harding's leadership style plants the seeds of significant changes in the organization and delivery of police services by HRPS.

The 1980s

A variety of innovative approaches to policing are implemented, including the **Village Constable Program** and a number of specific proactive initiatives.

- *1982*: A proactive policing squad is created in Aldershot, a high-crime area in the city of Burlington. Platoons in this area are split into proactive and reactive squads, each under the supervision of a sergeant. Proactive officers do problem-solving police work in collaboration with the community. This approach reduces the crime rate and receives strong support from community residents. A year later the program is implemented throughout Burlington. The split-platoon approach suffers from a number of operational difficulties, including a general absence of input from the community, and line officers receive little direction. This results in officers not fully supporting the initiative or being confused about management expectations. In short, "planning and implementation were limited and the impact uncertain" (Clairmont 1996, 43).
- *1982–1985*: Other programs are gradually phased in. Community conference committees are established and administered by constables. These are designed to give community members opportunities to interact with officers, discuss community problems, and voice their concerns. An auxiliary unit composed of volunteers is created, along with a summer youth program and special community events. The Children's Safety Village is established to educate children on safety practices.

  Also, a mission statement is created to reflect the new philosophy of policing. It states: "The Halton Regional Police Force [later changed to 'Service'] will respond to community needs through a combined strategy of preventative, proactive and reactive policing programs, using the concept of the Constable Generalist, the whole of which will be supported by a participatory management environment" (Halton Regional Police Force 1982).
- *1984*: The **Village Constable Program** is created. Officers are assigned to specific geographic areas, and partnerships are developed between officers and the community.

Positive results are obtained, particularly in high-trouble neighbourhoods such as Warwick Court, a low-income housing complex. This program peaks in 1990–1991, with 13 sites and 17 constables involved in community-directed patrol. Officers participating in the program experience marginalization within the organization.

- *End of the 1980s*: Studies suggest that despite all the above-noted initiatives, "the organization only modestly featured a participatory management style, the field officers were not particularly trained in or committed to CBP [community-based policing], and, apart from the village constables, there was little collaboration between the police and community in the sense of community-directed policing" (Clairmont 1996, 57). Commenting on the difficulties in developing substantive links with the community, Donald Loree (1988, 207) stated: "[the idea that] the community itself becomes a real partner in the provision of police services, not merely the recipient of programs developed and delivered in isolation … is probably the most difficult of the community policing ideas for police forces and their members to accept."

The 1990s

- *1990–1995*: A distinctive HRPS community-based policing model emerges. The commitment to CBP is widespread in the organization. HRPS continues to be a leading-edge police service, although concerns are expressed that the term CBP itself may carry too much historical baggage and may hinder the implementation of key principles, such as problem-oriented policing.
- *1990*: The HRPS community-based policing model is implemented and focuses on several key initiatives: the Village Constable Program, which involves officers working out of storefronts; community-directed patrol involving officers assigned to specific areas; and community consultation committees (CCCs). The adoption of this model is precipitated by a number of factors, including the following: village constables were only a small portion of the service and were at risk of being marginalized; the directive that patrol officers divide their time equally between proactive and reactive police work was not working; and many patrol officers still did not have a close relationship with the residents in the areas to which they were assigned. Efforts to create a service-wide community policing approach are hindered by insufficient training for officers and by an absence of officer participation in decision-making. Clairmont (1996, 67) notes the "widespread view that management policies in practice did not overly encourage strong officer-CCC linkages and that officers experienced both ambivalence and uncertainty with respect to their roles in the CBP system."
- *1993*: Reductions in provincial transfer payments and social contract legislation result in major changes in the police service. A comprehensive Organizational Review Project (ORP) is undertaken to eliminate, combine, or automate those activities of the police service that hinder effective policing.
- *1994*: A Community Policing Committee, an internal committee within the HRPS, examines the state of CBP in the police service and notes that, although the HRPS is widely recognized as a CBP police service, there are still problems in implementing CBP. Clairmont notes: "By the end of 1994 there were discernible cracks in HRPS's model of CBP. The number of village constables had declined … The CCCs in at least one district no longer had specific named constables assigned to them … Participatory management among patrol constables … was at a low ebb … The stress level had reached as high as 15 percent of the members" (Clairmont 1996, 78–79).
- *1995*: The ORP concludes and contains 170 recommendations. The chief of the HRPS states: "We believe that we must create a learning environment in which our employees will become increasingly empowered to provide service to the public without management interference. We will encourage them to participate more in designing changes to the way we do business" (Clairmont 1996). This provides the basis for what becomes known

as **Total Integrated Policing** (TIP), an approach designed to empower employees while at the same time holding them accountable for their work. To accomplish this, the organization is flattened and the traditional top-down command and control structure is altered.

- A community survey is conducted, soliciting feedback on citizens' perceptions of crime, experiences with the police, levels of satisfaction with the police, policing priorities, and expectations for the police service.
- A service delivery philosophy is developed, centred on proactive, reactive, and preventive policing and the development of police–community partnerships. The core components of the philosophy are problem-solving, continuity of service, communication among officers assigned to areas, and an ability to adjust to a changing environment. Officers are assigned to teams that concentrate on specific areas. Direction is provided by the Service Delivery Design Team (SDDT), which is to implement the TIP approach and the recommendations from the ORP.
- *1995–2000*: Emphasis continues on enhancing the organizational and operational requirements for community policing. As HRPS heads into the remaining years of the decade (and the century), there is increased emphasis on communication between management and patrol officers and on the participation of officers in decision-making. Team policing is becoming a cornerstone of service delivery.

Clairmont (1996, 102–3) notes that it may be useful to downplay the generic term *community policing* and to focus instead on those of its components that have widespread support in the community and among officers. These include police–community partnerships, problem-oriented policing, and team policing.

Nearly all of the 170 recommendations from the 1995 ORP report are implemented. A revised planning process is developed that includes a framework for producing a business plan. This includes environmental scans, an annual consultative process within the police service for identifying issues and goals, and business plans for each unit of the service.

The team concept has widespread support among officers and has been successfully implemented. An evaluation reveals that understaffing compromises its success and that, to succeed, teams require time and the support of supervisors. A comprehensive evaluation of all facets of HRPS concludes in 1999 that "the HRPS has demonstrated a successful community service orientation. Community consultation committees, periodic public surveys, the introduction of village constables, and the team approach have all buttressed the community-police partnership" (Taylor 1999, 59).

Lessons from the Halton Regional Police Service Experience

The HRPS experience illustrates the difficulty of effecting integrated, thorough-going CBP even in a very favorable policing environment where resources have been fairly plentiful, crime and reactive pressures fairly low, the population well-educated and appreciative, management positive and able, and the staff well-trained and young.
—D. Clairmont (1996)

Some important lessons can be drawn from the experience of the Halton Regional Police Service:

1. Community policing cannot be merely a set of programs; it must be built on a vision of what a police service should be. This vision must be communicated throughout the organization. It must be adopted as a philosophy governing the delivery of all policing services.
2. Implementing community policing does not occur overnight. It is a slow and gradual process that requires support and commitment. The Halton experience indicates that it is a combination of patience, commitment, ideas, and creatively constructed programs that allows for the success of a comprehensive community-based policing approach (Cooke-Scott 1998, 42).

3. Community policing requires significant changes in the organization of police services. Flattening the police organization by trimming upper-level management personnel displaces decision-making to front-line officers; this, in turn, empowers patrol officers to do community policing.

4. Implementing community policing requires police services to take risks, to learn from their mistakes, and to develop the capacity to adapt to changes in legislation, community expectations, and available resources. It is important that the police service document its efforts, thereby developing an organizational memory from which others may learn.

5. The innovation required for community policing must come from within the police service, and an organizational structure must be created to allow for change to be initiated from the bottom up rather than from the top down. Line officers in the HRPS often felt they were "thrown to the wolves" when upper management "imposed a program [on them] from above without any input from them, without any details about how or why they were supposed to go about implementing it … They expected us to carry something out that they [upper management] didn't even understand" (Cooke-Scott 1998, 130).

PLANNING FOR CHANGE: THE DURHAM REGIONAL POLICE SERVICE ORGANIZATIONAL RENEWAL PROJECT

The Adequacy and Effectiveness of Police Services Regulations have been in effect since 1 January 2001. We previously noted that these standards set out specific requirements for Ontario police services in a number of areas, including community policing. In anticipation of these new regulations, police services across the province engaged in planning exercises to develop the capacity for compliance. These exercises provide us with further insight into how organizational change can be initiated and directed. The **Organizational Renewal Project** of the Durham Regional Police (visit http://www.drps.ca/internet_explorer/businessplan.asp) illustrates how one police service planned to meet the new requirements.

At the outset, Durham's Police Services Board retained the services of a management research organization. The group followed a plan that addressed a number of implementation issues, each with sections on "What We Intend to Do" and "How We Intend to Do It." The approach taken by the Durham Regional Police (2004), which flowed from the consultants' report, is summarized below.

Implementation Issue 1. Defining Community Policing

- *What We Intend to Do:* Assist the Police Services Board to define, develop, communicate, and implement a stated board policy setting our approach to community policing and how it will be sustained.
- *How We Intend to Do It:* A research team will be established to meet this objective. Its role will be to create a definition of community policing so that the police service can measure programs and initiatives. This process will involve consultation with the community, community office, and unit leaders, and will include all our stakeholders. It will also review unit mandates, current practices, and resource materials.

Implementation Issue 2. Structural Changes

- *What We Intend to Do:* Establish accountability statements, competencies, and skills required for all positions listed in the consultant's report. Develop accountability statements, competencies, and skills required for all other roles within the organization.
- *How We Intend to Do It:* Establish a research team to examine each position identified on the organizational chart in the consultant's report and develop broad accountability statements, competencies, and skills required for all positions to the level of unit leader, in consultation with current incumbents, human resources, and involved stakeholders.

Implementation Issue 3. Communication

- *What We Intend to Do:* Develop a strategy for ensuring that effective internal and external communication can take place.
- *How We Intend to Do It:* Designate an internal/external communications research team with the responsibility for ensuring that the communication issues identified in the consultant's report are responded to.

Implementation Issue 4. Relationships with Associations

- *What We Intend to Do:* Address the issue of relationships with the two Durham Regional Police Associations, by identifying specific positions within the organization that will be responsible for improving the relationship with the associations through effective communication.
- *How We Intend to Do It:* For the positions of executive director of the Police Services Board, director of employee environment, and the chief of police, place specific tasks in the accountability statements to ensure effective communication with the associations. A research team will be established to meet this objective and the team will consult with the two associations to include their knowledge and expertise.

Implementation Issue 5. Leadership Development

- *What We Intend to Do:* Address the need of the police service to formulate a plan of leadership and career development for all members (both civilian and police) who aspire to meet its current and future succession needs. The plan will ensure that developmental roles are treated on a rotational basis to ensure optimal development and readiness of members to assume key leadership roles when they become available.
- *How We Intend to Do It:* Establish a research team that will be charged with formulating a plan of leadership and career development for the police service. This team will work closely with the team identified under Implementation Issue 6 (Training Development/ Certification), because leadership development will have a direct impact on the strategies of Team 6.

Implementation Issue 6. Training Development/Certification

- *What We Intend to Do:* The Learning Centre will be tasked with performing a needs analysis for formal learning and certification training requirements for each level within the organization, and with developing a strategy to present to the service to meet those requirements.
- *How We Intend to Do It:* Establish a research team tasked with developing a strategy to meet the identified formal learning and training requirements for each level, as well as identifying requirement standards. This team will work closely with the group identified under Implementation Issue 5 (Leadership Development), as the input of the team will have a direct impact on its work.

Implementation Issue 7. Resourcing Requirements

- *What We Intend to Do:* Ensure that the resourcing requirements under the five-year staffing and facilities plans are addressed.
- *How We Intend to Do It:* Establish a research team to analyze resource requirements and to make recommendations to the Police Services Board regarding the increased resource needs that will result from these initiatives. Develop a five-year resource plan to correspond to the five-year staffing and facilities plans and all demographic changes that are anticipated to occur within the region during the next five years. This will put the police service's administration and infrastructure in a better position for

supporting all resource areas as the service grows. This team will consult with and involve human resources, planning, information technology, the learning centre, the deputy chief of administration, and all operational units.

Implementation Issue 8. Change Management

- *What We Intend to Do:* Establish a project steering committee to ensure that change management issues are addressed on an ongoing basis. This team will ensure that new and existing initiatives work co-operatively and not in conflict with one another, and that they are in harmony with the spirit of the consultant's recommendations.
- *How We Intend to Do It:* Every quarter, the project steering committee will analyze the progress of the implementation of the recommendations from the consultant's report. It will also audit results and regularly review the position of the police service in relation to the Adequacy Standards, and it will plan for the police service's ability to respond to future internal and external changes.

As of 2003 the Durham Regional Police Service call response had increased by 37 percent and overall calls to the police service had increased by 24 percent over the previous five-year period. Demands on policing had also increased as a result of expanding legislative requirements requiring the police to deal with increasingly complex criminal investigations. By 2010, the population of Durham region was 620,427; it was expected to reach over 1 million by 2031. Durham Region's economic prospects also continued to grow, as evidenced by $1.7 billion in building permits issued in 2003, the highest in the Region's 30-year history.

It will be interesting to track the progress of the Durham Regional Police Service as it progresses through the various stages of organizational renewal, as well as both the successes and the trials it encounters on the path to implementing community policing. Our previous examination of the HRPS suggests that the journey of a police service to becoming a full-fledged community policing service is often filled with successes as well as setbacks, and that good intentions alone are not sufficient to achieve the ultimate objective.

REGIONAL POLICE SERVICES AND COMMUNITY POLICING

Regional police forces are a key feature of policing in the eastern regions of Canada. In Chapter 2, we discussed the large number of independent municipal police services that have been amalgamated into regional police services over the past 40 years in Ontario. A major issue concerning regionalization is compatibility among regional police services and the requirements of community policing. When a regional police service is created, a previously smaller, independent municipal police service becomes part of a much larger organization, and its officers are mixed with those from other police services.

Proponents of regional police services argue that these larger entities are more effective in providing a full range of services to the community, are more cost-effective than smaller independent police services, and create an equity situation where all of the municipalities involved contribute to the costs of policing services and receive equal protection. Critics argue that regionalization actually *increases* the costs of policing, both during the start-up phase when multiple police services are melded into one organization and later, when large regional police services have difficulty establishing partnerships with the community. Research suggests, however, that regional police services can achieve a number of efficiencies, including a reduction in per capita policing costs, increased police coverage, higher clearance rates, and increased flexibility in deploying officers (Griffiths, Whitelaw, and Parent 1999, 50).

Regionalization has not occurred without some difficulties. A report on the Niagara Regional Police Force documented a number of problem areas, including lack of lead time in planning regionalization, difficulties integrating officers from different police services into one organizational and operational structure, and an absence of loyalty to the regional police service (cited in Oppal 1994, D9–10). However, the report also found that over time, with strong leadership from senior administrators, these problems can be successfully addressed. Similar problems were encountered, and resolved, in the amalgamation of the police services in Halifax, Dartmouth, and Bedford, Nova Scotia.

Integrated Policing

In response to the difficulties noted with regionalization, many police services in Canada are electing to integrate specific sections of their police service with those of a neighbouring police service. Integration of police services and resources is becoming a much more common approach in delivering police services. Critical Perspectives 7.1 describes strategies many police services are implementing in an effort to enhance service. For example, by integrating key sections such as forensic services, emergency response teams, K-9 units, and other common specialized areas of policing, it becomes possible to provide a more efficient and effective response to the community's needs. This process also allows the policing service to retain its autonomy and loyalty to the local community, and in some instances, cost savings are also achieved. For example, the RCMP collaborates with a number of partners to provide integrated service delivery in several areas of policing. These include Integrated Homicide Teams; the Alberta Law Enforcement Response Teams; Drug Recognition Expert Training; and Integrated Border Enforcement Teams. Similarly, the Canadian Police Information Centre (CPIC) database, operated by the National Police Services, serves as a criminal intelligence database for police services across the country and provides this service at a cost that would otherwise be prohibitive for individual police services.

For purposes of this text, a major question is to what extent the regionalization of police services facilitates or hinders the implementation of community policing strategies and programs. Sensitivity to this issue is reflected by the Ottawa Police Service, discussed below.

Integrated First Nations Unit police car in Lower Vancouver

Source: Photo by Constable Jeff Palmer, WVPD

CRITICAL PERSPECTIVES 7.1

NEW ARRANGEMENTS FOR SERVICE DELIVERY: INTEGRATIONS, CONSOLIDATIONS, AND INTEROPERABILITY

Many police departments are exploring new and improved arrangements for the delivery of police services. In British Columbia, RCMP Communication Centres consolidated from several centres into three Operational Communications Centres (OCCs). In Calgary, Alberta, the Calgary Police Service, Calgary Fire Department, and Emergency Medical Services integrated their emergency 9-1-1 communications centre into one, called Calgary 9-1-1. Through the use of various technologies and training, the goal is to develop the knowledge and skills among employees to manage any type of emergency or nonemergency call regardless of whether they previously worked for fire, police, or emergency medical services. Across Canada, agencies like the RCMP in British Columbia are incorporating lower-priced personnel, called Community Safety Officers (CSOs), into their service delivery models to increase police visibility and provide dedicated resources for crime prevention initiatives. Alberta (as discussed in Chapter 3) has established provincial sheriffs with limited authority to perform traffic enforcement duties on rural highways as well as fugitive apprehension and province-wide surveillance.

Following 11 September 2001, recommendations made by the 9/11 Commission Inquiry called for greatly improved interoperability or the ability for emergency services to communicate with one another using shared radio systems. In British Columbia, a common radio system (called BC PRIME) became a legislated requirement. Similar efforts are currently under way in Alberta.

Since 9/11, integrated policing has also taken on a global scale, requiring the alliance of law enforcement agencies locally, federally, and internationally. According to former RCMP Commissioner Giuliano Zaccardelli, integrated policing requires that police agencies work together in five key areas:

1. The concentration on developing shared priorities, both domestically and internationally, to determine the best way to leverage and maximize police efforts and resources towards common objectives.

2. The free flow of intelligence, obtaining the right information, and providing it to the right people.

3. Implementing interoperable systems to ensure that intelligence and information systems are able to communicate across organizations and geographic locations.

4. Taking advantage of economies of scale to make the most out of the resources dedicated to policing, and focusing efforts on what police do best.

5. Ensuring seamless service delivery and eliminating duplicate services and activities as well as the fragmentation of functions.

As of 2012, there were a number of integrated teams across Canada, including integrated proceeds of crime units (IPOCs), which target money laundering; integrated border enforcement teams (IBETs), which protect the security of Canadian borders; integrated market enforcement units (IMETs), which are designed to protect the integrity of Canada's capital markets; and integrated national security enforcement teams, which investigate terrorist and extremist threats. As of 2008, and as part of the National Counterfeit Enforcement Strategy, the RCMP had established three Integrated Counterfeit Enforcement Teams (ICETs) to protect the integrity of Canadian currency. These teams, located in Montreal, Toronto, and Vancouver, also illustrate the RCMP's commitment to its strategic priorities (recall A Closer Look 6.4).

The Ottawa Police Service and Community Policing

The Ottawa Police Service (OPS) was created on 1 January 1995, bringing together police services from Gloucester, Nepean, and Ottawa. One of the biggest challenges facing the new police service, as noted by the first chief of police, was to work together as a unified and integrated police service while at the same time providing a decentralized police service through the deployment and delivery of services at the district and neighbourhood levels.

The OPS's formal submission to the Ontario Civilian Commission on Police Services (OCCPS) described the foundations on which police service delivery would be based. Problem-oriented policing was selected as the community policing philosophy for the new service, and a four-pronged approach was developed to incorporate this approach into the organization and delivery of policing services:

- to move in the direction of implementing a problem-oriented policing organization;
- to move as rapidly as possible to include the community as an active partner in problem-solving and prevention;
- to reassess the current community-based activities of the Ottawa Police Service; and
- to retain only those that would advance progress in the achievement of the above three priorities.

In addition, district-level policing was incorporated as a key strategy. This resulted in the decentralization of command and control structures and provided increased autonomy to line officers.

The new police service then set out a number of **service delivery principles** to provide the framework for providing police services to the new, expanded community. Those principles were as follows:

1. The Ottawa Police Service is organized around problem-oriented policing. Officers will work in teams to develop internal and external partnerships. These teams will be led by sergeants and staff sergeants and will engage in reactive and proactive and preventive activities.
2. The Ottawa Police Service is moving to district-level policing. Responsibility for policing, including patrol, resources, staffing decisions and hours of work, crime analysis, and general investigation, will reside at the district level. Front-line officers will be generalists and will assume responsibility for many types of investigations.
3. The Ottawa Police Service is front-loading supports. Front-loading support involves increased analytical and research support, improved technology, and increased training for officers in areas such as problem-solving, conflict resolution, and interpersonal skills.
4. The Ottawa Police Service is focusing on partnerships. The community will be involved in the design, delivery, and evaluation of policing services. Partnerships will enhance the problem-solving capacities of the police service.
5. The Ottawa Police Service is emphasizing its commitment to administrative efficiency. This commitment involves exploring ways to provide front-line officers with the time and support required to develop partnerships in the community, the use of auxiliaries and volunteers, and equitable distribution of workloads (Ottawa-Carleton Regional Police Service 1996, 25–27).

APPLICATION OF THE CORPORATE MODEL IN POLICING

In our discussion in Chapter 6, we noted that a key component of community policing is the use of strategies from the private sector. Police services are making increasing use of the corporate model for administrative and operational planning and performance assessment, as seen in materials from the Guelph Police Service and the Vancouver Police Department, described below.

Planning within a Community Policing Framework: The Guelph Police Service

The *Guelph Police Service Business Plan: 2010–2012* details the planning process carried out by a community-policing police service. The introduction, written by Chief Rob Davis, states that:

This Plan helps guide our response to the current issues of our community and our members. Moreover, it also assists us in preparing for future challenges that are likely to affect policing and the overall safety of our community. We cannot rest upon our past successes but instead need to continue striving to be a leader in developing new and innovative ways of addressing emerging issues … As recently documented in the new Statistics Canada "Crime Severity Index" data, Guelph is recognized as the safest city of its size in our Country which was mirrored in the responses of our community survey respondents, the majority of whom feel very safe in our community. As always, there are issues we need to be constantly mindful of and which are likely to be part of our long term focus. These include the positive development of our youth; maintaining a respectable standard for road and pedestrian safety; and continuing to develop strategies to address drug and associated crime through enforcement and as partners in the Wellington/Guelph Community Drug Strategy.

—Guelph Police Service (2010)

The Guelph *Business Plan* contains a number of sections, including:

- a review of the 2007–2009 business plan;
- an analysis of the socioeconomic trends in the community, including population and development trends, crime patterns and projections, and community priorities;
- discussions of police resource and workload trends, labour market and staffing issues, legislative changes, and changes in information and technology;
- a budget forecast, including a trends summary and implications for policing; and
- recommended corporate goals for 2010–12.

Let's take a brief look at each of these areas of the report to gain a better idea of how a community-policing police service does business.

A Review of the 2007–2009 Business Plan

A key part of the police service as a learning organization involves examining the outcomes of previous plans and initiatives. In fact, the 2007–2009 *Business Plan* clearly states that the business plan builds on the work of previous business plans—which is why the name "Partners in Excellence" has remained unchanged from previous plans. In this section, the GPS reviews its previous business plan and annual reports, lists the individual **corporate goals**, notes the major accomplishments found in yearly accomplishment reports, and identifies issues that remain to be addressed. In the same plan, the GPS also reviews its vision, mission, and values statements to ensure they are in line with the current philosophy and strategic direction of the department. In the 2004–2006 *Business Plan*, the vision, mission, and values were changed to ensure alignment with philosophy and strategic direction.

One corporate goal in the 2007–2009 *Business Plan*, under the heading "Neighbourhood Policing," is "Continue to seek solutions to neighbourhood issues in partnership with the community through crime prevention, education and enforcement."

Indications that this goal was met include:

- A multi-language survey was conducted in partnership with community agencies to determine the police-related needs of multicultural communities.
- The Traffic unit undertook successful initiatives targeting high-risk locations where pedestrian and/or motorist safety were jeopardized.
- A pre-charge diversion protocol was developed with local partners to facilitate referrals of persons with mental health issues to a diversion program, where appropriate, instead of being charged.
- The role of police in domestic violence and/or sexual assault incidents and investigations was discussed with community partners unit in 2008.

Socioeconomic Trends, Crime Patterns and Projections, and Community Priorities

Socioeconomic data presented in the *Business Plan* for 2010–2012 include:

- *Information on population*: population projections, population and age structures of the City of Guelph, population projections by age, and ethnocultural characteristics of the City of Guelph.
- *Residential, commercial, and industrial growth*: new residential units by type, including single detached, semidetached, townhouses, and apartments; industrial and commercial building construction.

   Crime data presented include:

- *Rates of police-reported criminal behaviour*: a summary of crime trends comparing national trends with trends in the City of Guelph relating to total crime, violent crime, property crime, and youth crime.
- *Crime severity rates*: an overview of the severity of crime in the City of Guelph.
- *Information on community perceptions and priorities*: as determined by community surveys and information from partner agencies.

Police Resource and Service Delivery Trends

Information presented on police resources and service delivery trends includes:

- Police resource and workload comparison, including population per police officer, per capita policing costs, and Criminal Code incidents per officer.
- Labour market and staffing issues, including changes in the labour force population and the anticipated shortage of police officers, changes in the occupations and industries in which people work, changes in the educational level of workers, and the alternative forms of work that are emerging.
- Legislative changes, including the impact of federal legislation (changes in the Criminal Code, sentencing reform, and gun control registration) and provincial legislation (the Adequacy Standards, downloading of the Provincial Offences Act, changes to seatbelt laws, and the Law Enforcement and Forfeited Property Management Statute Law Amendment Act).
- Information and technology changes and their impact on the delivery of policing services, including the growth of the Internet; the use of computers to gather, store, and process information; and the resource and financial implications of these changes for the police service.

   Table 7.3 outlines the policing resource indicators for the Guelph Police Service in a comparative context.

Trends Summary and Implications for Policing

Highlights include population and commercial and industrial growth in the community; the need for increased training of police officers to meet the requirements of legislation, changes in technology, and career enhancement; and the need to continue to adapt policies and procedures to ensure effective police services.

   A business plan includes a list of the corporate goals, key strategies for achieving these goals, and identification of the parties responsible for implementing the goals and strategies.

   Table 7.4 presents materials on one of the corporate goals identified by the GPS, called "neighbourhood policing," where the corporate goal focuses on seeking solutions to neighbourhood issues in partnership with the community through crime prevention, education, and enforcement.

Table 7.3 Municipal Policing Resource Indicators, Guelph and Selected Comparators

City	Population (2015)	Total police officers (2016)	Number of police per 100,000 population (2016)	Crime Severity Index	Clearance Rate*
Barrie	148,134	237	160	45.4	42.5
Chatham-Kent	105,322	159	151	86.6*	39.3
Durham Regional	661,190	861	130	51.3*	48.2
Greater Sudbury	164,266	264	161	63.5	39.7
Guelph	130,440	193	148	54.6	46.8
Halton Regional	559,213	690	123	37.5*	38.3
Hamilton	556,359	840	151	53.6	31.6
Kingston	130,490	201	154	55.2	41.3
London	391,925	582	148	68.4	46.7
Niagara Regional	449,098	706	157	50.3	35.5
Ottawa	956,710	1,239	130	51.3	41.2
Peel Regional	1,373,033	1,967	143	51.9*	42.3
Thunder Bay	116,311	232	199	85.9	44.9
Toronto	2,826,498	5,366	190	47,5	38.5
Waterloo Regional	542,511	767	141	61.2	44.4
Windsor	219,335	429	196	65.1	38.4
York Regional	1,139,738	1,598	140	43.2*	46.7

*Last reported available data Statistics Canada, 2011

Sources: Statistics Canada, Canadian Centre for Justice Statistics, Police Resources in Canada, Cat. No. 85-002-X (2016); Police Reported Crime Statistics in Canada 2016, Cat. No. 85-002-X (2016); Police Resources in Canada, Cat. No. 85-225-X (2011). Reproduced and distributed on an "as is" basis with the permission of Statistics Canada.

Table 7.4 2010 Guelph Police Service Neighbourhood Policing Accomplishments

The Guelph Police Service reports in its 2010 Accomplishments report that it achieved 26 objectives within its corporate goal of "neighbourhood policing." Here are three samples from that report.

Objective: Assist in the improvement of clearance rates for violent crime and property crime.

Importance: Guelph's clearance rate appears to be quite low in comparison to others, giving the appearance that the Service does not solve crimes as effectively as other police services.

Corporate Goal: Neighbourhood Policing

Objective Status: Achieved

Synopsis: A working group was formed early in 2010 to examine how crime statistics were being collected and forwarded to Statistics Canada and to examine how other police services were recording these data to ensure consistency in comparisons across services. The results did show some minor irregularities that could affect the final clearance rates. As a result of the review, new processes have been put in place that should improve clearance rates and response times to calls. A review of the changes to date shows an increase in clearance rates after the first six months of 2010, particularly in property crime where Guelph tended to be lower than comparators. The specialty units (persons crime and property crime) in the detective division are working well and the consistency in staffing and investigative processes is improving clearance. The GPS's clearance rates for violent crime are some of the highest in the province. The crime analyst is also increasing the information collected and shared with operational units on active crime types and locations leading to increased targeted enforcement and focused patrol. The overall results will be examined in more detail when the year-end review of crime data is conducted.

Objective: Ensure the GPS has excellent risk management procedures and processes in place.

Importance: It is important to identify and address high-risk activities to reduce organizational and member liability and increase member and community safety, both of which contribute to providing excellent service to the community.

Corporate Goal: Neighbourhood Policing

Objective Status: Achieved

Synopsis: The Risk Management Committee held regularly scheduled meetings during the year and the committee membership was updated to ensure adequate representation of the various work units. The minutes of the meetings were made available to all members of the GPS. A number of committee members attended a risk management training session presented by Gordon Graham.

The committee also spearheaded a proposal to provide patrol rifles to the platoons. This proposal was approved by the executive, and has been successfully implemented. The patrol rifles have the potential to assist our members and the community in critical firearms incidents.

In 2010 the Service complied with the implementation of the Bill 168 legislation (Workplace Violence and Harassment), including training our members and having an external risk assessment of the GPS conducted.

In addition, for the past year this Inspector (now overseeing a different division) has represented the Service on a community advisory committee for Project Wisdom, which has the goal to examine and understand elder abuse from a cultural perspective, thereby increasing cultural understanding and sensitivity to issues of elder abuse within ethno-specific communities. The project is made possible with funding from the New Horizon for Seniors Program, Human Resources and Skills Development Canada, and has partners from Trellis, Immigrant Services, County of Wellington Social Services, Women in Crisis, and the GPS. This work primarily supports the Service's Social Responsibility corporate goal.

Objective: Strengthen ties with formal Neighbourhood Groups by holding a series of Town Hall style meetings (community forums).

Importance: The discussion during these forums will build the collaborative relationship between the Police Service and the neighbourhoods.

Corporate Goal: Neighbourhood Policing

Objective Status: Achieved

Synopsis: Four community forums were conducted throughout the year, and issues and solutions raised during those forums were incorporated into operational planning for the Neighbourhood Services Division. All Neighbourhood Groups were invited to these forums, and representation from each group was achieved. City councilors and staff also attended the forums. Very positive feedback from the community, city councilors, and city staff about these forums was received.

To review all accomplishments see *Guelph Police Service, Business Plan 2010–2012, 2010 Unit Accomplishments*.

Source: Courtesy of Guelph Police Services. Found at http://www.guelphpolice.ca/en/resourcesGeneral/Guelph-Police-Service-2016-2018-Strategic-Business-Plan.pdf

Appendices

- Results of city service quality studies, conducted on households and businesses and comparing city services on a number of key performance indicators.
- Priorities identified by community partners in workshops, focus groups, and forums held in the community.

Guelph Police Service 2010 Accomplishments

The GPS prepares an Accomplishments report to assess how well it is meeting its corporate goals. This level of accountability to the community is a key feature of community-based police organizations. Table 7.5 outlines the GPS self-assessment of some its accomplishments for 2010.

The Vancouver Police Department Strategic Plan

The Vancouver Police Department (VPD) is an excellent example of a "best practices" police service organized on a corporate model. From 2003 to 2007, the VPD undertook a thorough review of all aspects of its service delivery model, including demands for service, ratio of civilian and sworn positions, and clearance rates, as well as an overall service-wide analysis of effectiveness and efficiencies. As a result of this extensive evaluation, the VPD adjusted a number of its call response performance targets and identified a number of positions that could be staffed by civilian employees rather than police officers.

The demands on policing in Vancouver, combined with the results of a very thorough analysis, made a strong case for change. These indicators, while specific to the

Table 7.5 Meeting the Needs of the Community: Strategies and Accountability

Objectives	Performance Measure
1. Review cruiser, foot and bike patrol patterns and resources available for community policing efforts along with an exploration of alternative scheduling and staffing models.	• Review of patrol & community policing patterns & demands (2010–2011) • Research alternative scheduling & staffing models (2010) • Strategies allowing for enhanced patrol & community policing initiatives developed (2010–2011), implemented & evaluated (2011–2012) • Amount of overtime hours* • Number and quality of community policing initiatives*
2. Maintain or improve violent and property crime clearance rates.	• Percent of members trained in investigations* • Resources available for investigations* • Clearance rates*
3. Maintain or improve response times for Priority One Calls for Service	• Percent of Priority One calls in queue • Response times • Alternate response strategies explored (2010) & implemented & evaluated as appropriate (2011–2012)
4. Enhance our collaboration with neighbourhood stakeholders on crime prevention, including Problem Oriented Policing (POP) initiatives.	• Number of members on committees* • Number of successful POPs* • Number of successful strategies implemented through partnerships*
5. Continue to improve the efficiency and effectiveness of officer involvement with mental health patients.	• Number of successful strategies developed by mental health partnerships* • Percent of members trained in mental health issues* • Amount of resources, including officer time, spent at hospitals*
6. Ensure the Guelph Police Service has excellent Risk Management and Emergency Preparedness procedures and processes in place.	• Quality of training, including training in relevant policies & procedures (2011) • Feedback received by Risk Management Committee*

* will be assessed annually

Source: Guelph Police Service, Business Plan 2010-2012, http://www.guelphpolice.com/business-plan, p.11.

Municipality of Vancouver, were very similar to those experienced by the Edmonton Police Service in the 1980s (refer to Table 7.2), and they required the VPD to balance its resources and services effectively to meet these current demands while at the same time adapting to future demands brought on by growth.

The VPD incorporated the research and findings from its review into a 2012–2016 strategic plan and a subsequent 2017–2021 strategic plan. As outlined in its 2017–2021 Strategic Plan, the VPD's overarching strategic goals, which are grouped into four categories, are to:

Support our people
- Foster a culture of employee engagement and effective communication
- Promote a healthy work environment

Engage our community
- Foster relationships, understanding, and trust with our diverse community
- Strengthen mental health programs and processes

Enhance public safety
- Address community concerns that affect public safety
- Improve road safety for everyone

Fight crime
- Fight violent crime and its causes
- Combat property crime and its drivers (VPD 2017a).

The Strategic Plan is intended to be a fluid document, adaptable to the needs of the VPD and the community. It outlines priorities and guides decision-making and is used to provide direction for budgets and annual business plans. The annual strategic business plan is important because it:

- sets strategies with associated activities and targets towards achieving long-term strategic goals and other organizational priorities;
- provides a basis for budgeting;
- promotes accountability;
- inspires innovation and action;
- assists in the efficient allocation of resources;
- communicates to stakeholders; and
- helps employees understand how they are being supported and how they can contribute to the success of the long-term Strategic Plan (VPD 2017b).

The 2017 Strategic Business Plan outlined below includes the eight overarching goals from the 2017–2021 Strategic Plan as well as strategies that will be undertaken by the VPD in 2017 towards achieving these long-term strategic goals.

> **Strategic Goal:** Foster Relationships, Understanding, and Trust with Our Diverse Community
>
> *2017 Strategy 1*: Continue to comprehensively engage with and provide direct support to vulnerable and marginalized women.
>
> *2017 Strategy 2*: Sustain and foster existing positive relationships with Aboriginal communities.
>
> *2017 Strategy 3*: Ensure the safety of the elderly population through community building and awareness.
>
> *2017 Strategy 4*: Develop trust and relationships with youth through outreach, education, and empowerment activities.
>
> *2017 Strategy 5*: Improve on existing relationships with the LGBTQ2S+ community and expand on the understanding of LGBTQ2S+ issues in policing

Strategic Goal: Strengthen Mental Health Programs and Processes

2017 Strategy 1: Continue to focus on youth mental health in schools and in the community with awareness campaigns.

2017 Strategy 2: Implement a tele-triage project in partnership with St. Paul's Hospital (SPH) that enables remote off-site mental health assessments of clients.

2017 Strategy 3: Work with external partners to develop and implement the Mental Health Hub and the Vancouver Police Foundation (VPF) Transitional Centre at SPH.

2017 Strategy 4: Continue to collaborate with health partners to reduce mental health apprehensions and hospital wait-times, and to improve patient care.

Strategic Goal: Fight Violent Crime and Its Causes

2017 Strategy 1: Increase the number of businesses participating in the BarWatch and Restaurant Watch programs.

2017 Strategy 2: Enhance information sharing between the Major Crime Section, Organized Crime Section, and Patrol.

2017 Strategy 3: Strategically target high-risk violent offenders utilizing a proactive approach.

Strategic Goal: Combat Property Crime and Its Drivers

2017 Strategy 1: Develop more robust processes within the Chronic Offenders Unit (COU) to target the most prolific offenders responsible for the majority of property crime.

2017 Strategy 2: Engage in multiple short-term investigation projects targeting theft-from-auto offences and those individuals responsible for the movement of stolen goods.

2017 Strategy 3: Continue to work with City of Vancouver (CoV) staff to develop amendments to building permits and licences to regulate the installation of crime prevention security measures.

2017 Strategy 4: Implement new public awareness prevention strategies to combat property crime.

2017 Strategy 5: Develop future business processes for the continued expansion of the Predictive Policing model and GeoDash.

Strategic Goal: Address Community Concerns That Affect Public Safety

2017 Strategy 1: Ongoing prioritization of liquor enforcement in the Granville and Gastown Entertainment Districts as well as on city beaches. Enforcement will focus on issues such as public drinking, intoxication, and monitoring of liquor establishments.

2017 Strategy 2: Work with the CoV and local non-profit organizations to manage disorder caused by illegal street vending.

2017 Strategy 3: Continue to assist the CoV with its efforts to end homelessness.

2017 Strategy 4: Focus concentrated efforts on combatting the fentanyl/opioid crisis currently plaguing the city of Vancouver as well as many other parts of Canada.

Strategic Goal: Improve Road Safety for Everyone

2017 Strategy 1: Participate in coordinated Provincial road safety campaigns.

2017 Strategy 2: Increase road safety initiatives and enforcement by Patrol members.

2017 Strategy 3: Leverage technology to address current and anticipated road safety enforcement challenges.

2017 Strategy 4: Ongoing commitment to road safety education and enforcement within the VPD Traffic Section.

Strategic Goal: Foster a Culture of Employee Engagement and Effective Communication

2017 Strategy 1: Improve communication between VPD Executive members and front-line staff.

2017 Strategy 2: Improve communication between VPD Divisions.

Strategic Goal: Promote a healthy work environment

2017 Strategy 1: Continue to support and foster employee wellness.

2017 Strategy 2: Enhance the professional development of VPD members.

2017 Strategy 3: Enhance employee management processes.

2017 Strategy 4: Enhance respectful work environments throughout the VPD.

2017 Strategy 5: Enhance employee safety and security at VPD facilities.

2017 Strategy 6: Ongoing comprehensive Operational Review of the VPD's staffing requirements. (VPD 2017b).

Sources: Vancouver Police Department, *2017–2021 Strategic Plan*, http://vancouver.ca/police/assets/pdf/vpd-strategic-plan-2017-2021.pdf; Vancouver Police Department, *2017 Strategic Business Plan*, http://vancouver.ca/police/assets/pdf/2017-business-plan-report.pdf. Used with permission of the Vancouver Police Department.

Chapter Summary

In this chapter, we have presented several case studies that illustrate the organizational and operational changes made by police services across the country to incorporate the principles of community policing. The Edmonton Police Service was one police service to embark on a major organizational reform, the outcomes of which have been positive for both the police service and the community. The Montreal Police Service and the Surrey, BC, detachment of the RCMP have undertaken similar structural reforms, and, although it is too early to assess the impact of these changes, it can be assumed that there will be positive outcomes in these jurisdictions as well.

In another case study, the successes and setbacks of the Halton Regional Police Service were traced through the decades-long implementation of community policing. Among the lessons of the Halton experience were that transforming police organizations takes time, patience, and vision on the part of leaders and front-line officers, as well as a capacity to adapt to changing demands.

The Organizational Renewal Project of the Durham Regional Police was then examined to illustrate the planning process of one police service designed to meet the requirements of the Adequacy Standards. This process involved identifying a number of implementation issues; for each issue the police service then set out a course of action for how the issue would be addressed.

The issue of regionalization, integrated policing, and community policing was examined, and the efforts of one regional police service—the Ottawa Police Service—to ensure that the principles and practices of community policing were at the core of the police service were discussed. Finally, the business plans of the Guelph Police Service and the Vancouver Police Department were presented to illustrate the planning process involved in implementing community policing.

These case studies provide important insights into the challenges that police services encounter in changing their organizational structures and their strategies for delivering police services. As police services wrestle with increasing costs and more stringent controls over police budgets, it is critical that they demonstrate effectiveness whether through reorganization or the provision of new services. The experiences of the police services that have been presented in this chapter leave little doubt that transforming police organizations is an all-encompassing process that does not happen overnight.

Chapter Review

Key Terms

- corporate goals, p. 234
- differential response model, p. 214
- empowerment, p. 216
- external communication strategy, p. 216
- intelligence-led police organization, p. 219
- internal communication strategy, p. 216
- new public management, p. 212
- Organizational Renewal Project, p. 228
- ownership, p. 216
- service delivery principles, p. 233
- Surrey Crime Reduction Strategy, p. 222
- Total Integrated Policing, p. 227
- Village Constable Program, p. 225

Key Points

- The experience of the Edmonton Police Service provides key insights into the challenges and outcomes of altering the organization and delivery of policing services.
- The Montreal Police Service and the Surrey RCMP detachment have recently undertaken major reforms in an attempt to implement the principles of community policing.
- The experience of the Halton Regional Police over three decades provides several lessons in the requirements for successfully adopting and implementing community policing.
- The Organizational Renewal Project of the Durham Regional Police is a good illustration of how a police service can plan to meet the requirements of the Police Services Act and the Adequacy Standards in the area of community policing.
- The regionalization of police services raises questions about the ability of amalgamated police services to implement the principles of community policing effectively.
- The service delivery principles established by the Ottawa Police Service illustrate how one regional police service set out to ensure that amalgamation did not prevent the development of a decentralized, community-focused police service.
- The planning approaches used by the Guelph Police Service and the Vancouver Police Department illustrate the use of a corporate model for organizing and delivering policing services.

Self-Evaluation

QUESTIONS

1. Describe the components of the **Edmonton Police Service differential response model**.
2. What role does **empowerment** of line officers play in the transformation to a community-policing police service?
3. What is meant by **ownership**, and what role does it play in a community-policing police service?

4. Define **internal marketing strategy** and discuss the role this strategy plays in implementing community policing. Provide examples.
5. Define **external marketing strategy** and discuss the role this strategy plays in implementing community policing. Provide examples.
6. Describe the **Village Constable Program** and the role this program played in the transformation of Halton Regional Police Service to community policing.
7. What is **Total Integrated Policing** and how is this approach to delivering police services illustrative of community policing?
8. Describe the key components of the **Organizational Renewal Project** of the Durham Regional Police.
9. What are the **service delivery principles** of the Ottawa Police, and how do they reflect community policing?
10. What are **corporate goals**, and what role do these play in a community-policing police service?

KEY IDEAS

1. Which demand on the Edmonton Police Service during 1980–1990 led the EPS to begin transforming itself into a community-policing police service?
   a. An increase in reported crime.
   b. An increase in the number of patrol constables.
   c. An increase in the elderly population.
   d. An increase in the number of motor vehicle incidents.

2. Which of the following was found by evaluations of the Edmonton Police Service?
   a. A decrease in citizen satisfaction with the police.
   b. An increase in officer morale, motivation, and job satisfaction.
   c. An increase in the levels of crime.
   d. A decrease in clearance rates.

3. In the Edmonton Police Service, senior police administrators secured the support and participation of line officers in the transformation into a community-policing police service. What strategy did they use in order to do this?
   a. co-optation strategy
   b. external marketing strategy
   c. internal marketing strategy
   d. devolution strategy

4. Which statement is true about the Montreal Police Service Neighbourhood Policing Project?
   a. It encountered considerable resistance from community residents.
   b. It is designed to increase foot and bicycle patrols in the community.
   c. It involved the creation of nearly 50 neighbourhood police stations.
   d. It was abandoned after a one-year trial period.

5. Which statement is true about the Village Constable Program?
   a. It was used by police services in Ontario until the mid-1970s.
   b. It was a key component of the Halton Regional Police community policing effort.
   c. It has been used by the Ontario Provincial Police for many years.
   d. It involves citizen volunteers patrolling the community.

6. Which of the following is indicated by the experience of the Halton Regional Police with community policing?
   a. Implementing community policing requires corporate sponsorship during the initial stages more than programs.
   b. Implementing community policing is a slow and gradual process.

    c. Implementing community policing requires federal funding in order to be successful.

    d. Implementing community policing can occur in a quick and efficient manner with proper planning.

7. In its Organizational Renewal Project, how did the Durham Regional Police Service propose to address its identified implementation issues?
    a. By creating audit teams.
    b. By creating statements of accountability.
    c. By contracting out certain police services.
    d. By using more volunteers.

8. What do research studies indicate about regional police services?
    a. That they increase the costs of police services.
    b. That they have difficulty establishing partnerships with the communities they police.
    c. That they reduce per capita policing costs.
    d. That they are able to provide more traffic enforcement than smaller police services.

9. What did the Ottawa Police Service do upon its creation in 1995?
    a. It based its policing philosophy on problem-oriented policing.
    b. It implemented district-level policing.
    c. It focused on building community partnerships.
    d. It focused on providing patrol officers with support and resources.

10. Which of the following is used by the Guelph Police Service and the Vancouver Police Department in applying the corporate model to the organization and delivery of police services?
    a. business partnerships
    b. environmental scans
    c. budgetary goals
    d. tactical response plans

11. Which of the following best exemplifies integrated policing?
    a. A strategic patrol technique.
    b. Shared computer-based systems and radio frequencies.
    c. An example of strategic policing.
    d. A traditional, paramilitary style of policing.

12. Which of the following factors is most true in terms of implementing a corporate model?
    a. A corporate model solves long-standing organizational problems.
    b. Corporate models indicate a police service has implemented a highly evolved community policing model.
    c. Corporate models need to be adapted to the realities of police work.
    d. Corporate models are necessary for generating revenue in policing.

EXERCISES: KNOWLEDGE INTO PRACTICE

Exercise 1. Leading-Edge Policing

The Halton Regional Police Service is widely regarded as a leading-edge police service, particularly in relation to community policing. From a review of the materials presented on the HRPS covering the 1970s to the 1990s, list what you would consider to be the elements that contribute to this police service being leading edge.

Now, using the same materials, list what you would consider to be the major obstacles confronting the HRPS as it transforms itself from a traditional police service into a community policing service.

Exercise 2. The Durham Regional Police Service Organizational Renewal Project

To prepare for the guidelines imposed by the Adequacy Standards as of 1 January 2001, the Durham Regional Police Service undertook the Organizational Renewal Project. This project identified a number of implementation issues and then set out what the police service planned to do about each of the issues and how it planned to do it. Four implementation issues are reproduced below.

Review the plans of the Durham Regional Police for addressing each of the implementation issues. Then, using the experience of the Halton Regional Police Service as a resource:

1. Identify what you would consider to be the major challenge(s) that the implementation issue poses;
2. Identify the potential difficulties that the Durham Regional Police might encounter in addressing each implementation issue; and
3. Suggest how the potential difficulties that might be encountered could be either avoided or successfully addressed.

Implementation Issue 1. Defining Community Policing
Challenges posed by this issue:

_____

_____

_____

_____

_____

Difficulties that may be encountered in addressing this issue:

_____

_____

_____

_____

How these difficulties could be avoided or successfully addressed:

_____

_____

_____

_____

_____

Implementation Issue 2. Structural Changes
Challenges posed by this issue:

_____

_____

_____

_____

_____

Difficulties that may be encountered in addressing this issue:

_____

_____

_____

_____

_____

How these difficulties could be avoided or successfully addressed:

_____

_____

_____

_____

_____

Implementation Issue 3. Communication
Challenges posed by this issue:

_____

_____

_____

_____

_____

Difficulties that may be encountered in addressing this issue:

_____

_____

_____

_____

_____

How these difficulties could be avoided or successfully addressed:

_____

_____

_____

_____

_____

Implementation Issue 4. Relationships with associations
Challenges posed by this issue:

_____

_____

_____

_____

_____

Difficulties that may be encountered in addressing this issue:

_____

_____

_____

_____

_____

How these difficulties could be avoided or successfully addressed:

_____

_____

_____

_____

_____

The Durham Regional Police Service 2005–2007 Business Report includes messages from the Chief of Police, Chair of the Durham Regional Police Services Board, and the Durham Regional Police Service Police Association, in addition to the message from the chief of police and the director of the police board. How do you feel about the police association providing a statement in a corporate document? What do you think this suggests about the strength of the relationship between the regional police service and the police association?

_____

_____

_____

_____

_____

REFERENCES

Bhayani, G., and S. Thompson. 2017. "SMART on Social Problems: Lessons Learned from a Canadian Risk-Based Collaborative Intervention Model." 1–16. Policing: A Journal of Policy and Practice 11(2): 168–84.

Burlington Post. 1976. "Experiment Spreads to Cover the Entire City." 4 February, 3, 5.

Charih, M., and L. Rouillard. 1997. "The New Public Management." In New Public Management and Public Administration in Canada, ed. M. Charih and A. Daniels. Toronto: Institute of Public Administration of Canada.

City of Surrey. 2006. Surrey Crime Reduction Strategy. http://www.surrey.ca/ NR/ rdonlyres/4D63836D-9691-44EA-9393-41320D92C105/33777/SurreyCrimeReduction Strategyweb.pdf

Clairmont, D. 1996. Community-Based Policing at Halton Regional: The Years 1980 to 1995. Ottawa: Solicitor General Canada.

Communauté urbaine de Montréal. 1997. Evolution. Montreal.

Cooke-Scott, L.A. 1998. "Community-based Policing in Ontario: Lessons from the Halton Regional Police Service." Canadian Public Administration 41(1): 120–46.

Durham Regional Police Service. 2004. 2005–2007 Business Plan. Whitby.

Edmonton Police Service. 1996. Community Policing in Edmonton, 1996. Edmonton: Community and Organizational Support Section.

—. 2002. Project Archimedes: Developing an Intelligence-led Policing Model for the Edmonton Police Service. Edmonton:.

—. 2007a. Delivering Service, Achieving Results: A New Patrol Service Delivery Model. Edmonton: Community Policing Bureau.

—. 2007b. Edmonton Police Service Citizen Survey: Highlights. Edmonton.

2017,

Griffiths, C.T., B. Whitelaw, and R. Parent. 1999. Canadian Police Work. *Toronto: ITP Nelson.*

Guelph Police Service. 2007. Partners in Excellence 2007–2009. *Guelph.*

—. *2010.* Business Plan 2010–2012. *Guelph, ON: Guelph Police Service.*

—. *2011a.* 2010 Annual Report. *Guelph.*

—. *2011b.* Business Plan 2010–2012, 2010 Unit Accomplishments. *http://www. guelphpolice.com/assets/2010-Accomplishments-Report-Yr-1-of-2010-2012-Business-Plan.pdf*

Halton Regional Police Force. 1982. Policing Philosophy *[internal document].*

Healey, S. and L. Bradburn. 2000. Our Policing Future: Business Plan 2001–2003. *Guelph: Guelph Police Service.*

Loree, D. 1988. "Innovation and Change in a Regional Police Force." Canadian Police College Journal *12(4): 205–39.*

Montreal Police Service. 2002. Annual Report. *Montreal.*

—. *2003.* Annual Report. *Montreal.*

Oppal, W.T. (commissioner). 1994. Closing the Gap: Policing and the Community. Policing in British Columbia Commission of Inquiry, *Final Report, vol. 1. Victoria: Attorney General of British Columbia.*

Ottawa-Carleton Regional Police Service. 1996. Ottawa-Carleton Police Amalgamation Report. *Ottawa: Ontario Civilian Commission on Police Services.*

RCMP. 2003. "Integrated Policing." Gazette *65(3).*

—. *2004.* Community Policing Surrey Style. *Surrey.*

—. *2017. "RCMP in Surrey: Your Surrey RCMP."* http://surrey.rcmp-grc.gc.ca/ ViewPage.action?siteNodeId=70&languageId=1&contentId=-1

Senge, Peter M. 2010. The Fifth Discipline: The Art and Practice of the Learning Organization. *New York: Crown Business.*

Statistics Canada. 2011. Police Resources in Canada, 2011. *Cat. no. 85-225-X. Ottawa: Canadian Centre for Justice Statistics.*

—. *2012.* Surrey, British Columbia *(Code 5915004) and* Greater Vancouver, British Columbia *(Code 5915) (table).* Census Profile. *2011 Census. Cat. no. 98-316-XWE. Ottawa.*

Sutherland, A. 1997a. "Right Up Their Alley: More Street Patrols Suits Officers, Residents and Merchants Just Fine." The Gazette *(Montreal), 20 February 20, G6.*

—. *1997b. "New Station Brings Policing Down to Street Level."* The Gazette *(Montreal), 13 March, F10.*

Taylor, K. 1999. Bringing into Focus—Policing in Halton Region: The Executive Summary. Oakville: Halton Regional Police Service.

Vancouver Police Department. 2017a. 2017–2021 Strategic Plan. Vancouver. http://vancouver.ca/police/assets/pdf/vpd-strategic-plan-2017-2021.pdf

—. 2017b. 2017 Strategic Business Plan. Vancouver. http://vancouver.ca/police/assets/pdf/2017-business-plan-report.pdf

Veitch, D. 1995. Community Policing in Edmonton, 3rd ed. Edmonton: Community and Organizational Support Section, Edmonton Police Service.

The Community Police Officer

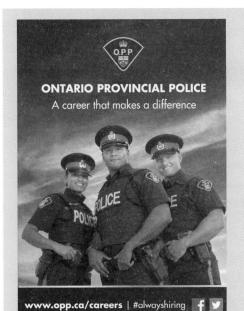

ONTARIO PROVINCIAL POLICE

A career that makes a difference

www.opp.ca/careers | #alwayshiring

Police services across Canada strive to ensure that the recruitment of police officers reflects the diversity of the communities they serve. "Branding" police work as an exciting and rewarding career is a key challenge faced by all police services.

Source: Ontario Provincial Police/Ministry of Community Safety and Correctional Services © Queen's Printer for Ontario, 2017. Reproduced with permission.

Learning Objectives

After completing this chapter, you should be able to:

- Discuss how recruitment and training of police officers has changed in recent years,
- Identify the basic and preferred qualifications for police recruits,
- Discuss the role of diversity in police recruitment,
- Identify and discuss the issues related to recruitment of gays, lesbians, bisexual and transgender individuals, members of First Nations, visible or cultural minorities, and women,
- Discuss the controversy over qualifications for women and members of cultural or visible minorities;
- Discuss the Recruit Training Program for Constables,
- Discuss the importance of in-service training,
- Describe the working personality of a police officer and its importance to the discussion of community policing,
- Describe what is meant by the community police officer as a generalist,
- Describe the relationship between reactive, proactive, and coactive policing, and
- Identify and discuss the sources of resistance to community policing.

INTRODUCTION

The success of community policing depends on the police officers who are responsible for implementing the programs. In essence, their attitudes, perceptions, and behaviors must be substantially changed before community policing can be put into practice.
—*A.J. Lurigio and W.G. Skogan (1994)*

The cornerstone of community policing is the front-line patrol officer, and it is this officer who ultimately plays a major role in the success of community policing. The task for senior police administrators is to create an organizational climate within which the line officer's role can be transformed from one of reacting to incidents and "crime fighting" (reactive role) to that of a proactive problem-solver who knows and understands the needs of the community he or she polices, and who works in partnership with the community to address these issues.

Community policing schemes result in more discretion and authority being vested in line officers, who can then solve problems instead of simply reacting to them. This makes it imperative that front-line patrol officers have an intimate knowledge of the communities and neighbourhoods they police and also have the time and opportunity to develop working partnerships with community residents.

RECRUITING POLICE OFFICERS

Community police officers must be creative in thinking and problem-solving. They must listen to community residents and mobilize them to address areas of concern, to identify the core issues related to a problem, and to develop intervention strategies for solving that problem. Understanding the root causes of crime and disorder, not to mention the complexity of social issues, has added to the difficulty of policing. Thus, applicants to police services should have some exposure to a university or college education that will assist them in developing research and critical thinking skills.

In addition, applicants should display good judgment and an ability to communicate. This will help the officer establish rapport with community residents and work collaboratively to solve problems. It is also essential that applicants have the personality and disposition to carry out the broad mandate given to community police officers, including the ability to work independently, take initiative, and be receptive to the varied duties of community policing officers (Carter 2000:1).

For anyone considering a career in a police service, there are certain **basic qualifications**. While some variation exists around the country (e.g., minimum age and post-secondary education requirements), generally an applicant must:

- be a Canadian citizen;
- be at least 18 years of age (although most applicants are between 25 and 32);
- be physically fit, in good health, and with the appropriate weight and height;
- be a grade 12 graduate or equivalent, supplemented with accredited post-secondary education (typically a minimum of two years of university or college);
- possess a valid Canadian driver's licence;
- be of good character and have a personal background of proper conduct; and
- show common sense and good judgment.

Preferred qualifications may result in an applicant's ranking being raised; knowledge of a second language or culture, related volunteer experience, and a university degree or college diploma may all serve to do this. Police services are seeking men and women who stand out in the crowd and who demonstrate the potential to work well under adverse circumstances and conditions. The New Westminster Police Department, in the Vancouver area, seeks individuals who have the ability to:

- manage conflict;
- make sound decisions under stressful conditions;

- make ethical decisions and take responsibility when things go wrong;
- plan and organize;
- manage risk;
- manage stress and be resilient;
- work in a team environment; and
- communicates exceptionally well.

Today's police recruit tends to have completed a post-secondary education while working part-time and volunteering in a related criminal justice area (e.g., community police station, crisis line, victim services). Pre-recruit employment and volunteer activities that allow the individual to interact with members of the public in a problem-solving environment provide valuable life skills.

Preferred qualifications also include an absence of inappropriate or questionable behaviour on the part of the applicant. Along with the company one keeps, individuals seeking a career in law enforcement must be mindful of the websites they visit and the posts they make on social media. Police recruiters conduct thorough background examinations by examining every aspect of an applicant's activities and conduct, noting that past behaviour is an indication of future behaviour. Desirable applicants are those who have demonstrated **ethical behaviour** in a consistent manner.

Education and the Community Police Officer

In Chapter 6, we discussed the police service as a learning organization. Related to this topic is the role of education in policing generally—more specifically, how education can enhance the performance of line officers. In a thorough examination of the issues relating to post-secondary education and strategic learning requirements for police officers, Donald Campbell (1992, 113) identified a number of benefits that post-secondary education should provide to a police service:

- Improved performance by individual officers due to enhanced job skills, improved attitudes, or both, and an interest on the part of officers in pursuing continuing education opportunities throughout their policing careers; and
- Improvements to the police service, including greater flexibility and adaptability, the capacity to anticipate, accommodate, and plan for change, and increased prestige.

The extent to which these expectations for individual officers and for police organizations are actually met by post-secondary education is unclear. On the one hand, it would be expected that regardless of the discipline pursued, successful completion of a college or university degree requires the ability to incorporate knowledge, think critically, express oneself orally and in writing, and appreciate the complexity of the issues that arise in society.

Research evidence, primarily from studies of policing in the United States, suggests that officers with higher levels of education:

- are more culturally sensitive to visible minorities;
- exhibit greater flexibility in carrying out policing tasks;
- generate fewer complaints from citizens than their less-educated police colleagues;
- have a greater ability to process information; and
- have better relations with the community (Fischer, Golden, and Heininger 1985).

Although the associations between higher education and these outcomes may be weak or at best moderate, they appear to be consistent: "The overall conclusion is that higher education is a generally beneficial but not highly significant factor in improving the performance of front-line officers" (Campbell 1992, 114). There is certainly a need for more research on the impact of education on police officer perspectives and performance, as well as on the types of educational experiences that are more beneficial to police officers working in various policing environments (Tomovich and Loree 1989).

Table 8.1 presents data on the education levels of Ontario police recruits.

Table 8.1 Educational Attainment of Ontario Police College Recruits, 1996-2016

	Frequency	Percent
No college or university courses completed	1,206	6.4
Some college or university courses completed	1,830	9.7
Law and security administration or police foundations (college program) completed	5,446	28.8
Other college program completed	3,137	16.6
University complete	5,705	30.2
University and college completed	1,560	8.3
Total	18,884	100.0
Missing	146	
Total	19,030	

Source: Ramona Morris, Table: Educational Attainment of OPC Recruits, 1996-2016, Ontario Police College Basic Constable Training Program Student Demographics 1996-2016. Policing Services Division, Ministry of Community Safety and Correctional Services, Ontario Police College (Ontario), 2017. © Queen's Printer for Ontario. Reproduced with permission.

The principal advantage of recruiting mature individuals is that they are more likely to have acquired significant life skills prior to joining the police. An individual with broader life experience is arguably more capable of coping with the various stressors of police work. Life skills also appear to be an important factor in an officer's ability to empathize with many of the troubled individuals encountered by the police. In addition, length of service, maturity, and general life experience may be important factors in the police use of force, including deadly force.

The Practice of Recruiting: Diversity and Today's Recruit

One of Sir Robert Peel's fundamental principles of modern policing, expounded in the early 1800s, and a key principle of community policing today, is that police services should reflect the diversity of the communities they police. Historically, police services displayed little interest in recruiting women, visible and cultural minorities, Indigenous people, and gays. Today, **diversity** is a key concept in policing (see In Your Community 8.1).

The adoption of community policing as the model for police service delivery has resulted in major changes in recruiting. In contrast to previous decades, police services are actively seeking female applicants and applicants from visible ethnic minorities. Police services are also recognizing that diverse groups such as gays, lesbians, and bisexual and transgender individuals are part of the communities they serve.

Police recruits today tend to be from a variety of educational backgrounds—many police services have officers who have law degrees, or college diplomas or university degrees in fields as diverse as business and biology. A typical police recruit is in his or her late 20s and may have related work experience (jail guard, probation officer, or CBSA officer) before being offered a position with a Canadian police service. Today's police recruits are mature and educated individuals who bring related work and volunteer experience along with practical life skills to policing. In addition, they must have a background that demonstrates integrity, as well as the ability to make sound decisions and work well with others.

This may appear to be a daunting list of pre-employment expectations, but note that policing has become one of the highest paid law enforcement professions in Canada. Police recruits are typically paid an starting salary of over $50,000 while they complete basic training. In 2017, most police services in Canada provided a base salary of $95,000 to officers with more than five years of service. When overtime is factored in, many lower ranking police officers in Canada are grossing more than $100,000 per year. Along with wages are benefits and a generous pension plan. All of this makes policing an attractive profession.

IN YOUR COMMUNITY 8.1

RCMP RECRUITMENT: COMMITMENT TO CULTURAL DIVERSITY AND EMPLOYMENT EQUITY

Employment Equity is of crucial importance in ensuring that the Royal Canadian Mounted Police has a diverse, innovative and responsible work force fully capable of achieving its mission. The RCMP remains committed to the principle that it should reflect the diverse population of Canada to ensure effective police/community relations and the effective delivery of police services. The RCMP has committed to ensure that all employment policies, practices, and standards are fully inclusive and provide all Canadians with equal and fair opportunities within the spirit of employment equity policies and legislation.

RCMP employment equity resources and actions continue to focus on practical measures in which employment equity contributes directly to effective community policing, quality of service and police/minority relations. Community Policing is a partnership between the police and the community in sharing the delivery of police services. The RCMP will continue to strive towards fully incorporating this policing philosophy in its strategic objectives, both external and internal.

For further information about employment equity in the RCMP you can access the following reports online through the Royal Canadian Mounted Police website at http://www.rcmp-grc.gc.ca/ee-eme/index-eng.htm.

Source: *Royal Canadian Mounted Police, Careers, http://www.rcmp-grc.gc.ca/recruiting-recrutement/rec/requirements-exigences-eng.htm.*

Within the framework of community policing, recruitment assumes a very important role. Police services must recruit individuals who have an interest in policing beyond the traditional "blue lights and siren" role and who understand the challenges that police officers encounter in policing in a diverse and highly accountable society. Police applicants tend to be recruited into policing after they have obtained some "life skills" beyond basic schooling. Most Ontario Police College recruits are at least 25 years of age (see Table 8.2).

Table 8.2 Age Distribution of Ontario Police College Recruits, 1996–2016

	Frequency	Percent
19–24 years	4,511	24.0
25–29 years	8,303	44.1
30–34 years	3,837	20.4
35–39 years	1,563	8.3
40 or older	619	3.3
Total	18,833	100.0
Missing	197	
Total	19,030	

Source: Ramona Morris, Table 8.2: Age Distribution of Ontario Police College Recruits, 1996 2016, Ontario Police College Basic Constable Training Program Student Demographics 1996-2016. Policing Services Division, Ministry of Community Safety and Correctional Services, Ontario Police College (Ontario), 2017. © Queen's Printer for Ontario, 2011. Reproduced with permission.

Demographic trends also play a significant role in police recruitment. Between 2004 and 2009, many police services conducted aggressive hiring campaigns to offset a retirement bulge. While recruitment has since slowed in response to recent economic changes, including government austerity, it is safe to assume that recruitment levels will continue to remain steady due to continued retirements and modest growth. You will recall from our review of trends in Chapter 2 that recruiting and retaining police personnel ranks in the top three objectives for almost all Canadian police agencies. Besides retirements, the difficulty of keeping police services fully staffed is compounded by the following factors:

- competition among all public safety agencies (e.g., Canadian Border Services Agency, Correction Service Canada, and Alberta Sheriffs) for a limited pool of potential candidates;
- limited federal and provincial funding for police officer growth positions; and,
- police personnel choosing to join another police agency or leave the police profession altogether (called the **attrition rate**).

Competition for qualified recruits, especially women and members of visible minorities, remains steady. In Your Community 8.2 highlights an innovative approach to recruitment in the virtual world.

As well, there is greater competition among police services to recruit police officers who are already serving. Increasingly, municipal and provincial police services and the RCMP are welcoming experienced and trained officers from other agencies. A trained and experienced police officer is usually exempt from a complete recruit training program and can often negotiate his or her entry level of pay, vacation leave, and preferred posting with the new police service. An experienced officer can be deployed in the field with minimal

IN YOUR COMMUNITY 8.2

VANCOUVER POLICE RECRUITING IN THE CYBERWORLD

In 2007 the Vancouver Police Department (VPD) launched a first-of-its-kind virtual recruitment drive on the online platform, Second Life. The VPD implemented the initiative through a partnership with the "Masters of Digital Media" program at Great Northern Way Campus. Police officers and campus staff created avatars and a meeting space for an information and recruitment seminar within the virtual campus already created by the Great Northern Way Campus. VPD recruitment officers showed videos and presentations to other avatars who visited this virtual world to show what it took to be a Vancouver police officer in the real world. "Technology is changing so fast. It's important we explore new audiences for recruiting our officers," said Inspector Kevin McQuiggin, who spearheaded the initiative. The increasing rate of change and innovation in technology continues, and recognizing this, most police departments now have various channels for online recruitment, such as online information sessions and applications, social media outreach, online mentoring, and even virtual ride-alongs.

Sources: *Vancouver Police Department, VANCOUVER POLICE RECRUITING IN THE CYBERWORLD (May 30, 2007), http://mediareleases.vpd.ca/2007/05/30/vancouver-police-recruiting-in-the-cyberworld/; CBC News, "Ontario Provincial Police turn to online recruiting as retirements loom" (6 September 2016), http://www.cbc.ca/news/canada/sudbury/opp-northeast-online-recruiting-1.3749365.*

training and at minimal cost—a substantial benefit to the police service doing the hiring. While it was uncommon in the past for police officers to leave their police agency and join another, many are now doing just that because of flexible hiring processes and career incentives. In particular, RCMP officers in unprecedented numbers have been leaving that service join the ranks of the Ontario Provincial Police, the Calgary Police Service, and other police services. Lower pay, northern postings, and a heavy workload have resulted in retention challenges for the RCMP. In other cases, retirement-eligible police officers retire and then join another law enforcement agency in order to receive both their pension and a new law enforcement salary—a practice referred to as **double-dipping**. In Your Community 8.3 outlines the basic steps in the Toronto Police Service recruitment process.

Cyber police recruits

Source: Vancouver Police Department, VANCOUVER POLICE RECRUITING IN THE CYBERWORLD (May 30, 2007). © Vancouver Police Services found at http://mediareleases.vpd.ca/2007/05/30/vancouver-police-recruiting-in-the-cyberworld/

There is increasing political pressure on police services to reflect the diversity of the communities they serve (recall Peel's principles from Chapter 1). In particular, visible ethnic minorities and women are generally in high demand. Many recruiting officers feel pressure from senior police administrators, politicians, and community groups to increase the numbers of these groups in policing. Police services have established a number of outreach programs with future recruitment from these groups as a primary goal. In Your Community 8.4 describes the RCMP's Aboriginal Pre-Cadet Training Program.

While minority groups have always existed in society, past recruiting practices generally promoted an all–white male profession. During the 1970s, this practice was so systemic that recruiting officers often made only minor attempts to recruit women and visible ethnic minorities. Police services across the country have made great strides in broadening out their recruiting processes, but they still fall far short of reflecting the diversity of Canadian society.

Today, the vast majority of recruiting officers are actively seeking out these minority groups as well as recognizing diversity in sexual orientation in an attempt to rectify the practices of the past and to ensure adequate staffing within police organizations. As the Canadian demographic landscape continues to change, police recruiting officers must make important inroads into communities that are underrepresented among the police.

Canadian police agencies have adopted employment equity practices in their recruitment of police officers. Employment equity is the practice of giving preference to a visible minority or member of a target group where two equally qualified candidates, one a visible minority and the other a male Caucasian, are ideally suited to a career in policing. Notwithstanding employment equity practices, the demand for new police recruits and their relatively limited supply means that almost all suitable candidates are hired.

Gays, Lesbians, and Bisexual and Transgender Individuals

Since the 1990s, police agencies have recognized that gays, lesbians, and bisexual and transgender individuals are part of the community they serve, and several Canadian police services are actively recruiting officers from these communities. There do appear to be

IN YOUR COMMUNITY 8.3

HOW DO I BECOME A TORONTO POLICE OFFICER?

The following points outline the process for becoming a police constable with the Toronto Police Service

- Complete online registration for a General Information Session (GIS),
- Attend General Information Session (GIS),
- Toronto Police Recruiter will be in contact with you,
- Complete online registration for one of our mentoring sessions,
- Attend your registered PREP, PATI or WCT mentoring session,
- Register for O.A.C.P. testing with Applicant Testing Services,
- Perform Test:
  - — PATI (Police Analytical Thinking Inventory),
  - — WCT (Written Communication Test),
  - — PREP (Physical Readiness Evaluation for Police),
  - — Vision and Hearing,
  - — BPAD (Behavioural Personnel AssessmentDevice for police).
- Obtain O.A.C.P. Certificate of Results,
- Submit Toronto Police Service online application,
- Pre-Screening,
- Pre-Background Questionnaire (PBQ),
- Blended Interview,
- Minnesota Multi-Phasic Personality Inventory (MMPI-2),
- Background Investigation,
- Psychological Assessment,
- Conditional Offer of Employment Pending Medical Examination,
- Cadet-in-Training.

Please be advised that the process for becoming a Police Constable is competitive and as such, an applicant may be declined at any stage of the process.

Source: Toronto Police Service, "How Do I Become a Toronto Police Officer?," http://www.torontopolice.on.ca/careers/uni_become_officer.php.

differences among police services across the country regarding the extent to which gays, lesbians, and bisexual and transgender individuals are actively sought as recruits and the degree to which these officers feel comfortable having their co-workers know about their sexual orientation.

Today, most police leaders acknowledge and support gay, lesbian, and bisexual and transgender police personnel in the workplace. This acceptance has been facilitated by human rights legislation and by positive workplace laws and policies, and has been accompanied by the creation of Hate and Bias Crime Units in many police services. Even with this support, however, many gay, lesbian, bisexual, and transgender officers are cautious of coming out—that is, publicly revealing their sexual orientation. Many of these officers feel that their sexual orientation is a very private matter. Though the police subculture is much more tolerant than in the past, there are stereotypes that have yet to be dismantled. Interestingly, lesbian police officers are sometimes accepted more readily because they are perceived as tougher and more macho than their straight female counterpart. The lesbian

IN YOUR COMMUNITY 8.4

THE RCMP ABORIGINAL PRE-CADET TRAINING PROGRAM

The Aboriginal Pre-Cadet Training Program (APTP) offers Canadian Aboriginal people aged 19–29 a paid opportunity to experience daily police work with the RCMP. The 3 week training component is completed at the RCMP's Training Academy (Depot) in Regina, Saskatchewan. The program pairs youth of Aboriginal ancestry with RCMP members and support staff to gain valuable work experience. The training consists of problem solving, law enforcement, public speaking, physical fitness, defensive tactics, drill, & cultural awareness. Upon completion, the pre-cadets are sent to an RCMP Detachment in their home province where they will spend the summer months assisting police officers in various aspects of community policing duties.

   Basic requirements for eligibility include:

- Be between 19 and 29 years of age;
- Be of First Nation, Métis or Aboriginal descent;
- Be a Canadian citizen;
- Be of good character;
- Be able to pass an enhanced reliability security check;
- Be in good physical condition;
- Completion of Grade 12 or equivalent; and
- Possess a valid Canadian driver's licence.

Source: *Royal Canadian Mounted Police, Class of 2016 – BC's Aboriginal Pre-Cadets, B.C., Aboriginal Policing Services (2016-07-25). Reproduced with the permission of the RCMP. http://www.bc.rcmp-grc. gc.ca/ViewPage.action?siteNodeId=2100&languageId=1&contentId=47482.*

police officer may also be viewed as a more reliable employee, in that she is less likely to become pregnant and to leave the agency to raise a family.

   In contrast, there remains the general perception within police circles that gay male police officers are soft and not macho. Given this, gay male officers may have difficulty assimilating into a police service comprised primarily of heterosexual males.

Members of First Nations

Due to a long history of suspicion and distrust, Indigenous people traditionally showed little interest in policing as a career. In addition, they were often categorized by police agencies as visible minorities and were thus rarely recruited. This situation has changed somewhat in recent years, and many police services are now actively seeking Indigenous recruits. The RCMP has perhaps been the most successful, having developed and expanded its Aboriginal Policing Program across Canada, designed to recruit Indigenous members and foster positive relationships. In Ontario, the OPP utilize the Aboriginal Policing Bureau (APB) to provide a variety of services and programs in relation to First Nation peoples. This includes support for First Nations communities receiving their policing through an OPP-administered Ontario First Nations Policing Agreement (OFNPA). The agreement provides for a First Nation to police its own community with First Nation Constables supported by the OPP. First Nation governments and the OPP also jointly administer the First Nations police service. There are currently 19 First Nation communities in Ontario using this model. You can read more about the OPP and the role of the Aboriginal Policing Bureau atgttp://www.opp.ca.This growth in autonomous Indigenous police forces has contributed to the opportunities available to Indigenous persons interested in a policing career.

Visible and Cultural Minorities

Depending on the police agency, an individual who is a visible ethnic minority may be considered a preferred applicant. Police agencies are under increasing pressure to hire, retain, and advance visible minorities. It has been argued that in order for a police force to be effective, it must represent the community it serves. For example, a police agency serving a large Indo-Canadian population will be less than effective in dealing with policing issues related to Indo-Canadians if it does not employ police officers with a similar background. Thus, if a community has a population base in which roughly 10 percent of the individuals are visible ethnic minorities, then 10 percent of its police officers should reflect those minorities. While this idea makes sense, more research needs to be done to test whether this belief is valid. For now, it is a guiding principle in the community-based policing recruitment process.

An applicant who meets all of the qualifications necessary to be a police officer and who is a visible ethnic minority may be considered an asset to the police agency due to his or her ethnic heritage. This may seem discriminatory on the surface; nonetheless, it is a reality faced by police agencies across Canada. The principles of community policing require police services to meet this challenge. Yet there is no guarantee that the community from which the visible-minority officers were recruited will openly accept them back into the community.

Even so, there is widespread agreement that minority hiring targets must not be achieved by lowering entrance standards. Visible-minority group representatives and police leaders all agree that only the best applicants should be hired. Anything else would be a disservice to the community and to the visible ethnic group represented by that individual. All applicants must therefore meet the minimum entrance standards, which are not lowered or compromised. Diversity hiring has increased over the past few years; by 2011 around 12 percent of the police officers in Toronto were visible minorities (Statistics Canada 2011; Toronto Police Service 2011).

Women

As with visible ethnic minorities, women may now be considered preferred applicants. Over the past 20 years, most police services have made great strides in hiring, retaining, and advancing female police officers. However, although women comprise roughly 45 percent of the labour force and 51 percent of the population, female police officers accounted for just 21 percent (14,545) of the national police population in 2016 (Statistics Canada 2016).

Interestingly, the number of female officers in police services across Canada continued to grow in 2016, while the number of male officers decreased. The growth in the number of female officers in recent years, especially within the higher ranks, represents a continuation of a longer-term trend. For example, in 2001 women represented 14 percent of all officers; by 2011, that proportion had risen to 20 percent. In 2011, Quebec had the highest percentage of female police officers at 24 percent. The lowest proportions were found in Yukon, the Northwest Territories, and Nunavut, with women accounting for 13 to 14 percent of total police officers in each jurisdiction (Statistics Canada 2011).

For all the increasing recognition that police services should reflect the diversity of the communities they serve, this is easier said than done. A look at the official record indicates some encouraging developments but also reveals the difficulties that police services have had in recruiting women and persons from cultural and ethnic minorities:

- Female officers are underrepresented at the senior management levels. However, over the past several years there has been a steady increase in female officers, particularly in the ranks of non-commissioned and senior officers. Over the past decade, the proportion of female officers within these ranks has almost tripled.
- In Toronto, female officers made up roughly 18 percent of police personnel in 2011 (Statistics Canada 2011; Toronto Police Service 2011).

These outcomes suggest that overall, the recruitment strategies designed to attract more women and members of visible minorities into policing have met with moderate success. The reasons while there hasn't been more success are complex, and include the failure of police services to devote the necessary resources to attract non-Anglo and female recruits; the negative perceptions of the police held by many visible minorities, based on experiences with the police in their country of origin; and the view that policing is not an honourable profession (Jain 1994).

The Controversy over Recruiting Standards for Women and Visible Minorities

Various suggestions have been made for increasing the numbers of women and visible minorities in policing. One is **hiring quotas**, which would require police services to give priority to these individuals in the recruitment and selection process and, if need be, waive or modify traditional hiring criteria, such as physical fitness requirements, that may act to discriminate against women and visible minorities. In the past decade, police services have abolished restrictions on height, minimum weight, and age that most likely would have been found discriminatory in a court of law.

An internal survey of a sample of RCMP officers from all ranks found a widespread perception that entrance standards had been lowered to accommodate women, Indigenous people, and members of cultural minorities (Mofina 1996). Moreover, for several years beginning in 1997, the RCMP did modify its recruiting standards, highlighting what is a very contentious issue in policing. Today this practice has changed, although hiring practices can be modified in keeping with the federal Employment Equity Act, which requires the RCMP to eliminate systemic recruitment barriers and to strive for a workforce that mirrors the complexion of the Canadian population. In 2008, the Supreme Court of Canada ruled that a criminal conviction cannot serve as a bar to employment in a police service (*Montréal [City] v. Quebec[Commission des droits de la personne et des droits de la jeunesse]*) 2008 SCC 48).

RECRUIT TRAINING

The big strong silent type who drives a race car and shoots straight is not the profile of tomorrow's police professional.

—*The Honourable Mr. Justice W.T. Oppal (1994)*

Training is also a cornerstone of community policing. As previously noted, it is important that officers receive training that will equip them to carry out their tasks within a community-based strategic policing framework. An underlying theme that appears throughout the training and promotion process in police services is **competency-based training**, which focuses on the acquisition of specific, measurable skills and knowledge that can then be transferred to the operational level.

To be effective, the training of police recruits in community policing should be based on a number of factors:

1. *Police officers should possess a sense of social history.* They should understand police history and the dominant approaches to policing. An understanding of the past allows the police to learn from history and, more importantly, to not repeat the mistakes of the past.
2. *Police officers should have a sense of society and community.* Police should know about changes that are occurring around them that affect the decisions they make. By being made aware of trends as well as local community factors, the police will be better at developing solutions for the community.
3. *Police officers should be equipped with the skills and knowledge for incorporating community policing into their work* (Palmiotto et al. 2000). The development of knowledge and skills requires an understanding of the broadened police role, including how to implement effective working relationships with community members. The goal is to achieve a mobilized community where the police provide support, guidance, and assistance.

Subject areas in the "ideal" curriculum for recruits would include:

- the philosophy of the police department;
- organizational structure of the police department;
- social, economic, and political make-up of the community;
- cultural diversity of the community;
- police history;
- police operations;
- police mission;
- police culture;
- police discretion;
- police misconduct;
- police values and ethics;
- problem-oriented policing;
- alternative dispute resolution;
- mental illness and crisis intervention;
- crime prevention; and
- community-oriented policing.

In Your Community 8.5 describes the recruiting process for the Ontario Provincial Police, as well as the training that occurs at the Ontario Police College; In Your Community 8.6 outlines the Ontario Police Fitness Award Program.

Community policing was once only one of many specialty subjects taught to recruits; today the philosophy and practice of community policing permeates all facets of recruit training. There are, as well, core areas in recruit training where community policing and problem solving are reinforced. The RCMP integrates the CAPRA problem-based model throughout its cadet curriculum (recall from Chapter 5 that CAPRA stands for *clients*, *acquire/analyze* information, *partnerships*, *response*, and *assessment*). The goal of this approach is to have police officers apply CAPRA to operational and organizational problems.

The community policing philosophy focuses on a number of questions, including the following:

- What is the best way to resolve this complex issue within the parameters of the law?
- What is best for the community and the individual?
- How can the police, as only one component of society, solve this problem best?
- How can the police best meet the needs of the community they serve?

The underlying theme of the training is problem-solving or problem-based learning and understanding the community that the police serve.

IN YOUR COMMUNITY 8.5

OFFER OF EMPLOYMENT – RECRUIT TRAINING WITH THE ONTARIO PROVINCIAL POLICE

Successful applicants will receive a phone call from OPP Uniform Recruitment staff, presenting them with a job offer conditional on acceptance of their detachment posting, which will be identified in two to three weeks' time.

Upon accepting a job offer, recruits attend the Provincial Police Academy in Orillia, Ontario for a one week orientation and introduction to the OPP.

Recruits receive academic instruction and physical training during their first week of orientation at the Provincial Police Academy. During this week, recruits will be required to challenge and pass the Ontario Police Fitness Award PIN test[see In Your Community 8.6].

Following the first week of orientation, OPP Recruits report to the Ontario Police College(OPC) in Aylmer, Ontario for 12 weeks of additional fundamental police training. OPP recruits will be intertwined with recruit constables from other police services in Ontario and will share common living quarters with up to nine pod-mates of the same gender.

OPC training is academically and physically rigorous. The Basic Constable Training Program is designed to provide candidates with the sound knowledge of the laws and procedures that front line-officers are required to apply in the performance of their duties.

Particular emphasis is placed on the core functions of the police services as found in section 4(2) of the Police Services Act:

- Crime Prevention
- Law Enforcement
- Assistance to Victims of Crime
- Public Order Maintenance
- Emergency Response

OPP recruits are expected to excel in all areas during training.

After completing 12 weeks of police training at OPC, Recruits return to the provincial police academy in Orillia for eight additional weeks of police training.

While at the academy, recruits will receive enhanced fitness, firearms and classroom training and instruction, including practical simulations that provide opportunities for recruits to apply concepts and theories learned during their training at the Ontario Police College. Practical simulations are designed to be as close to reality as possible, to ensure that recruits are operationally ready to serve and protect all citizens in Ontario in weeks to come.

Source: Ontario Provincial Police, Uniform Recruitment, Offer of Employment—Recruitment Training. © Queen's Printer for Ontario. Reproduced with permission. http://www.opp.ca/index.php?id=115&entryid=56b7c5868f94acaf5c28d17d$\num$sec6.

From the Academy to the Street: Operational Field Training

Becoming a police officer involves two distinct socialization processes: formal socialization is accomplished through the selection process and police training programs. These provide the new recruit with a vast amount of information on myriad subjects related to

IN YOUR COMMUNITY 8.6

ONTARIO POLICE FITNESS AWARD PROGRAM

The Ontario Police Fitness Award (OPFA) is a provincial incentive program developed to motivate Ontario police officers and police service employees to remain physically fit throughout their careers. The policing services division of the Ministry of Community Safety and Correctional Services and the Ontario Chiefs of Police sanction the OPFA program. The OPFA program is designed and implemented by Police Fitness Personnel of Ontario (PFPO).

In the policing profession, physical skills and abilities are important job prerequisites. Today, an applicant is required to successfully complete a PREP test or Physical Readiness Evaluation for Police, then again during Basic Constable training at the Ontario Police College. Once the recruit has returned to his or her respective police service, responsibility for individual and continuing fitness belongs to them.

Many police services offer incentives to officers completing or attempting the Ontario Police Fitness Award.

Source: *Ontario Police Fitness PIN Award Program. Used with permission. http://www.pfpo.org/index. php/2013-01-12-19-00-53/ontario-police-fitness-pin-award-program.*

policing. Informal socialization takes place as recruits interact with older, more experienced officers and with their peers on the job.

These two processes of socialization may conflict with each other, if only because of the differences between classroom learning and the skill development that comes with experience on the street. It was not uncommon in the past for new recruits to be told by veteran officers to forget what they learned in the training academy because they were now street cops. Somehow, street officers perceived an incompatibility with what was taught in the training academy and the way it "really" was on the street.

Today, police services are paying increasing attention to ensuring continuity between the training a recruit receives in the academy and the supervision provided once he or she is involved in operational policing. A model of instruction called **problem-based learning** has been implemented across Canada, including at RCMP Depot, the Justice Institute of British Columbia (JIBC), and the Calgary and Edmonton Police Services. This model presents actual problems that police officers will encounter on patrol and encourages them to apply their knowledge across a number of subject areas to solve the problem. This also helps establish limits on the acceptable use of police discretion.

The JIBC also utilizes competency-based education concepts in the training of municipal police recruits. Competency-based police education focuses on observable behaviours that reflect the recruit's actual skills, attitudes, and knowledge. It takes a case-based learning approach. Recruit class time focuses on mastering the competencies associated with police work. Further discussion of this topic and of **competency-based management human resource practices** is found later in this chapter during the discussion of performance evaluations and in A Closer Look 8.2.

On completing recruit training, the individual officer is usually assigned to general patrol duties for three to five years. After this initial indoctrination to the fundamentals of policing, that officer will receive additional in-service training. For the most part, in-service training is meant to complement both recruit training and the hands-on experience the new officer has received in the field.

It is during this second component of the training process, known as **operational field training**, that the recruit learns to apply the basic principles taught at the training academy. Under the guidance of a senior officer, the recruit is exposed to a wide variety of general police work. During this critical phase, the specially trained senior officer, who is specially trained (and who is often referred to as the "field trainer," "officer coach," or mentor), ensures that the recruit can handle the demands and challenges of police work. A primary objective of the field trainer is to enhance the skills and knowledge the recruit has learned at the academy. A good field trainer is vital to the ongoing learning and professional development of the new officer; even so, it is not uncommon to find inexperienced officers acting as coaches. This is due primarily to the significant levels of recruitment over the past several years, which has resulted in limited levels of experience among front-line patrol officers. In many instances, this is occurring among supervisory levels as well, which has caused many to observe a crisis in experience where it is needed most.

In-Service Training

Training provided to police officers over the course of their career—variously referred to as **in-service training**, refresher training, requalification training, advanced training, and career development training—is usually conducted by individual police agencies, at provincial training centres, or at the Canadian Police College in Ottawa.

A high level of demonstrated skill is expected during firearms training for recruit constables at the Police Academy and during annual firearm qualifications for all police personnel.

Source: © Atlantic Police Academy. P.E.I.

In-service training provides police personnel with ongoing professional development in operational, investigative, and administrative skills that are relevant to their current assignment or one they will soon be taking up. Typically, these training courses are highly sought after and are often viewed as a reward for competent and dedicated service to the police agency. In some instances, the in-service training may be necessary before the officer can be reassigned to a specialized section such as traffic enforcement or the drug section.

Advanced in-service training may include the following:

- *Administrative skills for police supervisors*: A course designed for police personnel who have recently been promoted or are soon to be promoted to a supervisory position.
- *Basic collision investigation*: A course designed to provide advanced skills and recommended techniques for traffic collision investigation.
- *Advanced collision investigation*: A course designed to provide technical knowledge in the area of crash science by facilitating investigative skills in collision analysis and collision reconstruction.
- *Control tactics instructor*: An instructor-level course designed to develop expertise in the area of use of force, handcuffing, weapons, compliance tools (e.g., pepper spray, baton), and handgun retention.
- *Crisis (hostage) negotiator*: A course designed to develop skills and techniques in negotiating the release of hostages or in the surrender of barricaded persons.
- *Drug investigator training*: A course designed to provide prospective drug investigators with the knowledge, skills, and techniques that relate to the search and seizure of drugs, including informant control, statements and confessions, and undercover operations.
- *Firearms instructor program*: An instructor-level course designed to develop expertise in the area of firearms and the instructional techniques needed to conduct firearms training in the police service.
- *Forensic DNA evidence*: A course designed to provide police officers with the necessary skills to investigate serious violent crimes and to accurately collect and process DNA evidence.
- *Forensic interviewing techniques*: A course designed to enable police officers to interview complainants, victims, witnesses, and suspects in order to obtain accurate, detailed, and relevant information that will aid in an investigation and that will be admissible in court.
- *General investigative skills*: A course designed for plainclothes police officers (detectives) in an investigative role, providing skills that include evidence handling, crime scene management, interviewing or interrogation, and forensic identification.
- *Media relations*: A course designed to enable police officers to disseminate information to the community via the print and electronic media, including skills to utilize when interacting with the media in general.
- *Police supervision skills*: A course designed to provide training in the necessary abilities, skills, and knowledge that are required for effective supervision and leadership.
- *Problem-oriented policing*: A course designed to enhance the operational police officer's skills and knowledge of community policing, the SARA model of problem-oriented policing, and crime analysis.
- *School liaison*: A course designed to provide police officers with the necessary intervention and prevention techniques related to youths, including skills that foster informal and formal interaction with youth in the classroom and in the community.
- *Search and seizure*: A course designed to provide police officers with knowledge pertaining to the search warrant process and skills essential to conducting a lawful search and seizure.

It is also important that officers have access to continuing education and information once they are on the job. There is a trend in Canadian police services towards integrating in-service training with career development and requiring that officers achieve certain educational and training competencies in order to apply for promotion. Many police services have developed in-service training programs to ensure that officers keep abreast of changes in legislation, policy, court decisions, departmental procedures, and societal issues.

Some of the trending training courses for Canadian police service personnel include:

- *Crisis intervention training*: These sessions provide front-line officers with the necessary knowledge and skills to deal with individuals in crisis. This includes subject assessment and situational awareness, allowing officers to defuse and de-escalate an incident involving a person experiencing a mental health crisis. This specialized training enhances both public and officer safety by emphasizing active listening skills and achieving resolution with the use of minimal force.

- *Implicit bias awareness training*: These sessions are designed to provide awareness to police and civilian personnel of the inherent bias they may have with regard to race, religion, gender, age, and sexual orientation. Implicit bias may distort an officer's perception and subsequent treatment of an individual or group. Reducing the influence of implicit bias is important to building relationships between police services and diverse Canadian communities.

- *Cybercrime investigation*: The Canadian Police College in Ottawa provides a 10-day training course on cyber-investigations. The course is designed to provide officers with the ability to investigate and prepare a cyber-related case for court that will result in a successful conviction. The topics include malware, DDoS attacks, penetration lab (inside the mind of the hacker), the preparation of expert reports, preparing for court, and investigating traditional crimes using online tools (e.g., Geofeedia, MediaSonar, and Echosec) (Canadian Police College 2017).

Police services are also utilizing learning technology, referred to as **e-learning**, to provide continual training to officers in the field. The Calgary Police Service, like most police services across Canada, has utilized a computer program called TRACCESS, in which organizationally important learning modules are developed. Police officers must work their way through the interactive programs and complete a test at the end of each module. Officers can work their way through a module any hour of the day. This mode of learning is ideal for ensuring that police officers clearly understand critical aspects of policing, such as pursuit policy, civil property disputes, and domestic violence.

Similarly, the Canadian Police Knowledge Network (CPKN) is a not-for-profit organization that provides online in-service training for Canadian police officers. CPKN was created by and specifically for members of the Canadian police community. Working with subject matter experts from police training academies and police services across Canada, CPKN provides training to meet police-specific situations, protocols, and tactics and is available to all police officers across Canada. The Canadian Police Knowledge Network is available online at http://www.cpkn.ca.

The RCMP has developed an online learning system to better serve its members, which is accessible athttp://www.rcmp-grc.gc.ca/ctb-fc/index-eng.htm. This "distance delivery" approach is excellent for reaching all members of the RCMP, whether they are stationed in remote parts of Canada or involved in international assignments.

ON THE LINE: THE NEW COMMUNITY POLICE OFFICER

The new police officer becomes a thinking professional, utilizing imagination and creativity to identify and solve problems … The police officer is encouraged to develop co-operative relationships in the community, guided by values and purposes, rather than constrained by rules and excessive supervision.

—E. Meese (1993)

Two key elements of community policing are the decentralization of decision-making and the empowerment of line officers to collaborate with community residents in problem-solving. This has been described as a coactive response. This term recognizes the importance of citizen–police partnerships. Either party can identify conditions that need to be addressed to increase the safety of a neighbourhood. This type of policing is coactive in the sense that citizens and police work collaboratively to define and design the response to threatening conditions. The coactive role of police officers in a community policing framework does not replace the reactive and proactive roles of the police; rather, it expands the role of the police by broadening the capacity of police officers to address the causes of crime and disorder. It is therefore essential that the necessary reforms be made to provide an opportunity for officers to assume a new role.

The Community Police Officer as a Generalist

Within the framework of community policing, the community police officer (CPO) is viewed as a **generalist** who is supported by specialists within the police service. The term "generalist" means that line officers have the authority, discretion, and skills to develop partnerships with the community in the area to which they are assigned and to apply various strategies to solve problems of crime and social disorder. Of course, in many police services, particularly smaller services, patrol constables have always been generalists. In large, urban police services, however, the trend over the past several decades has been towards increasing the specialization of officers.

The CPO is the primary conduit through which the police service reaches out to the community and engages residents in identifying and responding to problems. As well, CPOs are a primary referral source to other agencies and organizations that may be able to address specific concerns and issues. CPOs, however, cannot be expected to be experts in all areas, and the police service must provide the support of specialists when required. In addition, CPOs must have access to information gathered and analyzed by the police service. As Taylor (1999, 66) notes, "good community policing depends on gathering and analyzing accurate information."

For CPOs to succeed, the police service must meet a number of conditions:

- it must take a client-oriented approach to dealing with the community;
- it must focus on solving community problems;
- it must deploy patrol officers based on clear objectives;
- it must assign officers to defined areas where they can consult with residents and other agencies;
- it must provide resources and specialist expertise in support of patrol officers; and
- it must embrace demand-driven policing that considers short-, medium-, and long-term demands on police services (Taylor 1999:28–29).

Placing police officers in the role of generalists is, in the words of a certain baseball Hall-of-Famer, Yogi Berra, "déjà vu all over again." Check back to the description of the various roles that police constables played in communities in the early days of police forces. These officers were generalists as well and had an even wider range of responsibilities and activities, such as tax collector, chimney inspector, and animal pound keeper. And officers in rural and remote areas of the country have always assumed a variety of roles, both out of necessity and because many RCMP, OPP, and SQ detachments are quite small. It was mainly in the larger urban police services that officers slowly drifted away from contact with the community and tended towards increasing specialization. As noted in Chapter 1, the loss of contact with the community was precipitated largely by the introduction of the police patrol car and the demise of beat policing, which has now made a comeback within the framework of community policing.

THE POLICE PERSONALITY AND COMMUNITY POLICING

After completing academy and field training, the new officer becomes a full-fledged member of the police service and begins the process of adopting the attitudes that distinguish the occupation of police work. Research on the police occupation has resulted in the development of a number of key concepts that provide insights into the attitudes, perceptions, and behaviour of police officers. Many of these concepts are components of what Jerome Skolnick (1966) labelled the **working personality of police officers**, a set of attitudinal and behavioural attributes that develop as a consequence of the unique role that police officers play and the duties they are asked to perform. While Skolnick's findings may be dated, they remain relevant today.

Attributes of the Police Working Personality

Characteristics of the working personality include a preoccupation with danger, excessive suspiciousness of people and activities, a protective cynicism, and difficulties in exercising authority—that is, in balancing the rights of citizens under the Canadian Charter of Rights and Freedoms with the need to maintain order.

As a consequence of these personality attributes, many police officers:

- tend to view policing as a career and a way of life, rather than merely a nine-to-five job;
- value secrecy and practise a code of silence to protect fellow officers;
- exhibit strong in-group solidarity—often referred to as the *blue wall*—with other police officers due to job-related stresses, shift work, and an "us versus them" division between police and nonpolice (Goldsmith 1990);
- tend to hold conservative political and moral views; and
- exhibit attitudes that emphasize the high-risk/action component of police work—often referred to as the *blue-light syndrome*.

Although individual patrol officers have their own styles of policing, and although not every officer exhibits all of the characteristics of the working personality, it is a useful concept for understanding the police occupation and the behaviour of officers in certain situations, especially if the police organization is seeking to establish a major change initiative.

The extent to which this typology is useful for studying Canadian police services cannot be determined at this time. Not all police services are the same, and the police organizations in which officers carry out their tasks may differ on a number of key dimensions. What is clear, however, is that police officers and their style of policing are influenced by a number of environmental factors that combine to shape their perceptions. For example, since the 9/11 terrorist attacks, a much stronger commitment to national security, images of terrorism and terrorists, and perceptions of safety have imprinted themselves on the psyche of modern Canadian police in ways that have not been studied but that need to be understood. If attitudes drive behaviours, then many contemporary examples of police misconduct, particularly in relation to the use of force, are likely rooted in the "working personality" of police officers.

The Occupational Subculture of Police and Community Policing

In the four decades since Skolnick first proposed the existence of an occupational subculture of police and identified the components of the working personality of police officers, there has been a considerable amount of debate about the validity of his arguments.

One question relates to the extent to which the isolation of police officers, their in-group solidarity, and their traditional distrust and suspicion of the general public are being undermined by emerging trends in policing. These trends include the move towards community policing, the decentralization of traditional command and control structures, the empowerment of line officers, the growing number of partnerships being developed between police and communities, the increasing reliance on restorative justice approaches (see Chapter 9), and the changing face of police recruits. To counter negative aspects of the occupational subculture, police organizations have spent considerable time and effort developing codes of professional conduct and values statements, as well as ethics training to serve as guideposts for professional police conduct and service to the community. A Closer Look 8.1 examines the core values of Canadian police officers.

A second question relates to how the organizational and operational environment in which police officers carry out their work affects the various attributes of the police personality. For example, police officers assigned to community police stations or posted

A CLOSER LOOK 8.1

CORE VALUES IN POLICE SERVICES ACROSS CANADA

In Chapter 6 we examined mission statements as well as organizational values. The values of various Canadian departments are included below. Do you see similarities between them?

- Toronto Police Service: "Honesty, Integrity, Fairness, Respect, Reliability, Teamwork, Positive Attitude, Freedom from Bias"

- Edmonton Police Service: "Integrity, Accountability, Respect, Innovation, Courage, and Community"

- Ontario Provincial Police: "Professionalism, Accountability, Diversity, Respect, Excellence, Leadership"

- Vancouver Police: I CARE: "Integrity, Compassion, Accountability, Respect, Excellence"

- RCMP: "Integrity, Honesty, Professionalism, Compassion, Respect, Accountability"

Sources: Toronto Police Service; Edmonton Police Service; OPP © Queen's Printer for Ontario, 2017. Reproduced with permission; Vancouver Police Department; reproduced with the permission of the RCMP.

to small detachments in remote areas of the country have little choice but to interact with community residents. We have previously noted that police officers carry out their tasks in a variety of environments, ranging from small Inuit villages to large metropolitan areas.

Also, there may be two distinct subcultures within police services: one of senior police managers focused on delivering services within the framework of community policing, and the other of line officers focused on the operational realities of day-to-day police work (Dean 1995; Goldsmith 1990). There may be considerable distance between these two, even within the same police service. The success of police managers is often measured by the extent to which they can convince patrol officers to support the goals of the organization and incorporate its objectives into daily patrol practice.

In sum, the "us [police] versus them [public]" dichotomy is much too general to capture the variety of relationships that exist between the public and the police and the differences that exist among police officers themselves regarding how the police role is carried out (Herbert 1998).

The Positive and Negative Features of the Police Subculture

The subculture that exists among police officers has many positive features. Given the unpredictability of their work and the potential for violence, officers must develop camaraderie among themselves. This group solidarity helps individual officers cope with the more stressful aspects of police work; it is also a source of support.

Even so, there are a number of drawbacks, such as:

- police alienation from the general public and other agencies and organizations;

- police officer alienation from management;

- establishment of "symbolic" criminals; that is, people who "look like" criminals or terrorists; and

- resistance to change, including community policing, that could assist in addressing personal and organizational problems.

In sum, while it may not be possible to document the existence of a distinct police personality statistically, and while a considerable amount of mythology surrounds police work, many police officers believe they have a working personality that sets them apart as an occupational group. This belief may in itself make the working personality of police a reality. The occupational perspectives of police officers may have a significant impact on operational patrol work and decision-making (police discretion) in situations on the street and in case investigations.

This decision-making and the influence of the police subculture on the individual community police officer is a growing concern. Throughout Canada, there is a heightened awareness, and visibility, regarding the ethical conduct and professionalism of police officers.

For the new recruit, one factor that can reduce the "inward" influence of the police subculture is the maintenance of outside friendships, including taking part in community life outside of policing:

Outside friendships help to bring down the "blue wall" between police and those they serve, and to combat the insular nature of the police culture that can help corruption to breed. If you want to be a well-rounded officer, you must understand your community. Your community will keep you grounded.
     –Toronto Police Superintendent Keith Forde, Officer I/C, Charles O. Bick Police College

PATROL OFFICER RESISTANCE TO COMMUNITY POLICING

Departments converting to community policing might … be wise to recognize that there is a large body of research which suggests that rank and file police officers prefer the "law enforcement" role over the "order maintenance" and "service delivery roles."
     —K. Polowek (1995)

Experience suggests that many front-line patrol officers may resist the concept of community policing. This opposition may have several sources.

Distrust of Senior Police Leaders

Officers often distrust pronouncements about community policing made by senior police administrators. This response is based, in part, on experiences with past reforms and projects that produced few tangible results. In a survey of a sample of police officers in BC, 29 percent felt that community policing was "just a public relations" exercise (Murphy and Griffiths 1994). In a secret ballot conducted in Halifax in 1996, 87 percent of police officers indicated that they were in favour of returning to a "more traditional" style of policing (*Halifax Daily News* 1996, 4).

Fear of Being Marginalized

Patrol officers often fear being marginalized by other officers and some of their supervisors. Those officers who are extensively involved in community policing initiatives are often facetiously referred to as "the rubber gun squad" by other police officers who subscribe to a more traditional, crime-control model of police work. The term originated in the New York City police department, where officers who experience stress-related disorders have their working guns replaced with rubber ones. It can be anticipated that as the culture of police services changes from one centred on traditional police practices to one focused on community policing, the levels of marginalization will decrease.

Lack of Time

Many patrol officers feel that they do not have time to do community policing—a perception that is often grounded in reality. In the absence of a clear framework for implementation and clearly stated objectives, patrol officers may view community policing as merely adding to their workload. In fact, increasing call loads, excessive paperwork, and cutbacks in resources and in the number of police personnel may make it difficult for officers to work on establishing partnerships with the community and to solve problems. Generally speaking, if the police service has not adopted corporate practices such as strategic plans, business plans, and service performance indicators, and created the conditions for police to engage in proactive activities, then patrol officers are probably correct in feeling they don't have time.

In a study of community policing in BC, a high percentage of RCMP and municipal police officers indicated that they did not have time to do community policing, due to already heavy workloads (Murphy and Griffiths 1994). This reflects the widespread view that community policing is a programmatic "add-on" to the core activities of the police. It also reflects the reality that patrol officers are often not provided with the organizational and operational frameworks within which to become community police officers. Many police organizations across Canada have begun to address this issue by engaging in workload analysis studies to determine how busy police officers actually are and how workloads can be redistributed to make more time available for police officers. Recall our discussion in Chapter 7 about staffing to workload as opposed to staffing based on population to police officer ratios ("pop to cop"). The RCMP and the police services in Vancouver, Calgary, Edmonton, and Durham Region have all developed staffing models based on an analysis of workloads.

Performance Evaluations

Most performance evaluations currently used by police agencies do not reflect the work officers do. Evaluations typically consist of compliance audits, statistical comparisons, or descriptive summaries of events.

—*T.N. Oettmeier and M.A. Wycoff (1997)*

The implementation of community policing has resulted in an expansion of the role and activities of many police patrol officers, and of the expectations of both community residents and senior police administrators. The criteria used to assess the performance of line officers must reflect the myriad tasks and activities they are involved in. Many police services have implemented **competency-based performance evaluations**, which assess observable behaviours, knowledge, and skills directed towards the achievement of organizational objectives. Hay Group's *National Diagnostic on Human Resources in Policing, 2007* describes competency-based performance management in the following way:

> *… a competency as any skill, knowledge or other attribute, which leads to superior performance at work. The principle is that if we understand what separates "the best" from "the rest," then we can:*

- focus recruitment on finding people who will have what it takes to be a strong performer;
- focus performance management system towards individual acquisition of missing competencies so that they can be more like the best performers; and
- develop talent for the future that will leverage people's strengths and place them in roles where they are more likely to be successful thus developing a high performance organization (Hay Group 2007).

While consensus among police human resource professionals favours a competency-based developmental approach (see A Closer Look 8.2), there is still a tendency to recognize and reward officer performance based on reactive, law enforcement–oriented police work—despite the creation of mission and value statements that incorporate the principles of community policing, and despite the development of new programs in the community.

A CLOSER LOOK 8.2

THE CANADIAN POLICING COMPETENCY FRAMEWORK

The Police Sector Council collaborated with policing executives from across Canada to develop a competency framework and tools to support all aspects of strategic human resource management for the policing industry as a whole. This work involved leveraging existing best practices and knowledge within the policing sector to develop a nationally relevant system.

The **Policing Competency Framework** provides the policing industry with a common language and understanding of the work and underlying competency requirements associated with general policing duties for all ranks: Constable, Sergeant, Staff Sergeant, Inspector, Superintendent, Chief Superintendent, Deputy Chief, and Chief. This framework was developed by leveraging the best practices from police services across Canada and working with the policing community to fully analyze and document the job responsibilities of each rank. The resulting Framework includes Job Descriptions, Task Lists, Competency Profiles and a Policing Competency Dictionary.

Source: Police Sector Council, http://www.policecouncil.ca.

In a BC study, municipal police officers were asked to assign a relative weight (low, medium, high) to a number of factors they felt should be used in evaluating their performance. The responses of the officers for each factor are presented in Table 8.3.

The officers surveyed generally felt that the traditional measures of police performance, such as the number of tickets issued and arrests made and the number of criminal convictions, should not be used in evaluating their performance. Rather, the officers believed that more emphasis should be placed on the skills required to do the job and on the effectiveness of officers in solving community problems. When these same officers were asked to rank the importance of a number of police activities, 98 percent ranked "responding to emergency calls" and 65 percent ranked "building better relationships with the community" as "most important" or "important." To see an example of the extent of the duties and responsibilities of a police constable, see In Your Community 8.7.

Table 8.3 Officer Ratings of the Importance of Criteria for Assessing Performance

	Low	Medium	High
Number of tickets/arrests	26 percent	55 percent	17 percent
Number of criminal convictions	33 percent	47 percent	17 percent
Community involvement	16 percent	59 percent	22 percent
Skills (interviewing, report writing, etc.)	0.9 percent	27 percent	70 percent
Appearance	10 percent	55 percent	34 percent
Lack of citizen complaints	33 percent	43 percent	22 percent
Effectiveness in solving community problems	12 percent	45 percent	40 percent

Source: Dr. Christopher Murphy, *Policing in British Columbia: Commission of Inquiry*, table "Evaluating Police Officer Performance" (1994), 72. Copyright © Province of of British Columbia. All Rights Reserved. Reprinted with permission of the Province of British Columbia.www.ipp.gov.bc.ca. Found at http://www.llbc.leg.bc.ca/public/pubdocs/bcdocs/193531/communitybasedpolicing.pdf

IN YOUR COMMUNITY 8.7

WINDSOR POLICE SERVICE PATROL CONSTABLE JOB DESCRIPTION

Position Summary:

Under the supervision of the Platoon Sergeant will provide police response to prevent crime, protect life and property, preserve the peace, enforce and investigate violations of Federal, Provincial and Municipal laws, provide information and guidance to citizens and promote traffic safety. All sworn members are reminded they are responsible for preserving the peace, preventing offences and discharging all other duties as a Police Officer of the Windsor Police Service to the best of their ability, faithfully, impartially and according to law.

Position Duties:

- Remain current on Federal, Provincial, and Municipal laws, crime prevention and investigation techniques and comply with Service directives, memorandums and policies and procedures;
- Be familiar with the Windsor Police Service Business Plan and the stated objectives of the Windsor Police Service;
- Assume an active role in Community Based and Problem Oriented Policing initiatives adopted by the Windsor Police Service;
- Perform general patrol;
- Protect the life and property of citizens;
- Provide emergency service;
- Respond to calls for service;
- Enforce Federal, Provincial and Municipal laws;
- Provide traffic control and enforcement;
- Accident prevention and investigation;
- Investigate crime, provide crime prevention and detect and process offenders;
- Promote and maintain good community relations;
- Determine needs and direct efforts and correct or suppress crime, deal with traffic problems and answer other community policing needs consistent with Problem Oriented Policing principles;
- Gain the appropriate knowledge of the people and the area where they patrol and the impact of each on police service delivery;
- Prepare for and attend court when necessary;
- Prepare and submit detailed duty and investigative notes as required;
- Articulate the justification for the appropriate level of use of force;
- Attend community meetings as required;
- Undertake special projects or assignments as required and report on the results in a timely fashion;
- Remain current on all required technology;
- Attend training as required;
- Perform other duties as assigned.

The above job description outlines the principal function of the job identified and shall not be considered a detailed description of all the work requirements that may be inherent in this job.

Source: *Windsor Police Service. Found at http://www.police.windsor.on.ca/careers/officers-cadets/ Pages/Patrol-Constable-Job-Description.aspx.*

Lack of Training or Experience with Community Policing

Patrol officers may have little training or experience in how to do community policing and the strategies and skills required to work with community residents and organizations. Community police officers must have a variety of skills, ranging from those associated with case investigation and apprehending offenders to the ability to build partnerships with the community, to engage in problem-solving policing, and to meet the demands of policing in specific types of neighbourhoods. Officers who lack the personal attributes compatible with community policing, or who lack the necessary training to do community policing, may become frustrated and turn into an obstacle to the efforts of the police service. Initial and in-service training, combined with a supportive organizational environment, is critical to the success of individual CPOs. In addition, many officers still equate crime prevention and community relations activities with community policing—a misperception that can only be corrected by education and training. In response to this deficiency, several Canadian police services have worked with post-secondary institutions to develop community policing courses. Dalhousie University in Halifax, Nova Scotia, offers a Police Leadership Certificate, which includes two courses on community-based strategic policing. Across Canada, a number of post-secondary institutions have partnered with police agencies to augment learning opportunities in community-based policing. You can find more information about some of these programs by checking the following universities and the programs that they offer:

- University of Alberta—Management Development for Police Services
- Simon Fraser University—Police Studies Program
- University of Regina—Police Studies
- Wilfrid Laurier University—Policing

Absence of Patrol Officer Input into Community Strategies and Plans

Patrol officers may not have participated in the development of plans for service delivery, and there may be an absence of direction from senior management. Front-line officers must be intimately involved in the development of policing policies and programs. Often, police leaders have attempted to impose community policing and to implement various programs without adequate consultation with patrol officers. Senior police managers and front-line patrol officers may disagree about the extent to which community policing should be implemented. Officers in some police services feel they have not been empowered to identify and resolve problems in the communities they police.

Our discussion of community policing in Ontario in Chapter 3 revealed that there has often been a lack of communication between senior management and front-line officers, as well as a lack of training to provide patrol officers with the skills required to develop partnerships with the community and do problem-solving policing. As a result, patrol officers have often been confused about what exactly they are supposed to be doing and what expectations senior management and the community have of them. Ultimately, these problems will undermine attempts to adopt and implement community policing.

CHAPTER SUMMARY

In this chapter, we have focused on the community policing officer. Community policing places specific types of demands on police officers. This is reflected in the changes that have occurred in the recruitment of new police officers. Police services are increasingly expected to reflect the diversity of the communities they police, and this has resulted in an emphasis on hiring women, members of First Nations, and visible and cultural minorities, as well as gay, lesbian, bisexual, and transgender individuals. There has also been an emphasis on promoting women within the ranks and into senior officer positions.

Police training has also changed. Community policing permeates all facets of recruit training at the Ontario Police College and other police training facilities across the country. Despite this major change, the characteristics of the occupational subculture of police and the resistance of officers may undermine community policing efforts. Officers with the necessary skills, motivation, and organizational support can use a number of tools and techniques to implement community policing in the areas to which they have been assigned.

In Chapter 10, we will focus on how police officers can work with communities to establish partnerships and to identify and solve problems of crime and social disorder.

CHAPTER REVIEW

Key Terms

- attrition rate, p. 256
- basic qualifications, p. 252
- competency-based management human resource practices, p. 264
- competency-based performance evaluations, p. 272
- competency-based training, p. 261
- diversity, p. 254
- double-dipping, p. 257
- e-learning, p. 267
- ethical behaviour, p. 253
- generalist, p. 268
- hiring quotas, p. 261
- in-service training, p. 265
- operational field training, p. 265
- Policing Competency Framework, p. 273
- preferred qualifications, p. 252
- problem-based learning, p. 264
- working personality of police officers, p. 268

Key Points

- There is increasing pressure on police services to reflect the diversity of the communities they police.
- Police services are attempting with moderate success to recruit more women, members of First Nations, and visible and cultural minorities.
- Police services are competing with other law enforcement/public safety agencies for a limited pool of suitable applicants.
- Police training is becoming more centred on community policing and problems.
- Operational field training must complement the training received by recruits at the police academy/college.
- Community police officers are generalists who have the skills and knowledge to carry out a number of roles and mandates within the framework of community policing.
- CPOs can be effective only if they have the support of their police service and are given the discretion, autonomy, and resources they need to carry out their tasks.
- There are a number of sources of resistance to community policing among police officers that can undermine efforts of a police service to develop partnerships with the community and have officers be problem-solvers.

Self-Evaluation

QUESTIONS

1. What role does the concept of **diversity** play in the recruitment of police officers?
2. What is meant by **hiring quotas**, and why is this term often mentioned in discussions of police recruiting?

3. Describe the components of the **Recruit Training Program**.
4. What are the **basic qualifications** required by police services in the recruitment process?
5. Discuss what is meant by **preferred qualifications**, and note what role these play in the recruitment process.
6. What is **competency-based training**, and what role does it play in police training?
7. Describe the importance of **operational field training**.
8. What is **in-service training**, what types of courses are offered, and what role does it play in the training of police officers?
9. Discuss how the **decentralization** of decision making and the **empowerment** of line officers can result in effective problem-solving.
10. Describe what is meant by the **working personality of police officers**, and then note the importance of this concept for our study of community policing.
11. What is meant by the community police officer as **generalist?**
12. Discuss how core values within a police service serve to influence the police **subculture**.

KEY IDEAS

1. In the police recruiting process, what is the term for things such as citizenship, age, physical abilities, and common sense and good judgment?
   a. nonessential abilities
   b. preferred qualifications
   c. standard abilities
   d. basic qualifications

2. Which of the following have Canadian police services done in recent years?
   a. Attempted to avoid hiring people who are visible minorities.
   b. Continued to maintain regulations that prohibit the hiring of gays, lesbians, and bisexual and transgender individuals.
   c. Experienced moderate success in attracting qualified women and members of visible minorities.
   d. Hired large numbers of women, so that female officers now comprise nearly 30 percent of police personnel across the country.

3. According to recent figures, which province has the highest percentage of policewomen?
   a. Ontario
   b. Quebec
   c. British Columbia
   d. Nova Scotia

4. What percentage of police officers in Toronto are visible minorities?
   a. 12 percent
   b. about 5 percent
   c. 20 percent
   d. 15 percent

5. Overall, recruitment strategies designed to attract more women and members of visible minorities into policing have had moderate success. This is because of which of the following factors?
   a. The general lack of "specialty incentives" that exist once an individual is hired.
   b. Difficulties encountered in the physical testing process.
   c. The failure of police services to devote the necessary resources to attract non-Anglo and female recruits.
   d. Height requirements that tend to prevent many individuals from applying to become police officers.

6. How have some police services increased the numbers of women and visible and cultural minorities in policing?
   a. By reducing the entrance standards.
   b. By establishing hiring quotas.
   c. By raising pay levels.
   d. By offering a hiring bonus and covering expenses related to relocating.

7. What is the term for police training that focuses on the acquisition of specific, measurable skills and knowledge that can be transferred to the operational level?
   a. competency-based training
   b. hard skills training
   c. soft skills training
   d. intensive, professional training

8. Which of the following is true according to research studies on police services?
   a. Officers in some police services who participate in community policing initiatives are paid a bonus.
   b. Officers who participate in community police initiatives are guaranteed high status among patrol officers.
   c. In some police services, officer performance assessments are still based on traditional police work.
   d. In some police services, officer promotions are based upon community policing initiatives.

9. Which statement best defines the "working personality" of police officers?
   a. A term used to describe the attitudes and behaviours of police officers.
   b. One of many personalities that police officers may have while on duty.
   c. A discredited term that cannot be used to describe why police officers behave the way they do.
   d. The personality changes that occur from initial recruit training to working in the field.

10. What statement best describes "employment equity" hiring practices?
    a. A legislated "quota"-based hiring practice.
    b. A preferential hiring system focusing on visible minorities and other identified groups.
    c. A form of affirmative action to right the wrongs of systemic discrimination.
    d. A salary policy of "like pay for like work."

11. The RCMP integrates the CAPRA model throughout its recruit-training curriculum. The goal of this approach is to have police recruits deal with operational and organizational challenges by utilizing which of the following models?
    a. A theoretical model toward community-based policing.
    b. A problem-solving model.
    c. An individual decision-making model based upon education and experience.
    d. A corporate business practice model.

12. Competency-based police education _____
    a. is a standard method of training used throughout Canada for recruits.
    b. emphasizes observable behaviours that reflect recruit skills, attitude, and knowledge.
    c. emphasizes knowledge of the policies, procedures, and legislation that pertains to operational policing.
    d. is a standard method of in-service training used by Canadian Police Services.

The Community Police Officer: Situations and Strategies

Community Policing Implementation Checklist

There are a number of questions that should be asked to determine whether officers in a police service are being recruited, trained, and deployed within a community policing framework. These include:

Recruiting and Training

- In recruiting and screening prospective officers, does the police service emphasize individuals with the skills and interest to do community policing?
- Are new recruits trained in the principles and practices of community policing, including problem-solving skills, strategies for identifying and mobilizing community residents and resources, and communication skills?
- Do new recruits learn about a variety of crime attack strategies and crime prevention approaches and their effectiveness?
- Do new recruits receive cultural sensitivity training on the specific challenges in policing visible minority communities and neighbourhoods, and strategies for involving residents in these communities in police–community partnerships?
- Do new recruits learn about Indigenous history and cultures and how to police communities with Indigenous residents effectively?

Deployment of Officers

- Are officers responsible for policing, problem-solving, and establishing partnerships with residents in a specific zone or turf?
- Are officers assigned to a specific area for an extended period of time so that they have the opportunity to become familiar with the neighbourhoods and their residents?
- Do the residents in the community or neighbourhood know any of the officers by name?
- Do officers have the authority to establish committees composed of community members and to engage in problem-solving activities?
- Are officers familiar with the key strategies of community policing, including problem-oriented policing, situational crime prevention, and crime prevention through social development (see Chapter 9)?
- Do line officers understand the principles and practice of community policing, and do officers have access to ongoing training and information sessions?
- Do officers have the opportunity to participate in integrated service teams, working with professionals from other agencies and organizations?
- Are officers familiar with the resources and sources of support available within the community, including shelters, safe houses, youth street workers, and mental health workers?
- Are officers familiar with the philosophy and practices of community policing and how the principles of this model can be adapted to meet the needs and concerns of individual communities and neighbourhoods?
- If the officers are assigned to a neighbourhood with a high population of visible minorities or to a predominately Indigenous community, do the officers have an understanding of the history, culture, and dynamics of the particular community?
- Do officers receive departmental recognition for accomplishments in the community?
- Apart from the ordinary cynicism that arises on the job, do officers respect the communities and residents they police?
- Are officers highly motivated to make a difference in their policing activities, or are they more focused on working towards their retirement?

Performance Assessment

- Does the officer's performance review include assessments of problem-solving activities, contacts with the community, and involvement in specific crime prevention and response initiatives?

Case Studies

Case Study 1: Project Shock

The RCMP's response to 9/11 was called "Project Shock." It was one of the RCMP's first investigative and enforcement initiatives that was national in scope, with implications in one form or another for all divisions across the country. Under Project Shock, the RCMP worked closely with other government departments in the fight against terrorism—the Canadian Security Intelligence Service, the Department of Foreign Affairs and International Trade, Canada Customs and Revenue Agency, the Department of Justice, Transport Canada, Criminal Intelligence Service Canada, the Department of National Defence, and the Privy Council Office, among others.

This collaboration was underscored in the December 2001 federal budget, which funded a number of initiatives related to lawful access; emergency preparedness; marine security; border infrastructure; and chemical, biological, radiological, and nuclear (CBRN) technology.

The RCMP received $576 million under this budget, to be spread over six years. The funding from the December 2001 budget was earmarked for 17 specific national security projects and programs. Many of these initiatives leverage the expertise and resources of other federal government departments.

One such initiative was the Integrated National Security Enforcement Teams (INSETs), comprised of representatives from across the RCMP and partner agencies at the municipal, provincial, and federal levels.

After 9/11, the RCMP also created the Financial Intelligence Task Force, which has now expanded to become the Financial Intelligence Branch. This group tracks the criminal misuse of Canadian financial systems that may facilitate terrorist acts here and in other countries.

The task force works in close cooperation with the new Financial Transactions and Reports Analysis Centre of Canada (FINTRAC) to analyze information about the funding of terrorists and to prosecute individuals or groups who engage in terrorism.

Situation

You are in charge of an INSET when a prominent member of a Middle Eastern community comes forward and alleges that you are profiling his community based on race. How do you respond to this criticism? Justify your answer in terms of the main ideas you have learned about community-based strategic policing.

_____

_____

_____

_____

_____

_____

Case Study 2: R. v. Meiorin

In *R. v. Meiorin* ([1999] 3 S.C.R. 3), Ms. Meiorin was an employee of the BC Ministry of Forests and worked as a member of an initial attack forest firefighting crew. To ensure safe and productive work, employees in this category must be aerobically fit and have adequate levels of muscular strength and endurance to help combat fatigue, recover from high-intensity work, and cope with the added demands of heat and altitude.

In 1988 the BC Ministry of Forests instituted the US Forest Service Smoke Jumpers Test as the standard for physical fitness for its forest firefighters. The ministry contracted with the University of Victoria to see if other testing methods were available that would be more appropriate, and the university attempted to establish a test that reflected actual firefighting activities and the minimum fitness levels necessary to perform them properly. One element of the test was aerobic fitness, which was measured to a standard of 50 VO^2 max. Evidence submitted in the course of this arbitration showed that, due to physiological differences, women are on average less able to do aerobic work than men, and would therefore have more difficulty meeting the required standard than would men. In 1995 there were 800 to 900 initial attack crew personnel, of which 100 to 150 were female. Thirty-five percent of females passed the test the first time, as compared to 65 to 70 percent of males.

In 1994, the new fitness standard was introduced as mandatory. Recalled employees such as Ms. Meiorin were allowed to take the old test if they failed the new fitness test. Ms. Meiorin was given four opportunities to pass the aerobic aspect of the old test (a 2.5-kilometre run in 11 minutes or less) and failed on each occasion. As a result of her failure to meet the required physical fitness standard, she was suspended from work and, after further review, was laid off. The matter made its way through various appeals to the Supreme Court of Canada.

The Supreme Court ruled that a three-step test should be adopted for determining whether an employer has established, on a balance of probabilities, that a *prima facie* discriminatory standard is a *bona fide occupational requirement* (BFOR). First, the employer must show that it adopted the standard for a purpose rationally connected to the performance of the job. Second, the employer must establish that it adopted the particular standard in an honest and good-faith belief that it was necessary for the fulfillment of that legitimate work-related purpose. Third, the employer must establish that the standard is reasonably necessary to the accomplishment of that legitimate work-related purpose. To show that the standard is reasonably necessary, it must be demonstrated that it is impossible to accommodate individual employees sharing the characteristics of the claimant without imposing undue hardship upon the employer. The Supreme Court allowed Ms. Meiorin's appeal and reinstated her in her previous position.

This decision has had an important impact on the physical testing of prospective police officers. As a result, police agencies have had to ensure that they can meet the three-part test established by the Supreme Court and that physical entrance requirements do not discriminate against women. The full text of the *Meiorin* decision is available through the Supreme Court's website at www.scc-csc.gc.ca.

EXERCISES: KNOWLEDGE INTO PRACTICE

Exercise 1. Recruiting Criteria

You are a member of a recruitment team for your police service. Your department has recently adopted a new mission and value statement based on the principles of community policing. You and your colleagues on the recruiting team must develop new criteria for recruiting new members to the department. List what you would consider to be the most important criteria for hiring new recruits. Then, for each item, provide a rationale for why you feel it is important.

Criteria   Rationale

1. _____

2. _____

3. _____

4. _____

5. _____

6. _____

7. _____

8. _____

9. _____

10. _____

11. _____

12. _____

13. _____

14. _____

15. _____

Exercise 2. Assessing Officer Performance

Your police service has recently adopted a new mission and value statement based on the principles of community policing. You have been appointed by your chief to a committee tasked with developing new standards for the review and assessment of the performance of officers in the department. Develop a list of the criteria that you feel should be used to assess officer performance. Then, for each item, provide an example.

Criteria   Rationale

1. _____

2. _____

3. _____

4. _____

5. _____

6. _____

7. _____

8. _____

9. _____

10. _____

Exercise 3. Policing Remote Communities

As a member of the personnel division of the RCMP, you have responsibility for selecting officers to serve in remote Northern communities. Develop a list of criteria that you feel should be used for assigning officers to police these communities. Then, for each item, provide a rationale for why it is important.

Criteria   Rationale

1. _____

2. _____

3. _____

4. _____

5. _____

6. _____

7. _____

8. _____

9. _____

10. _____

Now, explain how these criteria differ from those used in selecting officers to police communities in more urban communities.

_____

_____

_____

_____

_____

Exercise 4. Recruiting Standards

Question: Should recruiting standards be modified in an attempt to attract more women, visible and cultural minorities, and members of the LGBT community to policing?

In 1997 the RCMP relaxed its fitness requirements in an attempt to allow more women to join. This was done in response to a review that indicated that a high percentage of female applicants were failing the Physical Abilities Requirement Evaluation (PARE), primarily due to a lack of upper-body strength. Up to 50 percent of the women who took the test during the review period failed, even after repeated attempts; 80 percent of the male applicants passed, most on the first attempt. At the time the decision was made, the Canadian Human Rights Commission was considering a complaint by a woman that the PARE test was discriminatory.

In 1998 the RCMP rewrote portions of its entrance exam in response to a concern that some Indigenous applicants and members of visible minorities scored lower than other potential recruits.

Consider the issues that have been raised by the actions of the RCMP and then answer the following questions:

1. Do you support or oppose the decision by the RCMP to modify the fitness rules for female applicants?

                    Support   Oppose
                       ☐   ☐

A. What are the primary reasons for your opinion?

_____

_____

_____

_____

_____

B. What assumptions about policing are reflected in your response?

_____

_____

_____

_____

_____

2. Do you support or oppose the decision by the RCMP to alter its entrance examination in response to lower scores by some groups of applicants?

Support   Oppose

☐   ☐

A. What are the primary reasons for your opinion?

_____

_____

_____

_____

_____

B. What assumptions about policing are reflected in your response?

_____

_____

_____

_____

_____

REFERENCES

Abernethy, T. 1995. Community Policing Review: Report. *Ottawa: Corporate Management, RCMP.*

Canadian Police College. 2017. Cyber Crime Investigator's Course (CCIC). *https://www.cpc-ccp.gc.ca/en/ccic*

Campbell, D.S. 1992. A Police Learning System for Ontario—Final Report and Recommendations. *Toronto: Ministry of the Solicitor General.*

Carter, D.L. 2000. "Human Resource Issues for Community Policing." *Ann Arbor: University of Michigan, Community Policing Center. (http://www.ssc.msu.edu*

Dean, G. 1995. "Police Reform: Rethinking Operational Policing." Journal of Criminal Justice *23(4): 337–47.*

Employment Equity Act. 2014. http://laws.justice.gc.ca/eng/acts/e-5.401

Eustace, C. 2007. "VPD: Virtual Police Department." *Vancouver Sun, 29 May.*

Fischer, R.J., K.M. Golden, and B.L. Heininger. 1985. "Issues in Higher Education for Law Enforcement Officers: An Illinois Study." Journal of Criminal Justice *13: 329–38.*

Goldsmith, A. 1990. "Taking Police Culture Seriously: Police Discretion and the Limits of the Law." Policing and Security *1(1): 91–114.*

Halifax Daily News. 1996. "Officers Also Want Return to 'More Traditional' Policing." *6 December, 4.*

Hay Group. 2007. A National Diagnostic on Human Resources in Policing, 2007. *Police Sector Council.*

Herbert, S. 1998. "Police Subculture Reconsidered." Criminology *36(2): 343–69.*

Jain, H.C. 1994. "An Assessment of the Strategies of Recruiting Visible-Minority Police Officers in Canada: 1985–1990." In Police Powers in Canada: The Evolution of Practice and Authority, *ed. R.C. MacLeod and D. Schneiderman. 138–64. Toronto: University of Toronto Press.*

Justice Institute of British Columbia. 2012. Police Academy Training Calendar 2012. *New Westminster.*

Lurigio, Arthur J., and Wesley G. Skogan. 1994. "Winning the Hearts and Minds of Police Officers: An Assessment of Staff Perceptions of Community Policing in Chicago" Crime and Delinquency *40(3): 315–330.*

Meese, E. 1993. "Community Policing and the Police Officer." Perspectives on Policing *15: 1–11.*

Mofina, R. 1996. "Force Fights Racism, Survey Reveals Problems." Calgary Herald. *27 September, A1.*

Montréal (City) v. Quebec (Commission des droits de la personne et des droits de la jeunesse), *2008 SCC 48.*

Morris, R. 2017. "Ontario Police College Basic Constable Training Program Student Demographics 1996–2016." Toronto: Policing Services Division, Ministry of Community Safety and Correctional Services, Ontario Police College.

Murphy, C., and C.T. Griffiths. 1994. "Community Based Policing—A Review of the Issues, Research, and Development of a Provincial Policy." Unpublished research report prepared for the Commission of Inquiry, Policing in British Columbia. Victoria: Ministry of Attorney General.

Palmiotto, M.J., M. Birzer, L. Unnithan, and N. Prabha. 2000. "Training in Community Policing: A Suggested Curriculum." Policing: An International Journal of Police Strategies and Management *1: 8–21.*

Police Sector Council. Policing Competency Framework. *http://www.policecouncil.ca*

RCMP. 2012a. "The Aboriginal Pre-Cadet Training Program." *http://www.rcmp-grc.gc.ca/recruiting-recrutement/aboriginal-autochtone/aboriginal-autochtone-cadet-eng.htm*

—. *2012b.* "RCMP-GRC Recruiting." *http://www.rcmp-grc.gc.ca/recruiting-recrutement/rec/requirements-exigences-eng.htm*

Skolnick, J. 1966. Justice without Trial: Law Enforcement in a Democratic Society. *New York: John Wiley and Sons.*

Statistics Canada. 2011. Police Resources in Canada, 2011. *Cat. no. 85-225-X. Ottawa.*

Statistics Canada. 2016. Police Resources in Canada, 2016. *Cat. No. 85-002-X. Ottawa: Minister Responsible for Statistics Canada.*

Swol, K. 1999. Police Personnel and Expenditures in Canada–1997 and 1998. *Ottawa: Canadian Centre for Justice Statistics.*

Taylor, K. 1999. Bringing into Focus—Policing in Halton Region: The Executive Summary. *Oakville: Halton Regional Police Service.*

Tomovich, V.A., and D.J. Loree. 1989. "In Search of New Directions: Policing in the Niagara Region." Canadian Police College Journal *13: 29–54.*

Toronto Police Service. 2011. More Minority Police. *(http://www.torontopolice.on.ca/modules.php?op=modload&name=News&file=article&sid=1219)I*

Restorative Justice within a Community Policing Framework

A component of restorative justice includes a healing process. Traditional healing practices in the Indigenous community attempt to restore peace and harmony in the community, the family, and the individual. The response to criminal behaviour occurs within a broader, holistic framework placing an emphasis on healing the victim, the offender, and, where required, the community.

Source: CP PHOTO/Winnipeg Free Press – Ken Gigliotti

Learning Objectives

After completing this chapter, you should be able to:

- Define restorative justice,
- Compare the principles of retributive justice and restorative justice,
- Compare the community decision-making models of circle sentencing, family group conferencing, and victim–offender mediation,
- Describe how victim–offender mediation works, including the four phases of mediation,
- Describe circle sentencing,
- Compare the adversarial criminal court process with the restorative justice process,
- Discuss the differences between criminal courts and community circles,
- Describe how family group conferencing works, and
- Describe how the Youth Criminal Justice Act includes principles of restorative justice.

INTRODUCTION

Our discussion of police strategies for responding to and preventing crime would not be complete without considering the emergence of **restorative justice**. Among the nations of the world, Canada has long assumed a lead role in the development and implementation of alternative justice policies and programs, including a number of innovative initiatives that place Canadian communities and jurisdictions at the forefront of the community and restorative justice movement. For example, the first modern-day victim–offender reconciliation project was established in Elmira, Ontario, in 1974, and since that time numerous jurisdictions worldwide have adopted and expanded on this practice. There are many victim–offender mediation programs operating across Canada, as well as nearly 300 in Germany and 130 in Finland. Canada has also contributed significantly to the development of restorative justice policy and practice for the United Nations.

More recently, Indigenous peoples and communities have served as the catalysts for the development of a wide range of innovative, community-based restorative justice practices. The Youth Criminal Justice Act also incorporates a number of the principles of restorative justice. Another factor that provides the impetus for the development of community-based restorative justice programs is the fiscal situation of governments. These programs hold the promise of addressing the needs of victims, communities, and offenders more effectively, and of doing so at less expense than the formal justice system (see Church Council on Justice and Corrections 1996; Galaway and Hudson 1996; Zehr 1995).

WHAT IS RESTORATIVE JUSTICE?

Restorative justice is an approach to problem-solving that involves the victim, the offender, their social networks, justice agencies, and the community. It rests on the fundamental principle that criminal behaviour injures not only victims but also communities and offenders, and that any efforts to address and resolve the problems created by the criminal behaviour should involve all of these parties. A widely used definition of restorative justice states: "Restorative justice is a process whereby parties with a stake in a specific offence collectively resolve how to deal with the aftermath of the offence and its implications for the future" (Marshall 1999, 5). The Canadian Resource Centre for Victims of Crime defines restorative justice as follows:

Restorative Justice (RJ) is not a program, but a way of looking at crime. It can be defined as a response to crime that focuses on restoring the losses suffered by victims, holding offenders accountable for the harm they have caused, and building peace within communities.

—Canadian Resource Centre for Victims of Crime (2011)

Principles and Objectives of Restorative Justice

Restorative justice is not a specific practice, but rather a set of principles that provides the basis for both a community and the justice system to respond to crime and social disorder. These general principles include:

- providing for the involvement of offenders, victims, their families, the community, and justice personnel;
- viewing crimes in a broad social context;
- a preventive and problem-solving orientation; and
- flexibility and adaptability (Marshall 1999, 5).

The primary objectives of restorative justice are:

- to address the needs of victims of crime;
- to prevent reoffending by reintegrating offenders into the community;

- to enable offenders to acknowledge and assume responsibility for their behaviour;
- to create a "community" of support and assistance for the victim and the offender and for the long-term interests of the community; and
- to provide an alternative to the adversarial system of justice (Marshall 1999, 6).

A key feature of restorative justice is that the response to criminal behaviour focuses on more than just the offender and the offence. There is also the involvement of crime victims and their families, the offender's family, community residents, and justice personnel, including police officers, both in the response to the behaviour and in the formulation of a sanction that will address the needs of all parties.

Retributive and Restorative Justice Compared

The concept of restorative justice is best illustrated by comparing it to the principles of **retributive justice**, on which our adversarial system of criminal justice is based. Several of these key differences are listed in Table 9.1.

THE DIMENSIONS OF RESTORATIVE JUSTICE

Among the more common restorative justice initiatives are victim–offender mediation, circle sentencing, community holistic healing programs, and **family group conferences**. There are critical differences among the various models of restorative and community justice, relating to their mandates and relationships to the formal adversarial system, the role of the crime victim and other co-participants, and the provisions and procedures for preparing for the event and for monitoring and enforcing the agreement (Van Ness and Strong 1997). The models also differ in terms of their objectives, the degree to which the model requires that the justice system share power with community residents, and the extent to which the model empowers the community and addresses the specific incident and behaviour in question. In addition, some restorative justice programs provide for police participation; others do not.

Victim–Offender Mediation

Victim–offender mediation programs (VOMPs)—also often referred to as victim–offender reconciliation programs, or VORPs—have been operating in Canada since the early 1970s and are widely used across the country. VOM takes a restorative approach by giving both the victim and the offender the opportunity to express their feelings and concerns. With the assistance of a mediator, who is a neutral third party, the offender and the victim resolve the conflict and the consequences caused by the offence, and ultimately learn to understand each other.

There are generally four phases of mediation: (1) intake of the case from a referral source; (2) preparation for the mediation, which involves the mediator meeting separately with the victim and the offender; (3) the mediation session; and (4) post-session activities, including ensuring the fulfillment of any agreement reached during the mediation session.

In recent years, VOM has been used in cases involving crimes of violence and in situations where the offender is incarcerated in a correctional facility. A recent analysis of VOM found that both victims and offenders reported greater satisfaction with restorative justice principles than with traditional non-restorative approaches (Latimer, Dowden, and Muise 2001).

Circle Sentencing: A Partnership between the Community and the Criminal Justice System

Circle sentencing originally developed in several Yukon communities as a collaborative initiative between community residents and territorial justice personnel—primarily RCMP officers and judges from the Territorial Court of Yukon (Stuart 1996).

In **circle sentencing**, all of the participants, including the judge, defence lawyer, prosecutor, police officer, victim and his or her family, offender and his or her family, and community

Table 9.1 Principles of Retributive Justice and Restorative Justice

Retributive Justice	Restorative Justice
Crime violates the state and its laws.	Crime violates people and relationships.
Justice focuses on establishing guilt ...	Justice aims to identify needs and obligations ...
... so that doses of pain can be meted out.	... so that things can be made right.
Justice is sought through conflict between adversaries ...	Justice encourages dialogue and mutual agreement ...
... in which the offender is pitted against the state rules and intentions outweigh outcomes, and ...	... gives victims and offenders central roles, and ...
... one side wins and the other loses.	... the outcome is judged by the extent to which responsibilities are assumed, needs are met, and healing (of individuals and relationships) is encouraged.

Source: From *Changing Lenses: A new focus for crime and justice* by Howard Zehr. Copyright © 1995, 2005 by Herald Press, Harrisonburg, VA 22802. Used by permission.

residents, sit facing one another in a circle. Discussions are designed to reach a consensus about the best way to dispose of the case, taking into account the need to protect the community as well as the rehabilitation and punishment of the offender. There are a number of important stages in the circle sentencing process, each critical to its overall success. An actual case that was handled in a sentencing circle is included as a case study at the end of this chapter.

Circle sentencing is premised on traditional Indigenous healing practices and has multiple objectives, including addressing the needs of communities and the families of victims and offenders through a process of reconciliation, restitution, and reparation. A fundamental principle is that the sentence is less important than the process used to select it.

There are a number of important stages in the circle sentencing process, each of which is critical to its overall success. It is generally only available to those offenders who plead guilty. The process is community-specific, meaning that it may (and should) vary between communities, and it relies heavily on community volunteers for its success (Stuart 1996). Offenders whose cases are heard in a sentencing circle may still be sent for a period of incarceration; however, many other sanctions are available, including banishment (generally to a wilderness location), house arrest, and community service.

Table 9.2 compares formal, adversarial criminal courts with the community-based, restorative approach. As you can see, there are some very significant differences between the two.

Circle Sentencing versus Adversarial Justice

There are some very significant differences between circle sentencing and the formal, adversarial system of criminal justice. These differences are outlined in Table 9.3.

Table 9.2 Formal Criminal Court Context and the Restorative Justice Process

	Court	Restorative Justice
People	Experts, non-residents	Local people
Process	Adversarial (state versus offender)	Consensus (community versus problem)
Issues	Laws broken	Relationship broken
Focus	Guilt	Identification of needs of the victim, offender, and community, and solution to the problem
Tools	Punishment and control	Healing and support
Procedure	Fixed rules	Flexible

Source: From GRIFFITHS. *Canadian Criminal Justice: A Primer*, 3E. © 2007 Nelson Education Ltd. Reproduced by permission. www.cengage.com/permissions

Table 9.3 Differences between Criminal Courts and Community Circles

Criminal Courts	Community Circles
The conflict is the crime	Crime is a small part of a larger conflict
The sentence resolves the conflict	The sentence is a small part of the solution
Focus on past conduct	Focus on present and future conduct
Take a narrow view of behaviour	Take a larger, holistic view
Avoid concern with social conflict	Focus on social conflict
Result (the sentence) is most important	Result is least important—the process is most important, as the process shapes the relationship among all parties

Source: Used with permission of Judge Stuart.

The Potential of Circle Sentencing

Circle sentencing is an example of how the principles of restorative justice can be applied within a holistic framework in which justice system personnel share power and authority with community residents. In contrast to the adversarial approach to justice, circle sentencing:

- reacquaints individuals, families, and communities with problem-solving skills;
- rebuilds relationships within communities;
- promotes awareness of and respect for the values and the lives of others;
- addresses the needs and interests of all parties, including the victim;
- focuses on causes, not just symptoms, of problems;
- recognizes existing healing resources and creates new ones;
- coordinates the use of local and government resources; and
- generates preventive measures (Hatch-Cunningham and Griffiths 1997, 240).

The majority of offenders whose cases have been heard by sentencing circles have been adults; however, more and more young offenders' cases are being handled by way of the legislated provisions contained in the Youth Criminal Justice Act. Circle sentencing has spawned a number of variations, including community sentence advisory committees, sentencing panels, and community mediation panels. Preliminary analysis suggests that this technique may be very effective in reducing or eliminating criminal and disruptive behaviour, particularly on the part of offenders who have lengthy records in the formal criminal justice system.

Judge Barry Stuart (1996) of the Territorial Court of Yukon, a pioneer in the development of circle sentencing, cautions that this approach is not appropriate for all offenders or crimes; the success of the circles depends on the cooperation of community residents and justice professionals, and it is imperative that the needs, rights, and interests of crime victims and offenders be protected. These concerns are particularly important in considering restorative justice initiatives for young offenders, who, due to their age and status in communities, often have many vulnerabilities.

Circle sentencing is a superb example of how the principles of restorative justice can be applied within a framework in which justice system personnel share power and authority with community residents. For police officers, it provides two important opportunities: (1) to participate in a community-based approach to addressing crime and disorder, and (2) to shift from a reactive mode to a coactive, problem-solving one. The principles and processes of circle sentencing complement those of community policing.

Although circle sentencing originated in the North, its principles and processes can be adapted to larger communities. In Yukon, both Indigenous and non-Indigenous residents have participated in circles, as victims and offenders, and in community support roles. Furthermore, as a point of interest, with the assistance of justice and community representatives from Yukon, a circle sentencing program has been successfully established in Minneapolis, Minnesota.

Family Group Conferencing

Family group conferencing (FGC) originated in New Zealand, was "exported" to Australia, and is now appearing in discussions of restorative justice in several Canadian jurisdictions. In 1989, Australia's Children, Young Persons, and Their Families Act identified the youth's family and extended family as key participants in addressing the problems of young people in conflict. The forum for discussing the issues surrounding the youth and his or her behaviour is the FGC, which incorporates the traditional restorative approach of the indigenous Maori people. Through the above-noted legislation, the FGC is now used as the basis of the entire youth justice system.

In Edmonton, a **community conferencing** program has been established to divert young offenders away from the justice system into a forum where they can be held accountable and where the victims of the offence can express their feelings and participate in the decision-making process. Personnel trained in mediation and communication techniques operate the program in conjunction with a community-based diversion program. The program is based on a partnership between the police service and a number of community agencies, including the Legal Aid Youth Office, the John Howard Society, the Victim Offender Mediation Society, and the Native Youth Justice Committee.

This program illustrates the potential for police involvement in restorative justice initiatives in urban and suburban areas, and is an excellent example of the types of police–community partnerships possible within an overall framework of community policing (Griffiths, Whitelaw, and Parent 1999). An actual case heard in a community conference is presented as a case study at the end of this chapter.

RESTORATIVE JUSTICE INITIATIVES IN INDIGENOUS COMMUNITIES

In recent years, Indigenous communities have become increasingly involved in developing community-based justice services and programs designed to address the specific needs of community residents, victims, and offenders. These initiatives have often been developed as part of a process of cultural and community revitalization and are part of the increasing efforts by Indigenous peoples and communities to reassert their authority over all facets of community life (Griffiths and Hamilton 1996). There has also been an attempt to explore alternatives to confinement in order to decrease the overrepresentation of Indigenous persons incarcerated in provincial and territorial correctional institutions. Indigenous people currently comprise roughly 4 percent of the Canadian population but make up 25 percent of the federal prison population; this emphasizes the need for innovation and reform. The Office of the Correctional Investigator noted that in the year 2016, there were approximately 3,500 Indigenous people in federal penitentiaries. In the Prairie provinces, 48 percent of federal inmates are Indigenous people; also, over 36 percent of women in Canadian prisons are of Indigenous descent (Correctional Investigator Canada 2016). A Closer Look 9.1 outlines Canada's Indigenous Justice Program (IJP).

The Supreme Court of Canada recognized the importance of restorative justice approaches in its landmark decisions *R. v. Gladue* (1999) and *R. v. Proulx* (2000). In *Gladue*, the Supreme Court supported restorative approaches found in the sentencing principles of Section 718.2 (e) of the Criminal Code, which states:

718.2 A court that imposes a sentence shall also take into consideration the following principles: … (e) all available sanctions other than imprisonment that are reasonable in the circumstances should be considered for all offenders, with particular attention to the circumstances of aboriginal offenders.

The *Gladue* decision directed the court system to take meaningful steps to counter the increasing reliance on incarceration in the sentencing of Indigenous offenders. Sentencing judges must consider the assessment of the Indigenous offender and all non-jail options

A CLOSER LOOK 9.1

THE INDIGENOUS JUSTICE PROGRAM

The Indigenous Justice Program (IJP) supports Indigenous community-based justice programs that offer alternatives to mainstream justice processes in appropriate circumstances. The objectives of the Indigenous Justice Program are:

- to assist Indigenous people in assuming greater responsibility for the administration of justice in their communities;

- to reflect and include Indigenous values within the justice system; and

- to contribute to a decrease in the rate of victimization, crime, and incarceration among Indigenous people in communities with community-based justice programs funded by the IJP.

    The Indigenous Justice Program consists of two funding components: the Community-Based Justice Fund and the Capacity-Building Fund.

Community-Based Justice Fund

The Community-Based Justice Fund supports community-based justice programs in partnership with Indigenous communities. Programs are cost-shared with provincial and territorial governments and designed to reflect the culture and values of the communities in which they are situated. The IJP currently funds 197 community-based programs that serve over 750 communities. The objectives of the Community-Based Justice Fund component are:

- to allow Indigenous people the opportunity to assume greater responsibility for the administration of justice in their communities;
- to help reduce the rates of crime and incarceration among Indigenous people in communities with cost-shared programs; and,
- to foster improved responsiveness, fairness, inclusiveness, and effectiveness of the justice system with respect to justice and its administration so as to meet the needs and aspirations of Indigenous people in the areas of appropriate models for:

  - diversion;
  - development of pre-sentencing options;
  - sentencing alternatives (circles);
  - use of Justices of the Peace;
  - family and civil mediation; and
  - additional community justice services such as victim support and offender reintegration services that support the overall goals of the IJP or, where affiliated with a successful program under any of the above.

Capacity Building Fund

The Capacity-Building Fund is designed to support capacity-building efforts in Indigenous communities. With a focus on building increased knowledge and skills for the establishment and management of community-based justice programs, the objectives of the Capacity-Building Fund are:

- to support the training and/or developmental needs of Indigenous communities that currently do not have community-based justice programs;
- to supplement the ongoing training needs of current community-based justice programs where the cost-shared budget does not adequately meet these needs, including supporting evaluation activities, data collection, and sharing of best practices and useful models;
- to support activities targeted at improved community reporting in IJP communities and the development of data management systems;
- to support the development of new justice programs, paying particular attention to:

  - the current geographic/regional imbalance in programming;
  - the commitment to develop new programs in the underrepresented program models, such as dispute resolution for civil and family/child welfare; and

- to support one-time or annual events and initiatives (as opposed to ongoing projects and programs) that build bridges, trust and partnerships between the mainstream justice system and Indigenous communities.

Sources: Department of Justice, Indigenous Justice Program, http://www.justice.gc.ca/eng/fund-fina/acf-fca/ajs-sja/index.html. Department of Justice Canada, 2017. Reproduced with the permission of the Department of Justice Canada, 2017.

that are appropriate and available in the local community. In *R. v. Ipeelee* (2012 S.C.C. 13), Justice LeBel, writing for the majority of the court, stated:

To be clear, courts must take judicial notice of such matters as the history of colonialism, displacement and residential schools and how that history continues to translate into lower educational attainment, lower incomes, higher unemployment, higher rates of substance abuse and suicide and, of course, higher levels of incarceration for Aboriginal Peoples[.]

Failing to take these circumstances into account would violate the fundamental principle of sentencing.

Restorative or community justice initiatives in Indigenous communities are often premised on customary law and traditional practices and may contain aspects of spirituality. Many involve elders and place a strong emphasis on healing the victim, the offender, and, where required, the community. Rather than focusing only on the offender and the offence, the response to criminal behaviour occurs within a broader, holistic framework. This facilitates the inclusion of crime victims and their families, the offender's family, and community residents in the response and also in the formulation of a sanction that accommodates the needs of all parties (Green 1997; 1998).

Another attribute of these initiatives is that the Indigenous band or community maintains a high degree of control over the disposition and sanctioning process, or these are shared, on a partnership basis, with justice system personnel. This is a significant departure from the manner in which justice services are typically provided by the criminal justice system.

CRITICAL PERSPECTIVES 9.1

INDIAN RESIDENTIAL SCHOOLS: A NATIONAL DISGRACE

Library and Archives Canada a123707

As part of the Government of Canada's policy of "aggressive assimilation," Indigenous children were forced to leave their homes on Indian reservations and forced to attend Indian residential schools. This policy existed from the late nineteenth century until 1996.

In the nineteenth century, the Canadian government believed it was responsible for educating and caring for the country's Indigenous people. The government of the day believed that an English education and the adoption of Christianity and European customs would result in the transmission of new customs, serving to diminish and eventually eliminate native culture. This belief was premised on the underlying assumption that Indigenous culture could not adapt to a rapidly modernizing Canadian society.

Relying on a policy called "aggressive assimilation," Indigenous children were bussed to church-run, government-funded industrial boarding schools, later called "residential schools," operated under the federal Department of Indian Affairs. They stayed there for 10 months of the year, and when they returned home to their reserves they had difficulty assimilating. In 1931, there were approximately 130 residential schools in Canada. The last residential school closed in 1996. In all, about 150,000 Indigenous, Inuit, and Métis children were removed from their communities and forced to attend the schools.

Following the Royal Commission on Aboriginal Peoples initiated in 1991, Canadian churches apologized to Indigenous people. Archbishop Michael Peers offered an apology on behalf of the Anglican Church of Canada in 1993, stating "I am sorry, more than I can say, that we were part of a system which took you and your children from home and family."

In 2007, two years after it was first announced, the federal government formalized a $1.9 billion compensation package for those who were forced to attend residential schools. Following the establishment of a Truth and Reconciliation Commission in 2008, Prime Minster Stephen Harper apologized to residential school students in Parliament on June 11, 2008.

Source: *CBC News, A history of residential schools in Canada (May 16, 2008) © CBC News. Found at http://www.cbc.ca/news/canada/story/2008/05/16/f-faqs-residential-schools.html*

Hollow Water's Community Holistic Circle Healing

Community Holistic Circle Healing was initiated in 1986 by the Hollow Water First Nation in Manitoba. It was designed as a community-based response to the high rates of sexual and family abuse in the community. It consists of a 13-phase process, depicted in Figure 9.1.

One of the phases of **community holistic healing** is the special gathering, which is a public event quite similar to the traditional justice case described in detail below. Traditional healing practices attempt to restore peace and harmony in the community, the family, and the individual. A healing contract is signed, and offenders apologize publicly to the victims and to the community for the harm done. The circle healing process is designed to consider the needs of all of the parties to the abuse—the victim, the offender, and the community—and is directed beyond merely punishing the offender for a specific behaviour. The notion of forgiveness may also be part of the healing process, allowing all of the involved individuals to come to terms with the offence that has occurred.

Figure 9.1 The Thirteen Phases of the Hollow Water
Community Holistic Circle Healing Process

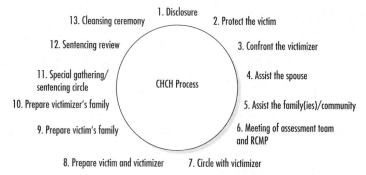

Source: Public Safety Canada, The Thirteen Phases of the Hollow Water Community Holistic Circle Healing Process. From Lajeunesse, T., and Associates Ltd., 1996. *Evaluation of Community Holistic Circle Healing: Hollow Water First Nation. Volume 1. Final Report.* Winnipeg: Manitoba Department of Justice., p. 33. http://www.publicsafety.gc.ca/res/cor/apc/apc-15-eng.aspx#holistic

Research findings suggest that the program may have a positive impact on offenders, victims, their respective families, and the community (Lajeunesse and Associates Ltd. 1996; Latimer et al. 2001).

Traditional Indigenous Justice

While many restorative justice initiatives such as circle sentencing involve partnerships between criminal justice system personnel and communities, sometimes communities themselves assume total control and take responsibility for the resolution of conflicts. These events are often not publicized, nor do they receive outside attention. And although local justice system personnel, such as the police, may be aware of the case and of the activities of the community in resolving it, there is little or no official intervention. One such case is presented as a case study at the end of this chapter.

RESTORATIVE JUSTICE PRINCIPLES IN THE YOUTH CRIMINAL JUSTICE ACT

On April 1, 2003, Canada's **Youth Criminal Justice Act** (YCJA) became law. It requires the criminal justice system to distinguish between violent and nonviolent offenders, with a focus on prevention and meaningful consequences for youth. One important aspect of this legislation is the provision of **extrajudicial measures** for dealing with young people who have committed offences, rather than court proceedings.

Before using the formal youth justice court system, police in Canada are now directed to consider whether one of the following options would be sufficient:

- to take no further action;
- to warn the young person;
- to administer a caution;
- to refer the young person to a program such as a community accountability program, a police-based diversion program, or an agency in the community that may help the young person avoid committing offences; or
- to refer the young person to an extrajudicial sanctions program due to the seriousness of the offence and the nature and number of previous offences committed, or other aggravating circumstances.

In keeping with the principles and objectives of restorative justice, the extrajudicial measures contained within the YCJA are designed to provide an effective and timely response to offending behaviour and to encourage young offenders to acknowledge and repair the harm caused to the victim and the community. Extrajudicial measures also encourage the involvement of families and members of the community in designing and implementing measures directed at the offending young person. Victims can also participate in these decisions and receive reparation.

CRITICAL ISSUES IN RESTORATIVE/COMMUNITY JUSTICE

Despite the success of many initiatives in restorative and community justice, both within a collaborative framework involving justice system personnel and community residents, such as circle sentencing, and within Indigenous communities on their own, there are a number of critical issues that must be addressed. Some of these are described below.

Restorative Justice in Urban Centres

In discussions about the potential for developing restorative justice initiatives, it is often argued that programs such as circle sentencing, which involve substantive community participation in a holistic framework, are suited only to rural and remote communities with a strong cultural identity and foundation. This assertion is often used to deflect suggestions that justice personnel in suburban and urban areas should explore the development of system–community partnerships for addressing the needs of offenders, their victims, and the community.

However, as was mentioned earlier, there is a community conferencing program in Edmonton, operated by not-for-profit community organizations and staffed by volunteers trained in mediation and communication skills and techniques. There are also a number of successful restorative justice initiatives currently operating in urban and suburban areas of Canada that, with additional funding, could be easily adapted to accommodate offenders (see Roberts and LaPrairie 1996 and http://www.publicsafety.gc.ca [search "restorative justice"]).

Crime Victims and Restorative Justice

Although crime victims are often excluded from the formal adversarial system of criminal justice, concerns have been expressed that restorative and community justice initiatives may not give adequate attention to the rights and needs of vulnerable groups, specifically women and female adolescents. As a consequence, crime victims may be "revictimized" by the process of restorative and community justice. Indigenous women, for example, have voiced concerns about the high rates of sexual and physical abuse in communities and have questioned whether restorative and community justice initiatives provide adequate protection for the victims of violence and abuse and also whether the sanctions imposed are appropriate.

Assessing the Effectiveness of Restorative Justice

There have been few evaluations of whether restorative justice strategies have achieved their stated objectives. Despite receiving widespread publicity at the national and international levels, for example, there have been no controlled evaluations of circle sentencing. Concluding a critique of circle sentencing, Roberts and LaPrairie (1996, 82–83) stated: "It has been claimed that sentencing circles have the following benefits: (a) they reduce recidivism; (b) prevent crime; (c) reduce costs; (d) advance the interests of victims; and (e) promote solidarity among community members. These are all measurable objectives and they should be put to empirical test."

Canadian research suggests that restorative justice approaches have been more successful than traditional, non-restorative approaches in the following areas:

- they are a more effective method of improving victim/offender satisfaction;
- they increase offender compliance with restitution; and
- they decrease the recidivism of offenders when compared to the more traditional criminal justice responses of incarceration, probation, and court-ordered restitution. (Latimer, Dowden, and Muise 2001)

In one Canadian study examining whether restorative justice approaches could be suitable in addressing serious crimes found that it could successfully be applied in the *pre-sentence stage* in serious crimes. Participants reported higher levels of satisfaction with the restorative approach, especially when compared to participants who had experienced only the traditional criminal justice system. Victims and offenders were offered the opportunity to participate in the decision-making process, in developing a reparation plan, and, in some cases, providing a sentencing recommendation. Overall, individuals affected by serious crime were empowered to achieve satisfying justice through a restorative approach (Rugge, Bonta, and Wallace-Capretta 2005). Another study examining recidivism rates and restorative justice found that restorative justice programs can have a small but positive impact on rates of recidivism: anywhere from 2 to 8 percent reductions in recidivism. More research is required to validate these findings.

The Restorative Action Program (RAP) is a community-driven initiative that helps youth develop and practise conflict management, relationship management, and leadership skills using an approach that focuses on prevention, intervention, and reconnection, with a goal of empowering youth and enabling them to be actively engaged in creating safe, respectful and caring communities. See http://www.rapsaskatoon.org.

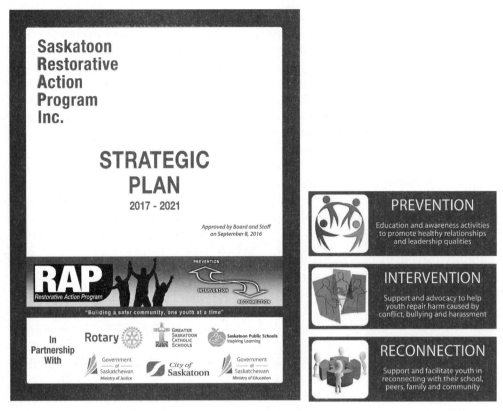

Source: Courtesy of Restorative Action Program (RAP).

Attempts to assess the effectiveness of restorative and community justice programs face a number of problems. One such problem is that the holistic approach and multifaceted objectives of many restorative justice programs require a broader evaluative framework than is used for traditional crime-control initiatives. Program objectives may encompass macro-level dimensions such as cultural and community revitalization and empowerment, as well as community, family, and individual healing.

The Dynamics of Community Justice

The significant role assumed by communities in restorative justice initiatives requires a close consideration of both the strengths and the potential pitfalls of community justice. Canadian observers have identified several critical issues that, if unaddressed, may undermine the efficacy of restorative justice initiatives. These issues include the general "health" of the community, including community leaders and those who would assume key roles in any restorative justice initiatives; the circumstance that within all communities there are power and status hierarchies that may threaten consensus-building and place certain residents, be they victims or offenders, in positions of vulnerability; and the need to protect the legal rights of offenders (Griffiths and Hamilton 1996).

There are often competing and conflicting goals in community justice, and even in relatively small communities it may be difficult to establish and maintain a consensus about how to respond to an offender.

THE ROLE OF THE POLICE IN RESTORATIVE JUSTICE

With the advent of community policing, the opportunities for patrol officers to become involved in restorative and community justice programs has increased. In fact, officers may assume a primary role in organizing and facilitating community conferences. This role can be described as coactive, because of the relationship it establishes between the police and the community. Patrol officers not only need to understand the principles of restorative and community justice, but also must develop the skills to bring together the various stakeholder groups, including the offender and the victim, their respective support groups, and other parties. We provide a case illustration of how to facilitate a community conference in one of the case studies at the end of this chapter.

Chapter Summary

In this chapter, we have examined restorative justice and considered its role within the framework of community policing. Restorative justice is based on the fundamental principle that in order to be effective, efforts to address and resolve the problems created by criminal behaviour must consider the victim, the offender, and the community. There are significant differences between restorative justice and the adversarial approach to responding to crime and offenders. Among the restorative justice initiatives developed over the past several decades are victim–offender mediation, circle sentencing, and family group conferencing. Canada's recent Youth Criminal Justice Act has embraced many of the principles and concepts found within restorative justice. The high rates of incarcerated Indigenous people in Canada emphasize the need for a new approach to traditional justice models. Many First Nations communities have developed programs premised on the principles of restorative justice in order to meet this need. The philosophy and practices of restorative justice complement community policing and provide patrol officers with an opportunity to participate in alternative forums for addressing crime. Restorative justice interventions also provide officers with the opportunity to engage in problem solving and to partner with communities to address issues of crime and social disorder.

Chapter Review

Key Terms

- circle sentencing, p. 289
- community conferencing, p. 292
- community holistic healing, p. 295
- extrajudicial measures, p. 296
- family group conferencing, p. 289
- restorative justice, p. 288
- retributive justice, p. 289
- victim–offender mediation programs, p. 289
- Youth Criminal Justice Act, p. 296

Key Points

- Canada has long assumed a lead role in the development of restorative justice programs.
- Restorative justice is based on the principle that criminal behaviour injures victims, offenders, and communities and that all three parties must be involved in resolving problems created by criminal behaviour.
- There are a wide variety of restorative justice programs across the country and within the legislated provisions of the Youth Criminal Justice Act.
- There are significant differences between retributive and restorative justice.
- Victim–offender mediation, circle sentencing, and family group conferencing are three common restorative justice initiatives.
- There are significant differences between the formal, adversarial process in the criminal courts and the community-based, restorative approach of circle sentencing.

- Many First Nations communities have developed community-based alternatives to the justice system based on the principles of restorative justice.
- There are a number of critical issues related to restorative justice that must be addressed in order to enhance its effectiveness as a response to crime and social disorder in communities.

Self-Evaluation

QUESTIONS

1. Define **restorative justice**.
2. Compare **retributive justice** and restorative justice.
3. Describe how **victim–offender mediation** programs operate.
4. Describe **circle sentencing** and then compare it to the adversarial court process.
5. What is **community holistic healing** and how does this program reflect the principles of restorative justice?
6. Describe the key features of **family group conferencing**.
7. What is **community conferencing**?
8. Discuss the use of **extrajudicial measures** within the **Youth Criminal Justice Act**.
9. Canadian research suggests that restorative justice approaches have been more successful than traditional, nonrestorative approaches in which areas?
10. Discuss the critical issues that exist within the current framework of restorative and community justice.

KEY IDEAS

1. Which statement best describes restorative justice programs in Canada?
   a. They generally exclude the police.
   b. They have only been developed in the past five years.
   c. They vary widely in the types of offences and offenders processed.
   d. They operate primarily as diversion programs.

2. One approach to justice views crime as a violation of the state. Laws focus on establishing guilt and result in one side winning and the other losing. What is the term for this approach?
   a. retributive justice
   b. winner-take-all justice
   c. restorative justice
   d. community justice

3. One approach to restorative justice provides an opportunity for the key individuals in this process to express their feelings and concerns with the assistance of a mediator. What is the term for this approach?
   a. circle sentencing
   b. family group conferencing
   c. crisis counselling
   d. victim–offender mediation

4. Where did circle sentencing originate?
   a. Yukon
   b. Minnesota
   c. Ontario
   d. Newfoundland

5. One restorative approach views crime as part of a larger conflict and the sentence as a small part of the solution. What is the term for this approach?
   a. victim–offender mediation
   b. retributive justice
   c. community circle sentencing
   d. distributive justice

6. Which statement describes the experience of restorative justice programs in Canada?
   a. They are generally unsuccessful in dealing with serious offences.
   b. They work best in rural and remote communities.
   c. Their participants have been generally limited to the residents of First Nations.
   d. They can work in both rural and urban areas.

7. Which of the following has been found by research studies on restorative justice initiatives?
   a. Restorative justice programs are highly successful with young offenders, but less successful with adult offenders.
   b. Restorative justice programs are most successful when the police are not involved.
   c. Due to a lack of research it is difficult to determine the extent to which restorative justice programs have achieved their objectives.
   d. Circle sentencing is not effective with serious offenders.

8. Which of the following factors can undermine the effectiveness of restorative justice initiatives?
   a. Power and status hierarchies within the community.
   b. Lack of private funding and support.
   c. Lack of focus and direction.
   d. The multicultural and diverse make-up of the community.

9. In keeping with the principles and objectives of restorative justice, the extrajudicial measures contained within the YCJA are designed to _____
   a. ensure that youth are aware of their responsibilities.
   b. provide an effective and timely response to offending behaviour.
   c. ensure that young offenders are not publicly identified.
   d. provide a process that incorporates options and choice for youth.

10. Which of the following things did the *Gladue* decision direct the Canadian court system to do?
    a. Provide separate holding cells for individuals arrested by the police that fall within the jurisdiction of the Youth Criminal Justice Act.
    b. Utilize community conferencing principles when dealing with young persons.
    c. Take meaningful steps to counter the increasing reliance on incarceration in the sentencing of Indigenous offenders.
    d. Utilize victim–offender mediation programs (VOMP) in cases involving domestic violence.

Restorative Justice: Situations and Strategies

Case Studies

Case Study 1. Community Conferencing in an Urban Centre

The following is the report of a community conference facilitated by a police officer in a Canadian urban centre.

The Case

The case involved a 14-year-old boy who sprayed pepper spray in the hallway of his school. At the time, there were approximately 50 students and 10 staff members in the school, most of whom were affected by the spray. After discharging the substance, the boy gave the pepper spray container to another student, who was unaware of the incident. This student subsequently led police to the boy, who admitted spraying the pepper spray. A police constable discussed the option of community conferencing with the principal, who was interested in the idea. The offender agreed to participate and gave the officer the names of several people he wanted to attend.

The Offences

Sec. 90, Canadian Criminal Code—Possession of a Prohibited Weapon
Sec. 430 (1)(a), Canadian Criminal Code—Mischief

The Offender

The Indigenous youth came from a broken home and had had three different stepfathers and two different stepmothers. He had 12 siblings and, at the time of the offence, was living with his 23-year-old sister, who was providing him with a stable home. The constable's impression of the youth was that he was a good boy who had very difficult issues to deal with, including the substance abuse by his parents. In his case study report, the constable wrote: "He is struggling to do the right thing most of the time, and I believe he needs people in his life to support him. He has no criminal record."

The Process

On the date of the offence, the constable met with all the staff at the school and explained the concept of community conferencing. He gathered the names of six staff members who had been affected by the incident and were willing to participate in a conference. The names of six mature and responsible students who were affected by the incident were also obtained. The following morning, the constable met with the students and explained the concept of community conferencing. The students were all interested and willing to be involved.

The offender had informed the constable that he wanted his birth father, his sister, and a good friend of the family to be at the conference. The constable met with these three individuals, described the incident, and prepared them for the conference. The conference was scheduled to be held approximately 48 hours after the offence had occurred.

The Conference

The conference lasted 1.5 hours. Almost all of the participants were Indigenous and were aware of traditional Indigenous ways. Two Indigenous elders (wife and husband) attended the conference and provided invaluable input. One conducted a sweet grass ceremony to begin the conference. This ceremony was significant because it gave the process a sense of legitimacy and respect.

The offender was the first to speak and said he had found a canister of pepper spray earlier that day. He openly admitted that he brought the spray to school and sprayed it, in a hallway near some exit doors, in front of two unidentified students. He then ran upstairs and gave the spray to an acquaintance and told him to hold on to it until the end of the day. When the constable questioned him about whom he thought was affected, he indicated he did not know.

After the offender had spoken, the constable asked each of the victims (staff and students) to describe how they were affected by the incident and how they felt at the time. Some people were very expressive and eloquent in their description of their experience with the pepper spray. One teacher, who had asthma, disclosed how she urinated during severe coughing. Another teacher described how her special needs students were extremely traumatized by the disruption in their normally routine day. The students described how the spray made them feel physically and also described the initial anxiety they felt as a result of not knowing what was happening.

The offender's father spoke after the victims. He described the fear and anxiety he felt when the constable had first contacted him to tell him about the incident. He also became emotional when he talked about how, in some way, he was responsible for his son's actions. The participants were all moved by what the father had to say. The offender's sister then spoke and described her reaction to finding out about the incident. She was also very supportive of the offender and spoke about how responsible he usually was.

After all the participants had the opportunity to speak, it was time for the group to decide on an appropriate outcome. An agreement had to be reached regarding how the offender would be responsible for "making things better." After discussions, the following agreement was arrived at:

1. The offender would make a public apology to the student body and staff at an assembly to be held in the school's library.

2. He would meet with the principal every morning 45 minutes before class for counselling and work projects.

3. He would meet with the arts and crafts teacher one day per week for one-on-one counselling.

4. He would assist the janitor in his duties for one week.

The offender agreed to the noted sanctions, which resulted from group consultation and consensus. No time limit was specified for the second and third items because the group wanted the offender to prove himself. The time limit would be set by the offender's behaviour and progress.

When the formal part of the conference was completed, there was a symbolic "breaking of bread." This part of the process was very meaningful because it provided the opportunity for the participants to talk informally. The principal had prepared some bannock (traditional Indigenous bread). This event allowed the individuals involved to move on from the incident and look towards a more positive future. It also provided the constable with time to prepare the written agreement with the four sanctions, which all participants subsequently signed. Copies of the agreement were given to the offender, his father, and the principal.

Summary of the Conference (the Constable's Observations)

I believe this community conference was a success. Time will tell, however, if the four outcomes will be completed by the offender. A positive outcome of this process is the many people who have agreed to monitor the offender's progress and, as a result of this, the offender has a newfound community within the school. Prior to the incident he had only attended this school for a couple of months and had not established much of a support network. In fact, this offender has now established a new peer group made up of some of the more responsible students in the school. This is a peer group that, under normal circumstances, this offender would not have associated with. During the informal snack time after the conference, it was clear that he had made some new friends, both among his peers and the staff. It was also interesting to note that the offender's father connected with one of the teachers. This teacher will attempt to provide some counselling for him and his son in the future.

General feedback from the participants was very positive. The sense that the victims of this incident could actually have a say in the justice process proved to be very satisfying for them. They believed they were ensuring that the offender took responsibility for his actions and that he was correcting the wrong. Victim satisfaction was very real and tangible. I sensed that the offender believed he had his work cut out for him; however, it was not so much a punishment he felt but accountability to his community. That community I speak of is the community within his school and those who care for him.

On a personal note, I was surprised by my own reaction as I heard the many different ways that people had been affected by this incident. I had no idea that they had suffered in the ways that they described during the conference. In conclusion, compared to the mainstream justice system where this youth would most likely have received a sentence of 20 to 30 hours of community service, I believe this approach is much more meaningful to the offender, the victims, and the supporters of the victims and offender. Community conferencing made a positive difference in the participants' lives. This approach will not be appropriate in all cases; however, I feel we can divert many youths to this model and thereby create a system of responding to youth crime that is meaningful and will hopefully prevent future criminal behaviour.

Source: *International Review of Victimology*, September 1999, Vol 6, No 4, 279–294. copyright © 1999 by International Review of Victimology. Reprinted by Permission of SAGE.

Case Study 2. Family Group Conferencing in an Indigenous Community

The following describes a successful family group conference that was held in Lennox Island Reserve after the theft of candy vending machines from the reserve's main building.

Since one of the two offenders connected to the incident was on probation, the constable convinced community members to attempt to resolve the issue through restorative justice. After hearing how paying restitution would financially affect the offenders' families and the band, the vending machine company representative dropped the price of machine repairs by $200. "The session was very emotional and the offenders heard the disappointment, embarrassment, and lack of trust they had caused," stated the constable. "At the end of the session, the whole mood of the group was relief. There was no pent-up anger or unresolved feelings." The penalty determined by the community was 10 hours of community service and repayment of repair costs.

Source: Ramsey, K., 1997. "A Return to Wisdom: Restorative Justice Revisited." Pony Express, the RCMP's National News Magazine (April): 16–19.

Case Study 3. Circle Sentencing: A Case Study

The following is an actual case that was resolved through the use of circle sentencing.

The victim—the wife of the offender, who admitted to abusing her physically during two recent drunken episodes—spoke about the pain and embarrassment her husband had caused her and her family. After she had finished, the ceremonial feather (used to signify who would be allowed to speak next) was passed to the next person in the circle, a young man who spoke about the contributions the offender had made to the community, the kindness he had shown towards the elders by sharing fish and game with them, and the offender's willingness to help others with home repairs. An elder then took the feather and spoke about the shame the offender's behaviour had caused to his clan, noting that in the old days the offender would have been required to pay the woman's family a substantial compensation.

Having heard all this, the judge confirmed that the victim still felt that she wanted to try and work things out with her estranged husband and that she was receiving help from her own support group (including a victims' advocate). Summarizing the case by again stressing the seriousness of the offence and repeating the Crown counsel's opening remarks that a jail sentence was required, the judge then proposed that sentencing be delayed for six weeks until the time of the next circuit court hearing. If, during that time, the offender had (1) met the requirements presented earlier by a friend of the offender who had agreed to lead a support group, (2) met with the community justice committee to work out an alcohol and anger management treatment plan, (3) fulfilled the expectations of the victim and her support group, and (4) completed 40 hours of service to be supervised by the group, he would forgo the jail sentence. After a prayer in which the entire group held hands, the circle disbanded and everyone retreated to the kitchen area of the community centre for refreshments.

Source: G. Bazemore and C.T. Griffiths, "Conferences, Circles, Boards, and Mediations: The 'New Wave' of Community Justice Decision Making." *Federal Probation* (June 1997) 61(2): 25–37; Canadian Resource Centre for Victims of Crime (2000) p. 25. http://www. crcvc.ca/docs/ restjust.pdf.

Case Study 4. A Traditional Indigenous Justice Ceremony

On December 4, 1993, a significant event was held in the gymnasium of an Indigenous community on the west coast of Vancouver Island. The community held a traditional justice ceremony and potlatch (ceremonial feast), during which a man from the community who had sexually abused women in the community over a 35-year period faced his victims, their families, and invited witnesses. The event was made possible by one of the man's victims, known as The One Who Broke the Silence, who could no longer bear to return to the community, see the offender, or endure the pain of silence.

The One Who Broke the Silence approached her eldest brother and the speaker and told them of her desire to resolve this long-standing crisis through a traditional justice ceremony rather than through the Canadian justice system. Subsequently, three additional women publicly disclosed that they, too, had been sexually assaulted by the offender and that they would also participate in the ceremony. At the time of the ceremony, the age of the four victims ranged from late teens to mid-40s. All now had children, and three were married.

Prior to the start of the ceremony, three chairs were situated at one end of the gymnasium: one for the speaker, one for the eldest brother of The One Who Broke the Silence, and one for the offender. The victims, female elders, and female relatives sat in the front row of a semicircle. Behind them, in ever-widening semicircles, sat the witnesses from the village and from neighbouring Indigenous communities. Witnesses play a very important role in this Indigenous nation. The proceedings were initiated by the speaker, who explained to the assembly both the reasons for the ceremony and the sequence of events that would occur during the ceremony. He then presented his cousin, the offender, to the assembly. The offender entered and took a seat between the speaker and the eldest brother of The One Who Broke the Silence. It was the desire of The One Who Broke the Silence that the entire ceremony should be videotaped so as to provide a record for the community and for others.

The offender in this case was a highly respected member of the community, a historian and a ritualist, singer, mask carver, dancer, painter, and name giver. He was also highly respected in the Indigenous communities along the west coast of Vancouver Island. He rose and spoke to the assembly, admitting guilt for his offences, describing in detail the crimes he had perpetrated upon the four victims, and relating how, through intimidation of the victims and their families, he had managed to silence their pain and suffering for so many years. The offender then begged for their forgiveness—not for them to forget but, within the traditions and customs of the First Nation, to forgive.

Following this, the offender approached each of the victims individually. Next to their feet stood a washbasin filled with water and, at the side, a towel. In the culture of this nation, the feet of women are washed during puberty ceremonies to signify their ascension to womanhood. Because of the pain and anguish inflicted on them by the offender, to that day the women had been denied their full womanhood. Now, in a symbolic gesture, the offender would wash the feet of the four victims, beginning with The One Who Broke the Silence.

The offender approached each of the victims individually, spoke to them, and apologized. The washing of the victim's feet followed. The washing began the process of transformation for each of the women from sexual assault victim to sexual assault survivor.

The washing was the beginning of the process of renewal, a process that would allow the women to live full lives within the village. The washings took place before all of the assembled witnesses. The water from the washings was then transported outside, where it was placed in a fire, along with the basins and towels.

Following this, The One Who Broke the Silence approached the offender and removed a mask from his face. This mask, which had been carved by the offender, symbolized the persona of the offender at the time the offences were committed and until the present moment. Masks are among the most highly treasured possessions in this Indigenous culture and are normally used in dances to demonstrate social status. The One Who Broke the Silence took this mask and placed it, face up, on the fire. As the fire consumed the mask, the speaker, accompanied by a rattle, chanted a prayer. The burning of the mask was the pivotal moment of the entire ceremony. At this juncture the ceremonial conversation involving the speaker, the victims, and the offender ended and the public conversation began. The victims were now survivors of sexual abuse and were spoken of as such. The mask burning terminated the ceremonial formalities of the event.

The offender, survivors, and witnesses then returned to the gymnasium, at which time the witnesses were asked to ratify the events that had occurred. For the next several hours, women in attendance spoke about the crimes and the victims, and offered support for the victims and the action they had taken. A feast was then held, and then the men in attendance spoke.

This ceremony was planned and carried out by the people in the community, without the assistance of the police, lawyers, the judiciary, or outside government. The objectives and process of this ceremony could not be more different from the adversarial system of criminal justice. The offender was held directly accountable to the victims of his crimes and was required to come before them and an assembly of witnesses to confess these crimes and to ask for forgiveness. The ceremony also provided an opportunity to begin the healing process for the victims, the offender, and the community. The victims were supported by their families, community members, and witnesses from neighbouring bands. The offender had the support of his family.

Source: From *Restorative Justice: International Perspectives,* edited by Burt Galaway and Joe Hudson. Copyright © 1996 by Lynne Rienner Publishers, Inc. Used with permission of the publisher.

How to Run a Community Conference

One of the biggest obstacles to the use of community conferences is the inexperience of line officers with this form of dispute resolution. Once the participants have been identified, it is important that the officer create a forum where the interests of all of the parties to the incident can be heard and addressed. The following is a suggested "script" that gives an idea of how to organize a successful conference.

Welcome, everyone. My name is ___. Before the conference begins, I would like to introduce everybody here and indicate their reason for being here." [Introduce each participant and indicate his or her relationship to the victim and the offender.]

At this stage, I would like to thank you all for making the effort to attend this conference. This is difficult for all concerned and your presence here will help us deal with the matter that has brought us together.

This conference will focus on an incident that happened on ___. It is important to understand that we will focus on what ___ did and how his/her unacceptable behaviour has affected others.

___ has admitted his/her part in the incident and so we are not here to determine guilt or innocence. Our primary objective is to explore the ways in which people have been affected by the behaviour and, hopefully, work toward repairing the harm that has resulted from his/her actions. As well, we need to consider the interests of the general community or neighbourhood. We also want to try to ensure that no further harm is done to the victim or to the community and that the needs of ___ are addressed as well.

If at any stage of the conference, [offender], you no longer wish to participate, you are free to leave; however, you must understand that if you do, the matter will then have to be dealt with by other means. If you participate to the end, this matter will be finalized subject to your satisfaction and your compliance with the conference agreement. Do you understand?" [Ask offender's parents and caregivers also.]

"This conference is an opportunity for all of you here to be involved in repairing the harm that has been done and to formulate a plan that will decrease the likelihood of it happening again in the future.

Offender

Ask the perpetrator to tell the story of what happened. If there is more than one perpetrator, each is asked to speak in turn, taking up the story at different intervals:

- "To help us understand what happened and who has been affected by this incident, we'll begin by asking ___ to tell us what happened. How did you come to be involved?"
- "Tell us what happened."
- "What were you thinking at the time?"
- "What have you thought about since the incident?"
- "Who do you think has been affected by your actions?"
- "In what way do you think they have been affected?"

Victim

The victim is then asked to describe the incident as he or she experienced it. If there is more than one victim, each is asked to speak.
  Key questions include:

- "What did you think at the time? Immediately afterwards?"
- "How has this incident affected you (in terms of health, emotions, physical harm, employment, relations with others, patterns of activity)?"
- "How did your family and friends react when they heard about the incident?"

Victim's Supporters

The victim's supporters, in turn, are then asked:

- "How did you find out about the incident?"
- "What did you think when you heard about it?"
- "What has happened since?"
- "In your view, how has the incident affected the victim?"

Offenders' Supporters

The offender's supporters are then asked for their reactions. Begin with the parents (keep mother for last unless father is very angry), caregivers, and then the other supporters in turn.
  To the parents/caregivers:

- "It must be very difficult for you to hear this." [Give the person time to respond at this point. Do not interrupt until he or she has finished speaking.]
- "What did you think when you heard that this had happened?"
- "What has happened since?"

Offender

Give the offender a chance to respond, having heard the stories from all participants.

- "Before we move on, is there anything you want to say to ___ or anyone else here?"

Agreement

Restitution and reparation are now negotiated.

1. Begin with the victim. "You've heard all that has been said here. What do you want to see happen out of this conference?"

2. Ask the same question of the victim's supporters. Allow plenty of time for discussion at this point. Plans to repair the harm may begin to develop.

3. As the group begins to develop a plan, be sure to ask the offender if he or she thinks it is fair.

4. To the offender's supporters, ask if they think it is a fair arrangement.

5. Ask the group if everyone is happy with the plan.

6. Make sure the agreement includes arrangements for monitoring and follow-up.

Closing the Conference

The facilitator summarizes the outcome(s) of the conference regarding restitution and reparation:

Allow me to read back what you have agreed upon [at this point read the agreement aloud]. Completion of this agreement will go a long way to putting right the wrong and allowing all of us to learn from this unhappy experience. Is there anything else you want to say? No? Thank you all, again, for coming and participating in the conference. Although it has been difficult at times, we hope it's been worthwhile for everyone.

The facilitator writes up the agreement, which the participants sign, and then makes photocopies for anyone related to the incident or just for the key people. Where appropriate, refreshments can be served while the agreement is being written up, signed, and photocopied. Do not hurry participants out of the conference room, as informal reintegration can begin after the conclusion of the conference.

Case Study 6. Graffiti Vandalism: The Art of Tagging

Graffiti, known as mischief under S.430.[1] of the Canadian Criminal Code, has serious financial and emotional costs to victims, businesses, and communities. If left unchecked it can seriously damage the reputation of a community and adversely impact the economy and quality of life enjoyed by the residents. It may open the door for other property crimes and create an environment that tolerates more serious crimes.

The vast majority of graffiti vandalism is the result of "tagging," committed by juveniles for the main reason of recognition. Taggers are not necessarily gang members, they do not reflect any specific socio-economic background, and they come from all neighbourhoods. In some instances, the individuals responsible for writing illegal graffiti are expressing complex behaviour, requiring intervention and help.

The Vancouver Police Department's Anti-Graffiti Unit (AGU) found that the driving force behind individuals engaged in graffiti outweighed the deterrent effect of the criminal justice system. Given the high rates of recidivism and the complicated nature of the problem, the AGU collaborated with researchers from Simon Fraser

University and restorative justice advocates to create a unique response to graffiti. The resulting program, titled "RestART," is based on successful restorative justice practices in correctional and community settings, as well as the AGU's work within the graffiti subculture.

The RestART initiative is a restorative justice response to graffiti and is a collaborative effort by the Vancouver Police Department, the City of Vancouver, and community members. http://mediareleases.vpd.ca/2016/07/28/restart-for-artistic-youth/

Source: © Vancouver Police Department

There are three main objectives of RestART:

1. To use processes based on the values and principles of restorative justice to:
   - bring together varying perspectives including youth, art community, victims, police, local business representatives, community and social service resources, legal graffiti artists, restorative justice advocates, and academics;
   - create an environment where all participants feel safe, equal, and respected;
   - raise awareness of the impacts of graffiti;
   - create an sense of connection that can facilitate reintegration and acceptance into community; and
   - promote collective responsibility in finding solutions to the current situation of illegal graffiti.
2. To increase youths' skills and channel these abilities and talents towards legal opportunities.
3. To use a creative, interactive, and experiential approach to learning.

When police apprehend a youth or adult for illegal graffiti and it is decided that the formal court process is not appropriate, the following steps may occur:

- The individual can be referred to additional programs such as drug and alcohol counselling, psychological testing, or art therapy.
- The individual may be asked to complete various tasks related to their offence, such as an apology letter to the victim, cleaning up graffiti, victim reconciliation, or forms of related volunteer work.
- The individual participates in the four-day RestART workshop, which includes the production of a mural on a public wall commissioned by the city.

REFERENCES

Bazemore, G., and C.T. Griffiths. 1997. "Conferences, Circles, Boards, and Mediations: The 'New Wave' of Community Justice Decision Making." Federal Probation (June) 61(2): 25–37.

Canadian Resource Centre for Victims of Crime. 2011. "Restorative Justice in Canada—What Victims Should Know." http://www.crcvc.ca/docs/restjust.pdf

Church Council on Justice and Corrections. 1996. Satisfying Justice: Safe Community Options That Attempt to Repair Harm from Crime and Reduce the Use or Length of Imprisonment. Ottawa: Church Council on Justice and Corrections.

Correctional Investigator Canada. 2016. Annual Report of The Office of the Correctional Investigator, 2015-2016. http://www.oci-bec.gc.ca/cnt/rpt/pdf/annrpt/annrpt20152016-eng.pdf

Galaway, B., and J. Hudson. 1996. Restorative Justice: International Perspectives. Monsey: Criminal Justice Press.

Green, R.G. 1997. "Aboriginal Community Sentencing and Mediation: Within and Without the Circle." Manitoba Law Journal 25(1): 77–125.

—. 1998. Justice in Aboriginal Communities: Sentencing Alternatives. Saskatoon: Purich.

Griffiths, C.T., and R. Hamilton. 1996. "Sanctioning and Healing: Restorative Justice in Canadian Aboriginal Communities." In Restorative Justice: Theory, Practice, and Research, ed. J. Hudson and B. Galaway. 175–91. Monsey: Criminal Justice Press.

Griffiths, C.T., B. Whitelaw, and R. Parent. 1999. Canadian Police Work. Toronto: ITP Nelson.

Hatch-Cunningham, A., and C.T. Griffiths. 1997. Canadian Criminal Justice: A Primer. Toronto: Harcourt Brace.

Lajeunesse, T., and Associates Ltd. 1996. Evaluation of Community Holistic Circle Healing: Hollow Water First Nation, vol. 1. Winnipeg: Manitoba Department of Justice.

Latimer, J., C. Dowden, and D. Muise. 2001. The Effectiveness of Restorative Justice Practices: A Meta-analysis. Ottawa: Department of Justice.

Marshall, T.F. 1999. Restorative Justice: An Overview. London: Research Development and Statistics Directorate, Home Office.

Ramsey, K. 1997. "A Return to Wisdom: Restorative Justice Revisited." Pony Express: The RCMP's National News Magazine. April, 16–19.

Regina v. Gladue [1999] S.C.R. 688.

Regina v. Ipeelee *[2012] 1 S.C.R. 433.*

Regina v. Proulx *[2000] 1 S.C.R. 61.*

Roberts, J.V., and C. LaPrairie. 1996. "Sentencing Circles: Some Unanswered Questions." Criminal Law Quarterly *39(1): 69–83.*

Rugge, T., J. Bonta, and S. Wallace-Capretta. 2005. Evaluation of the Collaborative Justice Project: A Restorative Justice Program for Serious Crime. *User Report 2005-02. Ottawa: Public Safety Canada.*

Spicer, V. 2005. "Couch Surfing in Vancouver: An Aggregate Study of the Vancouver Graffiti Suspect Network." Unpublished MA thesis, School of Criminology, Simon Fraser University.

Stuart, B. 1996. "Circle Sentencing: Turning Swords into Ploughshares." In Restorative Justice: International Perspectives, *ed. B. Galaway and J. Hudson. 193–206. Monsey: Criminal Justice Press.*

Truth and Reconciliation Commission of Canada. 2012. http://www.trc.ca

Van Ness, D., and K.H. Strong. 1997. Restoring Justice. *Cincinnati: Anderson Publishing.*

Wickins, R. 1998. Community Conferencing: The Edmonton Model: Justice for Victims, Justice for Offenders, Justice for Citizens. *Edmonton: Edmonton Police Services.*

Youth Criminal Justice Act. S.C. 2002, c.1. http://www.canlii.org/ca/sta/y-1.5

Zehr, H. 1995. Changing Lenses: A New Focus for Crime and Justice. *Scottsdale: Herald Press.*

The Community and Community Policing

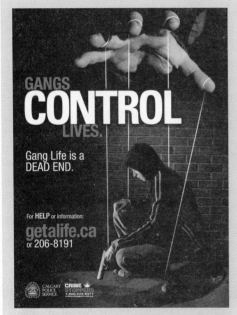

Gang violence has become common in most Canadian communities. Combating gang violence requires community awareness. The Calgary Police Service invited students to participate in gang suppression strategies by designing posters such as this one.

Source: © Calgary Police Service.

Learning Objectives

After completing this chapter, you should be able to:

- Identify the key issues relating to community involvement in community policing,
- Describe Ontario's Mobilization and Engagement Model of Community Policing and explain its purpose,
- Discuss the issues relating to cultural and visible minority and Indigenous communities and community policing,
- Describe the nine steps for building working relationships with the community,
- Describe the strategies used to gather information on and facilitate partnerships with the community,
- Discuss the role of integrated service teams in community policing,
- Identify and discuss the potential obstacles to police–community partnerships,
- Describe the role of volunteers in community policing, and
- Describe the various types of community policing committees.

INTRODUCTION

In the philosophy and practices of community policing, the **community** is paramount. The general public is viewed as a partner in the effort to create and maintain safe and secure communities. The model of community policing provides community residents with increased opportunities for involvement in crime prevention programs, community police stations, and consultative committees. In Ontario, both the Police Services Act and the Adequacy Standards include specific directives to involve the community in the design and delivery of policing services.

THE COMMUNITY IN COMMUNITY POLICING

Most discussions and research studies on community policing focus on only one part of the police–community equation: the police. Very little attention has been given to the role and responsibilities of community citizens in the development and implementation of community policing. In fact, at first glance, it would seem that soliciting the participation of the community in the police effort would not be difficult. Public opinion surveys and field research studies have found that:

- most adults and youth have a positive perception of the police;
- in general, community residents prefer proactive policing to reactive policing;
- community residents desire more, not less, contact with police officers;
- there is strong support for increased visibility and accessibility of the police;
- foot patrols are favoured by community residents;
- community police stations are viewed positively by the general public; and
- there are resources in all communities that, if properly mobilized and channelled, can play a significant role in addressing problems of crime and disorder.

The "how to's" of getting the community interested and involved as a partner in policing, however, have proven to be a challenge for police services. In short, there are a number of important issues surrounding the "community" portion of the police–community equation. These are considered below.

Issue 1. Whose Responsibility Is It to Get the Community Involved?

It is one thing to declare that communities are actively responsible for policing their own neighbourhoods as a key principle of community policing; it is another to achieve this involvement. Among the questions that must be addressed are the following:

- Whose responsibility is it to ensure that communities become involved? The police? The community? The local or provincial government?
- Where will the resources come from to encourage and sustain community involvement? The police? The community?

You will recall in our earlier discussion of problem-oriented policing (see Chapter 5) that the police and the community perform important roles in the identification of problems. While the police are very good at demonstrating leadership in problem-solving, long-term sustainment for community improvements requires a mobilized and engaged community. In many communities in Canada, this can be difficult to achieve.

Issue 2. Who and What Is the Community?

Although the term community appears often, the "who" and "what" remain unspecified. Two sociological definitions of community are widely recognized: (1) community as a locality, and (2) community as "networks of human interactions and social ties" (Gusfield 1975, xvi). It is often assumed that all of a community's people have a common interest and live in the same neighbourhood. Little consideration is given to the opportunities and obstacles presented by culturally, economically, and socially diverse communities composed of many different neighbourhoods. In Your Community 10.1 highlights how a community of interest can help the police service solve crime.

Traditionally, the geographic boundaries of policing zones or districts have been established by the police alone rather than in consultation with community residents. Most often, these boundaries are arbitrary and are set to meet organizational needs rather than community ones. Needless to say, community residents may define the boundaries of their neighbourhoods differently than the police organization, whose boundaries are generally meaningless to citizens. For example, a police zone or boundary may have a river as one border. Residents on one side of the river may be policed by different groups of officers than residents on the other side, even though residents on both sides of the river view the river collectively and would be considered a community.

It is also important to recognize that a neighbourhood may be only a portion of a community or may comprise an entire community, particularly in urban centres populated by cultural and ethnic minorities. In Edmonton, for example, the Edmonton Federation of Community Leagues has identified 155 communities (EFCL 2012).

The City of Vancouver is home to many gays, lesbians, and transgender or bisexual individuals, who together constitute a community. Earlier in our discussion, we pointed out that police officers carry out their duties in a wide range of policing environments—from urban neighbourhoods to remote Indigenous communities—and that many of these communities reflect the cultural diversity that is a defining feature of Canadian society. This requires that the philosophy and practices of community policing be adapted to the specific needs and concerns of individual communities; this, in turn, makes it imperative that police officers have knowledge of the people and communities they are policing.

IN YOUR COMMUNITY 10.1

ENLISTING COMMUNITIES OF INTEREST TO SOLVE CRIME: THE CASE OF THE STOLEN NISSAN SKYLINE

On 26 March 2008, two men visited a specialty car dealership in Calgary, Alberta. They asked to test-drive a 1991 Nissan Skyline GT-R, a rare performance car made primarily for the Japanese market and rarely seen in North America. They left with the car and did not return with it. A police report was filed. The owner of the car also posted the theft on www.beyond.ca, a website for Canadian auto enthusiasts, to spread the word.

Car enthusiasts connected on the Internet and began actively looking for it. Sightings were posted to the website almost immediately. One person, who had seen the Skyline on the website, pulled up alongside it at a light and gave the driver a "rock out" sign. When the driver looked at him he was able to snap a photo using his cellphone and post it onto Google and Facebook. Within 15 minutes, a forum member added a link to a Google map with directions to the suspect's house. Other members scrambled to narrow their Facebook searches for the suspect to the closest high school. At about 11 p.m., a link to the Facebook profile of the thief appeared online.

In a little more than 24 hours from the time of the first post, members of the forum had spotted the car and assembled a name, photo, home address, and Facebook profile for the person seen behind the wheel of the Skyline. The police were called and the individual was arrested. Had the police established an operation to collect the evidence, which the Beyond. ca community was able to do, investigative costs would have been several thousand dollars. The arrest has been profiled on a number of social media websites including YouTube and was also featured in the *New York Times* and in *Wired*.

(continues)

> This example illustrates how a mobilized community can assist the police in crime detection, investigation, and apprehension. It remains to be seen what deterrent effect social media websites may play in the future. The Beyond.ca site has also played a role in earlier cases of what might be called "open-source crime solving," including a hit-and-run collision from 2002. Already, many police agencies are turning to websites like YouTube for help identifying suspects in unsolved crimes.
>
> For additional information related to this case, use the search term "stolen Calgary Skyline GTR" at www.youtube.com. You can also read about it at www.beyond.ca.

Issue 3. What Is the Level and Distribution of Community Participation?

It is important to consider both the level of participation in a community and the distribution of that participation (Skogan 1995, 15). There may be an "unrepresentativeness" among the community representatives involved in any community policing initiative: people representing certain community interest groups, such as businesspeople, may be more active than people at lower socioeconomic and income levels. Little is understood about the conditions that facilitate or hinder substantial community involvement in community policing initiatives. Ironically, the community residents who are most likely to be "policed" are those who are the least likely to have access to the police, to influence police policy and practices, and to participate in police–community initiatives. This is often the case in communities where there are low levels of homeownership and where the residents are working hard to get out of the community.

There is also the question of what the community is supposed to do. Community residents may not clearly understand the principles of community policing and, like police officers, may equate it with crime prevention. Where community committees do exist, their roles and responsibilities may not be clearly defined or may be focused on a single issue. Traditionally, the hierarchical structure of police services has hindered community input into and involvement with police services. Community policing provides the opportunity for community residents to become involved in a partnership with the police.

Issue 4. Who Trains the Community?

Although police services have taken steps to ensure that community policing is a cornerstone of both recruit and in-service training, little attention has been given to training community residents to assume a role as equal partners in preventing and responding to crime and social disorder. This is referred to in the police literature as "community empowerment"—that is, giving to communities the necessary tools and knowledge to respond effectively to crime and social disorder at the local level. Generally speaking, citizen education initiatives are limited to ride-alongs, citizen academies, Neighbourhood watch programs, and citizen foot patrol, all of which will be discussed later in this chapter. Such programs are often presented as "Get to Know Your Local Police" programs. These programs do provide citizens with some insights into police work, but they are insufficient, on their own, to prepare citizens for a significant role in dealing with problems.

Training community residents requires the development of workshops and forums on leadership, community building, and problem-solving, as well as on strategies for identifying and mobilizing community resources. These programs can be offered under the auspices of the police, municipal or provincial governments, or community organizations. The objective is to build a solid foundation for substantive citizen involvement in police–community partnerships. One such initiative is featured in In Your Community 10.2, which focuses on Vancouver's Community Policing Centres, which exist throughout that city.

IN YOUR COMMUNITY 10.2

POLICE–COMMUNITY PARTNERSHIPS

Vancouver's ten community policing centres hold a unique position among crime prevention initiatives in North America, because of their strong partnership with the community. Unlike their counterparts in other cities, these centres are not satellite police stations—they are actually operated, staffed, and governed by members of the community.

Source: *Courtesy of the Vancouver Police Department*

Vancouver Aboriginal Community Policing Centre Society

The Vancouver Aboriginal Community Policing Centre Society (VACPCS) was incorporated in 2006 as a non-for-profit society by the Vancouver Indigenous community. It was created to address social justice issues, improve safety for Indigenous people, and build the relationship between the Vancouver Police Department (VPD) and the Indigenous community through education, awareness, and open dialogue.

The positive link between the Vancouver Indigenous community and the VPD provides an avenue to engage and support Indigenous people so that they better understand and utilize the services of the VPD. This link is supported by the presence of an assigned member of the VPD, a Neighbourhood Police Officer at VACPC who participates in activities and is available to support the specific needs of the Indigenous community in Vancouver.

VACPCS is governed by a board of directors elected by and from members of the Vancouver Indigenous community. Working in partnership with Indigenous community members, Indigenous and non-Indigenous organizations, and all levels of government, VACPC seeks to provide resources, services, and programs that support the safety and security of Vancouver's Indigenous community.

Source: *Courtesy of Vancouver Aboriginal Community Policing Centre Society*

Issue 5. The Potential and Limits of Community Involvement

A key question that has generally remained unaddressed in discussions of community policing is whether the community *wants* to become involved in police–community partnerships. There are a variety of reasons why community residents may not become involved in community policing initiatives, including fear of retaliation from the criminal element, apathy, lack of time, hostility to and distrust of the police, a lack of understanding on the part of community residents as to their role, and the diversity of needs among community residents (Grinc 1994). In addition, neighbourhoods are becoming increasingly fluid as residents move regularly in pursuit of educational and employment opportunities and for other personal and professional reasons. Furthermore, research studies have found the following:

- Many citizens understand little about the role and activities of community policing initiatives such as community police stations.
- Community residents rarely access the services offered by community police stations.
- Police services have experienced considerable difficulties in generating and sustaining community interest and involvement in community policing initiatives. (Hornick et al. 1990; Liou and Savage 1996; Polowek 1995)

There is also a flip side to this issue: What about segments of the community that may want to become *too* involved in partnerships with the police?

In recent years, police services have been relying increasingly on the private sector and community groups to fund certain police activities and initiatives, referred to as **P3s**, for "public–private partnerships." The goal off these is to offset the high costs of policing through partnerships with the private sector. The Winnipeg Police Service, for example has constructed new police stations using P3s to support the high costs of facilities. The Ottawa Police Service has received assistance from the private sector for a number of initiatives. The companies involved include:

- Brinks, an armoured car company that pays for the police to investigate armoured car and other robberies;
- Corel, a computer company that finances "cop cards"—baseball-like cards with pictures of police officers on them—as part of a police program for youth; and
- local car dealers that donate money for the police to combat auto theft (*Ottawa Citizen* 1996, A6).
- In some jurisdictions, local car dealerships have provided the vehicles used for patrol.

Critics of the practice of private funding for police programs contend that a dangerous precedent is being set—that is, only special interest groups with financial resources will be provided with police service. Supporters of private funding reply that the increasing involvement of the private sector in funding police services is not only a consequence of reduced operating budgets but also an important component of the police–community partnership within the framework of community policing. You will have an opportunity to wrestle with this issue in Exercise 1 later in the chapter.

THE ONTARIO MOBILIZATION AND ENGAGEMENT MODEL OF COMMUNITY POLICING

In 2010, the Ontario Association of Chiefs of Police introduced a new community policing model called **Ontario's Mobilization and Engagement Model of Community Policing** (access the student resource website to see an illustration of the model). This model incorporates the key ideas we have been discussing throughout the text. The model outlines the roles and responsibilities of both police services and community members in addressing crime and safety. For example, the idea that community policing is tailored to the individual needs of communities is clearly reflected by the degree to which a community requires police assistance. For this reason, the model serves as a diagnostic tool that the police and community leaders apply in order to assess how much support is required to achieve a safer community.

The model has four key areas:

- enforcement and crime suppression;
- community mobilization and crime prevention;
- community safety and consultation; and
- community engagement and liaison.

The Ontario Provincial Police identify three pillars supporting this model of community policing:

1. **Engagement**:
   Reducing crime and victimization in communities requires collaborative and comprehensive planning to combat the root causes of crime and social disorder. Police will work towards connecting partners, creating community partnerships, identifying and mobilizing community assets, supporting social development, and leading crime prevention, to increase community safety and well-being.

2. **Education**:
   The model is structured to direct the community's safety efforts towards addressing whatever type of crime or social disorder affects the community. It also supports the use of data and analysis to assess and plan for addressing the crime and/or social disorder affecting the community. Police will partner with local community partners to educate the public by suggesting and assisting with situational crime prevention measures, media releases, sharing of crime data, and town hall meetings on relevant and current information.

3. **Enforcement**:
   Responding to emergency situations and crime management are some of the fundamental police functions in our society. By analyzing crime, practicing targeted enforcement, monitoring crime reduction strategies and initiating problem solving strategies in partnership with communities and agencies that have mandates to address the underlying issues, police can begin to reduce risk and crime where there is a high need for police assistance.*

Police officers meet with community leaders and determine how a community rates across these four dimensions. For example, in communities having high repeat calls for police service, there is typically a requirement for a high level of attention from police to establish order through frequent high-visibility policing and enforcement.

The model also helps identify strategies that help maintain or improve overall community safety. For example, in communities requiring a high level of police support, police-led and -initiated strategies such as "hot spot" policing and targeting prolific offenders are necessary to reduce crime and disorder. These strategies place significant demands on the police. The strategy in this stage of community development is to stabilize neighbourhood problems and begin developing the community's capacity (ability) to take ownership for many problems that lead to feelings of insecurity. The police must apply principles of problem-oriented policing at this stage to ensure that positive outcomes are sustained.

The goal for both the police and the community is to reduce the amount of assistance the former need to provide. The process may be initiated by the police, who identify community leaders capable of sustaining and building on progress in addressing many of the community's crime and disorder problems. Over time, by applying community-based policing strategies, intelligence-led policing efforts (see Chapter 3), situational crime prevention efforts (e.g., target hardening), CPTED, and crime prevention through social development, the community will be better equipped to manage its own problems and thereby lessen its reliance on the police.

*OPP, Community Mobilization and Engagement: the three pillars that support this philosophy. © Queen's Printer for Ontario, 2016. Reproduced with permission. Found at https://www.opp.ca/index.php?&lng=en&id=115&entryid=56b7979b8f94ac0d5c28d174

As you review the model, try to relate key ideas you have learned from each chapter. This will help you understand how community policing has become much more strategic. At the end of this chapter, you will find an example of community mobilization planning utilized by the OPP. Check out the source of policing problems related to one Ontario municipality, the Main Action Plan (MAP) that was initiated, and the evaluation summary.

CULTURAL AND VISIBLE MINORITY COMMUNITIES AND COMMUNITY POLICING

Canada's cultural diversity presents major challenges to police services. They must increase the number of police recruits from cultural and ethnic minorities, ensure that officers receive training that makes them culturally sensitive and aware, and implement strategies that will facilitate police–community partnerships. Several Canadian police agencies have recently undertaken "implicit bias" training, during which officers are taught how to recognize their own biases with regard to ethnicity, socioeconomic background, class, religious affiliation, sexual orientation, gender, age, and more. The training offers suggestions and methods for overcoming any bias the officer may have during his or her interactions with the public. For more information, visit the website pertaining to fair and impartial policing at http://www.fairimpartialpolicing.com.

Increased immigration and the migration of Indigenous people have fuelled rapid population growth in a number of urban centres such as Vancouver, Montreal, and Toronto. Police agencies in cities (notably the Greater Toronto Area, which is Canada's fastest growing region) face the challenge of developing police–community partnerships with a variety of "communities" within the area.

In recent years, there have been several highly publicized incidents involving police officers and members of racial and ethnic minorities. Police have also confronted individuals suffering from mental illness, at times using force to end the conflict. These issues have increased pressure on the police from community groups and politicians and led to a number of commissions of inquiry into police actions.

In 1995, the Commission on Systemic Racism in the Ontario Criminal Justice System issued its report on racism in the provincial justice system. Among other findings, the commission reported that both Anglo and non-Anglo residents of Toronto believe that the police do not treat all groups of citizens the same and that Blacks are more likely to feel they were treated unfairly the last time they were stopped by the police (Gittens and Cole 1995).

Distrust of the police among community residents may undermine community policing initiatives. In 1996, for example, the RCMP opened a community policing office in the Black Cultural Centre in North Preston, Nova Scotia. This is a community near Halifax with a history of tension and conflict between residents and the police. Melees and standoffs between the police and angry mobs have challenged both the community and the police to bridge the gap between the RCMP and the community.

Canadian police are involved in far fewer fatal police shootings per capita than their US counterparts (around 19 per year in Canada versus around 987 per year in the United States); nonetheless, what happens in the United States often impacts policing north of the border and places greater scrutiny on Canadian policing and issues surrounding the use of force (Parent, 2016). Recently, controversial fatal police shootings of Black men in the United States have resulted in the creation of the "Black Lives Matter" (BLM) movement, which now has chapters in Canada as well. Following its US counterpart's playbook, the Canadian BLM protested the police involvement of the deaths of two black men—Abdirahman Abdi by Ottawa police in July 2016 (the officer was later charged with manslaughter) and Andrew Loku by Toronto police in July 2015. In the case of Loku, BLM held a 15-day protest outside Toronto Police Headquarters after the officer involved was cleared of criminal wrongdoing (Gillis 2017; Nease 2017).

In Canada, the Toronto Police Service (TPS) has been confronted over its practice of "carding." Also known as "street checks," carding is a means of intelligence-gathering and typically involves police personnel stopping, questioning, and documenting the movements of individuals when no particular offence is being investigated. Civil libertarians and critics of the process lobbied the Ontario government suggesting that carding is a form of racial profiling and should be discontinued by the police.

On 1 January 2017, the Ontario government enacted regulations requiring police in Ontario to advise individuals that they have a right not to talk with police and that refusing to cooperate or walking away from the police cannot be used as a reason to obtain information. The regulations allow police to continue to gather personal information during routine traffic stops or when someone is being arrested or detained, or when a search warrant is executed. The new rules do not apply to police undercover operations, and police can still stop and collect information when investigating a specific crime. Some critics remain uneasy with the current situation, suggesting that the new rules do not go far enough and may leave room for abuse.

The new regulations also require the police to maintain a written record of any carding interactions with the public, including the name and badge number of the police officers involved. At least once a year, the Chiefs of Police in the Province of Ontario will have to conduct a detailed review of a random sample of entries in their database to verify that it was collected in compliance with the regulation. The chiefs must also issue an annual public report on the number of carding incidents and on the collection of personal information, including the gender, age, and race of the individuals stopped and the neighbourhoods where the information was obtained.

In addition to allegations of racial profiling, the TPS was involved in a highly publicized incident in which 18-year-old Sammy Yatim was shot and killed by a TPS officer on 27 July 2013 after brandishing a knife on a streetcar. Cellphone video of the incident as it unfolded gave the public a first-hand look at a fatal police shooting. This resulted in international media coverage and allegations that the police had used excessive force.

This controversial shooting resulted in the police officer being charged with the murder of Sammy Yatim. The matter went to trial, and on 25 January 2016 the jury found the officer not guilty of second degree murder and manslaughter but guilty of attempted murder. The jury accepted the officers' argument that he had been justified in firing the first three shots from his gun, but also found that he had not been justified in firing a second round of shots; thus, he was guilty of attempted murder. The complex court ruling was appealed.

These examples illustrate that it may take many years to address and overcome the profound suspicions and distrust of the police that are held by some community residents, and that the resolve of the police and the community to develop a true partnership will be severely tested along the way.

Police services require community support in order to establish and maintain positive relationships with the public and with the communities they have been hired to serve. In line with Peel's Principles (see Chapter 1), and with regard to the issue of police legitimacy, it is important for police personnel to be courteous, fair, and respectful when performing their duties. Public satisfaction with policing helps build and maintain community trust and confidence. Satisfaction levels with police performance are often reflected in public opinion surveys and in the number and severity of complaints lodged against officers. A 2014 survey revealed that the majority of Canadians felt that police were doing a good job at being approachable and easy to talk to (73%), ensuring the safety of citizens (70%), promptly responding to calls (68%), treating people fairly (68%), enforcing the laws (65%), and providing information on crime prevention (62%) (Cotter 2015).

However, while the majority of those surveyed believed that the police were doing a good job, police performance was perceived more poorly among those who had had contact with the police, and those who had been victims of crime, as well as among Indigenous people (Cotter 2015). Police services across Canada are striving to do better. Having learned from the business sector and from psychology, police in Canada are focusing more and more on "customer service" initiatives that enhance the delivery of policing. Exceptional customer service requires officers to be compassionate, caring, and service-oriented in their approach to their duties. The Canadian Police Knowledge Network (CPKN) offers a course on customer service in the police environment that is designed to provide insight regarding the delivery of "exceptional" customer service. Also, many Canadian police services are recruiting service-oriented individuals and promoting an organizational mindset that reinforces providing the highest quality of service.

In addition, police often have specialized units dedicated to responding to issues related to diversity and cultural conflict. In Calgary, for example, the Diversity Resources Unit maintains a number of portfolios that respond to cultural and interest-based diversity (e.g., the gay community). It is important to maintain these units, for at times when cultural tensions are high, these units can be highly effective in defusing racial or interest-based tensions. Calgary's Diversity Resources Unit has addressed community concerns when citizens have been killed by police, in high-profile use-of-force incidents, in allegations of racial profiling, and in a high-profile police raid on a gay bathhouse.

Similarly, the Ottawa Police Service has established the Community Development Section (CDS) with the following mandate:

- to develop sustainable partnerships and engagement strategies within the community;
- to work with communities, agencies, and members of the organization to identify problems, opportunities, and potential solutions; and
- to promote trust and confidence in policing by expanding and enhancing educational opportunities related to community policing (Ottawa Police Service https://www.ottawapolice.ca/en/about-us/Community-Development.asp?_mid_=18607).

INDIGENOUS COMMUNITIES AND THE POLICE

Relations between Indigenous peoples and the police, historically and in contemporary times, have often been characterized by a high degree of mutual suspicion and hostility. Numerous task forces and commissions of inquiry conducted over the past two decades have documented instances in which police officers acted in a discriminatory manner against Indigenous people. This has led to initiatives on the part of the RCMP and provincial and municipal police forces to improve the training and cultural sensitivity of police

---

IN YOUR COMMUNITY 10.3

THE RCMP: SERVING CANADA'S INDIGENOUS PEOPLE

Since the earliest days of the North-West Mounted Police in the 1870s, the RCMP has been a law enforcement partner of Indigenous communities. The RCMP continues to develop a unique and important relationship with Indigenous people in Canada.

Contributing to safer and healthier Indigenous communities is one of the five strategic priorities of the RCMP. Delivering culturally competent police services provides the foundation necessary to build relationships and partnerships with the more than 600 Indigenous communities the RCMP serves.

The RCMP's shared and unique history with Canada's Indigenous peoples allows an environment in which it can work collaboratively to improve community health and wellness.

The RCMP is committed to continue building upon these relationships as it encourages, sustains, and fosters honest and open dialogue among its Indigenous partners. Working together, the RCMP is in a position to assist and advocate for Indigenous communities at a local and national level.

The RCMP contributes to safer and healthier Indigenous communities by:

- promoting and encouraging the recruitment of Indigenous people as potential employees and police officers.

- working collaboratively with the communities to ensure enhanced and optimized service delivery by developing relevant and culturally competent police services.

- contributing to the development of community capacity to prevent crime through ongoing social development.

- maintaining and strengthening partnerships with Indigenous communities, our policing and government partners, stakeholders, and Indigenous organizations.

- promoting and using alternative/community justice initiatives for Indigenous people.

- demonstrating value for service through the development, management, and evaluation of the detachment performance plan created in collaboration with the local Indigenous communities.

- contributing to public policy development and implementation to assist in building safer and healthier Indigenous communities.

National Aboriginal Policing Services (NAPS)

The RCMP's National Aboriginal Policing Services (NAPS) is responsible for planning, developing, and managing the organization's strategies and initiatives. NAPS works closely with Indigenous groups to develop innovative policing approaches that meet their distinctive needs.

Programs

NAPS oversees a number of Indigenous programs and initiatives, including the following:

- Commissioner's National Aboriginal Advisory Committee;

- Aboriginal Perceptions Training;

- Inuit Perceptions Training; and

- Annual Performance Plans, which address an offence or negative social issue that concerns the community.

NAPS also provides support on the First Nations Policing Policy to its partners in the Indigenous Policing Directorate of Public Safety Canada, serving First Nations, Inuit and Métis groups. The RCMP maintains ongoing dialogue with the:

- Assembly of First Nations;

- Inuit Tapiriit Kanatami (Canada's national Inuit organization);

- Métis National Council;

- National Association of Friendship Centres;

- Native Women's Association of Canada; and the

- Congress of Indigenous Peoples.

(continues)

Reproduced with the permission of the Royal Canadian Mounted Police.

Each spring, the RCMP erects a tipi at National Headquarters in Ottawa in celebration of our Indigenous communities.

Sources: *RCMP, Strategic Priorities, found at http://www.rcmp-grc.gc.ca/prior/index-eng.htm#ac Reproduced with permission of the RCMP. and Serving Canada's Indigenous People. www.rcmp-grc.gc.ca/aboriginal-autochtone/index-eng.htm Reproduced with the permission of the RCMP.*

officers, to establish better lines of communication with Indigenous communities, and to support the Indigenous police forces that have been created (see In Your Community 10.3). In recent years, Indigenous bands have developed community-based criminal justice services and programs. These initiatives have been designed to address the overrepresentation of Indigenous people at all stages of the criminal justice system—from arrest to incarceration—in most regions of the country. This trend has provided an opportunity for Indigenous peoples not only to create autonomous police services, but also to establish partnerships between Indigenous and non-Indigenous police services.

COMMUNITY POLICING AND SOCIAL DEVELOPMENT

Police agencies such as the Waterloo Regional Police and the Calgary Police Service have adopted an innovative approach to community policing, centred on the concept of social development. The strategy involves focusing not on the problems within a community but rather on building capacity within a specific area of the community. The police agency and the community work together in a partnership, drawing on existing strengths for the purpose of benefiting the overall health of the municipality.

As was noted early in the text, community problems are often complex and deeply rooted, which typically rules out the option of a quick fix. When the unique strengths and resources within the individual community are recognized, the chances of success in resolving the problem are far greater.

Schools are often a key area for implementing positive change. Research studies have demonstrated a relationship between school performance and criminal offending in youth. School performance can be a significant predictor of both adolescent and adult criminality. Delinquents tend to be less successful in school than those who are not delinquents; they also have lower attendance rates and are more likely to leave school early. School dropouts are far more likely to be in trouble with the law and are more likely to be unemployed or underemployed.

These factors underscore the need to keep Canada's youth in school. In its discussion paper "Crime Prevention through Social Development: A Literature Review," the John Howard Society of Alberta notes:

There is growing recognition within both Aboriginal and non-Aboriginal communities of the need to stress prevention, rather than remedial strategies, if problems such as literacy and low educational levels are to be banished from our society. Within this prevention strategy, two factors are recognized. The first is that communities and families, not experts and governments, possess the creative energies necessary to find and manage durable community-based prevention initiatives. The second factor is that most human development problems are the result of multiple and intertwined factors or deprivations. Since people are shaped by their total environment, strategies must address this whole environment, not just one specific aspect of it.
— *CCSD (1991), 17, quoted in John Howard Society of Alberta (1995)*

A useful way of setting out the particular strengths and capacities of a community is with a community assets map, like the one in Figure 10.1.

DEVELOPING POLICE-COMMUNITY PARTNERSHIPS

In Chapter 7, we discussed the strategies that police services use to implement the philosophy and principles of community policing. These include preparing a business plan, conducting environmental scans, developing partnerships with communities and neighbourhoods, incorporating best practices, and assessing the effectiveness of programs and interventions. Many of these same techniques are also used in problem-oriented policing (see Chapter 5).

Figure 10.1 Community Assets Map

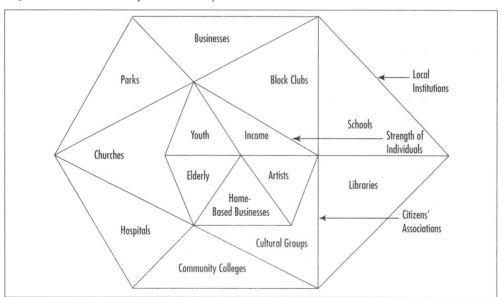

Source: *Building a Safer Canada: A Community-Based Crime Prevention Manual, p. 18.* Department of Justice Canada, 1996. Reproduced with the permission of the Minister of Public Works and Government Services (2017).

Community policing requires that individual police officers use many of these same approaches in carrying out their duties. The specific demands placed on community police officers (CPOs) will, of course, depend on the area to which they have been assigned. As well, the ability of CPOs to establish community partnerships, to solve problems, and to develop programs will be affected by the level of support provided by the police service. This includes ensuring that officers have the necessary resources to carry out their tasks.

There are a number of steps that police services and CPOs must take to build working relationships with the community.

Step 1. Identify Potential Partners

The first step involves preliminary discussions with community groups, government and not-for-profit agencies and organizations, and the business community. Potential partners should represent a cross section of the neighbourhood or community and include persons and groups that have traditionally been marginalized, such as low-income residents and youth. CPOs should also make a concerted effort to visit agencies and organizations in the community and introduce themselves. There is no substitute for face-to-face meetings.

Step 2. Develop a Clear Understanding of the Neighbourhood or Community Being Policed

When first assigned to a zone or area, the police officer should review any environmental scans that the police service has conducted, as well as other reports from provincial or municipal ministries and departments relating to current and projected socioeconomic developments; crime patterns; commercial and industrial features; and social, health, and mental health issues and problems. This includes reviewing materials on interventions carried out by officers previously assigned to the area. The officer should not assume that this information will automatically be made available.

It is also recommended that the new CPO meet with officers who have previously policed the area. This will provide the new officer with vital information on current issues and problems, on initiatives that are currently under way in the community, and on interventions that have been attempted in the past. Meeting with these officers will enhance the cumulative experience of officers policing the area and provide the incoming officer with information on key community groups and resource persons as well as on troublesome individuals and issues.

Based on this information, the CPO can develop a community profile that will provide useful information for addressing community concerns and problems.

Step 3. Initiate Dialogue

Every opportunity should be taken to interact with community groups and residents in a non–law enforcement capacity. Informal conversations with residents can provide the CPO with important information on community sentiment, the problems and issues faced by the various stakeholder groups in the community, residents' perceptions of previous policing efforts, and past experiences of residents in collaborating with police.

In many communities, youth problems consume a considerable portion of the public's concern and police attention. This includes parties; drag racing; loitering; drinking in public places such as school playgrounds and parks; and vandalism, including "tagging" (graffiti). The CPO should make time to visit places and spaces where youth congregate, be they the local youth centre, the skateboard park, or the 7-Eleven parking lot, to meet youth in a non–law enforcement context.

Experienced police officers make an effort to meet youth, not only to connect names to faces, but also to develop a rapport that will be useful in enforcement situations. Youths can be a valuable source of information about their friends and acquaintances, and they can also help officers defuse potentially explosive situations at house parties and during parking lot confrontations and drinking incidents. An excellent way to meet young people is to co-sponsor events with the local youth centre or community service organization. This includes police–youth sports events such as softball, basketball, pool events, and volleyball tournaments. In addition, police services are using social media to engage youth, prevent crime, and respond to specific offences such as cyberbullying and gang activity. Twitter, Facebook, YouTube, and other social media platforms allow police to provide information regarding youth safety and criminal activity, serving to connect youth with police services. The use of apps and smartphone technology enhances engagement.

Lower profile youth offences, such as bullying, intimidation, and exclusion, also require a strategic response by the CPO. The national bullying strategy calls for early intervention into the lives of young people by addressing issues of antisocial behaviour. In this regard, police personnel, teachers, social workers, parents, and community members require a coordinated effort in dealing with youth violence in the community. For example, in Alberta, youth care workers, school administrators, and the police have made it a common practice to assess potentially violent behaviour in students before a tragedy occurs.

Finally, CPOs must be aware of "multi-disciplinary collaborative responses" to threat-making and other forms of violent behaviour in the community environment. The CPO needs to establish a protocol using what is referred to as the four-pronged assessment model. This model encourages the evaluation of potential threats and threat-making behaviour by examining risk factors such as the personality of the youth, family dynamics, social dynamics, and school dynamics. Police personnel, as well as community agencies (social service offices, the school administration), are equipped with strategies for intervening in extreme cases of violent youth behaviour.

Step 4. Organize Community Meetings

Community meetings provide a forum for citizens to express their concerns about problems in the community. They also enable CPOs to identify citizens who may be interested in serving on a community committee. There are a number of different types of community meetings, including general forums, meetings with specific stakeholder groups, and meetings with community policing committees. We will examine the important issues relating to community meetings in Exercise 1.

Step 5. Identify Issues

CPOs should work with the community to identify the issues that are of greatest concern and the highest priority. They should try to isolate those issues on which there is consensus and that have the greatest potential to be resolved through police–community collaborative efforts.

Step 6. Formulate a Plan or Develop an Action Plan

The police and the community should formulate a plan that considers all facets of the issues that have been identified and that sets out a clear course of action that has been agreed upon by all parties. Developing an action plan would include:

- determining the level of intervention;
- selecting participants;
- identifying prevention strategy options;
- selecting the best strategies;
- setting goals and objectives; and
- preparing a work plan.

Figure 10.2 provides an outline of the strategies and actions that could be considered.

Figure 10.2 Selecting Strategies and Approaches

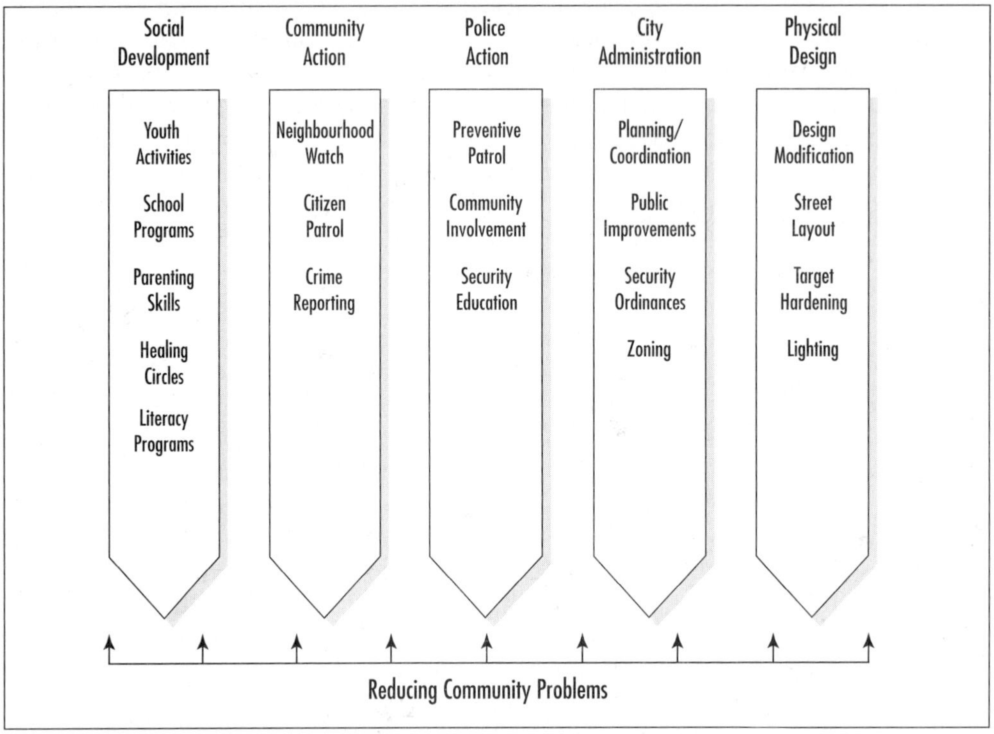

Social Development	Community Action	Police Action	City Administration	Physical Design
Youth Activities	Neighbourhood Watch	Preventive Patrol	Planning/ Coordination	Design Modification
School Programs	Citizen Patrol	Community Involvement	Public Improvements	Street Layout
Parenting Skills	Crime Reporting	Security Education	Security Ordinances	Target Hardening
Healing Circles			Zoning	Lighting
Literacy Programs				

Reducing Community Problems

Source: *Building a Safer Canada: A Community-Based Crime Prevention Manual, p. 19.* Department of Justice Canada, 1996. Reproduced with the permission of the Minister of Public Works and Government Services (2017).

Step 7. Take Action

Both the police and the community must be involved in implementing the plan of action. The intervention should closely follow that plan. Taking action may require building community support through personal contact. An effective communication strategy is vitally important to ensure that information and ideas are shared among all the interested parties and, as well, to prevent misunderstandings that might undermine the initiative.

Step 8. Maintain the Partnership

One of the greatest challenges facing CPOs is how to sustain community interest and involvement in the partnership. There are a number of strategies that can be used to sustain the police–community partnership, including choosing problems with a high likelihood of success (at least at the outset), publicizing the successes of the partnership, and giving community residents a substantive role to play in addressing the identified issues. Other strategies could include providing ongoing training for all participants to ensure that interest remains high, and creating websites and newsletters to disseminate information, highlight activities, and increase the visibility of the partnership in the community. Rewards and incentives such as public commendations, block parties, and awards dinners can also be offered.

Step 9. Document Activities

The police–community interventions and their outcomes should be recorded. This will create a written record of activities that can be referred to in the future. An evaluation of impacts and outcomes will also suggest whether resources are being used effectively and whether any changes are required in the strategies.

Each CPO should create a personal business plan that outlines the key priorities to be addressed, sets out timelines, and determines the goals and objectives for the year. Among other things, this will provide documentation to supervising officers that can be used for the officer's annual performance assessment.

Figure 10.3 sets out a planning model for community problem-solving that can be used to address problems of crime and social disorder.

DETERMINING COMMUNITY PRIORITIES AND CONCERNS: THE COMMUNITY POLICING TOOLBOX

In the past, many police services assumed that the police themselves were in the best position to determine how communities should be policed and resources allocated. Furthermore, there were few if any mechanisms for the community to offer feedback to the police on how well the police were doing in addressing the needs and concerns of community residents.

Community policing requires that the police service develop the capacity to determine the priorities and concerns of the community being policed, if such a capacity does not already exist. In addition, it is essential that police services develop ways to solicit continual feedback from the community, so that policies and initiatives can be enhanced, modified, or, if found to be ineffective, discontinued. Police services must also develop mechanisms to communicate with other criminal justice and social service agencies.

Community input is a core component of community policing, which strives to develop true partnerships between the community and the police. The difficulties of fulfilling this mandate should not be underestimated. Community residents often overestimate the abilities of the police to address problems of crime and social disorder; they may also have conflicting expectations of the police or believe that the police should be

Figure 10.3 A Community Problem-Solving Planning Model

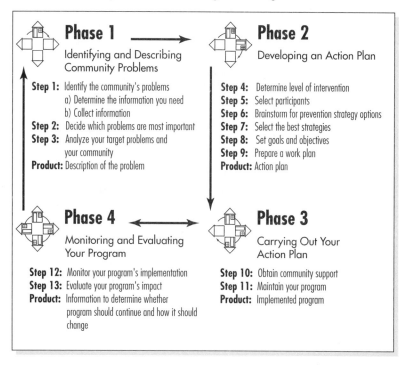

Source: *Building a Safer Canada: A Community-Based Crime Prevention Manual, p. 19.* Department of Justice Canada, 1996. Reproduced with the permission of the Minister of Public Works and Government Services (2017).

equally concerned with law enforcement, crime control, crime prevention, community policing, and order maintenance. For most community residents, knowledge of the police is limited to the often-distorted images presented on television, in movies and social media, or in encounters with officers during traffic stops.

The Ottawa Police Service has established a program—"Partnership in Action"—designed to nurture and strengthen relationships with the community and to work collaboratively on common problems. For more information, visit "Community Partners" on the OPS website, http://www.ottawapolice.ca.

Developing a Community Profile

One of the best ways to determine the needs, concerns, and perceptions of community residents is to construct a **community profile**. This can include information on the demographic characteristics of the community, crime rates, and community issues and concerns, as well as residents' perceptions of crime and of the effectiveness of the police and criminal justice system. Figure 10.4 depicts the possible information sources for a community profile.

A number of techniques can be used to gather information for a community profile. These include community surveys, focus groups, public forums, and community consultative committees.

Figure 10.4 Possible Information Sources for a Community Profile

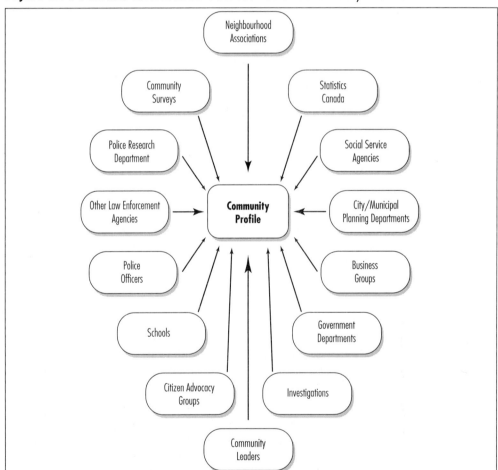

Source: Linda Reid, *Developing a Community Profile: A Manual for the Development and Implementation of Community Profiling for Police Planners and Managers, Community Policing Series.* Ministry of Solicitor General of Canada and Ministry of the Solicitor General of Ontario (1993), p. 3. © Queen's Printer for Ontario, 1993. Reproduced with permission.

Community Surveys

Community surveys are a cost-effective way to gather information from community residents in order to improve service delivery. These surveys are most often conducted by telephone or through the Internet, but they can also be carried out by mail or by visiting individual households in the community. The Policing for Results Survey, created by the Ontario Provincial Police and discussed in Critical Perspectives 6.2, illustrates a technique used by one police service to gather information from the community in order to enhance policing effectiveness. Community policing teams in any neighbourhood can use this same technique.

Focus Groups

Focus groups are a widely used, cost-effective technique for obtaining information from various groups of citizens in the community. Focus group discussions bring together individuals who share a common attribute, be it age (adult or youth), gender, or experience (victim or offender). A facilitator, preferably a person from outside the community, runs the session and leads a discussion related to the topic at hand. Generally, the intent is to gather information on the perceptions, experiences, and observations of the group; the focus is not on providing a forum for individual residents to relate specific details of their personal situation. A focus group discussion may last several hours. A research assistant, who also attends the session, takes down participants' comments. Throughout the discussions, the facilitator can draw out the experiences and opinions of the group members and identify the major issues relating to the specific topic.

Focus groups are also valuable in securing the involvement of community residents in the dialogue about how policing services are organized and delivered. They make it possible to include diverse groups. One cannot assume that everyone has the same view of the police, so it is important to include groups that may be more likely to have contact or potential conflict with the police. Among the different groups in a community are:

- high school students;
- high school-aged youth who are not in school;
- the elderly;
- members of the business community;
- members of visible/cultural minority communities; and
- general community residents.

The topics that might be addressed in a focus group discussion include:

- general perceptions of community life;
- the key issues confronting the community;
- perceptions of crime and social disorder in the community;
- the role of the police in the community;
- citizens' experiences with and expectations of the police;
- how to improve the delivery of policing services;
- the nature and extent of involvement in community activities generally and crime prevention initiatives specifically; and
- the potential for increased community involvement in preventing and responding to crime and social disorder.

Focus groups are not designed to solicit the personal experiences of community residents with the police, but rather to gather more general information on a variety of community and policing-related topics. As such, focus groups are not oriented towards documenting specific case incidents.

Public Forums

Public forums (also known as town hall meetings) can raise the profile of community concerns and provide police with a venue where they can explain their goals and objectives. In staging or participating in public forums, the police make themselves available to hear the concerns and priorities of community residents. Potentially, they can establish ongoing lines of communication.

Public forums, however, can be counterproductive. If the forum is dominated by one specific community interest group, or by specific individuals, little progress will be made. Individual citizens may attend public forums with a specific agenda, such as criticizing police actions, relating personal stories and experiences with the police, or preventing other groups from the community from expressing their concerns and needs.

If public forums are to succeed and not be hijacked by personal agendas, the focus of the forum should be clearly defined and communicated to the community. All parties with a vested interest in the topic at hand should be invited, and a neutral third party—that is, someone not connected to the police—should moderate the proceedings. Other obstacles to establishing partnerships with the community are identified and discussed below.

Multi-Agency Meetings and Liaison Groups

Developing police–community partnerships involves breaking down the barriers that have long separated justice agencies and organizations. Problem-solving requires more than a focus on law enforcement. Many of the difficulties experienced by individuals, families, neighbourhoods, and communities are the result of poverty, mental disabilities, health problems such as fetal alcohol syndrome (FAS), and other environmental, psychological, or physical challenges.

Increasingly, police services and their officers are collaborating with other agencies and organizations. This includes developing **integrated service teams** made up of representatives from the police, social and mental health services, health agencies, and community organizations. Many police services have Children At Risk Response Teams (CARRTs) composed of a social services worker and a police officer working together in a patrol car to respond to any call where the health, safety, and welfare of a child or youth is deemed to be at risk. Integration is a key feature of the developing model of community based strategic policing.

EDUCATING THE COMMUNITY

One of the biggest challenges facing police services is to develop strategies to educate the community about community policing and the potential for police–community partnerships. Research has found that community residents, even those who have been the victims of crime, tend not to become involved in community policing initiatives and generally have little knowledge of police activities.

Police services have developed a number of initiatives to address the problems of citizen apathy and lack of interest. Larger Canadian police services offer "citizen police academies" to educate citizens about policing, its limitations, and its possibilities. Smaller police services such as the Cornwall Community Police Service (see In Your Community 10.4) actively engage community groups by way of police presentations, displays, and "Fact Sheets" that inform members of the public. The Toronto Police Service, through its Community Mobilization Units, offers a one-day workshop designed to strengthen community problem-solving and crime prevention. There are also observer programs in which community residents accompany a police officer for a shift. These programs provide the public with a glimpse into operational front-line policing. In Calgary, for example, citizens are able to ride in HAWC1 or HAWC2, the Calgary Police Service patrol helicopters.

IN YOUR COMMUNITY 10.4

CRIME REDUCTION AND COMMUNITY PARTNERSHIPS

DO YOU KNOW 5 DIFFERENT
THE FIRST NAME OF AT LEAST 5 NEIGHBOURS?

WOULD YOU BE ABLE TO TELL POLICE THE ADDRESS OF THE
HOUSE BEHIND YOU IN THE EVENT YOU WITNESS A BREAK-IN?

WOULD YOUR BACK DOOR NEIGHBOUR KNOW YOUR ADDRESS?

If you answered **NO** to any of these questions, use the chart on the back of this card - to get to:

KNOW YOUR NEIGHBOURS

KEEP YOUR NEIGHBOURHOOD SAFE

**Courtesy of Cornwall Community Police Service, http://www.
cornwallpolice.ca/en/sections-and-units/crime-reduction-and-
community-partnerships.html.**

Taking crime down and crime reduction are high on the list of priorities with the members of the Cornwall Community Police Service.

Our Crime Reduction and Community Partnerships Division is actively engaged in presentations and displays to many community groups in order to educate our community members in taking crime down.

These officers also serve as a liaison to many community-oriented programs including: Halloween safety patrol with Laidlaw Transit Ltd., Neighbourhood Watch, Operation Lookout, V.I.P. (Values, Influences And Peer pressure) Program, and the Adopt-A-School Program.

The officers also present lectures in local schools, community groups and businesses on such topics as: Bicycle Safety, School Bus Safety, Drinking And Driving, Drug Abuse, Traveling Alone, Robbery Prevention, Theft Prevention, Personal Safety and Home Security to mention a few.

The Cornwall Community Police Service offers the following one and two page Fact Sheets on a variety of topics in order to educate and assist the community with crime prevention. The Fact Sheets are comprised of crime prevention advice that will assist you in lessening your chances of becoming a victim of a crime. The Fact Sheets cover topics such as auto and vehicle theft, elder abuse, and robbery prevention.

Source: *Courtesy of Cornwall Community Police Service. http://www.cornwallpolice.ca/en/sections-
and-units/crime-reduction-and-community-partnerships.html*

Another important means for educating the public is through the strategic use of the media. Police services require a proactive and strategic communication plan if they are to educate the public and, importantly, provide a balanced response to hostile or anti-police media stories. Key individuals such as front-line supervisors and senior police administrators must practise effective communication skills when addressing the media. Communications must also be a strategic part of the planning process, to ensure that new programs and changes to departmental policies are announced and clearly articulated to the public in a timely manner. Within this framework, many police services delegate a full-time officer who is trained in media relations, to act as the spokesperson for the police service. By keeping an open dialogue and taking a strategic communications approach, the police service can avoid many of the pitfalls associated with distorted, negative, or absent media attention. For example, the Toronto Police Service has established a Corporate Communications section, which is responsible for internal and external communications, providing content, and maintaining the service's Internet and intranet websites. The TPS is also active on social media, providing a platform for designated Toronto police officers to regularly tweet and post to Facebook and YouTube. Visit the TPS social media Web page "The Way Forward" at http://www.torontopolice.on.ca/TheWayForward/social-media.php. In Vancouver, the Metro Vancouver Transit Police has developed a free app that allows transit users to connect to all Transit Police services through one channel. Transit users can report crimes and non-emergencies on the transit system, receive alerts about transit disruptions, plan trips, and connect to the transit police on social media, all by using this single mobile app.

POTENTIAL OBSTACLES TO ESTABLISHING PARTNERSHIPS WITH THE COMMUNITY

It is important to reiterate that even where a police service is committed to a community policing model and to establishing partnerships with the community, it may encounter obstacles. Many have been noted earlier, such as citizen apathy and lack of interest and domination of the police–community dialogue by special interest groups.

In addition, government policies or initiatives that are beyond the control of the police agency may challenge partnerships with the community. For example, Bill C-58 and federal legislation requiring a national gun registry was fraught with controversy and criticism. More than $2 billion was spent on this program, which placed police agencies at the centre of a heated debate concerning the registration of firearms by law-abiding individuals such as farmers, ranchers, and hunters. Bill C-19, Ending the Long-Gun Registry Act, came into effect on 5 April 2012.

Other barriers to effective police–community partnerships are:

- antagonistic feelings towards the police among some groups in the community;
- antagonistic feelings among police officers towards some groups in the community;
- officers who feel ill-equipped in terms of training and resources to establish relationships with the community; and
- officers burdened by heavy workloads who do not have the time to plan or implement community policing strategies (Ministry of the Solicitor General and A.R.A. Consultants 1991b, 7).

ROLES AND ACTIVITIES FOR COMMUNITY RESIDENTS

In community policing, community residents can play a variety of roles. The most common way for citizens to contribute to the police effort is as volunteers—for example, by serving as police auxiliaries. The business sector may also provide support for police activities. In addition, community residents may be members of service clubs, businesses, and other agencies that enter into partnerships with the police.

Serving as Volunteers

In Chapter 2, we identified the increasing involvement of volunteers in police services as a major trend in Canadian policing. The framework of community policing calls specifically for the participation of the community in a wide range of activities. **Volunteers** assist the police in developing partnerships with the community, provide an opportunity for the community to take ownership of problems, are a continual source of new energy and fresh ideas, and help reduce the workload on patrol officers.

Volunteers fall into two groups: internal volunteers, who work directly with a police service supporting police-sponsored programs, and external volunteers, who assist with various groups in the community that have the support of the police. For example, an internal volunteer would be involved in assisting in a police-run activity such as seating guests at a police graduation or fundraiser, while an external volunteer would staff neighbourhood projects such as Neighbourhood Watch or Block Parents.

Citizen volunteers serve in a wide range of capacities, including staffing victim services units and storefronts, serving on community policing committees, participating in special police–community projects, conducting citizen patrols, serving as extra "eyes and ears" for the police, and serving as police auxiliary constables. The Waterloo Regional Police Service utilizes volunteers in a variety of programs such as Victim Services, the Citizens Police Academy, Crime Stoppers, Neighbourhood Watch, and the Community Advisory Committee.

Another example of volunteer involvement was the 1988 Winter Olympics, when the Calgary Police Service recruited hundreds of volunteers to assist at various events and activities. After the Olympics, nearly 400 volunteers remained with the police service; they now constitute the Special Projects Team. These volunteers assist with many police activities, including police graduations, mock crime scenes, fundraisers, traffic control, and warrant and subpoena programs. Many of these volunteers are seniors who donate many hours of their time to ensure that programs succeed.

There is considerable variation across Ontario in the numbers and activities of volunteers (for one example, see In Your Community 10.5). The guidelines governing the involvement of volunteers in police work are generally developed and enforced by individual police services. Another resource with regard to police agency volunteers is Volunteer Canada's website at http://www.volunteer.ca.

The Goals of Volunteer Programs

Most police services operate volunteer programs with goals that include:

- focusing on community participation and the use of civilian volunteers to assist police in meeting the needs of the community;

IN YOUR COMMUNITY 10.5

VOLUNTEER OPPORTUNITIES IN THE OTTAWA POLICE SERVICE

You can help keep our community safe. Become an important part of a unique organization: become a police volunteer. *An experience you'll never forget!*

The Ottawa Police Service believes in Community Policing—solving community problems with the assistance of members of the community. Community Police Centres rely heavily on trained volunteers. Most volunteers assist at centres in their neighbourhoods. They answer questions about the police service and crime statistics for their area. They may also run crime prevention programs depending on a community's needs. Individuals are selected on the basis of their ability to perform assignment requirements.

(continues)

Volunteers must be a minimum of 18 years of age, have no police record and be available to commit a minimum of 4 hours per week for a minimum of 1 year. The screening process includes an interview with the supervising officer, a reference check, and a background check performed by our organization, at no cost to the applicant. If volunteers are between the ages of 14 and 18, they can participate in the **Venturers** program or **High School Cooperative Education** program.

Source: *Used with permission of Ottawa Police Service, found at https://www.ottawapolice.ca/en/careers-and-opportunities/Volunteer.asp.*

- enhancing public safety through civilian volunteers working together with police throughout the community in the areas of crime prevention, education, special projects, short-term assignments, and other tasks;
- providing assistance to police in delivering complete and efficient service to the community; and
- developing creative programs with and for the community within the economic and budgetary constraints that police face.

In addition to these general types of goals, a police service may develop specific goals and objectives for particular programs that are staffed by volunteers. These are generally set out in a volunteer management manual developed by the police service. The goals of the Winnipeg Police Service Volunteer Program are set out in In Your Community 10.6.

IN YOUR COMMUNITY 10.6

WINNIPEG POLICE SERVICE: VOLUNTEER PROGRAMS

The Winnipeg Police Service is not only committed to working with and serving the community of Winnipeg, they value and appreciate the contributions made by their volunteers.

Working within a team environment each volunteer brings with them different life skills and abilities they draw upon and utilize while assisting members of the public.

The Winnipeg Police Service has two separate and distinct volunteer programs. Each program provides a volunteer with the opportunity to interact with the public and contribute to the community.

Victim Services Volunteer

Victim Service Volunteers work closely with one another and with assigned Police Officers in assisting victims of crime. This is achieved primarily by telephone contact with victims offering them support and resource information on social and judicial material.

The duties of a Victim Services Volunteer include:

- Answering telephones and providing short-term emotional support to victims of crime and tragedy.
- Provide referrals to appropriate community resources.

- Provide crime prevention information.
- Provide information to victims regarding their occurrences by accessing police data base.
- Obtain and provide court information to victims of crime.
- Provide Criminal Justice information regarding Victim Bill of Rights, Victim Impact Statements and Compensation for Victims of Crime.
- Conduct personal home visits when required.
- Volunteer at various Police related events.

Community Volunteer

Under the direction of the Volunteer Coordinator and the assigned Constable, Community Volunteers staff the front counter at the Public Safety Building/Police Headquarters, the East District Station, the West District Station and the Winnipeg Police Museum in the City of Winnipeg.

The duties of a Community Volunteer include:

- Greet the public, question as to the reason for their attendance
- Ensure the person has the proper document(s) to conduct business
- Answer the telephone and redirect calls / forward messages
- Provide administrative support for the Block Parent Program
- Provide direction/referrals concerning WPS and outside agency programs
- Ensure pamphlets are available to the public
- Accept payment & applications for Alarm Permits
- Accept applications for a Criminal Record Search
- Assist in the preparation of a Constable taking a report

Source: *Courtesy of the Winnipeg Police Service. http://www.winnipeg.ca/police/policerecruiting/volunteer/*

Recruiting and Screening Volunteers

Police services recruit volunteers in a variety of ways, including by contacting schools and community service organizations and placing advertisements in newspapers, on radio and television stations, and on the Internet. Current and former volunteers are another good source of names of potential candidates. Strategies are often designed to attract Indigenous volunteers as well as volunteers from visible and cultural minorities. Every effort should be made to ensure that volunteers reflect the diversity of the community being policed. In addition, volunteers should be recruited from all segments of the community, including youth and senior citizens.

Candidates for volunteer positions complete an application form that includes personal information; education and training; employment history; qualifications and special skills, such as languages spoken other than English; availability; a list of family members including full name, date of birth, and place of birth; and personal references. Applicants may also be required to indicate why they wish to volunteer with the police service and what they expect from the experience.

Applicants generally undergo a security check and a criminal records check, and sign a number of documents including a disclaimer for liability. A volunteer coordinator or a patrol officer responsible for the volunteer program then interviews the applicant.

Training and Retaining Volunteers

Once appointed, volunteers generally undergo an orientation during which they receive background information about the police service. They also receive additional training related to the specific positions and activities they will be involved in, such as victim services. Volunteers who will work in storefronts or community policing offices receive training in the proper procedures for taking citizen complaints and completing occurrence reports. Most police services have developed print materials and brochures that provide volunteers with information on police procedures and resources.

A major challenge for police services is retaining volunteers, particularly in light of the competing demands on the time of community residents. Police services use various strategies to reduce turnover and maintain a stable cadre of volunteers, including:

- providing initial and in-service training;
- providing organizational support and resources;
- setting a clear agenda and specific lines of authority and communication;
- ensuring that volunteers are treated as co-workers, not just as free help;
- organizing workshops and conferences for continuing education;
- giving volunteers responsibility and discretion to carry out tasks;
- providing volunteers with the opportunity to assist in goal setting and program development;
- formally recognizing volunteer contributions through awards banquets, press releases, community newsletters, and interdepartmental memos; and
- informally recognizing volunteer contributions through one-on-one meetings, informal lunches, letters of recognition, and telephone calls.

Volunteer Canada has developed a handbook on screening volunteers. For additional information you can contact Volunteer Canada by telephone or visit its website at http://www.volunteer.ca.

Auxiliaries

Auxiliaries, also known as **"reserve" police officers**, have been a feature of Canadian police services for many years. Citizen volunteers are provided with training, a uniform, and "sworn" peace officer status while accompanied by a full-time police officer. The application process to become an auxiliary is competitive, and candidates must undergo a background and security check. Often, people involved in auxiliaries are interested in a career in policing and view the position as an opportunity to learn about the role and activities of the police. Others are motivated by a desire to contribute to the overall well-being of the community.

In addition to on-the-job experience, auxiliaries receive basic police training and are often allowed to participate in more advanced in-service training courses. The OPP provides ongoing conferences and workshops for the auxiliary police officers attached to the service. The OPP Auxiliary members' mission is "to provide fully trained volunteer Auxiliary members to assist in the delivery of traffic safety and community-based crime prevention initiatives and; to perform police duties only in special circumstances, including an emergency that the police officers of the OPP are not sufficiently numerous to deal with." (Ontario Provincial Police, 2016b)

In the field, the tasks performed by auxiliaries may include accompanying a regular member on patrol and assisting with traffic duties at sporting events, parades, and other community events, and in emergency situations where additional personnel are required. Auxiliaries generally do not have access to firearms while on duty. Rather, the primary role of the auxiliary is to serve as an additional pair of "eyes and ears" for regular police members. (In 1999, BC's attorney general determined that auxiliary members of the

RCMP in that province could no longer wear sidearms—a practice that had been allowed under earlier RCMP guidelines.)

Many police auxiliaries have years of experience and an intimate knowledge of the community, especially in more rural settings. These auxiliary members are a particularly important source of information and assistance for police in regional and provincial services, and for RCMP officers who have recently been transferred into the community.

The International Association of Chiefs of Police (IACP) coordinates the Volunteers in Police Service (VIPS) program in the United States. The program enables agencies to develop volunteer programs and allows citizens to volunteer with a community law enforcement agency (International Association of Chiefs of Police 2017).

Corporate Sponsorship

Although the private sector is an enthusiastic supporter of police services, its involvement has been controversial. Supporters of private funding argue that the increasing involvement of the private sector is a consequence of reduced operating budgets and an important component of the police–community partnership. Critics argue that this threatens to set a very dangerous precedent in which police services are provided only to special-interest groups with financial resources, and that accepting donated vehicles and other resources compromises the independent role of the police.

For these reasons, corporate funding is often provided through privately operated organizations such as Crime Stoppers. The creation of police foundations is one idea under consideration by police services across the country. Donations would be made to the foundation, which would then disburse money through a board. This would help maintain the arm's-length relationship between the police service, which must remain independent, and private-sector donors.

COMMUNITY POLICING COMMITTEES

Community policing committees are one of the best ways to establish and sustain a working partnership with the community. The composition and role of a particular committee depends on a number of factors, including the needs and interests of the community. For example, the Toronto Police Service Community Consultative Committee (CCC) has drawn members from various organizations within each of these communities to reflect both inclusiveness and credibility within that community. The committees serve as voices on wider policing issues that include training, recruiting, Professional Standards and community mobilization. The service has created committees with communities such as the Aboriginal, Black, Chinese, French, Gay/Lesbian-Bisexual/Transgender/Transsexual, Muslim, South and West Asian and Asia Pacific communities. The mandate of the CCC is to work in partnership with community representatives to identify, prioritize, and problem-solve policing issues by:

- being proactive in community relations, crime prevention, education, mobilization, and communications initiatives ;
- acting as a resource to the police and the community ; and
- developing a strategic long-term vision through building knowledge, education, tolerance and understanding (Toronto Police Services http://www.torontopolice.on.ca/community/ccc.php).

Types of Community Committees

There are three general types of committees:

- *The **consultative community policing committee:*** As the name implies, this type of committee advises the police, who assume primary responsibility for responding to the specific issue at hand. Consultative committees focus on gathering information, which they then pass along to the police. They require minimal structure, and meetings can be scheduled on a regular basis or as needed.

- *The **multifunctional community policing committee:*** The activities of this type of committee extend beyond providing advice and recommendations to the police. Multifunctional committees partner with the police to identify areas of concern and to develop problem-solving responses. Committee members represent a broad cross section of the community. These committees usually have an executive consisting of a chair, vice-chair, secretary, and treasurer. As well, there may be one or more standing subcommittees responsible for finances, media relations, production of a newsletter, and other areas as required. These committees meet regularly, and as their scope and activities expand, they may consider incorporation as a non-profit or charitable organization. This status assists the committee in fundraising, raises its profile in the community, and limits its liability for insurance purposes.

- *The **interagency community policing committee:*** These committees are composed of the police and other agencies and organizations in the community and have a mandate that includes a broad range of community and social issues. These committees formulate plans of action that maximize the expertise and efforts of the participating agencies and organizations. Interagency committees are the most complex type of police–community committee and require a formal operating structure, including an executive, standing committees, and subcommittees. They are often incorporated as not-for-profit or charitable organizations to assist in fundraising and increase their profile in the community, and for liability insurance purposes (OPP 1997a, 3; 1997b, 4.2–4.3).

Other types of committees can be established to address community issues and concerns, such as short-term problem-solving groups that address a specific issue in the community (e.g., graffiti or traffic). Within the framework of community policing, the possibilities for police–community partnerships are limited only by the imagination of the police officers and community residents.

Committee Membership and Member Responsibilities

It is a challenge for patrol officers to create a committee composed of residents and officers who are willing to spend the time and energy to find solutions to community problems. It requires identifying individuals in the community who have a special expertise or skill that can be used by the committee, including someone from the legal profession, someone with access to and knowledge of computer technology, someone with a background in training or education, someone with analytical or evaluation skills, and someone who is familiar with community clubs, businesses, and organizations (OPP 1997b. 4–5).

Once members for the community policing committee have been selected, the responsibilities associated with committee membership must be set out. These include, but are certainly not limited to:

- maintaining the confidentiality of sensitive materials;
- attending meetings regularly and being on time;
- understanding committee procedures;
- being willing to volunteer for committee projects;
- controlling the "yap factor" (not engaging in spreading rumours); and
- not engaging in promoting hidden agendas (OPP 1997b, 4–7).

Operating Effective Committees

Community policing committees can be an integral component of the police–community partnership only if they operate effectively. The requirements for effective community policing committees are described below.

The goal of the Community Policing Committee in Amherstburg is to work with the citizens and both public and private organizations to identify and resolve issues that could affect the quality of life in Amherstburg. Volunteers are made up of a diverse group of citizens, and are involved in prevention initiatives, providing public feedback and input. The committee seeks to educate the public about police work in a variety of ways, including: publications, websites, town meetings, and committee meetings.

Source: Courtesy of the Town of Amherstburg. Found at https://www.amherstburg.ca/en/town-hall/Community-Policing-Committee.aspx

Running Effective Meetings

For an example of how to run an effective meeting, see Case Study 1.

Defining the Role of Community Policing Committees

Community interest and involvement can be sustained only if the role of the community policing committee is clearly established and community members can be substantively involved in addressing problems and concerns that have been identified as priorities. In the absence of such an arrangement, patrol officers will likely have difficulty recruiting residents to sit on committees and, over time, community involvement will dissipate.

Generating Officer Support and Participation

Community residents must feel that members of the police service are available through the community consultative committees. Every effort should be made to ensure that there is good police presence at the committee meetings and that officers do not leave meetings abruptly to answer outside calls for service, which can be irritating to community attendees. As well, it is important that there be good community representation at the meetings.

CHAPTER SUMMARY

This chapter has focused on the community portion of community policing, an area that has historically received very little attention. A number of key issues were identified that provided the backdrop for the materials presented in this chapter, including defining who and what is the community, the level and distribution of community involvement in policing, and the potential and limitations of community involvement. Ontario's Mobilization and Engagement Model of Community Policing, developed in 2010, attempts to address many of these issues, particularly in framing the roles for both the police and the community. The chapter also discussed the particular difficulties that have been encountered in soliciting the participation of people from Indigenous communities and from visible and cultural minorities.

There are a number of specific steps that patrol officers must follow to build working relationships with the community, from identifying potential community partners to organizing meetings to developing strategies to sustain community involvement. Community police officers have a number of techniques at their disposal that can be used to determine community priorities and concerns, including community profiles, surveys, focus groups, public forums, and integrated service teams. Officers must also address the potential obstacles to establishing effective partnerships.

Citizens can play a variety of roles in community policing, including serving on community policing committees, volunteering for a wide range of activities, and serving as auxiliary police officers. Police services have developed procedures for screening, recruiting, training, and retaining volunteers.

The discussion concluded with an examination of community policing committees. The various types of committees were identified, the issues surrounding committee membership and member responsibilities were examined, and the strategies for operating effective committees were noted.

CHAPTER REVIEW

Key Terms
- auxiliaries or "reserve" police officers, p. 338
- community, p. 314
- community profile, p. 330
- community surveys, p. 331
- consultative community policing committee, p. 339
- focus groups, p. 331
- integrated service teams, p. 332
- interagency community policing committee, p. 340
- multifunctional community policing committee, p. 340
- Ontario's Mobilization and Engagement Model of Community Policing, p. 318
- P3s (public–private partnerships), p. 318
- public forums, p. 332
- volunteers, p. 334

Key Points
- There are a number of critical issues relating to the community portion of community policing.
- Ontario's Mobilization and Engagement Model of Community Policing serves as an important tool for both the police and the community to assess the degree of police support necessary create safe communities.
- Specific strategies are required to engage members from diverse communities, including Indigenous, LGBT, and cultural minority communities, in partnerships with the police.
- Patrol officers must take several key steps to develop partnerships with the community.

- Community profiles, community surveys, focus groups, public forums, and inter-agency collaboration can be used to determine community priorities and address community concerns.
- Integrated service teams and collaboration with other agencies and organizations are effective approaches for developing partnerships.
- There are a number of potential obstacles to establishing effective police–community partnerships.
- The most common way that citizens become involved in partnerships with the police is by volunteering.
- Police services have developed procedures for recruiting, screening, training, and retaining community volunteers.
- Several types of community committees can be created to identify and address community concerns and problems.

Self-Evaluation
QUESTIONS

1. What are the key issues surrounding the **community** portion of the community policing equation?
2. Discuss the concept behind **community empowerment**.
3. What is a **community profile**, how are community profiles developed, and what role do they play in community policing?
4. Describe the use of **community surveys** in the development of police–community partnerships.
5. What are **focus groups**, and what role do they play in identifying the priorities and concerns of a community?
6. What are the benefits and limitations of **public forums** as a way to gather information from the community?
7. Describe Ontario's Mobilization and Engagement Model of Community Policing and explain how it serves as a diagnostic tool.
8. Describe the role of **integrated service teams** within the framework of community policing.
9. Describe the role of **volunteers** in Ontario policing, noting the key issues surrounding recruitment, screening, training, and retention.
10. Describe the role of **auxiliaries** in Canadian police services.
11. Compare the three types of community policing committees: **consultative community policing committees**, **multi-functional community policing committees**, and **inter-agency community policing committees**.

KEY IDEAS

1. Which of the following statements describes Ontario's *Police Services Act* and the Adequacy Standards?
   a. They make no mention of the role of the community in policing.
   b. They specifically limit the policing activities that citizens can become involved in.
   c. They direct police services to involve the community in the design and delivery of policing services.
   d. They specify how police services are to involve members of Indigenous and cultural and visible minority communities.

2. Which of the following is true of community involvement in community policing?
   a. The role of the community is typically well defined.
   b. Representation from all segments of the community may not exist.

    c. Residents who are most likely to be "policed" are often the same individuals who are likely to become involved in police–community relationships.

    d. The vast majority of individuals within a community want to be involved with their police agency and community policing initiatives.

3. Which of the following is indicated by public opinion surveys and field research studies?

    a. Most adults and youth are skeptical of their police agency.

    b. Community residents would like to have more opportunities to volunteer their services with a police agency.

    c. The public is largely unaware of local community police stations.

    d. There are resources in communities that can be mobilized to address problems of crime and social disorder.

4. What has been revealed by research on Indigenous and visible- and cultural-minority communities?

    a. These communities typically embrace police–community partnerships.

    b. Many people in these communities share the view that the police do not treat all groups of citizens equally.

    c. Establishing police–community partnerships with these communities is relatively simple and straightforward.

    d. These communities may require initial federal funding as a result of the requirement for translation services.

5. One information-gathering technique brings together individuals in the community who share a common attribute, such as age or gender, in order to provide an opportunity for them to relate their perceptions, experiences, and observations. What is this technique called?

    a. community profile

    b. focus group

    c. community survey

    d. public forum

6. Which of the following is a potential barrier to the development of effective police–community partnerships?

    a. Citizen apathy and disinterest.

    b. A lack of police resources.

    c. Legislation limiting the types of police–community relationships that can be developed.

    d. Opposition by police unions.

7. Integrated service teams comprise representatives from which of the following?

    a. Minority groups within the community.

    b. Various crime prevention programs existing in the area.

    c. Various police agencies existing in a geographic area.

    d. The police, health services/health agencies, and community organizations.

8. Which of the following statements is true about volunteers in police services?

    a. They are typically limited by departmental policy to a small number of activities.

    b. They are engaged in a wide variety of activities.

    c. They need not have a background or security check.

    d. They must have a college or university degree.

9. Which of the following is not one of the three general types of community policing committees?
   a. The consultative community policing committee.
   b. The multi-functional community policing committee.
   c. The legislated community policing committee.
   d. The interagency community policing committee.

10. Which statement is true about the membership of community policing committees?
    a. Persons from the legal profession should be excluded.
    b. Membership should be given only to those persons with previous volunteer experience.
    c. Membership on the committees should be limited to a one-year term.
    d. Membership selections should require a background check.

The Community and Community Policing: Situations and Strategies

Community Mobilization Planning in Ontario

The Ontario Provincial Police provides mandatory training for all uniform officers in community mobilization. The following is an example of a community mobilization initiative from one Ontario municipality.

Problem Identification:

A local resident of the Municipality of XXXXX had become a source of policing problems in the Municipality. The person of interest between September 2014 and 5 January 2015 had made 25 plus non emergent 911 calls.

Date: January 2015

Address

Street Number: XX

Street Name: XXXXXX

City/Town: Municipality of XXXXXX

Province: XXXXXX

Postal Code: XXXXXX

Analysis Summary (Socio Demographic, Public Buildings, Community Resources)

- The resident between September 2014 and 5 January 2015 had made 25 plus non emergent calls to 911

- These calls were non-emergent, belligerent in nature and had become a nuisance.

- The calls to police were requesting officers to pick up prescriptions or cigarettes for the caller, or they wanted a "hug", or they just wanted to argue and yell at dispatchers.

- A few calls involved the person's mental health.

- The person resides on a busy cottage road with permanent residents.

- The resident has access to a motor vehicle.

- The calls for service usually came in around the start or end of shift change.

- Neighbours were involved to assist in keeping the person safe from themselves.

Risk Factors:
- All the 911 calls for service are two officer calls.

- Time consuming and depletes resources for other policing functions.

- The person has a long history with police involving addiction abuse with alcohol, mental health issues and is a victim of sexual assault.

- Officer safety is an issue for officers.

- Each time the officers would attend the person would be extremely intoxicated and a danger to themselves. They were belligerent, rude, and offensive and swore at officers.

- As the calls increased, the person was becoming a danger to themselves. They would be extremely intoxicated, smoking, dropping lighters/cigarettes, or trying to light candles or tipping them over.

- Officers spent a great deal of time trying to deal with the situation to keep the subject safe by way of getting a neighbour to attend or take them somewhere to be looked after. This avenue in the neighbourhood was becoming exhaustive.

- The person was taken to the general hospital and kept there till sober in the morning.

- This took up an emergency bed in the hospital.

- It took an ambulance bus out of service.

- An ambulance bus had to leave another "zone" to cover while the other was out of the area.

- The person refused to participate in mental health services, addiction services or counselling.

- Cost of policing for the Municipality.

Protective Factors:
- OPP are required to attend 911 calls to assist, and investigated within their community.

- Available mental health services, addiction services or counselling.

Previous or Ongoing Community Mobilization Efforts: (PFR Survey, Reports of Social Disorder, Proactive Identification, Statistical Analysis, Complaints, Formal Requests)

- Officers and Shift supervisors attended and spoke with person warning and advising of the proper use of 911.

- The person was warned of possible Criminal charges.

- The person was warned through Probation officer.

- The person would not allow family involvement to assist.

Main Action Plan (MAP):

- Speak with person and warn possible criminal charges.

- Speak with probation about setting up a plan i.e. attending addictions.

- Detachment members were advised of a plan to charge the person with Fail to Keep the Peace and Be of Good Behaviour pertaining to their current probation order if calls continued.

- The person was breached with one criminal charge.

- Plan was to get the person before the courts and into the Mental Health Diversion Court System.

- A plan would be put in place involving Mental Health Services and Addictions Services, and Probation.

Partnerships / Traditional and Non:

- Probation and Parole

- Court Mental Health Diversion

- Addictions Services

Evaluation Summary (PFR, Anecdotal, Calls for Service, Meeting dates, Milestones, Lessons Learned):

- Mental Health Court Diversion and Probation are now more involved.

- OPP have checked in with Probation officer.

- Officers have stopped at residence to check on the wellbeing of the person.

- The person is being monitored through Probation to participate and attend Mental Health and Addictions Services.

- January 16 2015 to present, the 911 calls or calls for service has been 0 to date involving this person.

Source: © Queen's Printer for Ontario, 2017. Reproduced with permission.

The Community and Community Policing Implementation Checklist

Among the key questions that should be asked to determine whether the community is involved as a partner with the police are the following:

- Has the police service identified the neighbourhoods and groups that make up the community it serves?

- Does the police service have an active program for recruiting, screening, training, and supervising volunteers?

- Are community residents generally aware of the activities of the police and of opportunities available to them to participate in crime prevention and response initiatives?

- Are there training programs for community residents in such areas as community building, problem solving, crime prevention and response strategies, and building partnerships between the community and the police?

- Are materials on how to become a member of a community consultative committee widely available in the community?

- Are specific groups within the community, including youth, people who are visible minorities, Indigenous people, and the elderly, aware of the programs sponsored by the police in partnership with the community?

- Are there mechanisms in place to allow the residents to participate in identifying problems and concerns?

- Are all sectors of the community represented on community policing committees?

- Is the community involved in addressing substantive areas of concern, including issues related to the activities of the police such as the use of force or dealing with people who are mentally disabled?

- Are there identifiable mechanisms for ongoing community input and feedback into police policies and programs?

Case Studies

Case Study 1. How to Run a Community Meeting

Knowing how to run a community policing committee meeting is essential to developing and sustaining partnerships with the community. It is also important for sustaining the interest, motivation, and participation of community volunteers. Effective meetings are those that:

- take place in an appropriate meeting space where the privacy and confidentiality of discussions are assured;

- are conducted without interruptions from telephones, cellphones, and pagers;

- begin on time;

- have a clear (as opposed to a hidden) agenda;

- provide an equal opportunity for all committee members to participate;

- deal with substantive issues;

- make the best use of committee members' time by ensuring that the meeting is required and that the topics are substantive;

- do not meet just for the sake of meeting;

- have an established procedure for conducting discussions and making decisions; and

- end on time.

The OPP Community Policing Development Centre has identified the key factors that contribute to effective community meetings. These are discussed below.

The Chairperson

- *Prepare*: Develop the agenda; confirm meeting particulars, including location, time, guest speakers, and refreshments; distribute the agenda.

- *Know the committee members*: Be familiar with their skills, time availability, and community contacts.

- *Motivate*: Offer encouragement as well as constructive criticism.

- *Delegate authority*: Ensure that committee members understand their roles and responsibilities.

- *Preside at meetings*: Establish clear guidelines for running the meeting; follow the set agenda; involve all members in discussions and decision-making; complete the agenda within the declared time frame.

- *Evaluate progress*: Solicit feedback from committee members on the quality and effectiveness of meetings; be open to constructive suggestions for how meetings might be improved.

The Agenda

The agenda is the set of items to be covered during the meeting. There should not be too many items to cover during a single session, and the items should not be too different from one another. Meetings are most productive when committee members can focus their attention and discuss one general topic for most of the meeting time. All committee members should have the opportunity to contribute items to the agenda, and the chairperson must not be seen as pursuing a personal agenda by including some items but excluding others.

A typical agenda follows this outline:

- Call the meeting to order.
- Seek approval of the agenda.
- Read the minutes of the last meeting.
- Seek approval of the minutes of the last meeting.
- Present officers' reports (president, treasurer, etc.).
- Present standing committees' reports.
- Present special committees' reports.
- Discuss unfinished or postponed business.
- Discuss any new business.
- Set date for the next meeting, including time and location.
- Adjourn.

Meeting Dynamics

The OPP offers the following advice for improving the effectiveness of meetings:

- Schedule meetings early in the morning, when committee members are likely to be more alert.
- The attention span of committee members usually drops after 15–20 minutes; a good strategy is to place an item of general interest at this stage to revive attention.
- Organize the agenda in descending order of importance to ensure that important items are dealt with first.
- Place time limits on the discussion period and decision making for agenda items.
- Guest speakers and special presentations are a good way to maintain interest.
- Schedule breaks in the agenda.
- Ensure that there is continuity from discussions and decisions taken in previous committee meetings.

Group Decision-Making

Ideally, the interests, experience, and skills of members enhance the effectiveness of committee meetings. For these talents to be put to good use, however, the meeting environment should encourage the expression of individual views and opinions while at the same time facilitating consensus. Effective group decision making is enhanced when:

- the issues are clearly identified;
- alternative courses of action are discussed;
- the pros and cons of alternative courses of action are discussed;
- a solution is chosen by consensus, show of hands, or secret ballot;
- responsibilities for implementing the solution are assigned to committee members;
- the outcome of the solution is evaluated within a set period; and
- the outcome of the solution is shared.

Committee members are more likely to remain motivated to participate in meetings if the committee makes decisions that result in positive outcomes and if individual members are given the responsibility for implementing the solutions that are formulated.

Physical Set-Up

A comfortable group will likely be a productive group.

—*OPP Community Policing (1997)*

The physical setting in which the meeting takes place can have a significant impact on effectiveness. A meeting site should have the following characteristics:

- a room that seats all members comfortably,
- comfortable seating that allows everyone to see and hear one another,
- adequate lighting,
- proper temperature and ventilation,
- writing materials and space,
- access to washrooms,
- coatrooms,
- audiovisual equipment if necessary,
- refreshments,
- convenient parking or accessibility, and
- few outside distractions.

Patrol officers must make an effort to develop the skills required to create, manage, and sustain community policing committees to ensure the effectiveness of this core component of the police–community partnership.

Case Study 2. "Cop Camp"–A Summer Program for Youth

One of the more innovative community policing programs is Cop Camp, a week-long educational program that provides youth and their parents with the opportunity to learn about policing and police officers. These camps are often offered in conjunction with police school liaison programs, with youth participants recruited from the student body. In British Columbia, versions of Cop Camp have been operated in the Greater Vancouver area for several years by the RCMP, and on lower Vancouver Island by police agencies such as the Saanich Police Department. In recent times, Cop Camp has evolved as a strategic means of long-range recruiting, inspiring young people to pursue a career in policing and to remain loyal to the sponsoring police service.

In most instances, the camp is restricted to a specific number of individuals. Youths who are selected for the camp are screened to ensure they will be able to complete the program. The parents or guardians of the youth must also sign a waiver allowing them to participate in the program.

The camp is generally restricted to one or two groups of 24–48 youths, depending upon the resources available. Camps may be offered for four different age groups: junior (ages 6, 7, and 8), intermediate (ages 9, 10, and 11), teens (ages 12, 13, and 14), and young adults (ages 15, 16, and 17). Due to the complexities involved in running such a program, as well as the scarce resources that often exist, an agency may offer only teen or young adult camps. (For more information regarding Cop Camp, check out the Chatham–Kent Police Service at http://ckpolice.com/cop-camp-for-kids).

A major obstacle to operating a police camp is committing financial resources and personnel to a program that can only be operated during the summer months, when school is not in session. This is typically a time when police services and community groups experience staff shortages due to scheduled holiday leaves. One solution is for summer students or Neighbourhood Watch volunteers to coordinate the camp. The Hamilton–Wentworth Regional Police have operated such a camp since 1994 in collaboration with parents and community organizations.

A Day in the Life of a Cop

The camp is run by police officers who serve as instructors on police-related topics. They describe a typical day in the life of a police officer. Both classroom learning and hands-on experience are involved. Among the topics covered at a typical camp are:

- life-saving skills, such as first-aid training and swimming;

- forensic sciences and crime investigation, including methods of photographing a crime scene, detecting evidence by lifting fingerprints, and engaging a crime artist;

- a tour of the communication centre and 911 dispatch centre;

- a traffic squad presentation on the use of a roadside-screening device, how a breathalyzer works, and how serious motor vehicle accidents are investigated, as well as the all-time favourite—the use of radar and road screening devices;

- general duty patrol, including attending calls for service and patrolling the community;

- bike squad, including the methods employed by bike officers and the advantages of being out of a patrol car;

- emergency response team, including the equipment used and an overview of the strategies employed when dealing with critical incidents;

- a use-of-force presentation on the compliance tools and physical force options used by police officers;

- drug squad, including marijuana-growing operations;

- dog squad;

- victim services; and

- community police stations.

Cop camps may also include field trips to various government agencies and facilities. For example, an organized tour may include a brief visit to the local police training academy, a crime lab, or the local courthouse where evidence is being given in a court case. It may also include visiting the emergency ward of the local hospital. In addition to providing youth with the opportunity to become familiar with organizations and resources in the community, Cop Camp serves as an outreach program for youth in the community, providing valuable life skills and positive role modelling.

Case Study 3. How Not to Do It: Community Policing Horror Stories

The following stories illustrate community policing gone wrong (Woods 2000).

Horror Story 1. Collaboration Requires Community Input

New community policing officers (CPOs) are often a little anxious and intimidated before their first community meeting. One CPO, George, had a full agenda and was eager to get started. His community policing training had taught him about the difficulty in developing effective community resource groups. Often, initial meetings are encumbered by miscellaneous complaints and bickering until individuals learn to function as a group. George hoped to avoid unnecessary complications by beginning his meeting by declaring, "I have a lot to cover, so I won't listen to any complaints. We are going to stick to the issues. If I hear any complaints, I'm leaving."

- **Community's Perception:** The police are not interested in community input.

- **Discussion:** It will come as no surprise that George's project was unsuccessful. He took control of the meeting and determined the agenda. The participants were not given the opportunity to be equal or active partners.

- **Moral of the Story:** Although it may be difficult for officers to relinquish control, the committee members must feel that their input is valued. This will ensure the success of the collaborative effort.

Horror Story 2. Collaboration Requires Community Involvement

Shortly after proclaiming a community policing philosophy, the Thomasville Police Department declared it had a problem with unregistered bicycles. Two officers were assigned to confiscate any unlicensed bikes. To carry out the assignment, the officers needed to work with dirty, oily bikes, so they were given permission to work in civilian clothes. The department did not have a marked vehicle large enough to hold the bicycles, so an unmarked van was used to transport the seized bikes. When the officers found an unlicensed bike, it was confiscated and placed in the van.

Several children had their bicycles confiscated and were told to walk home. The police department was flooded with calls from angry parents complaining of thugs who were stealing their children's bicycles.

- **Community's Perception:** Community policing is merely rhetoric. The police department does not actually consult the public before they respond.

- **Discussion:** Aside from the obvious flaws in this problem-solving strategy, this example points out the importance of community participation in problem identification. Clearly, the police department would have benefited from community input before carrying out this initiative. Community involvement might have refocused police concerns, foreseen the shortcomings of this particular strategy, and helped formulate a more appropriate response to the problem.

- **Moral of the Story:** Involve the community in the identification of and response to problems of crime and social disorder in the community.

Horror Story 3. Collaboration Requires Developing Appropriate Instruments for Acquiring Community Input

In an effort to canvass public opinion, the Forest Township Police Department assigned officers to distribute and collect questionnaires. About 1,500 surveys (4 percent of the population) were completed and returned to the department. The surveys were then placed in a file cabinet and forgotten, and no changes were made to police policies or activities.

- **Community's Perception:** Although community policing involves public relations, there is no substantive change in police behaviour.

- **Discussion:** Every individual wants to think that his or her opinion is important. The goodwill achieved by soliciting public opinion dissipates when citizens realize that their input does not matter. In this example, the public's concerns were dismissed without consideration. The survey process wasted the time and efforts of citizens and officers alike.

- **Moral of the Story:** A department contemplating a public survey should ask itself the following questions:
  —What are we trying to learn?
  —Do we have the expertise to develop, conduct, and analyze a useful survey? If not, who does?
  —Is a survey the best means of obtaining the information we seek?
  —Are we prepared to act on the results?

EXERCISES: KNOWLEDGE INTO PRACTICE

Exercise 1. The Limits of Community Involvement: The Issue of Corporate Sponsorship

Newspaper Editorial

"Buddy, can you spare a sponsorship?" It hasn't quite come to that. But it's a shock that community police stations in some Vancouver suburbs are all but panhandling local businesses for vehicles, bicycles, and cellphones that they can't afford in exchange for discreet advertising. It's a disturbing sign of the times.

What happens if a patrol cruiser festooned with Acme Pewter Fork's logo pulls over a speeding car that happens to be driven by Acme's president? Where will it end? Could we trust the RCMP (Royal Canadian Manufacturers' Police) to track down international commercial frauds, in cooperation with the FBI (Federal Bureau of Investments)? (Editorial, *Vancouver Sun*, 28 March 1998, A22)

List what you consider to be the positive features of corporate sponsorship of police services.

_____

_____

_____

_____

_____

What limits, if any, would you place on corporate sponsorship of police services?

_____

_____

_____

_____

_____

Do you think the police should accept donations of patrol vehicles from a private business?

Yes   **No**

Why?

_____

_____

_____

_____

_____

From a private citizen?

Yes   **No**

Why?

_____

_____

_____

_____

_____

Exercise 2. Community Surveys

Many police services, including the Ontario Provincial Police, the Calgary Police Service, the RCMP, and the Peel Regional Police, use community surveys to determine community levels of satisfaction with police services (see Chapter 6). Design a survey to be administered to a sample of community residents in order to assess police performance. Consider the following.

List the major categories of information that should be included on the survey.

1. _____

2. _____

3. _____

4. _____

5. _____

6. _____

7. _____

8. _____

9. _____

10. _____

List ten questions that you would include on the survey, and provide a rationale for why each question was included.

Question   **Rationale**

1. _____

2. _____

3. _____

4. _____

5. _____

6. _____

7. _____

8. _____

9. _____

10. _____

How would the specific questions you include on the survey be affected by the following:
A. The socio-demographic makeup of the community, such as age groups, economic levels, and ethnicity.

_____

_____

_____

_____

_____

B. The location of the community—that is, is it an urban, suburban, regional, city, rural, or remote community?

_____

_____

_____

_____

_____

Note the strengths and limitations of the various ways of administering the survey:

A. By telephone—calling households in the community

_____

_____

_____

_____

B. In person—visiting households and having an occupant complete the survey

_____

_____

_____

_____

_____

C. Through various groups in the community—visiting schools, seniors' retirement homes, service clubs such as the Lions Club.

_____

_____

_____

_____

Final Exercise

The following exercise challenges you to apply the main ideas and concepts you have been studying throughout all nine chapters of this book. Good luck.

Creating the Ideal City Police Service

As an expert in community policing, you have been hired by a municipality to create a municipal police service in Ideal City. Residents of Ideal City are unhappy with their current police service. Several police officers have recently been charged with criminal assault in a number of very visible cases on social media. In addition, a number of high-profile cases, including a murder investigation and child pornography investigation, have recently been thrown out of court because of serious Charter breaches that the police could have easily avoided. Many residents feel they have no voice in terms of deciding the police service's priorities.

Accessing the police has proven problematic. The police take considerable time to arrive at complaints and then seem disinterested while at the scene. Officers are commonly quoted as saying there is little they can do. Recent press releases advise that minor thefts, marijuana-growing operations, stolen cars, and all cheque frauds must be reported in person at police stations, yet police stations are not always open. Case numbers will be assigned, but no investigation will occur. In the last community survey, many citizens stated they wanted improved access to the police service, including the online ability to report crime.

The residents of Ideal City perceive that the quality of life has dropped in their community. There is more graffiti on buildings, and frightening-looking people loiter in public areas and ride public transit. Transit stations have developed a reputation for being unsafe, with considerable drug-dealing taking place. Seniors, many of whom depend on public transit, are too afraid to ride.

Ideal City has a population of 350,000 people and a current policing budget of $35 million. The average cost per police officer in the municipality is $125,000, including salary and benefits. People under 19 make up 25 percent of the population, and 23 percent are over 60. The city is experiencing significant growth of approximately 23,000 people per year, due primarily to immigration, although a significant number of people are moving into the city from adjoining municipalities.

Crime rates have generally been decreasing, although in the past few years there seems to be greater coverage of violent crime in the media, and a number of high-profile crimes (shootings, car-jackings) have been linked to gang "turf wars." A number of criminal organizations are suspected of having infiltrated the municipal infrastructure. Some of these groups are highly visible, such as outlaw motorcycle gangs. Other groups are believed to be at work, including the Mafia and Eastern European criminals. White-collar crime is seldom reported, but business analysts agree that economic losses due to white-collar offenders are outstripping costs related to property crimes and crimes of violence.

Ideal City is experiencing significant demands on its social services. Many people have difficulty accessing available social services and are seeking alternative ways of coping with problems. The roads have become congested due to increasing urban density, and the local media are reporting numerous examples of road rage. In addition, there has been a considerable rise in the number of motor vehicle accidents.

The Task: Your company, Public Safety Consulting, has been hired to propose improved policing services for Ideal City. What steps would you recommend to the local government to improve policing in Ideal City? What should the Ideal City police service look like in terms of (a) organizational structure, (b) mission and value statements, (c) recruitment and training, (d) administrative features, (e) operational strategies, and (f) performance assessment?

PARTING THOUGHTS: CREATING THE COMMUNITY POLICING POLICE SERVICE

The materials presented in this text have highlighted the key requirements for creating a police service based on the principles and practices of community policing, which are listed below. These criteria can be used to evaluate police services and to make recommendations for how the service can adopt and implement community policing.

1. Continued reliance on random, preventative patrol should be minimized. Random, preventive patrol should be used only when police visibility is an issue.
2. Citizens will accept a range of response times for different types of calls.
3. Differential police response strategies should be implemented to improve the effective management of the dispatch function.
4. Effective management of the patrol function depends on intelligent management of the dispatch function.
5. Effective management of criminal investigations depends indirectly on intelligent management of the dispatch function and relates directly to management of the patrol function.
6. Case management systems must be developed and implemented to fit the needs of various investigative functions.
7. Work demand and resource allocation studies are necessary to ensure equitable deployment of personnel.
8. Crime and operational analysis procedures are vital in managing patrol and investigative functions.
9. The use of directed and self-directed patrol activities for officers should increase when and where appropriate.
10. Officers assigned to the patrol function must be actively involved in criminal investigations (e.g., conducting follow-up investigations, recommending early case closures).
11. Patrol officers need enhanced status and enriched job responsibilities.
12. Attention must be devoted to reassessing the purpose and function of existing beat configurations.

13. The police must take steps to identify citizen service expectations and work with citizens in addressing and resolving neighbourhood crime and disorder problems.
14. To facilitate the development of stronger ties with the community, policies requiring frequent rotation of officers across shifts must be seriously considered.
15. Regular public forums should take place so that the police and the public (preferably patrol officers and neighbourhood residents) frequently exchange information.
16. Performance measurement systems should serve as a management tool that guides personnel development and facilitates organizational change.
17. More meaningful performance evaluation criteria must be developed to reflect the changes in officers' roles and responsibilities.
18. Training curricula must be designed so that they are more relevant and supportive of patrol and investigative operations.
19. Disciplinary processes must become part of a system that incorporates education, training, and counselling as strategies designed to assist officers experiencing behavioural problems.
20. Management styles must adapt to varying situations and personalities.
21. Managers must begin directing their attention towards the qualitative aspects of service delivery processes and outcomes.
22. Police agencies must cultivate leaders who are comfortable and effective working in an environment characterized by constant demands for change (Oettmeier and Wycoff 1997).

REFERENCES

Cotter, A. 2015. Spotlight on Canadians: Results from the General Social Survey Public Confidence in Canadian Institutions. *Statistics Canada, Cat. no. 89-652-X. http://www.statcan.gc.ca/pub/89-652-x/89-652-x2015007-eng.htm.*

Edmonton Police Service. 1996. Community Policing in Edmonton, 1996. *Edmonton: Community and Organizational Support Section, Edmonton Police Service.*

EFCL (Edmonton Federation of Community Leagues). 2012. http://www.efcl.org/Home/tabid/348/Default.aspx.

EPS (Empowered Student Partnerships). 2012. http://www.esponline.ca.

Gillis, W. 2017. "Police officer who shot Andrew Loku says he feared for his life." Toronto Star, *14 June. https://www.thestar.com/news/gta/2017/06/14/inquest-to-hear-from-officer-who-shot-andrew-loku.html.*

Gittens, M., and D. Cole. 1995. Report of the Commission on Systemic Racism in the Ontario Criminal Justice System: A Community Summary. *Toronto: Queen's Printer.*

Grinc, R.M. 1994. "'Angels in Marble': Problems in Stimulating Community Involvement in Community Policing." Crime and Delinquency 40(3): 437–68.

Gusfield, J. 1975. The Community: A Critical Response. *New York: HarperCollins.*

Hornick, J.P., B.A. Borrows, I. Tjowvold, and D.M. Phillips. 1990. An Evaluation of the Neighbourhood Foot Patrol Program of the Edmonton Police Service. *Ottawa: Solicitor General.*

International Association of Police Chiefs. 2017. "Volunteers in Police Service." http://www.iacp.org/vips.

John Howard Society of Alberta. 1995. Crime Prevention through Social Development: A Literature Review. *Calgary: Wild Rose Foundation.*

Liou, K.T., and E.G. Savage. 1996. "Citizen Perceptions of Community Policing Impact." Public Administration Quarterly *20(2): 163–79.*

Metro Vancouver Transit Police. 2017. https://transitpolice.ca/advice-info/see-something-say-something/on-duty-app.

Ministry of Aboriginal Affairs. 2005. "Ontario's New Approach to Aboriginal Affairs." http://www.aboriginalaffairs.gov.on.ca/english/policy/newapproach/newapproach03.asp#justice.

—. 2007. "Ontario's Support for First Nations Policing." http://www.aboriginalaffairs.gov.on.ca/english/news/2007/may31bg3_07.asp.

Ministry of the Solicitor General and A.R.A. Consultants. 1991a. "Developing a Community Profile: A Manual for the Development and Implementation of Community Profiling for Police Planners and Managers." In Ontario Provincial Police: Shaping Our Future. *Toronto: Solicitor General.*

—. 1991b. "Working with the Community. A Manual for Building Police-Community Partnerships." In Ontario Provincial Police: Shaping Our Future. *Toronto: Solicitor General.*

Nease, K. 2017. "Ottawa police officer charged with manslaughter in man's 2016 death." CBC News, *6 March.* http://www.cbc.ca/news/canada/ottawa/abdirahman-abdi-ottawa-police-siu-findings-1.4008142.

Oettmeier, T., and M.A. Wycoff. 1997. Personal Performance Evaluations in the Community Policing Context. *Washington, DC: Community Policing Consortium.*

Ontario Provincial Police. 1997a. "Community Partnerships." CPDC News *2 (August), 5.*

—. 1997b. Community Policing "How Do We Do It" Manual. *Oakville: Community Policing Development Centre.*

—. 2000. Annual Report, 1999. *Oakville.*

—. 2016a. "Community Mobilization and Engagement." www.opp.ca/index.php?&lng=en&id=115&entryid=56b7979b8f94ac0d5c28d174.

—. 2016b. "Auxiliary Policing Program." https://www.opp.ca/index.php?id=115&entryid=56b758c48f94ac9e5828d172.

Ottawa Police Service. 2017a. "Community Development." https://www.ottawapolice.ca/en/about-us/Community-Development.

—. 2017b. "Careers and Opportunities: Volunteer." https://www.ottawapolice.ca/en/careers-and-opportunities/Volunteer.asp.

Parent, R. 2016. "Police Use of Deadly Force Much Higher in US Than Canada." Vancouver Sun, 22 July. http://vancouversun.com/opinion/opinion-police-use-of-deadly-force-similarities-and-differences-in-canada-and-the-u-s.

Polowek, K. 1995. Community Policing: Is It Working and How Do We Know? An Introductory Guide for Police Managers and Police Boards. Victoria: Attorney General.

Prairie Research Associates Inc. 1996. Building a Safer Canada: A Community-Based Crime Prevention Manual. Ottawa: Department of Justice.

Skogan, W.G. 1995. Community Participation and Community Policing. Chicago: Center for Urban Affairs and Policy Research, University of Chicago.

Toronto Police Service. 1999. Partners in Community Safety. Toronto.

—. 2008. "Community Mobilization." http://www.torontopolice.on.ca/communitymobilization.

—. 2017. "Community Consultative Committees." http://www.torontopolice.on.ca/community/ccc.php.

Vancouver Sun. 1998. Editorial. 28 March, A22.

Woods, D.J. 2000. "Community Policing Pages." http://www.concentric.net/~dwoods

Index